SELECTED SPIRITUAL WRITINGS OF ANNE DUTTON

EIGHTEENTH-CENTURY, BRITISH-BAPTIST, WOMAN THEOLOGIAN

Baptists
History, Literature, Theology, Hymns

General editor: *Walter B. Shurden*, Mercer University.

John Taylor. *Baptists on the American Frontier: A History of Ten Baptist Churches.* Edited by Chester Young (1985).

Thomas Helwys. *A Short Declaration of the Mystery of Iniquity (1611/1612).* Edited by Richard Groves (1998).

Roger Williams. *The Bloody Tenant of Persecution for Cause of Conscience.* Historical introduction by Edwin Gaustad. Edited by Richard Groves (2001).

James A. Rogers. *Richard Furman: Life and Legacy* (1985; reprint with new forewords, 2002).

Lottie Moon. *Send the Light: Lottie Moon's Letters and Other Writings.* Edited by Keith Harper (2002).

James P. Byrd, Jr. *The Challenges of Roger Williams: Religious Liberty, Violent Persecution, and the Bible* (2002).

Anne Dutton. *Selected Spiritual Writings of Anne Dutton, Eighteenth-Century, British-Baptist, Woman Theologian.* Five volumes. Edited by JoAnn Ford Watson. 1. *Letters* (fall 2003). 2. *Discourses, Poetry, Hymns, Memoir* (fall 2004). 3. *The Autobiography* (summer 2006). 4. *Theological Works* (spring 2007). 5. *Miscellaneous Correspondence* (fall 2007).

David T. Morgan. *Southern Baptist Sisters: In Search of Status, 1845–2000* (fall 2003).

William E. Ellis. *"A Man of Books and a Man of the People": E. Y. Mullins and the Crisis of Moderate Southern Baptist Leadership* (1985; reprint, fall 2003).

Jarrett Burch. *Adiel Sherwood: Baptist Antebellum Pioneer in Georgia* (winter 2003).

Anthony Chute. *A Piety above the Common Standard: Jesse Mercer and the Defense of Evangelistic Calvinism* (spring 2004).

William H. Brackney. *A Genetic History of Baptist Thought* (September 2004).

Henlee Hulix Barnette. *A Pilgrimage of Faith: My Story* (November 2004).

Walter B. Shurden. *Not an Easy Journey: Some Transitions in Baptist Life* (Spring 2005).

Marc A. Jolley, editor. *Distinctively Baptist: Essays on Baptist History: Festschrift Walter B. Shurden* (Spring 2005).

Keith Harper and C. Martin Jacumin. *Esteemed Reproach: The Lives of Rev. James Ireland and Rev. Joseph Craig* (2005).

Charles Deweese. *Women Deacons and Deaconesses: 400 Years of Baptist Service* (BH&HS, 2005).

Pam Durso and Keith Durso. *Courage and Hope: The Stories of Ten Baptist Women Ministers* (BH&HS, 2005).

W. Glenn Jonas, Jr., editor. *The Baptist River: Essays on Many Tributaries of a Diverse Tradition* (November 2006).

SELECTED SPIRITUAL WRITINGS OF ANNE DUTTON

EIGHTEENTH-CENTURY, BRITISH-BAPTIST, WOMAN THEOLOGIAN

Volume 4
THEOLOGICAL WORKS

compiled and with an introduction by
JOANN FORD WATSON

MERCER UNIVERSITY PRESS
MACON, GEORGIA USA
MARCH 2007

ISBN 978-0-88146-029-2   MUP/H722

Selected Spiritual Writings of Anne Dutton.
Eighteenth-Century, British-Baptist, Woman Theologian.
Volume 4. *Theological Works*
Copyright ©2007
Mercer University Press
Printed in the United States of America
First edition, March 2007

Library of Congress Cataloging-in-Publication Data

[CIP data is available from the Library of Congress]

CONTENTS

Volume 4. THEOLOGICAL WORKS

ANNE DUTTON
from the frontispiece to
Selections from Letters on Spiritual Subjects /etc./ (1884)

PREFACE

I thank Dr. Russell Morton, research librarian, and Ms. Sylvia Locher, head librarian, of Ashland Theological Seminary Library for their assistance. I thank Ms. Kathleen Slusser, graduate assistant, Ashland Theological Seminary, for typing and preparing the manuscript, and Dr. Dawn Morton, for assistance with the index. I also thank my parents for their support.

I thank Mr. Mark Holland, publisher and vice-president, Gale Group, United Kingdom, Reading, England, for permission to publish the following manuscripts. I thank Mr. Martin Zonis of GaleGroup/Primary Source Microfilms/Research Publications, Woodbridge, Connecticut, for assistance in obtaining permission to publish the following from the Eighteenth Century Gale Collection. Permission has been granted to publish the following in a rekeyed format.

Hints of the Glory of Christ, as the Friend and Bridegroom of the Church: From the Seven Last Verses of the Fifth Chapter of Solomon's Song. In a Letter to a Friend. By A. D. (Eighteenth Century, reel 10676. no. 2, unit 306).

A Treatise on Justification: Shewing the Matter, Manner, Time and Effects of It by the Rev. Thomas Dutton [pseudonym] 3rd ed. Glasgow. Printed by Mr. William Smith for Archibald Coubrough, 1778 (Eighteenth Century; reel 9566, no. 7; unit 274).

A Discourse concerning the New-Birth: To which Are Added Two Poems: The One on Salvation in Christ, by Free-Grace, for the Chief of Sinners: The Other on a Believer's Safety and Duty. With an Epistle Recommendatory, by the Reverend Mr. Jacob Rogers, B.A. London: Printed and sold by John Oswald; and Ebenezer Gardner, 1740 (Eighteenth Century; reel 2524, no. 3).

A Discourse concerning God's Act of Adoption. To which Is Added a Discourse upon the Inheritance of the Adopted Sons of God. London: Printed and sold by E. Gardner, 1737 (Eighteenth Century, reel 5786, no. 07, unit 166).

Three Letters on I. The Marks of a Child of God. II. The Soul Diseases of God's Children; and Their Soul-Remedies. And III. God's Prohibition of His Peoples Unbelieving Fear; and his Great Promise Given for the

Support of Their Faith, unto Their Time-Joy, and Eternal Glory. By One Who Has Tasted that the Lord Is Gracious. London: Printed by J. Hart and sold by G. Keith and J. Fuller, 1761 (Eighteenth Century, reel 7212, no. 02, unit 207).

The manuscripts have been rekeyed but retain the original spelling except that the "long, descending, or medial s" (*f*) is now a regular "s" (for example, "la*f*t Ver*f*es" becomes "last Verses"). In the introduction, references to Dutton's works cite the original page numbers, not the page numbers in this reproduction.

This volume is dedicated to my daughter, Christina Lucille Watson, and to my husband, Dr. Duane F. Watson, for their unending love and support. With deep gratitude and appreciation.

JoAnn Ford Watson

INTRODUCTION

These theological works of Anne Dutton display her ability as a thinker and writer on the major themes and tenets of the Baptist faith and tradition. The doctrines of Jesus Christ, election, grace, adoption, inheritance, new birth, justification, sanctification, and holiness are developed in the various treatises, discourses, and other writings presented in this volume.

1. Hints of the Glory of Christ

Dutton's *Hints of the Glory of Christ* was published in 1748.[1] Prefixed is a thirty-eight line poem, "To Mr. *E.H.*," signed "*A.D.*," on "Bridegroom," and love, and addressed to "my dear Friend."[2] Dutton bases this discourse on the Song of Solomon 5:10-16. She writes to her "friend":

> *SIR,* I Beg leave to acquaint you, that it is on my Heart, to put you in Remembrance of that *Description* the *Spouse* gave of her *Beloved*, in the Fifth Chapter of *Solomon's* Song, from the tenth Verse, to the Close of the Chapter.[3]

This piece was written very early in Dutton's correspondence and publishing career. She speaks of her own weak ability to write of noteworthy things, and gives her writing to the power of God to speak through it. She confesses:

> And as I have a deep Sense of my own Inability to say any Thing worthy of your Regard, or for your Advantage; so have I a much more humbling Sense of my exceeding Unfitness to say any Thing worthy of the Notice, or becoming the Glory of my great LORD![4]

Dutton continues:

---

[1] Full Title: *Hints of the Glory of Christ; As the Friend and Bridegroom of the Church from the Seven Last Verses of the Fifth Chapter of Solomon's Song. In a Letter to a Friend* (London: printed by J. Hart in Popping's-Court, Fleet Street, and Sold by J. Lewis, in Bartholomew-Close, near West-Smithfield, 1748).

[2] *Hints of the Glory of Christ*, 3-4.

[3] *Hints of the Glory of Christ*, 5.

[4] *Hints of the Glory of Christ*, 6.

What then can be expected from such a *Babe* as I, who am the *Least,* and *Last* of all? So that I should even sit down in *Silence,* if *He* had not said, *With the* last, *I am* HE. But, believing his infinite Grace, and depending on his Almighty Power, I shall proceed to take a little Notice of the Church's Description of her *Beloved,* which we have Song 5.10, *&c.* And attempt to *lispe out* somewhat of *his Glory* from thence. . . . For surely, my *Soul loves him*; from that Heart-attracting, Soul-overcoming *Display* I have had of his infinite Beauties, his adorable Excellencies![5]

Dutton attributes the authorship of the Song of Songs or Song of Solomon to Solomon himself.

Of a divine Original, being given, as all the other Parts of the Scriptures of Truth, by the immediate *Inspiration* of the *Holy Spirit-of God:* and dedicated to his Servant *Solomon,* who was the Penman thereof.[6]

And she says that Song of Solomon 5:10-16 is an "*Epithalamium,* or *Marriage Song.*"[7] She uses the relationship between the spouse and her beloved in Song of Solomon 5:10-16 to compare the relationship of the heavenly marriage between Christ and the church. She states that this Song

in the Mystery, and Spirituality thereof, respects the Heavenly *Marriage* between *Christ,* and the *Church.* And if it should be allow'd, that some Parts of this Song, were literally true, of King *Solomon's Marriage* with *Pharaoh's* Daughter. Yet even in those Parts, a *Greater* than *Solomon* is *here.* Even no less a Person, than the *Christ of God,* the *Prince of Peace,* God's *King Solomon,* whom he has set upon his holy Hill of *Zion,* and given to be the *Bridegroom* of his *Church.*[8]

In her hermeneutics, Dutton assumes that because the text is inspired it was intended to move beyond the immediate reference to Solomon and his bride to describe the deeper relationship between Christ and his bride, the church.

But, for my own Part, I chuse to take this Song, as it was given by the immediate Inspiration of the Holy Ghost, and stands upon Record, as a

---

[5]*Hints of the Glory of Christ,* 7-8.
[6]*Hints of the Glory of Christ,* 9.
[7]*Hints of the Glory of Christ,* 9.
[8]*Hints of the Glory of Christ,* 9.

Part of the sacred Scriptures, for the Edification of the Church in all Ages; as *independent* upon the Glory of *Solomon*, and *his Queen*; and as wholly relating to the super-excellent Glory of *Christ*, and *his Spouse*.[9]

Dutton further comments on the deeper relationship of Christ and the church found in the Song of Solomon:

But this much may suffice, as to the Nature of the *Book*: That it is a *Song*, a *Marriage-Song*, of *Christ*, and *his Spouse*. In which, we may observe, That as these are the *chief Speakers* herein, so they alternately *commend* one another's Love, Beauty, and Excellency.[10]

Dutton expounds on each of the verses of Song of Solomon 5:10-16, giving both text and commentary on the text. She states that the spouse describes her beloved in these verses. In verse 10, the beloved is described as: "*White and ruddy*. . . . Of all Beauties, He is the fairest, a glorious Beauty, transcendently *above* and beyond *all* others."[11] Dutton correlates this to the person of Jesus Christ and applies the characteristics of "white" and "ruddy" to him.

He's *White:* with Regard to the *Glory of his Deity. Ruddy:* with Respect to the *Truth of his Humanity.* His Divine, and Human Nature, Hypostatically united, are hereby intended. He is *White*, with Regard to the *Glory of his Deity.* The Lord Jesus Christ, the Church's Beloved, is so great a Person, that has all the immense Glories of the *Godhead*, radically in Himself.[12]

She adds: "He is *White*, in regard of the *Purity* of his Human Nature, and the Whole of his Obedience therein. . . . And *Ruddy*, with respect to his *Sufferings*."[13] "*Ruddy*. This respects his *Sufferings*. Oh astonishing Mixture, *White and Ruddy!* What must this *sinless* One, *suffer!* this *spotless* Lamb, *die!*. . . . His Bride had sinn'd, and was under the Sentence of Death; and die she must, if He had not dy'd for her, in her Room."[14]

---

[9]*Hints of the Glory of Christ*, 14.
[10]*Hints of the Glory of Christ*, 14.
[11]*Hints of the Glory of Christ*, 17.
[12]*Hints of the Glory of Christ*, 18-19.
[13]*Hints of the Glory of Christ*, 25.
[14]*Hints of the Glory of Christ*, 33.

Linking "white" to the current glory of Christ, Dutton writes, "The Spouse's *Beloved*, is *White* and *Ruddy*, in his *heavenly Glory*. He is *White*, in that personal, and relative *Glory*, He now wears in Heaven, as the great *Head* of the Church; and *Ruddy*, as the exalted *Saviour*."[15] She argues that the future glory of Christ will reverse his previous earthly humiliation.

> When Christ, the Bridegroom, *appears in Glory*; the Church, the Bride, shall likewise *appear with him*.—The last View the World had of *Christ*, was, as Hanging on the *Cross*, and laid in a *Tomb*. They saw him in the Depth of his Humiliation; disbeliev'd his *Messiahship*, despised, and rejected him. But when he comes again, they shall see him in his *Glory*.[16]

Dutton comments that the Church, having followed Christ will also be glorified with him:

> the *Church*, the Bride, the Saved of the Lord, that had followed the Lamb whithersoever he went, and come up out of great Tribulations; with her Resurrection-Body, exactly conform'd to Christ's glorious Body, and her white Robes of Glory, her Bridal Garments on, advanc'd to sit with Him on His Throne.[17]

As she expounds further, Dutton gives commentary on the bridegroom's excellencies and beauties as given in Song of Solomon 5:11-16. Allegorical interpretation abounds. For example, from verse 13 she connects "cheeks" with Christ's manifestations to his church:

> *His Cheeks are as a Bed of Spices, as Sweet Flowers:* The *Cheeks* in Nature, when they are full, and comely, are a special Part of the Beauty of the *Face*. And by the *Cheeks* of Christ, we may understand, those *Manifestations* he makes of *Himself* to his Spouse, either in Grace, or Providence.[18]

Regarding verse 14, "*His Hands are as Gold-Rings set with the Beryl: his Belly is as bright Ivory overlaid with Sapphires*," Dutton writes:

> As the Hands of Christ are compar'd to Gold-Rings, for the Excellency of their *Matter*: So, as I conceive, it may likewise respect their *Form*. Gold

---

[15] *Hints of the Glory of Christ*, 50.
[16] *Hints of the Glory of Christ*, 57.
[17] *Hints of the Glory of Christ*, 58.
[18] *Hints of the Glory of Christ*, 74.

is excellent, and Rings of Gold, are *round*, and enclose the Finger on which they're put: And so the precious *Hands of Christ*, gloriously *enclose* his *People*.[19]

Verse 16 states, "*His Mouth is most sweet: Yea, he is altogether lovely. This is my Beloved, and this is my Friend, O ye Daughters of* Jerusalem."[20] Regarding "*Yea, He is altogether lovely*," Dutton writes:

> The Spouse had been describing the Glories of her *Beloved*, in his particular *Parts*, by resembling them to the *chiefest* Beauties, the *greatest* Excellencies in *Nature*; and likewise summed up the *Whole*, general Glory of his *Person*. . . .[21]

Dutton elaborates on verse 16 as a call to greater devotion on the part of all the church:

> *This is my Beloved, and this is my Friend, O Ye Daughters of* Jerusalem! Here she exults, and glories in *Her Beloved: This! This is* HE! . . . And 'tis as if she should say, "O Daughters of *Jerusalem*, look upon my *Beloved*, until you're *enamour'd* with his infinite Glory!"[22]

Dutton concludes the letter with her hope that the description of the bridegroom will engender greater devotion to Christ on the part of the recipient:

> Thus, Sir, as enabled, I have gone over this *Description* the *Spouse* gives of her *Beloved*: And leave it with the eternal *Spirit*; who can give you a Display of *Christ's Glory*, even by the *Lispings of a Babe*: To the attracting of your Soul into the Strongest *Desires* after him, and the nearest *Coalition* with him; to your present *Felicity,* and *endless Glory!*—I subscribe myself, *Sir, Yours*, &c. *A.D.*[23]

---

[19]*Hints of the Glory of Christ*, 77, 79.
[20]*Hints of the Glory of Christ*, 91.
[21]*Hints of the Glory of Christ*, 94
[22]*Hints of the Glory of Christ*, 98-99.
[23]*Hints of the Glory of Christ*, 100.

2. A Treatise on Justification

In 1778 the third edition of *A Treatise on Justification* was published.[24] The first two editions of this work from 1740 and 1743 are anonymous. The third edition used in this volume is ascribed to the Reverend Mr. Thomas Dutton, a pseudonym for Anne Dutton. This edition was published posthumously, for Dutton died in 1765. This third edition states that Anne Dutton is the author of two other works attributed to Mr. Dutton: *A Discourse concerning the New Birth to Which Are Added Two Poems; The One on Salvation in Christ, by Free-Grace, for the Chief of Sinners: The Other on a Believer's Safety and Duty* and many famous religious letters, notably her tracts *Letters on Spiritual Subjects Sent to Relatives and Friends*. The third edition includes an advertisement and a preface not included in previous editions. The preface is dated "Glasgow, Oct. 24th 1777."[25]

The advertisement emphasizes the central point of the doctrine of justification. It offers this definition of justification: "The scripture doctrine of the free justification of guilty sinners, thro' the meritorious obedience and imputed righteousness of the adorable Redeemer, received by faith."[26] The advertisement stresses the centrality of the doctrine of justification for the Christian faith as "of the utmost importance in itself, so it has ever been one of the received articles of all the reformed churches, and is still held, by all true protestants, as one of the most essential doctrines of Christianity."[27] The advertisement further notes that, "The small tract now offered to the public, needs no recommendation: the worthy author of it was well known; and the performance, when read, will sufficiently recommend itself."[28]

The advertisement provides the outline of the discourse as the matter, manner, time, and effects of justification:

---

[24]Full title: *A Treatise On Justification: Shewing The Matter, Manner, Time, and Effects of it*. By the Reverend Mr. Thomas Dutton, late minister in London, and author of the *Discourse on the New-Birth*, and *Religious Letters*. It is God that justifieth. Rom. vii.33. The third edition. Glasgow: printed by William Smith, for Archibald Coubrough, bookseller; and sold at his shop, above the Cross. 1778.

[25]*A Treatise on Justification*, x.

[26]*A Treatise on Justification*, iii.

[27]*A Treatise on Justification*, iii.

[28]*A Treatise on Justification*, iii.

The author's plan in the discourse is shortly this;—To consider the doctrine of the justification of a sinner, in the sight of God, in the MATTER of it, *viz.* the complete *obedience* of Jesus Christ, exclusive of all works of the creature;—in the MANNER of it, as, with respect to God, it is by *imputation*, and with respect to ourselves, by *faith*;—in the TIME of it, as it respects the whole *body* of the *elect*, and every individual person of God's *chosen*;—and in the EFFECTS of it, with respect to the SOUL, as it regards its *peace*, its *state*, and its *obedience*.[29]

In the preface the publisher emphasizes the importance of the doctrine of justification when he writes:

> *This is not only the scripture doctrine of justification, but also the doctrine of all our reformed churches; and was of such great account with our protestant reformers, that Luther said of it, "That the church either stood or fell, as this doctrine was maintained, or rejected."*[30]

In his preface the publisher also highlights the literary ability and previous publications of "Mr. Dutton." For example, he writes, "*The Rev. Mr. DUTTON, author of the following Treatise, on the important doctrine of Justification, was also the author of some other Tracts. We have seen his discourse concerning the NEW BIRTH, and his LETTERS on religious subjects.*"[31] The publisher endorses this treatise in the strongest of terms, describing the hermeneutic as "scripture interpreting scripture": "*In the following Treatise on Justification, he has endeavored to exhibit to his readers, a scriptural view of his subject, in the words of the Holy Ghost, comparing spiritual things with spiritual.*"[32]

In the introduction, Dutton gives the organization of the discourse as follows:

> In the *justification* of a sinner, in the sight of God, I shall consider four things principally. As, 1. The *Matter* of it. 2. The *Manner* of it. 3. The *Time* of it. And, 4. The *Effect* of it, with respect to the soul. And then, 5.

---

[29] *A Treatise on Justification*, iv.

[30] *A Treatise on Justification*, v.

[31] *A Treatise on Justification*, v.

[32] *A Treatise on Justification*, vi.

In the last place shall add something by way of *Use*. I shall consider each of these in the order laid down.[33]

Section I deals with the matter of justification and is based on Jeremiah 23:6: "This is the name whereby he shall be called, the Lord our righteousness."[34] Dutton focuses on the active and passive obedience of Christ. Jesus Christ on the cross as God-man both frees us from the curse of the law and, through his obedience, offers us the blessings of righteousness.[35] She writes, "that the *active* and *passive* obedience of our Lord, or both these *branches* of his righteousness, were absolutely necessary, to make us completely *righteous* in the sight of God, and of his holy law."[36]

In Section II, the manner of justification is discussed as based upon Romans 1:17, 4:6, and 10:10.[37] Dutton sums up the manner of justification this way: "*God imputeth righteousness without works.—The righteousness of God is revealed from faith to faith.—With the heart man believeth unto righteousness*."[38] It is Christ's imputed righteousness by God for us, by faith, not by our own works, that justifies us. Dutton states:

> Thus, a poor soul, when stript *naked* of all its own *righteousness, looks* by faith unto Christ's, as its only justifying robe. And the eye of a believer is *single* towards Christ, in this respect; it does not look partly to *Christ*, and partly to its own *works*, to make it righteous in the sight of God.[39]

God imputes justification to those who have faith. Dutton comments that "the *manner* of justification, as with respect unto *God*, it is by *imputation*; and with respect to *ourselves*, by *Faith*."[40]

Section III focuses on the time of justification as based on Romans 3:26, 4:25, and 1 Timothy 3:16.[41] The time of justification is immanent or transient. The time of justification is immanent because God, in his divine mind in eternity was in Christ to deliver and justify the elect. Dutton writes:

---

[33] *A Treatise on Justification*, 12.
[34] *A Treatise on Justification*, 12-28.
[35] *A Treatise on Justification*, 24.
[36] *A Treatise on Justification*, 26.
[37] *A Treatise on Justification*, 41-95.
[38] *A Treatise on Justification*, 41.
[39] *A Treatise on Justification*, 71.
[40] *A Treatise on Justification*. 95.
[41] *A Treatise on Justification*, 96-100.

THE next thing proposed to be considered, was, The *time* of justification. As justification is God's act, so it is to be considered, either as *immanent*, or *transient* and timed accordingly. I. As *immanent*, or an act of God's will, that always abideth the same in his divine mind, from eternity to eternity: and so it was from *everlasting*; as 2 Cor. v.19. *God was in Christ.*[42]

Dutton understands transient time that justification of the elect would not actually occur in time until the Holy Spirit applied Christ's righteousness to the elect.

The act of justification is to be considered as *transient*; or, as it is an act of God that passeth upon the creature in time. . . . Though, from eternity, God *decreed* to justify all the elect; yet they are not *actually* justified, until the Holy Spirit doth, in due time, apply Christ, and his righteousness, unto them.[43]

Section IV focuses on the effect of justification and is based on Romans 4:7, 5:1, and 2 Corinthians 5:14.[44] Dutton states:

THE next thing I am to consider, is, the *effect* of *justification* with respect to the soul. And this is three-fold; and has respect, 1. Unto the soul's peace. 2. Unto its state. 3. Unto its obedience.[45]

Dutton shows that justification brings peace, righteousness, and obedience.
Dutton uses Malachi 3:16-18 to show that the privilege of justification is righteousness and obedience which is found acceptable to God and will effect peaceful assurance forever with God. Dutton writes:

It being the peculiar privilege of the *justified* ones, to have all their *obedience*, thus *accepted* and *rewarded:* so that, though the good *works* of the saints do not go to the flock of their justifying *righteousness*; yet as they go to the treasure of their filial *obedience*, which is so *acceptable* to God, and shall be so *rewarded* by him. . . . *The effect of righteousness shall be peace, quietness, and assurance for ever*, Isaiah xxxii.17.[46]

---

[42]*A Treatise on Justification*, 96.
[43]*A Treatise on Justification*, 97.
[44]*A Treatise on Justification*, 101-30.
[45]*A Treatise on Justification*, 101.
[46]*A Treatise on Justification*, 128-29.

Section V deals with an objection against justification by faith alone. Dutton affirms that it is by faith alone that sinners are justified and not by works also. Dutton cites texts that might be used to support the contrary, like James 2:21 ("*Was not Abraham our Father justified by works, when he had offered Isaac his Son upon the altar,?*")[47] and James 2:24 ("*Ye see then how that by works a man is justified, and not by faith only*")[48] as well as 1 John 3:7.[49] Dutton responds: "To which I answer, *Answ*. That the truth laid down, of justification by faith alone, is not in the least shaken by this *objection*, founded upon these *texts*."[50] Jesus Christ in his perfect obedience is perfectly righteous before God and he imputes this righteousness to us and imparts justification to us by his perfect righteousness. So we are not righteous based on our actions, but Christ's justification imparted to us.[51] Based on Romans 3:27, Dutton again writes: "[T]hat is, by the *doctrine* of faith, the *gospel*; which reveals the *obedience* of Christ to be the only justifying *righteousness* of a sinner before God, as it is *imputed* to him, of the freest *grace*, and *received* by *faith* alone."[52]

Section VI deals with the insufficiency of legal obedience to the justification of a sinner and is based on Romans 3:20."[53] Dutton states that it is impossible for a sinner to be justified by the works of the law or by manmade efforts. It is an affront to the free grace of God for human attempts of obedience to the law to bring about salvation. It is not human obedience to the law or manmade efforts that result in salvation, but salvation is solely based upon the free gift of the grace of God in Christ.[54]

"AND now, to shew the *impossibility* of a sinner's being *justified* before God, by the *works* of the law, or by his own obedience to the law."[55] She writes that

---

[47]*A Treatise on Justification*, 130, 135.
[48]*A Treatise on Justification*, 130-31, 138.
[49]*A Treatise on Justification*, 130-33.
[50]*A Treatise on Justification*, 131.
[51]*A Treatise on Justification*, 131-32.
[52]*A Treatise on Justification*, 137.
[53]*A Treatise on Justification*, 141-61.
[54]*A Treatise on Justification*, 159.
[55]*A Treatise on Justification*, 141.

if a sinful creature sets aside the *perfect* obedience of Christ, by introducing his own *imperfect* obedience in the stead thereof; or presents his own *filthy rags*; to join with Christ's spotless, glorious *robe*, in order to obtain *life* by the *works* of his own hands, when God has declared, that it is only to be had by his *free gift*; it is a most daring affront to the *grace* of God in the *gospel*, and to the *justice* of God in the *law*."[56]

Dutton concludes this section:

> Thus, as it is the *duty* of the creature, man, to *do* whatever his Creator commands in his holy law, which yet he *cannot* do: so it appears to be utterly *impossible* for him to be *justified* by his own obedience; and the *misery* of man, with regard to the *law*, is exceeding great indeed: and therefore, the good news the *gospel* brings must needs be *glad tidings*.[57]

Section VII is the conclusion of the treatise on justification.[58] Dutton offers five main points in the concluding section and sums up with the words:

> And in short, as it was God's design to get himself *glory*, in the *justification* of sinners, by the *righteousness* of Jesus Christ; so the *display* thereof, throughout the whole gospel, lays *them* under the highest *obligation* to *live* to his *praise*.[59]

The preface and appendix were additions to the later 1778 edition. The appendix concludes with various verses on justification.[60]

---

[56]*A Treatise on Justification*, 159.
[57]*A Treatise on Justification*, 161.
[58]*A Treatise on Justification*, 162-79.
[59]*A Treatise on Justification*, 178.
[60]*A Treatise on Justification*, 180-85.

3. A Discourse concerning the New-Birth

A Discourse concerning the New-Birth[61] was published in 1740. The work begins with a preface by Jacob Rogers, a London clergyman who knew Dutton and endorsed the work. Rogers writes:

> *AS I have read over the ensuing Discourse concerning the* New-Birth, *with some Pleasure and Satisfaction to my own Soul; so I wou'd take the Liberty to recommend it likewise to thy serious and impartial Perusal.*[62]

Rogers is very complimentary of Dutton's work and briefly mentions her correspondence with George Whitefield and Mr. Seward:

> *The Author is well known to me, and I think it my Duty to acknowledge that I have been much strengthen'd and comforted, under God, by conversing with one, whose Communication is indeed good to the Use of Edifying, and powerfully ministers Grace to the Hearers. The Reverend Mr.* Whitefield, *and Mr.* Seward, *now with God, who both held a Correspondence with the Author, have also frequently declar'd with what Savour and Sweetness, the reading of the Author's Letters, has been accompanied to their Souls; which gives me Hopes that all who have the Taste and Spirit of those Servants of the most high God, will not only be inclin'd to read this Discourse, when it comes to their Hands, but likewise receive that spiritual Edification from it.*[63]

Dutton begins her discourse with an assessment that the doctrine of the

---

[61]Anne Dutton, *A Discourse concerning the New-Birth: To Which Are Added Two Poems; the One on Salvation in Christ, by Free-Grace, for the Chief of Sinners: the Other on a Believer's Safety and Duty. With an Epistle Recommendatory, by the Reverend Mr. Jacob Rogers, B.A.* (Printed; and sold by John Oswald, at the *Rose* and *Crown* in the *Poultry*, near *Stocks-Market*; and Ebenezer Gardner, at *Milton's* Head in Grace-Church-Street. 1740).

This was also published as *A Discourse concerning the New Birth to Which Are Added Sixty-four HymnS; Compos'd on Several Subjects; with an Epistle Recommentatory by the Reverend Mr. Jacob Rogers, A.B.* (London: J. Hart, 1743). The poem on Believer's Safety and Duty also appears in the 1743 edition of *A Discourse upon Justification; Shewing the Matter, Manner, Time, and Effects of It. To Which Are Added Three Poems* (London: printed by J. Hart; and sold by J. Lewis; and E. Gardner, 1743). Whitebrook, *Ann Dutton*, 16 no. 4.

[62]*Discourse concerning the New Birth*, preface, 1.

[63]*Discourse concerning the New Birth*, 1.

new birth was once known, but was in her day foreign to many. "THE Doctrine of the *New Birth*, is a Doctrine of the Bible, clearly taught, and necessary to be known; and yet Multitudes are ignorant of it."[64] She writes the *Discourse*, then, to reacquaint readers with the spiritual importance of the doctrine of new birth: "And since many think the New-Birth, a strange, and unnecessary Thing, being at a Loss to know what it is, or, what it is to be born again, I shall give some Hints concerning it, in the following Method."[65] Dutton defines her method of explaining the new birth as follows:

> *First*, I shall shew, What the New-Birth is, or, What it is to be born again, by giving a Definition thereof.
> *Secondly*, Endeavor to explain, and prove it from the Word of God.
> *Thirdly*, Shew, What we may learn from this Phrase of being Born again. And
> *Fourthly*, With some Uses, conclude the whole.[66]

In the first part Dutton defines the new birth and demonstrates her astute theological mind:

> to be Born Again, is, a supernatural Work of the Holy Spirit of God, by the Word, upon the Soul of a Man; creating it a-new in Christ Jesus, in all the Powers and Faculties thereof; by which he produceth an abiding Principle of spiritual Life; which contains in it all Kinds of Grace, every way fitted for, and acting towards their proper Objects.[67]

In the second part Dutton "proves" the new birth from the Bible. She writes: "That it is a Work of the Holy Spirit of God, by the Word, appears plain, from what our Lord asserts, in his Discourse with *Nicodemus*, John iii."[68] She focuses on John 3:8 and affirms that the new birth is entirely a work of the Spirit of God: "That the Soul herein is *Passive* to the Spirit, before it *acts*; just as the Objects blown upon are to the Wind, before they move."[69] There is an irresistible grace before which corrupt human nature is helpless: "That the Spirit works by an *irresistible* Power in the New-

---

[64]*Discourse concerning the New Birth*, 1.
[65]*Discourse concerning the New Birth*, 2.
[66]*Discourse concerning the New Birth*, 2.
[67]*Discourse concerning the New Birth*, 2-3.
[68]*Discourse concerning the New Birth*, 3.
[69]*Discourse concerning the New Birth*, 5.

Birth; which corrupt Nature can no more *resist*, than moveable Things can *withstand* an irresistible Wind."[70] The new birth is fully the work of the Holy Spirit that supercedes his other work in the individual. "And as the New Birth is a Work of the Holy Spirit of God; so, likewise, it is a *supernatural Work*; or a Work that is wholly above his *common* Operations in the Hearts of natural Men: Yea, even above what he wrought in the Heart of perfect *Adam*."[71]

Further, Dutton refers to John 3:5 and states that the new birth is accomplished by the Spirit and the Water and the Word. She states:

> And the Word is set forth by Water, to shew the cleansing Efficacy thereof in the Hand of the Spirit; for as Water cleanseth the Body from natural Filthiness, so doth the Word of God cleanse the Soul from spiritual Uncleanness.[72]

She believes that the newborn soul in Christ grows daily in Christ's grace and grows toward his image. She writes:

> The New-Born Soul, in Respect of *Grace*, and the compleat Glory of Christ's Image in it, is just like a New-Born Infant in Nature, which has all the *Parts* of a Man, tho' it wants the full *Stature* of a Man; and therefore *increaseth* until it arrive unto the *Perfection* of Manhood.[73]

Dutton states that the life-giving power of the Holy Spirit pours the grace of Christ into the unregenerate soul and cleanses it and makes it new. She uses Titus 3:3-6 and speaks of the washing of regeneration.

> Efficacious Grace (*says he*) made new Men of us; it cleansed our Souls of that Earthliness, Sensuality, and Vileness, which filled our Affections; and made them Heavenly, Spiritual, and Pure, by the washing of Regeneration, and the renewing of the Holy Ghost; that is, by the cleansing Efficacy of Christ's Blood.[74]

She further defines the grace of faith as a "leading Grace."

---

[70]*Discourse concerning the New Birth*, 5.

[71]*Discourse concerning the New Birth*, 6-7.

[72]*Discourse concerning the New Birth*, 9.

[73]*Discourse concerning the New Birth.*, 15.

[74]*Discourse concerning the New Birth*, 27-28.

And, as in Nature, a Child is first formed and quickned in the Womb, in order to its Birth and Life in this World; so in Grace, the Soul is first formed anew and has a Principle of Life, or of every Grace given it, in order to its being brought forth into the Liberty of the Gospel, and the visible Actings of every Grace.[75]

For Dutton, the soul in new birth grows and progresses in the course of life, yet it awaits the hope of eternal life in God.[76] She illustrates the hope of the martyrs of the Church such as Stephen.[77] Referring to the martyrs of the history of England, she writes: "And the *Martyrs* in the *Flames*, even here in *England*, in Queen *Mary's* Days, have been fill'd with inconceivably more Pleasure in their Torments for Christ's Sake, than their Enemies could have in heaping Fire and Faggots upon them."[78]

Dutton offers characteristics or principles of the spiritual life produced by the new birth. One example is humility:

Humility, is another Grace, contained in that Principle of Spiritual Life, produc'd by the Spirit, in the Souls of the New-born, at the Time of their Regeneration."[79]

She also writes that

the Grace of *Humility* in the Souls of the *Regenerate, acts* towards God, in *depending* on his *Power.* . . .
　　Once more, this Grace of *Humility, acts* towards God its *Object*, in *submitting* to his *Dominion* in *Providence*, as well as *Grace*.[80]

To discuss the spiritual quality of meekness, Dutton uses the story of the Canaanite woman in Matthew 15:22-28. She writes of the Canaanite woman's words as found in verse 27:

As if she should say, Lord, I acknowledge I am *Vile*, that I deserve no better Name than that of a *Dog*, that I am unworthy of *Children's Bread*, or to be dealt with as thou dealest with thy *own*; but let me have *Crumbs*

---

[75]*Discourse concerning the New Birth*, 31-32.
[76]*Discourse concerning the New Birth*, 51.
[77]*Discourse concerning the New Birth.*, 52.
[78]*Discourse concerning the New Birth*, 53.
[79]*Discourse concerning the New Birth*, 60-61.
[80]*Discourse concerning the New Birth*, 81-82.

of Mercy, the Off-falling of that rich, and plenteous Board thou spreadest for thy *Children*. Oh the amazing *Meekness* of this Woman's Spirit![81]

In reference to verse 28, Dutton notes that Jesus feeds her, heals her, praises her faith, and calls her daughter.

> His *Wisdom*, in trying her Faith, Patience, Humility, and Meekness; that so, in granting her Request, he might do it in such a Way, as to put a peculiar Honour upon her to all Generations.[82]

Dutton goes on to the third main part of her discourse, that is, to show what can be learned from the phrase "to be born again." She states:

> That as no Man can give himself an Existence in *Nature*, or the *First-Birth*; so neither can any Man give himself a Being in *Grace*, or the *New-Birth*. As God, as the God of *Nature*, is the sole *Author* of the one; so God, as the God of *Grace*, is the sole *Author* of the other. This appears, from John i.13.[83]

She further states that the things of God are spiritual: "The Things of Christ's Kingdom are *spiritual*; and therefore the *natural Man*, with all his highest Attainments, cannot *know* them, I *Cor*. ii.14."[84]

Concluding the discourse on the fourth topic, Dutton offers a three-point discussion of the usefulness of the doctrine of the new birth.[85] She gives three points and states, First, the new birth gives "all the *Glory* of your *heavenly Birth*, unto God, your *Heavenly Father*, who was the sole Author of it. You are *his Workmanship, created in Christ Jesus unto good Works*, Eph. ii.10. Your *New-Life*, was a Work of *Almightiness*."[86] Second, Dutton writes, "Learn hence, you *New-Born* Souls, the Necessity of your *Growth*."[87] And third, Dutton declares, "From this Doctrine of the *New-Birth*, you who are *New-Born*, may learn, the Security of your *State*, for endless Life and Glory."[88]

---

[81]*Discourse concerning the New Birth*, 90-91.
[82]*Discourse concerning the New Birth*, 92.
[83]*Discourse concerning the New Birth*, 96.
[84]*Discourse concerning the New Birth*, 102.
[85]*Discourse concerning the New Birth*, 108.
[86]*Discourse concerning the New Birth*, 109.
[87]*Discourse concerning the New Birth*, 110.
[88]*Discourse concerning the New Birth*, 112.

Dutton beautifully writes about the essence of the new birth. She offers:

> And as Christ is our Life, as the Ocean-fulness of it dwells in him, so
> it is and shall be communicated from him, by his holy Spirit; who, having
> taken Possession of our Souls, *abides* there, as the Spring of our Life, or
> as a Well of living Water, springing up unto everlasting Life.[89]

On the usefulness of the doctrine of the new birth to the unregenerate, she admonishes: "[M]ake use of all the *Means* of Grace, which God affords him."[90]

Dutton concludes the discourse by calling persons to wait upon the grace of the gospel: "And yet, as was said, it is the *Duty* of every Creature to *obey* his Creator's *Command*, and as Law-condemn'd, and Self-ruin'd, to *wait* upon the God of all Grace under the *Gospel*."[91]

The discourse ends with a herald to God's grace from Zechariah 4:7.[92]

Two Poems and a Hymn

Two poems and a hymn are found added to the end of *A Discourse concerning the New-Birth*.

"A Poem on Salvation in Christ by Free Grace, for the Chief of Sinners."

Dutton prefaces "A Poem on Salvation in Christ by Free Grace, for the Chief of Sinners," with

The DEDICATION.

To th' Soul that sees its Need of Christ,
And longs in him t' have Interest,
And 'cause its vile, is full of Fear,
The following Lines presented are;
Being a *Poem*, made by One,
Sav'd by Free Grace, thro' God's dear Son.
The Author wishes 't may be blest,
To give some Soul a Glimpse of Christ.[93]

---

[89]*Discourse concerning the New Birth*, 114.
[90]*Discourse concerning the New Birth*, 119.
[91]*Discourse concerning the New Birth*, 120.
[92]*Discourse concerning the New Birth,* 121.
[93]*Poem on Salvation,* 122.

The poem itself begins with the lines,

> COME, trembling Soul, Oh! come and see,
> What Grace there is in Christ for Thee."[94]

The poem is 132 lines long and focuses on the salvation of the grace of Christ in the sinner's soul. The following are some select lines on sin and grace.

> But come to Christ, *just* as thou art. . . .
> I come, *Lord Jesus*, in my *Need*,
> To Thee, who did for Sinners *bleed*.
> I come to *th' Fountain, ope* [open] *for Sin*;
> Oh *wash* my filthy Soul therein!
> I come to Thee for *Righteousness*,
> And for Supply of every *Grace*.[95]

Dutton writes of God's love in Christ's grace that he poured out to save the church:

> I *joy* to *save* thee, Oh my *Bride!*
> This was the *End* for which I dy'd. . . .
> I, in my Love, will *rest* in thee;
> Who art for ever *one* with me.[96]

"A Hymn on the Mercy and Grace of God in Christ."

After the poem on salvation is found a hymn entitled, "An HYMN on the Mercy and Grace of God in Christ." It is ninety-six lines long with twenty-four stanzas or verses. It begins:

> POOR *Sinners*, hark! what Voice is this
>   That soundeth in your Ears?
> JEHOVAH speaks, in boundless Grace,
>   To banish all your Fears.[97]

In stanza 9 Dutton writes of God's grace and mercy:

---

[94] *Poem on Salvation,* 122.
[95] *Poem on Salvation,* 124.
[96] *Poem on Salvation,* 125.
[97] *Hymn,* 126.

Unto JEHOVAH, who will shew,
    On Him his *Mercy* Free,
And to that *God, who pardon will,*
    And that *Abundantly.*[98]

She concludes the hymn with the words

Oh *venture* on his boundless *Grace!*
    However *vile,* and *poor*;
And he'll thee *save* from *Death* to *Life,*
    To *praise* him evermore.[99]

"A Poem on the Safety and Duty of a Believer"

After the hymn, Dutton adds another poem entitled, "A POEM on the Safety and Duty of a Believer." The poem is long—455 lines. It begins,

HOW is it, Soul? hast thou to *Jesus* fled
For *Refuge,* from that Wrath hung o'er thy Head?
Hast ventur'd in to Him, the *Hiding place,*
Prepar'd for Sinners, by the Father's *Grace*?

She writes of a believer's safety in Christ. God is a refuge from sin through his grace. God hides us in Jesus. By our faith he brings us into salvation:

So *Christ* hid *Thee,* when in thy Place he stood.
And being entered into *Him* by Faith,
There, thou art *safe,* out of the Reach of Wrath:
Thou'rt pass'd from *Death to Life,* ev'n full Salvation.[100]

Dutton continues in the poem to discuss the duty of a believer. She writes of the need to offer sacrificial love to Christ at all times. She states,

Now then, dear Soul, if thou God's *Glory* love,
If *this,* ev'n this *alone,* thy Soul doth move;
Then rise in Haste, from all base *Selfishness,*
To *love* thy God, and him at all Times *bless.*[101]

---

[98]*Hymn,* 127.
[99]*Hymn,* 128.
[100]*Poem on the Safety,* 129.
[101]*Poem on the Safety,* 137.

The poem concludes with:

> A Life of *Faith* and *Love*, till thou art *crown'd!*
> Thus *walk* with God, in every *Dispensation*;
> Thy Course will *end*, in glorious full SALVATION!
>   Now, I commit thee to the *Grace* of Christ;
> Oh may his *Spirit* always on thee rest!
> That thou in all good *Works*, may'st fruitful be,
> Till thou shalt *rest*, in blest ETERNITY![102]

4a. *A Discourse concerning God's Act of Adoption*

In 1737 Dutton published *A Discourse concerning God's Act of Adoption*.[103] Her preface to this discourse begins:

> *As to the Publication of my Thoughts upon the ensuing Subjects, what I have freely received of the Lord, I have freely imparted to the dear Saints.*[104]

Regarding herself she says:

> *And tho' I* am less than the least of *them* all, *yet have I humbly offer'd my* Mite, *endeavouring to* speak the Truth in Love, *Eph.* 3.8 and 4.15.[105]

Then she states her purpose for writing:

> *And if the Lord will please to use me, tho' one of the least Members, to do any Service to his Body, by what I have wrote, verily I have my Reward.*[106]

Dutton defines adoption as a privilege of grace for the elect who have been chosen by God in Christ for salvation. She writes of God's adoption as "a special gracious Privilege conferr'd upon the Elect of God."[107] In this

---

[102]*Poem on the Safety*, 140.

[103]Full Title: *A Discourse concerning God's Act of Adoption. To Which Is Added, a Discourse upon the Inheritance of the Adopted Sons of God* (London: printed for the Author: and sold by E. Gardner in Coleman-street near the Old Jewry, 1737).

[104]*Discourse concerning God's Act of Adoption* (3).

[105]*A Discourse concerning God's Act of Adoption* (3), iv.

[106]*A Discourse concerning God's Act of Adoption*, iv.

[107]*A Discourse concerning God's Act of Adoption*, 9.

discourse on adoption, she will, first, "Give a Definition of it, (according to the Measure of Light received). *Secondly*, Endeavour to explain it. And, *Thirdly*, Improve it."[108] She defines adoption this way:

Adoption, is a gracious, immanent, eternal Act of God's Sovereign Will: Whereby he has taken a certain Number of Persons from among Mankind, as consider'd in the pure Mass, into a Supernatural, and Covenant-Relation of Children to himself, by Christ Jesus, to the Praise of the Glory of his Grace.[109]

She uses various Scriptures to create her definition: 2 Corinthians 6:18; Ephesians 1:3-5; Colossians 1:9; 2 Timothy 1:9; Titus 1:2; and 1 John 3:1.[110]

Dutton describes the immediate effect of adoption upon the persons chosen. The elect are chosen and made in Christ and brought into a supernatural covenant of grace.[111] She states that they are "taken by Adoption" and it "is, a Supernatural and Covenant-Relation: It is a Relation unto God by Grace, which is far superior unto that we had by Nature."[112] She continues that God predestined and chose the elect to be in the covenant of grace. She writes:

That it was a certain Number of Persons from among Mankind, which were taken into this Relation. *For whom he did Foreknow, them he did Predestinate*, &c. *Rom.* viii.29. Here is the determinate Number exprest, by their being said, to be [Foreknown]: Which was by God's eternal Choice of 'em *in Christ, Eph.* i.4.[113]

Further emphasizing God's foreknowledge, she says, "And it was none but those whom God thus Foreknew, which he did *Predestinate to be conform'd unto the Image of his Son, Rom.* 8.29."[114] For Dutton, God adopts the elect through Jesus Christ whom God predestined unto salvation through his Son. She states, "That Christ Jesus was the Pattern by which

---

[108]*A Discourse concerning God's Act of Adoption*, 9-10.

[109]*A Discourse concerning God's Act of Adoption*, 10.

[110]*A Discourse concerning God's Act of Adoption*, 14-15.

[111]*A Discourse concerning God's Act of Adoption*, 33.

[112]*A Discourse concerning God's Act of Adoption*, 34.

[113]*A Discourse concerning God's Act of Adoption*, 40.

[114]*A Discourse concerning God's Act of Adoption*, 41.

God did proceed in this Act of Adoption: *Having predestinated us unto the Adoption of Children by Christ Jesus,* Eph. i.5."[115]

Secondly in the discourse, Dutton further explains adoption and election in Christ Jesus. She makes a distinction between secret and open adoption. Secret adoption in Christ refers to the eternal act of God's will in establishing the everlasting covenant with his Son for the salvation of the elect. Open adoption is the visible activity of God in time. It is when God's grace actually passes upon the elect to save them in Christ. In time, the elect can enjoy the privileges of their covenant relation of salvation and grace in Christ. The elect who are already in God's eternal will are now saved in time in Christ. The elect's salvation is made manifest in time when Christ's grace passes over them and they can enjoy the fruits of Christ's redemption. Dutton states:

> We are to distinguish between secret and open Adoption: The one is the Foundation of the other. Secret Adoption respects the Relation itself, bestow'd of mere Grace. . . . Open Adoption respects the Visibility, or Manifestation thereof by a transient Act in Time: Which I look upon to be no new Act in God, but only his eternal Will herein, in the Declaration of his Word, passing upon an elect Vessel at the appointed Season; whereby the Person is admitted into the enjoyment of all the Privileges of this Relation, as a Fruit of Christ's Redemption, and free Justification by his Blood.[116]

Thirdly in the discourse, Dutton focuses on the improvement of the doctrine of adoption. She emphasizes themes of freedom, love, and fellowship as children of God's grace. She writes:

> How shall [We] Sin against that Love, that will never Disinherit us! Oh, what Childlike Ingenuity, should this work in our Hearts towards our dear Father, since we are *no more Servants*, to return to Servitude, *Gal.* 4.7. but Sons, *Free* Children that shall *Abide in the House for ever. Joh.* 8.34, 35.[117]

She continues:

---

[115] *A Discourse concerning God's Act of Adoption,* 44.

[116] *A Discourse concerning God's Act of Adoption,* 57-58.

[117] *A Discourse concerning God's Act of Adoption,* 70.

We are called to walk in daily Fellowship with the Family of Heaven, as such that are *no more Strangers and Foreigners, but Fellow Citizens with the Saints, and of the Household of God, Eph.* 2.19.[118]

Near the end of the discourse, Dutton states her last point:

Lastly, Was God's ultimate End in this Act of Adoption, the Praise of the Glory of his Grace, both as display'd and ascrib'd:
Then let's Admire that Grace which illustriously Shines forth herein."[119]

4b. A Discourse upon the Inheritance of the Adopted Sons of God.

The 1737 edition of *A Discourse concerning God's Act of Adoption* included *A Discourse upon the Inheritance of the Adopted Sons of God*. Dutton begins this discourse by summing up the major emphases of the previous discourse on adoption and then by explaining the second discourse's purpose and focus:

---

[118]*A Discourse concerning God's Act of Adoption*, 71.
[119]*A Discourse concerning God's Act of Adoption.*, 76-77.

HAVING in the foregoing Discourse, chiefly insisted upon God's Act of Adoption, predestinating us into a supernatural Relation: And also therein given some Hints, of what the Inheritance is that was settled upon the Sons of God, as standing in that Relation: I shall now farther take it into Consideration, and make it a distinct Head of Discourse.[120]

She then outlines the main points she will make about the inheritance of the adopted sons of God:

> *First*, To prove that the adopted Sons of God have an Inheritance.
> *Secondly*, To enquire what their Inheritance is, or wherein it consists.
> *Thirdly*, When it was made theirs.
> *Fourthly*, How it was settled upon them.
> *Fifthly*, Which Way they come to enjoy it.
> *Sixthly*, When they enter upon the Possession of it. And,
> *Seventhly*, Something by Way of Reflection.[121]

Dutton uses various Scriptures to show the validity of her points, particularly Psalms 37:18; Ephesians 1:11, 14; and 1 Peter 1:4.[122]

Dutton asks, "What then is the Inheritance?" She answers what it is not and then what it is.[123] She states: "[T]heir Inheritance doth not consist in the perfect Enjoyment of outward and temporal Blessings since the Fall."[124] Inheritance consists rather in God himself, that is, "It is no less than GOD HIMSELF, as the God of all Grace and Glory, making over himself to them, as their Eternal ALL."[125] She continues, "That *Jehovah*, is the God and Portion of his People, is a Truth oft inculcated in the Sacred Scriptures."[126] She supports her definition of inheritance with scripture references such as Genesis 15:1; Numbers 18:20; Psalms 73:26; Isaiah 41:10; Lamentations 3:24; and Hebrews 8:10.[127]

Using Romans 8:17, Dutton says we are joint-heirs with Christ and share in his riches. She writes:

---

[120]*Inheritance*, 81-82.
[121]*Inheritance*, 82
[122]*Inheritance*, 82-83.
[123]*Inheritance*, 84.
[124]*Inheritance*, 85.
[125]*Inheritance*, 85-86.
[126]*Inheritance*, 88.
[127]*Inheritance*, 88-89.

The Riches of Christ, as Mediator, and Ours in him are Unsearchable, as the Man Christ, stands personally United to the Godhead; and we United to the Person of Christ. Christ stands in [God], the infinite Ocean of Grace and Glory; and we in [Him] as the *Medium* of Communication.[128]

To explain this further, she quotes Dr. Owen's book, *Communication with God*.[129]

Describing God's attributes, Dutton shows those communicable attributes that he gives to us and the incommunicable attributes ascribed to him alone. For example, she writes of communicable attributes that "he is also Light to us, when as *the Father of Lights*, Jam. i.17. He communicates Light, by creating a Divine Principle of Light in our Hearts."[130] Of God's incommunicable divine attributes, she writes:

> Again, Is our God the omnipresent Being, *Psal.* 139.7, 8, 9. and *Jer.* 23.24. He fills all things for us: The World with his general [presence], the Church with his gracious [presence], and Heaven with his glorious Presence; yea, and Hell with his wrathful Presence.[131]

Using Romans 8:30, Dutton shows that God glorifies the elect:

> And if we take this Word, *Glorified*, to intend either, 1. The Settlement, or, 2. The Conveyance of a glorious Inheritance, or both, it will afford a full Proof to the Point in Hand: That God hath glorify'd none but those whom he eternally Predestined unto Life. They were all *Known by* [*Name*] in God's Electing, and adopting Love.[132]

Dutton states the relation of Adam to the lostness of the human race due to the Fall. Yet God's election of his chosen remnant in Christ is sure and certain:

---

[128]*Inheritance*, 93-94.

[129]*Inheritance*, 94-95, quoting Owen, *Of Communion with God the Father, Son, and Holy Ghost, Each Person Distinctly: In Love, Grace, and Consolation. or, The Saints Fellowship with the Father, Son, and Holy Ghost Unfolded. By the Reverend John Owen D.D.* (London: William Marshall, 1700) 78-79.

[130]*Inheritance*, 100.

[131]*Inheritance*, 107.

[132]*Inheritance*, 114-15.

So that, if the Inheritance of the Sons of God by supernatural Grace, had been put into *Adam's* Hands, it had been lost: for he lost all he was entrusted with.

But this was the unspeakable Privilege of the Children of God, the elect remnant, that they were, not only chosen in *Christ,* but, *Blessed in Christ* too, *Eph.* 1.3, 4.[133]

For Dutton, Jesus Christ is the Mediator of Salvation for the elect by the way of his sufferings on the cross. She writes:

Nor was *Christ* to have all this Glory as the just Reward of his meritorious Sufferings for himself only, but for us also, according to the decreed Proportion of Head and Members: so that, having obtained Life, Glory, and a Kingdom, by the infinite Worth of his Obedience unto Death; he was to be the Donor of this *Life,* Glory, and Kingdom, as being his own Right by Price, *to as many as the Father gave him,* John 17.2, 22.[134]

Later in the discourse, Dutton further states of Jesus that

3. *Christ* is the Way, in which the Sons of God come to enjoy their Inheritance in respect of Communication: *Christ was set up from everlasting,* as the great Mediator between God and all his Creatures.[135]

Speaking of Christ's eternal benefits unto the elect, Dutton especially focuses on his mediation as a way to God. She writes: "And as in the Kingdom-State, so unto the endless Ages of Eternity, we shall admire Christ, both as our Way to the Father, and the Father's Way unto us."[136] Christ accomplished this "when he ascended to Heaven as their great Representative."[137]

Dutton understands that the souls of Christians take possession of their inheritance at death, but await the resurrection for the full possession of their inheritance. She states:

The Sons of God, do enter upon the compleat Possession of their Inheritance, in their Soul-part, at the Time of their Death. . . . [Y]et so, as

---

[133]*Inheritance.*, 121.
[134]*Inheritance*, 134-35.
[135]*Inheritance*, 156.
[136]*Inheritance*, 161.
[137]*Inheritance*, 162.

that it is but partial, respecting their Souls only. For their Bodies remain still in the Grave, under the Dominion of Death.[138]

She continues:

> That the Time when the Sons of God, in their whole Man, shall enter upon the compleat Possession of their Inheritance, will be at *the Resurrection of the Just*, Luke 14.14. Then their Bodies shall be raised from the Dead, reunited to their Souls, and so their whole intire Persons, taken up into the Enjoyment of that Glory which is prepared for them. And that, 1. In the Glory-Kingdom of *Christ:* And, 2. In the ultimate State of Glory after the last Judgment.[139]

5. Three Letters

The "Three Letters" were written during the end of Dutton's life, and published together in 1761 (Dutton died in 1765).[140] Here, each of the letters will be briefly discussed. They are included here, in Dutton's "theological works," because of their rich theological content.

Letter I.
The Marks of a Child of God.

Dutton addresses letter 1 simply to *"Dear Sir,"*[141] and offers seven genuine marks of a child of God. They are given as follows.

1. The first mark of a child of God is that he recognize himself as a sinner in God's eyes and a breaker of God's laws.

2. The second mark of a child of God is that he knows Christ Jesus as his Savior by faith.

---

[138]*Inheritance*, 165, 165-66.

[139]*Inheritance*, 166.

[140]Full title: *Three Letters on I. The Marks of a Child of God. II. The Soul-Diseases of God's Children; and Their Soul-Remedies. And II. God's Prohibition of His Peoples Unbelieving Fear; and His Great Promises Given for the Support of Their Faith, unto Their Time-Joy, and Eternal Glory. By One Who Has Tasted That the Lord Is Gracious* (London: printed by J. Hart, in Popping's-Court, Fleet-Street: and sold by G. Keith, at the Bible and Crown, in Grace-church-street; and J. Fuller, in Blow-bladder-street, near Cheapside, 1761).

[141]*Three Letters*, 3.

3. The third mark of a child of God is that he believes his salvation in Christ is sealed by the promise of the Holy Spirit.

4. The fourth mark of a child of God is that he loves the Lord fervently because he has been adopted in him by his grace by the Holy Spirit.

5. The fifth mark of a child of God is that once he has been brought into God's love he hates sin.

6. The sixth mark of a child of God is that he now resides in God's love and seeks after holiness.

7. The seventh mark of a child of God is that he now desires to be with Christ in eternal bliss, that is,

> A Child of God is one, That "*Desires* to depart, and to be with Christ:" In his Spirit, at his Body's Dissolution: And that *Loves*, and *looks* for, Christ's Appearance: "Unto his full Salvation." When in his entire Person, in the Glory of the First Resurrection, he shall "See CHRIST as HE is; and be like him:' In perfect Holiness, unto GOD's external Praise, and to his external Bliss.[142]

Letter II.
The Soul-Diseases of God's Children;
and their Soul-Remedies.

Dutton again writes to "*Reverend and Dear Sir.*"[143] She addresses the diseases of the soul that the Reverend addressed to her. He senses that God is distant and withholding his grace from him. She writes:

> So I mourn with you, for your present Distress, for your Bridegroom's Absence, in which you set your Soul-Diseases, your Weakness, Deadness, Coldness, towards the God of Grace in Christ.—You ask me the Causes, Sir, "Why the Lord speaks not to you by his blessed Spirit & Word, as formerly? Why Reading and Meditation, are not so comforting as they were? And, Why Prayer is begun and ended coldly, & in a very languid manner?"[144]

She continues that the Lord may withdraw because he wishes for a Christian to more fully comprehend his own depravity and so that he can more fully

---

[142]*Three Letters*, 3-8; quotation on 8.
[143]*Three Letters*, 11.
[144]*Three Letters*, 13.

acknowledge dependence upon Christ and seek greater holiness. In his sovereignty God may withdraw

> To shew them more fully, their own universal Depravity; that they may confess & bewail it, to his Glory: Their own Nothingness and Vileness; their Need of continual Dependance, upon His All-Sufficiency; to endear the more, Christ and His Fulness; and to make them Partakers of His Holiness.[145]

Dutton attributes the cause of soul-disease to the depravity of human nature. "But, You ask me, Sir, "To point out the *Cause* of these *Diseases*."—And in General, I wou'd answer: I. That the proper *Cause*, of every *Soul-Disease:* Is the *Universal Disorder*, of our *whole* Nature."[146]

The effective remedy for soul-disease is the grace of God given according to his will. She writes: "I. Effectual Remedies for Soul-Diseases, are Those which respect *Divine Bounty.—*The *Grace of God the Father.* . . . The *Grace of God the Son*: . . . the *Grace of God the Holy Ghost* . . . convey'd according to Divine Appointment, by & thro'."[147]

Offering instrumental remedies for soul diseases, Dutton calls forth spiritual duty and discipline. She highlights the essential practices for growth and healing in the spiritual life. She lists seven in order: (1) self-examination; (2) confession of sin; (3) deep humiliation; (4) earnest supplication; (5) believing, patient expectation; (6) reading and meditation; and (7) soul-trust in the God of our salvation.[148]

Letter III.
God's Prohibition of His People's Unbelieving Fear;
and His Great Promise Given for the Support of Their Faith,
unto Their Time Joy, and Eternal Glory.

Dutton again addresses a "*Dear Sir*" and responds to a letter received from him and mentions a previous letter she had written to him concerning the Bible.

Dear Sir, [she writes]

---

[145]*Three Letters*, 13-14.
[146]*Three Letters*, 18.
[147]*Three Letters*, 20.
[148]Three Letters, 20-21.

YOURS I received with Joy, and give Thanks to GOD with you, That my Letter on *The Application of the Holy Scriptures*, is so sweet and precious to your Soul. How blessed are *you*, in that you are an *Heir of Promise!*[149]

Noting of "Dear Sir" that he has said he longs to have her thoughts on Isaiah 41:10,[150] she focuses her letter on that Isaiah text, she writes:

Briefly, then, Sir, I humbly think, That these Words, are the LORD's *Prohibition* of his Peoples unbelieving *Fear*; and His great *Declaration*, and All-comprehending *Promise of Grace*, unto their Time-Joy, and eternal Glory.[151]

Then, throughout the letter, Dutton focuses on five points:

1. *Who* the People of God are, which are here spoken to. 2. That these People are subject to unbelieving *Fear*, and sinful *Dismayment*. 3. That nevertheless, it is their unspeakable Privilege, To have God *with them*, and an Interest in HIM, as *their God*. 4. That as their God, HE hath given his great Word, That He will *strengthen* them, yea, *help*, and *uphold* them. And 5. That in dispensing all this Grace, HE engages to do it, With the *Right Hand* of his *Righteousness*."[152]

Dutton closes the letter with the joy of God's promise:

Of which, by this great Promise, You have & shall have, a most firm Asxsurance, a most certain Earnest, & a most sweet Foretaste. And may the Lord fill you thereby, with *Joy unspeakable, & full of Glory!*—I am, Dear Sir,

Yours in Christ forever, &c."[153]

---

[149]*Three Letters*, 27.

[150]*Three Letters*, 27-28.

[151]*Three Letters*, 28.

[152]*Three Letters*, 28.

[153]*Three Letters*, 36.

BIBLIOGRAPHY

Primary Sources: Anne Dutton[154]

A Brief Account of the Gracious Dealings of God, with a Poor, Sinful, Unworthy Creature, in Three Parts . . . With an Appendix. And a Letter Prefixed, on the Lawfulness of a Woman's Appearing in Print. London: John Hart, 1750.
   This autobiography was published in three parts over a period of years. Part 1 and part 2 were originally published together with separate titles as *A Brief Account of the Gracious Dealings of God, with a Poor, Sinful, Unworthy Creature, Relating to the Work of Divine Grace on the Heart, in a Saving Conversion to Christ, and to Some Establishment in Him* and *A Brief Account of the Gracious Dealings of God, with a Poor, Sinful, Unworthy Creature, Relating to a Train of Special Providences Attending Life, by which the Work of Faith was Carried on with Power.* London: John Hart, 1743. Part 3 and the "Letter" were included with the 1750 publication (see above). Part 3 is entitled *A Brief Account of the Gracious Dealings of God, with a Poor, Sinful, Unworthy Creature, Relating to Some Particular Experiences of the Lord's Goodness, in Bringing Out Several Little Tracts, to the Furtherance and Joy of Faith.*
   The publications referred to in the title ("Several Little Tracts") are pamphlets published by John Hart before 1750.
   (Parts 1 and 2 [1743] are available in the United States at Harvard University and Baylor University. The complete work [1750] is in the British Library, London.)
Brief Hints Concerning Baptism. London, 1746. May be identical to *Letters on the Ordinance of Baptism* (1746). (Whitebrook, 18 no. 25.)
Brief Hints on God's Fatherly Chastisements, Showing Their Nature, Necessity and Usefulness, and the Saints' Duty to Wait upon God for Deliverance When under His Fatherly Corrections. 1743. (Whitebrook, 17 no. 14.)
A Caution against Error When It Springs Up together with the Truth, in a Letter to a Friend. 1746. (Whitebrook, 17 no. 24.)

---

[154]"Whitebrook" refers to the bibliography of John Cudworth Whitebrook, in his *Ann Dutton: A Life and Bibliography*, 15-20, as offprinted from "The Life and Works of Mrs. Ann Dutton," in *Transactions of the Baptist Historical Society* 7:129-46.

A Discourse Concerning God's Act of Adoption. To Which is Added a Discourse upon the Inheritance of the Adopted Sons of God. London: E. Gardner, 1737. (British Library, London.)

A Discourse Concerning the New-Birth: To Which Are Added Sixty-Four Hymns; Compos'd on Several Subjects; with an Epistle Recommendatory, by the Reverend Mr. Jacob Rogers, B.A. London: John Hart, 1743. (Yale University Beinecke Rare Books Library.)

A Discourse Concerning the New-Birth: To Which Are Added Two Poems: The One on Salvation in Christ, by Free-Grace, for the Chief of Sinners: The Other on a Believer's Safety and Duty: with an Epistle Recommendatory, by the Reverend Mr. Jacob Rogers, B.A. London: John Oswald and Ebenezer Gardner, 1740. (British Library, London.)

A Discourse upon Justification: Shewing the Matter, Manner, Time and Effects of it. To Which are Added Three Poems: I. On the Special Work of the Spirit in the Hearts of the Elect. . . . III. On a Believer's Safety and Duty. London: printed by John Hart and sold by J. Lewis and E. Gardner, 1740, 1743. (The 1743 edition is at Harvard University Libraries.)

A Discourse upon Walking with God: In a Letter to a Friend. Together with Some Hints upon Joseph's Blessing, Deut. 33.13, &c. As Also a Brief Account How the Author Was Brought into Gospel-Liberty. London: printed for the author and sold by E. Gardner, 1735. (Gale Group.)

Divine, Moral, and Historical Miscellanies in Prose and Verse. Edited by A. Dutton. 1761. (British Library.)

Five Letters to a Newly Married Pair. 1759. (Whitebrook, 18 no. 33.)

Hints of the Glory of Christ: As the Friend and Bridgroom of the Church: From the Seven Last Verses of the Fifth Chaper of Solomon's Song: In a Letter to a Friend. London: printed by John Hart and sold by J. Lewis, 1748. (British Library, London.)

Originally published as *Meditations and Observations upon the Eleventh and Twelfth Verses of the Sixth Chapter of Solomon's Song.* 1743. (Whitebrook, 16 no. 13; 18 no. 27.)

The Hurt that Sin Doth to Believers, etc. 1733. Second edition, 1749. (Whitebrook, 18 no. 30.)

A Letter from Mrs. Anne Dutton to the Reverend Mr. G. Whitefield. Philadelphia: printed and sold by William Bradford, 1743. (Library Company of Philadelphia.)

A Letter on the Application of the Holy Scriptures. Poppings Court: printed by John Hart and sold by J. Lewis, 1754. (Whitebrook, 18 no. 31.)

A Letter on the Divine Eternal Sonship of Jesus Christ: . . . Occasioned by the Perusal of Mr. Romaine's Sermon . . . Entitled, A Discourse Upon the Self-Existence of Jesus Christ. With Three Letters on Assurance of Interest in

Christ: . . . Written as the Author's Thoughts, on Part of Mr. Marshal's . . . The Gospel-Mystery of Sanctification. And Two Letters on the Gift of the Holy Spirit to Believers . . . By One Who Has Tasted that the Lord is Gracious. London: printed by John Hart and sold by G. Keith, 1757. (Oxford University Bodleian Library.)

A Letter on the Duty and Privilege of a Believer to Live by Faith, and to Improve His Faith unto Holiness. 1745. (Whitebrook, 17 n. 21.)

A Letter on Perseverance, against Mr. Wesley. 1747. (Whitebrook, 18 no. 38.)

A Letter to All Men on the General Duty of Love among Christians. 1742. (Whitebrook, 16 no. 7.)

A Letter to all the Saints on the General Duty of Love: Humbly Presented, by One That is Less Than the Least of Them All, and Unworthy to be of Their Happy Number. London: printed by John Hart and sold by Samuel Mason, 1742; printed by John Hart and sold by J. Lewis and E. Gardner, 1743. Philadelphia: Joseph Crukshank, 1774. (Harvard University Andover; Harvard Theological Library has the 1743 edition.)

A Letter to All Those That Love Christ in Philadelphia. To Excite Them to Adhere to, and Appear for, the Truths of the Gospel. 1743(?). (Whitebrook, 17 no. 19.)

A Letter to the Believing Negroes, lately Converted to Christ in America. 1742. (Whitebrook, 16 no. 9.)

A Letter to Christians at the Tabernacle. 1744(?). (Whitebrook, 18 no. 37.)

A Letter to Mr. William Cudworth, In Vindication of the Truth from his Misrepresentations: With Respect to the Work of the Spirit in Faith, Holiness, The New Birth &c. Being a Reply to his Answer to the Postscript of a Letter Lately Published, &c. 1747. (Whitebrook, 18 no. 26.)

A Letter to the Reverend Mr. John Wesley. In Vindication of the Doctrines of Absolute, Unconditional Election, Particular Redemption, Special Vocation, and Final Perseverance. Occasioned Chiefly by Some Things in His Dialogue between a Predestinarian and His Friend; and In His Hymns on God's Everlasting Love. London: printed by John Hart and sold by Samuel Mason, 1742. (Pitts Theology Library, Emory University.)

A Letter to Such of the Servants of Christ Who May Have Any Scruple about the Lawfulness of Printing Anything Written by a Woman. 1743. (Whitebrook, 17 no. 18.)

Letters against Sanddemanianism and with a Letter on Reconciliation. (Whitebrook, 18 no. 36.)

Letters on the Being and Working of Sin in a Justified Man. 1745. (Whitebrook, 17 no. 20.)

Letters on the Ordinance of Baptism. 1746. May be identical to *Brief Hints Concerning Baptism.* London, 1746. (Whitebrook, 18 no. 25.)

Letters to the Reverend Mr. John Westley [*sic*] *against Perfection as Not Attainable in This Life*. London: John Hart, 1743. (Pitts Theological Library, Emory University; John Rylands Library, University of Manchester.)

Letters on Spiritual and Divers Occasions. London: G. Keith, 1749. (Whitebrook, 18 no. 29.)

Letters on Spiritual Subjects, and Divers Occasions, Sent to Relatives and Friends. London: printed and sold by John Oswald and Ebenezer Gardner, 1740. London: printed by John Hart and sold by J. Lewis, 1748.

Letters on Spiritual Subjects and Divers Occasions, Sent to the Reverend Mr. George Whitefield And others of his Friends and Acquaintance. To Which is Added, A Letter on the Being and Working of Sin, in the Soul of justify'd Man, as Consistent with His State of Justification in Christ, and Sanctification Through Him: With the Nature of His Obedience, and of His Comfort, Consider'd: As the One is from God, and the other to Him; notwithstanding his Corruptions may be great, and His Graces Small in His Own Sight. As Also, A Letter on the Duty and Privilege of a Believer, To Live by Faith, and to Improve his Faith unto Holiness. By One Who Has Tasted that the Lord is Gracious. London: John Hart, 1745. (Pitts Theology Library, Emory University. Incomplete copy.)

Letters on Spiritual Subjects Sent to Relations and Friends. Two parts. Second revised edition. Edited by Christopher Goulding. London: T. Bensley, 1823–1824. (Duke University Library.)

Letters Sent to an Honourable Gentleman, for the Encouragement of Faith. By One Who Has Tasted that the Lord is Gracious. London: printed by John Hart and sold by J. Lewis and E. Gardner, 1743. (Boston Athenaeum.)

Meditations and Observations upon the Eleventh and Twelfth Verses of the Sixth Chapter of Solomon's Song. 1743. Published later as a pamphlet entitled *Hints of the Glory of Christ as the Friend and Bridegroom of the Church: From the Seven Last Verses of the Fifth Chapter of Solomon's Song, &c.* 1748. (Whitebrook, 16 no. 13; 18 no. 27.)

Mr. Sanddeman Refuted by an Old Woman: or Thoughts on His Letters to the Author of Theron and Aspasio. In a Letter from a Friend in the Country to a Friend in Town. London: John Hart, 1761. (Brown University Library.)

A Narration of the Wonders of Grace, in Six Parts. I. Of Christ the Mediator, as Set Up from Everlasting in All the Glory of Headship. II. Of God's Election and Covenant—Transactions Concerning a Remnant in His Son. III. Of Christ's Incarnation and Redemption. IV. Of the Work of the Spirit, Respecting the Church in General, throughout the New Testament Dispensation, from Christ's Ascension to His Second Coming. V. Of Christ's Glorious Appearing and Kingdom. VI. Of Gog and Magog; Together with the Last Judgment. To Which Is Added, A Poem on the Special Work of the Spirit in the Hearts of the Elect, also, Sixty One Hymns Composed on Several Subjects. A new edition. Revised, with a preface and collected memoir of the author, by John Andrews Jones. London: John Bennett, 1833. Pages xxxii + 115. (Covenant Theological Seminary, St. Louis.)

Second edition. "Corrected by the author, with additions." London: printed for the author and sold by John Oswald, 1734. Pages viii + [9-]143.

First edition. London: printed for and sold by the author, 1734. Pages viii + 139.

Occasional Letters on Spiritual Subjects. Seven volumes. Popping's Court: John Hart and Bartholomew Close: J. Lewis, 1740–1749.

A Postcript to a Letter Lately Published, on the Duty and Privilege of a Believer to Live by Faith, &c . . . Directed to the Society at the Tabernacle in London. . . . As Also, Some of the Mistakes of the Moravian Brethren. . . . By One Who Has Tasted that the Lord is Gracious. London: printed by John Hart and sold by J. Lewis and E. Gardner, 1746. (Union Theological Seminary, New York.)

Selections from [Occasional] Letters on Spiritual Subjects: Addressed to Relatives and Friends. Compiled by James Knight. London: John Gadsby, 1884. (Turpin Library, Dallas Theological Seminary.)

A Sight of Christ Necessary for All True Christians and Gospel Ministers. 1743. (Whitebrook, 16 no. 11.)

Thoughts on the Lord's Supper. London, 1748. (Whitebrook, 18 no. 28.)

Three Letters on I. The Marks of a Child of God. II. The Soul-Diseases of God's Children; . . . III. God's Prohibition of His Peoples Unbelieving Fear: . . . By One Who Has Tasted that the Lord is Gracious. London: printed by John Hart and sold by G. Keith and J. Fuller, 1761. (Oxford University Bodleian Library.)

A Treatise on Justification: Showing the Matter, Manner, Time, and Effects of It. Third edition. Glasgow: printed by William Smith for Archibald Coubrough, 1778. The author is listed as "the Rev. Mr. Thomas Dutton," presumably one of Anne Dutton's pseudonymns. (British Library, London.)

Primary Sources: Dutton's Contemporaries

B. D. [Benjamin Dutton]. *The Superaboundings of the Exceeding Riches of God's Free Grace, towards the Chief of the Chief of Sinners, &c.* No publisher, no date.

Baker, Frank, ed. *The Works of John Wesley.* Volume 26. *Letters II (1740–1755).* Oxford: Clarendon Press, 1982.

Bunyan, John. *The Holy War.* London: printed for Dorman Newman and Benjamin Alsop, 1682.

_____. *Pilgrim's Progress.* 1678. Repr.: Ulrichsville OH: Barbour Publishing, 1985.

_____. *The Works of John Bunyan: With an Introduction to Each Treatise, Notes, and a Sketch of His Life, Times, and Contemporaries*. Three volumes. Edited by George Offor. Repr.: Edinburgh and Carlisle PA: Banner of Truth Trust, 1991. Original: Glasgow: W. G. Blackie and Son, 1854.

Cudworth, William, *Truth Defended and Cleared from Mistakes and Misrepresentations*. See Arthur Wallington, "Wesley and Ann Dutton," 48.

Middleton, Erasmus. *A Letter from the Reverend Mr. [Erasmus Middleton] to A[nne] D[utton]*. 1735. (British Library, London.)

Wesley, John. *A Dialogue Between a Predestinarian and His Friend*. London: W. Stratan, 1741.

_____. *Wesley's Standard Sermons*. Two volumes. Edited by Edward H. Sugden. Fifth edition. London: Epworth, 1961.

_____. *The Works of John Wesley*. Fourteen volumes. Third edition. Edited by Thomas Jackson et al. London: Wesleyan Conference Office, 1873–1893. Repr.: Grand Rapids: Zondervan, 1958-1959.

_____. *The Works of John Wesley*. Volume 19. *Journal and Diaries II (1738–1743)*. Edited by W. Reginald Ward and Richard P. Heitzenrater. Nashville: Abingdon Press, 1990.

Wesley, John and Charles. *Hymns of God's Everlasting Love*. Bristol: S. and F. Farley, 1741.

_____. *The Poetical Works of John and Charles Wesley*. Thirteen volumes. Edited by George Osborn. London: Wesleyan-Methodist Conference Office, 1868–1872.

Whitefield, George. "A Letter to the Rev. Mr. John Wesley in Answer to His Sermon Entitled 'Free Grace' " (24 December 1740). In [Whitefield's] *Journals*, 571-88. London: Banner of Truth Trust, 1960.

_____. *The Works of the Reverend George Whitefield*. Six volumes. London: Edward and Charles Dilley, 1771–1772.

Secondary Sources

Austin, Roland. "The Weekly History." *Proceedings of the Wesley Historical Society* 11/2 (June 1917): 239-43.

Burder, Samuel. See under Thomas Gibbons.

Dana, Daniel. See under Thomas Gibbons.

A Dictionary of Hymnology. Edited by John Julian. New York: Scribner's, 1892.

Gibbons, Thomas. *Memoirs of Eminently Pious Women, Who Were Ornaments to Their Sex, Blessings to Their Families, and Edifying Examples to the Church and World*. Two volumes. London: printed for J. Buckland, 1777.

    (2) Dana's abridged edition: "Abridged from the large work of Dr. Gibbons, London, by Daniel Dana." Women and the Church in America 9. Newburyport MA: printed for the subscribers by Angier March, 1803.

(3) Jerment's expanded edition: "Republished [with some omissions] in 1804, with an additional volume by George Jerment." Two volumes. (Volume 1 contained all of Gibbons's material, originally in two volumes; volume 2 contained additional material by Jerment.) London: printed by W. Nicholson for R. Ogles, 1804.

(4) Burder's new and further expanded edition: "A new edition, embellished with eighteen portraits, corrected and enlarged by Samuel Burder." Three volumes. (Volume 1 comprises the original material of Gibbons; volume 2 is Jerment's 1804 addition; volume 3 adds Burder's new material.) London: Ogles, Duncan, and Cochran, 1815.

(Gibbons's *Memoirs* is most readily available today in the following Burder edition. Consequently, *Memoirs* is routinely cited in the literature under "Burder" as author.)

(5) Reprint of the Burder expanded edition: "From a late London edition, in three volumes; now complete in one volume." One volume. Philadelphia: J. J. Woodward, 1834ff. (This is the edition routinely cited herein, and that in its 1836 reprinting.)

Green, Richard. *Anti-Methodist Publications: Issued during the Eighteenth Century: A Chronologically Arranged and Annotated Bibliography of All Known Books and Pamphlets Written in Opposition to the Methodist Revival during the Life of Wesley; Together with an Account of Replies to Them, and of Some Other Publications. A Contribution to Methodist History.* London: C. H. Kelly, 1902. Repr.: New York: Burt Franklin, 1973.

Haykin, Michael. "The Celebrated Mrs. Anne Dutton." *Evangelical Times* (April 2001). (The third in an extended series of articles under the general title "A Cloud of Witnesses.") Now available online at <http://website.lineone.net/~gsward/pages/adutton.html>.

Heitzenrater, Richard P. *Wesley and the People Called Methodists.* Nashville: Abingdon, 1995.

Herbert, George. *The English Poems of George Herbert.* Edited by C. A. Patrides. London: S. M. Dent and Sons, 1991.

Jerment, George. See under Thomas Gibbons.

Johnson, Dale A. *Women and Religion in Britain and Ireland: An Annotated Bibliography from The Reformation to 1993.* ATLA Bibliography Series 39. Lanham MD: Scarecrow Press, 1995.

MacHaffie, Barbara J. *Her Story: Women in Christian Tradition.* Philadelphia: Fortress, 1986.

The Oxford Dictionary of the Christian Church. Second edition. Edited by F. L. Cross and E. A. Livingstone. Oxford: Oxford University Press, 1974. Third edition. 1997.

Robinson, H. Wheeler. *The Life and Faith of the Baptists*. Revised edition. London: Kingsgate Press, 1946; first edition, 1927; repr.: Wake Forest NC: Chanticleer, 1985. The section on Anne Dutton appears on pp. 50-56: "Studies in Baptist Personality: (6) A Baptist Writer (Ann Dutton)."

Starr, Edward, editor. *A Baptist Bibliography*. Rochester NY: American Baptist Historical Society, 1959. (Section D, 201-204, lists about seventy works by Anne Dutton.)

Stein, Stephen. "A Note on Anne Dutton, Eighteenth-Century Evangelical." *Church History* 44/4 (December 1975): 485-91. Now available online (to those with licensed access) at the JSTOR: Church History website.

Wallington, Arthur. "Wesley and Anne Dutton." *Proceedings of the Wesley Historical Society* 11/2 (June 1917): 43-48.

Watson, JoAnn Ford, "Anne Dutton: An 18th Century British Evangelical Woman." *Ashland Theological Journal* 30 (1998): 51-56.

Whitebrook, John Cudworth. *Ann Dutton: A Life and Bibliography.* London: A. W. Cannon and Co., 1921; 20 pp. Appears also as "The Life and Works of Mrs. Ann Dutton," in *Transactions of the Baptist Historical Society* 7 (1920–1921): 129-46. (*Transactions*, 1908–1921, became the *Baptist Quarterly*, 1922 to date.)

Whitley, William Thomas. *A Baptist Bibliography: Being a Register of the Chief Materials for Baptist History, Whether in Manuscript or in Print, Preserved in Great Britain, Ireland, and the Colonies*. Two volumes. London: Kingsgate Press, 1916, 1922. Repr.: Two volumes in one: Hildesheim: Georg Olms, 1984.

HINTS

OF THE

GLORY of CHRIST;

AS THE

Friend and *Bridegroom* of the *Church:*

FROM THE

Seven last Verses of the Fifth Chapter of
Solomon's Song.

In a L E T T E R to a F R I E N D.

By *A. D.*

L O N D O N:

Printed by J. HART, in *Popping's-Court, Fleet Street:*
And Sold by J. LEWIS, in *Bartholomew-Close,*
near *West-Smithfield.* 1748.

[Price stitch'd Nine-Pence.]

To Mr. *E. H.*

S ir, as the after Letter, to you I've sent,
These Lines before it, I likewise present.

My Friend, read of a *Friend*, that doth all Friends *exceed:*
A Friend, *that* loves His, *in all Times of* Need:
A *Friend,* whose Kindness and his Truth ne're *fails;*
A *Friend,* whose Power and Int'rest e're prevails.
Read of a *Bridegroom*, that doth all *excel:*
And may you, with the *Virgins, love him* well!
May you, with *Salem's* Daughters, *seek* him too:
And never *rest*, till *Christ*, as *yours*, you know!
And may the Spirit, to you Christ's Glory *shew*,
By some one Line, your Friend did write for *you!*
How *blest* wou'd be that *Morn*, that Day how *bright,*
If *Christ*, and *you*, were *join'd* in *Love's Delight!*
Were you so *join'd*, that you might never *part;*
'twould be the Joy, and Gladness of my Heart.
Oh! might *He* have you, as his *Bride:* Then *I*,
As th' Bridegroom's *Friend*, should joy exceedingly!
T'endear your Soul to *Him:* This was my *End*,
In what, from th' *Spouse's Lips,* for *you*, I penn'd.
And might I see you marry'd to the LORD,
'twou'd be my Life, my Crown, my great Reward!
Read then, my Friend, This Story of Christ's Love:
Who knows but th' Spirit, may tell you't from above?
If while you read Christ's Beauties, *Him* you spy:
'twill make you *happy* to Eternity!
For his sweet Bridegroom's fill'd with *Love* to th'
And lets none *die*, who fall in Love with *Him:* [*Brim:*
To them, he gives himself, his Life, his Store!
And makes them *blest*, both now, and evermore!

And now, that *Christ*, your happy *Lot* may be:
That you may *share* his full Felicity:
That *His* may be the Glory: *Ours* the Joy:

So, my dear Friend, your Friend for you, doth pray!
So be't! I say. LORD! say, *So shall it be.*
And we'll raise *Hallelujahs* unto thee!
We'll bless thy Name, thy Grace we'll magnify:
While Time doth last, and to Eternity!

My Friend, I'll here, no longer you detain:
Grace be with you! Your Friend, I still remain,

A. D.

H I N T S

OF THE

Glory of Christ, &c.

In a LETTER to a FRIEND.

SIR,

I Beg leave to acquaint you, that it is on my Heart, to put you in Remembrance of that *Description* the *Spouse* gave of her *Beloved*, in the Fifth Chapter of *Solomon's* Song, from the tenth Verse, to the Close of the Chapter. And tho' I am conscious of my own Weakness, and utter Inability, as in, and of myself, to say any Thing worthy of your Notice, or for your Profit: Yet I intreat the Favour of you to read this Epistle, however tedious it may seem; and patiently attend to the Chatterings of a Child, that cannot speak, the Lispings of a Babe; for such I am in Knowledge. And the Lord grant you an *Interpreter, one among a Thousand*; even the blessed *Spirit of God*, who alone can teach you to *profit*. He can give you the Sense of my broken Language, and make my half Words, plain, and intelligible to you: Yea, He can give you the Meaning of his own Words, in a far higher Sense, than I am yet capable of conceiving, or expressing them. This glorious, Almighty Agent, can *take of the Things of Christ*, and *shew them unto you*; so as to make them stand forth to the Eye of your Soul, in their Reality, Excellency, and Glory, with the highest Evidence, and greatest Demonstration. His Teachings are efficacious Teachings; vastly different from ours. Ours are external, his internal. He can irradiate the darkest Soul in an Instant, and reveal to the weakest Babe, those glorious Mysteries of Grace and Salvation, in and by Christ, which are hidden from this World's *wise* and *prudent* Ones. He can shine in upon the Soul, and give it to know the Truth of God in his own Light; as the Being, and Brightness of the Sun's Body, is known by its glorious Rays. Yea, he can give us to know the *Truth as it is in Jesus*, not only in the Reality, and Excellency of its Being; but in its Life-giving Efficacy, its Soul-transforming Glory. Therefore pray to the *Father of Glory*, that he would *give unto you, the Spirit of Wisdom and Revelation in the Knowledge of Christ:* Whom to *know*, is *Life eternal.*

And as I have a deep Sense of my own Inability to say any Thing worthy of your Regard, or for your Advantage; so have I a much more humbling Sense of my exceeding Unfitness to say any Thing worthy of the Notice, or becoming the Glory of my great LORD! The *Glory of Christ*, is a Theme so *High*; that the loftiest Notes of glorify'd Saints above, of Angels, and Arch-Angels, in their most exalted Strains of Praise, can never *warble it forth*. The Infinity of its Height, is past created Knowledge, Conception, and Expression: And 'tis infinite Condescension in this great LORD, to behold the Worship of *Heaven*, in their most raised Hallelujahs, and humble Adorations. Who, or what am *I*, then, a Worm of the *Earth*, a vile, sinful Worm, that I should attempt to speak of his Incomprehensible Glory! And what an amazing Stoop of divine Favour is it, that the great JEHOVAH, should have a gracious Regard to the Worship and Service of his Children, that *dwell in Houses of Clay, whose Foundation is in the Dust!* Yea, that have a Body of Sin dwelling in 'em, which renders their highest Service imperfect, and as coming from them, a low, inconsiderable Thing! There is such a vast Disproportion between the *Glory of Christ,* the *Head of the Church,* and the *Capacity* of that Part of his *Body* to take it *in*, who dwell in this low Land; That the greatest Saints on Earth, when they speak in the Commendation of *Him* whom their *Souls love*; (tho' according to their clearest Conceptions, their aptest Expressions, and most ardent Affections, are yet so far from *delineating* his Glory, that they rather draw a *Vail* over his infinite Excellencies. So that it may be said of the brightest Displays thereof, made by them, *There was the Hiding of his Glory.* As the Prophet said, when he had a View of the Glory of God, as having *Horns* coming out of his *Hand:* (which were an Emblem of the infinite Strength of Him, who is wonderful in Counsel, and mighty in Work) *And there was the Hiding of his Power*, Hab. 3.4. Because the *Almightiness* of *Jehovah*, in itself, was infinitely beyond the brightest Displays that could be made of it. And so is the *Glory* of *Christ*, infinitely beyond the brightest Conceptions, or Expressions of the greatest Saints on Earth. What then can be expected from such a *Babe* as I, who am the *Least*, and *Last* of all? So that I should even sit down in *Silence*, if *He* had not said, *With the* last, *I am* HE. But, believing his infinite Grace, and depending on his Almighty Power, I shall proceed to take a little Notice of the Church's Description of her *Beloved*, which we have Song 5.10, &c. And attempt to *lispe out* somewhat of *his Glory* from thence, that can never be fully told; no, not by the Tongues of Men, nor of Angels, to the innumerable Ages of a blest Eternity! For surely, my *Soul loves him;* from that Heart-attracting, Soul-overcoming *Display* I have had of his infinite Beauties, his adorable Excellencies! And yet I am asham'd that I know so little of him, am so like him, and can do, or say so little for him. But as it's the Nature of Love, to delight in lisping out the Praises, and commending the apprehended Worth of the beloved Object; even so, would I humbly attempt what I first propos'd, while herein, I *serve the* LORD *with Fear, and rejoice with Trembling.*

SONG V.10, 11, 12, 13, 14, 15, 16.

My Beloved is white and ruddy, the chiefest among ten thousand.

His head is as the most fine gold, his locks are bushy, and black as a raven.

His eyes are as the eyes of Doves, by the rivers of water, washed with milk, and fitly set.

His cheeks are as a bed of spices, as sweet flowers: his lips like lilies, droping sweet smelling myrrh.

His hands are as gold-rings set with the beryl: his belly is as bright ivory overlaid with sapphires.

His legs are as pillars of marble, set upon sockets of fine gold: his countenance is as Lebanon, excellent as the cedars.

His mouth is most sweet: yea, he is altogether lovely. This is my beloved, and this is my friend, O daughter of Jerusalem.

This is the Account the *Spouse* gives of her *Beloved*. But before I take any particular Notice hereof, I would just give a Hint of the *Nature* of this *Book*, and of the *Occasion* of this *Account*, the Spouse here gives.

As to the *Book* itself, it is agreed upon, by those that fear God, and have a spiritual Understanding to discern his Word, and to know his Mind therein: That it is a Part of the *Sacred Records*. Of a divine Original, being given, as all the other Parts of the Scriptures of Truth, by the immediate *Inspiration* of the *Holy Spirit of God:* and dictated to his Servant *Solomon*, who was the Penman thereof. The Nature of this *Book*, is a *Song*; and on Account of the Excellency of it, as such, it is stiled, *The Song of Songs*, which is *Solomon's*, Ch. 1.1. His *Songs*, we are told, were *a thousand and five*, 1 Kings iv.32. But of all those many Songs, this was the most *Excellent:* The *Song of Songs*. And among the various Kinds of Songs, This is, an *Epithalamium,* or *Marriage Song*. Which, in the Mystery, and Spirituality thereof, respects the Heavenly *Marriage* between *Christ*, and the *Church*. And if it should be allow'd, that some Parts of this Song, were literally true, of King *Solomon's Marriage* with *Pharaoh's* Daughter. Yet even in those Parts, a *Greater* than *Solomon* is *here*. Even no less a Person, than the *Christ of God*, the *Prince of Peace,* God's *King Solomon*, whom he has set upon his holy Hill of *Zion*, and given to be the *Bridegroom* of his *Church*. Who was espoused to him in the everlasting Covenant, by God the Father's Gift of her to him as his Bride, and his own voluntary Acceptance of her as such, at his Father's Hands. When, in boundless and unchangeable Love, he engag'd to take her into an indissoluble Union to Himself, in the Conjugal Relation; and to raise her up in Time, into an actual Love-Union, and Communion with Himself here in Grace, upon the Bottom of her mystical Union with him from Everlasting. And who is also espoused to him in all her Individuals, or the particular Members of the invisible Church; when being given him of the Father in the New Birth, and receiv'd by him, as giving up themselves unto him by Faith on their Part, He gives Himself to them in Covenant-Faithfulness on his Part; and raiseth them up into a collective Body, a Church visible, that openly adheres to him in Love as his Spouse, and makes Profession of Him, her glorious Lover, as her Lord and Husband. And for the Church thus espoused unto Christ, and engaged for by him before Time began; and thus espoused to him, and raised up by him in Time, unto a visible, professed Adhesion to Him as his Bride, and Subjection to him as her Bridegroom: He likewise of old engaged, That at the End of Time, he would raise her up to the highest Union and Communion with Himself in Glory; even to an eternal Participation of all those immense Riches of endless Life and Bliss, which he had in Himself, and settled upon Her before Time began.

And this he resolv'd to do, whatever it cost him. Aye, tho' he foresaw all that Guilt and Defilement, that Death and Wrath she would bring upon herself, and be expos'd to, by her Fall in the first *Adam*. Yet so great was his *Love*, that he resolv'd to put Himself, his Great SELF, in her Room. To take her Nature, to stand in her Law-Place, to bear her Sin, and die in her Stead; that so he might set her free, deliver her from Death, and raise her up to perfect Life and Glory, in and with Himself for ever. He resolv'd that nothing should separate her from that Love Union, on his Part, he had taken her in to Himself, nor from any of the glorious Fruits of it in Communion, which his great Love had ordain'd. He would *die* for her, rather than *lose* her irrecoverably in the Fall. When she had deserved *Death*, was under the Sentence of Death, and must have dy'd eternally; *his Love, strong as Death*, endures it for her, even the strong Death of the *Cross*, to give *her Life*. And thus, in his Godlike Strength, his glorious Faithfulness, his infinite and unchangeable Love, he breaks out, in Old Testament Times, in the Views of those vast Depths of Misery she had plung'd herself into, and in the Fore-Prospects of those mighty Enemies, he had to conflict with, and those mighty Sufferings he must endure, if he wou'd fetch her thence; resolving to conquer all. *I will ransom them from the Power of the Grave: I will redeem them from Death: O Death, I will be thy Plagues; O Grave, I will be thy Destruction; Repentance shall be hid from mine Eyes,* Hos. 13.14. "*O Death*, as if he should say, *Thou* has conquer'd *my Bride:* but *I'll* be *thy Plagues.* I, who am the *Prince of Life*, will give my self to thy Stroke. Thou shalt try thy Strength upon ME: I'll open my Bosom to thy sharpest Darts; a Thought of *parting* with my *Bride*, of *leaving her* under *thy Conquest*, is a much keener Dart, to wound my Heart, than any *Thou* hast in thy Quiver. And therefore, strike ME thro', Body, and Soul; and when thou hast done thy worst, and brought Me into the Dust of Death, I'll thereby, in the infinite Merit of *my Death*, satisfy God's Law and Justice, and thereby be *thy Plagues, thy Death.* And in the Infinity of *my Life*, having conquer'd *Thee, O Death*, I'll take *my Bride* into *my Embraces,* out of *thy cruel Hands.*"—And so, "*O Grave, I'll be thy Destruction.* Thou hast got a legal *Victory* over *mine:* But *I'll* become *thy Captive*, I'll take a Lodging with my *Bride* in the *Tomb*. And by becoming a Captive, I'll be *thy Conqueror*. I'll break thy Bars and Gates, and by the Power of *my endless Life*, I'll set *her free*. Thou canst not hold ME; *I'll rise* from under *thy Dominion*, and raise *her up mystically* in my self; as the Foundation of her *personal Resurrection* from under *thy Power* at the latter Day, to an *endless Life*, and *Glory* with me. When in most glorious *Triumph*, I'll be thy *full*, and *everlasting Destruction.*" Thus the Love of Christ's Heart, work'd towards his Bride, from the Dates of Everlasting, and all along, throughout the successive Ages of the Old Testament; until the appointed Time of his Incarnation came on.

And then, in the same infinite Grace and Faithfulness, he stoops down, to take her Nature into Union with his divine Person; and therein fulfills all his ancient Engagements. The *Lord of Glory*, becomes a *Servant*, to set *her free*. He, *Jacob* like, *served for a Wife*. Aye, not *seven Years* only, but his *whole Life* he spent in *Service*, which seemed unto *Him* but a *few Days*, for the *Love* he had to her. But, oh, the transcendent Glory of *Christ's Love!* He serves, but not, as *Jacob,* for a *beautiful* Bride, that had a *native* Glory in her, to attract his Heart. But for a most *deformed* Object, that he might put his *own Beauty* upon her. For a most *lothsom, filthy* Creature, that he might *cleanse*, and make her *lovely*. For one that was fill'd with *Enmity* against him, that he might conquer *her Hatred*, and secure *her Love*, by the amazing, all conquering Displays of his *own infinite Favour*. Thus he served for his Bride. Aye, perform'd *such* a Piece of Service for her, in bearing her Sin, and enduring divine Wrath in her Stead; that *none* of the *Creatures*, in both *Worlds*, had they join'd all their Forces together, were *capable* of doing. And had he not had the Strength of the *Godhead* in him, both as to Love, and Power, he could never have *gone thro' it*. But, Oh, Behold him on the Cross, crying out, *It is finished!* When he had drank up the Cup of Wrath, at one mighty Draught; which would have cost his Bride an Eternity of Misery, to have been sipping off, and never could have come at the Bottom! Then, lo, He *bows the Head,* and *gives up the Ghost: The Prince of Life, dies! For when we were yet without Strength, in due time Christ dy'd for the Ungodly,* Rom. 5.6. *He loved the Church, and gave himself for it; That he might sanctify and cleanse it with the Washing of Water, by the Word, That he might present it to himself a glorious Church, not having Spot or Wrinkle, or any such Thing; but that it should be holy, and without Blemish,* Eph. 5. 25, 26, 27. And having satisfy'd divine Justice, by his meritorious *Death*, and thereby obtain'd *eternal Redemption* for his Bride; he *rose* in his mighty Love, and God-like Strength, as a triumphant *Conqueror* over Sin, Death, and Hell; and *ascended to Glory* for her, and there sits at *God's Right Hand*, to save her by his *Life*, or to redeem her by Power, in the Virtue of his having redeem'd her by Price, from out of the Hands of all her Enemies, from under all Deaths and Miseries, to perfect Glory, and endless Life and Bliss in the Enjoyment of himself for ever. When, to the endless Wonder of Men and Angels, he'll openly *marry her* at the *latter Day*, in the Face of *all the Creatures*. And having kept his Marriage-feast a while *below*, He'll *ascend*, with his glorious *Mate*, to his *Father's House*, his Palace Royal, in Heaven, Where the Heavenly Bridegroom and his Bride, shall spend a long *Eternity*, in the mutual Love-Delights of that Glory-Union, and Communion, which is yet *unknown!*

Well, this is the happy *Marriage*, and These the glorious *Pair*, which are the *Subject* of this *Song* of *Solomon*. And if any should think, That some Expressions herein, might be literally true of the Glory of the earthly *Solomon:* Yet, we must not rest here; but rise in our Thoughts, to the transcendent Glory of *Christ*, the heavenly *Solomon*; which was the spiritual Intendment thereof; and take, even *these*, as spoken only by way of *Allusion* thereto. But, for my own Part, I chuse to take this Song, as it was given by the immediate Inspiration of the Holy Ghost, and stands upon Record, as a Part of the sacred Scriptures, for the Edification of the Church in all Ages; as *independent* upon the Glory of *Solomon*, and *his Queen*; and as wholly relating to the super-excellent Glory of *Christ*, and *his Spouse*. And certain it is, that there are some Parts of it, which can't be literally apply'd to, or spoken of King *Solomon* and *his Bride*. As in this Description the *Spouse* gives of her *Beloved*, Chap. 5. and the Commendation He gives of his *Bride*, Chap. 6. and 7. 'twould be rather a monstrous Description of *Solomon's Queen*, than a Commendation of her Beauty, to set her forth, As having an *Head like Carmel:* A *Nose like the Tower of* Lebanon, *looking towards* Damascus; as having *Teeth like a Flock of Sheep, every one bearing Twins:* and a *Neck like the Tower of* David, *builded for an Armory, whereon hang a thousand Bucklers, all Shields of mighty Men,* &c. Which makes it evident, that this Song must be taken *mystically*, and not *properly*. Besides, the *Majesty* of its *Stile*, and that divine *Power* with which it is attended in the *Hearts* of God's People, are most certain *Evidences* of the super-excellent Glory of its *Subject*, and the Sublimity of its *Scope*.—But thus much may suffice, as to the Nature of the *Book:* That it is a *Song*, a *Marriage-Song*, of *Christ*, and *his Spouse*. In which, we may observe, That as these are the *chief Speakers* herein, so they alternately *commend* one another's Love, Beauty, and Excellency; and mutually *express* their ardent Desire after, and Complacency in each other; according to that Nearness of Relation, and Dearness of Love, in which they stand.—Again, the *Daughters of Jerusalem*, are likewise brought in, as bearing a Part in this heavenly Musick. And this brings me to speak of the *Occasion* of that Account which the *Spouse* gave of her *Beloved*.

And this we find, Song 5.9. What is thy beloved more than another beloved, O thou fairest among Women? What is thy beloved more than another beloved, that thou dost so charge us? This Speech is made by the Daughters of Jerusalem; as is manifest, by the Charge the Spouse gives them in the preceding Verse, with their applying it to themselves, as so given in this. And by these Daughters of Jerusalem, as I take it, we are to understand, young Converts, newly converted unto Christ; (to the Person of Christ, and not merely to the Doctrine of Christ) that have had a Principle of saving Faith, special Faith, the Faith of God's Elect, wrought in their Hearts: And from thence have had some discerning of the Glory of Christ, and of his Church; tho' not such a full Knowledge of Him, or Communion with him as his Bride hath. And these are stiled Daughters of Jerusalem, because they are the Children of the Church. As they're such that have been born of God, so likewise, born in Zion. And the Lord promiseth to his Church, That these her Daughters, shall be nursed at her Side: And milk out, (of the Breasts of her Consolations) and be delighted with the Abundance of her Glory, Is. 60.4. and 66.11. And it's plain, that these Daughters of Jerusalem, had been favour'd with some special Acquaintance with Jesus Christ; or the Spouse wou'd never, when under Desertion, the hiding of her Bridegroom's Face and Favour, have sent a Message to him, by them. As we find she did, Ver. 8. I charge you, O Daughters of Jerusalem, if ye find my Beloved, that ye tell him, that I am sick of Love. If ye find him: It's plainly imply'd in these Words, that they were such that had found him, were wont to find him, and that might find him in special Manifestations of Favour, which might give them an Opportunity of delivering her Message, even before she herself, had that Happiness. And therefore, if ye find my Beloved, tell him, that I am sick of Love. And this, she not only desires them to do, but gives them a most solemn Charge concerning it: I charge you, &c. Whereupon, Seeing the Spouse in such a Fit of Languishment, or Love Sickness for her *Beloved*, they perceiv'd that vast Estimation she had of him, and those vehement Desires she had after him, as being just ready to faint, and die for want of his Presence: And thus they reply: Ver. 9. *What is thy Beloved more than another Beloved, O thou Fairest among Women? what is thy Beloved more than another Beloved, that thou dost so charge us?*

In these Words, we may observe, 1. This *Compellation*, with which they address the Spouse, the *Name* they call her by, *Fairest among Women:* And this being usher'd in, with an *O; O!* Thou Fairest: It informs us, That these Daughters of *Jerusalem*, had a Discerning of the *Church's Beauty*, as shining forth in the *Glory of Christ*, her Royal Bridegroom; and as such admir'd her superlative Fairness. And, 2. Upon this, they *interrogate* her: *What is thy Beloved, more than another Beloved?* 'tis as if they should say, 'thou art such a great, such an excellent *One*, of such bright Knowledge, and sublime Affection, HE must be a glorious Person indeed, that thus ingrosseth *thy Heart*, that thou canst not *live* without him. And therefore, *tell us*; What is thy Beloved?' They say not, *Who* is thy Beloved: Because they had a certain *Knowledge* of his Person, and, in some *Degree*, of his Excellency. But they look'd upon their *own* Knowledge, in Comparison of *hers*, to be as nothing; and having their Hearts fir'd with Love to him, and a Desire after a greater Display of his Glory, They say, *What* is thy Beloved? "Tell us, what excellent Glories thou hast seen in *Him*, which have thus struck thy *Heart?* We have had but little Knowledge of him, and Communion with him. But thou, his Royal Bride, that hast been favour'd with the most intimate Familiarity, and Bosom-Communion with him, as thy own; What hast *Thou* found in *Him?* Tell us his personal Excellencies. Yea, Tell us, his super-excelling Glories: What is *thy* Beloved more than *another* Beloved? What hast *thou* seen, and found of *his* transcendent Excellency? Wherein is HE, above *all others?* *What is thy Beloved more than another Beloved, that thou dost so charge us?*" And this gives Occasion to the Spouse, to *describe* her *Beloved*, in the following Verses. For lo, she *replies:*

Ver. 10. *My Beloved is white and ruddy, the chiefest among ten thousand.* In these Words, the Spouse gives a General Description of the Glory of her Beloved; *White and Ruddy, the chiefest among ten Thousand. White and Ruddy:* a due Mixture of which Colours, make a perfect *Beauty* in Nature, an *amiable, delightful* Object. *The Chiefest among ten Thousand:* Of all Beauties, HE is the fairest, a glorious Beauty, transcendently above, and beyond all others.

My Beloved] This the Spouse sets first, The *Person* of her Beloved, before she describes his *personal Glories*. Because her Heart was so intensely fixt upon him, that she delights to make mention of *Him*; and that under this endearing Character, of a *Beloved:* Yea, as *her* Beloved. *My Beloved:* One that *loves Me*, one that *I love*, one in the nearest Conjunction with me, even in an indissoluble Union, of Relation, Love and Glory. It's *my Beloved*, that I'm going to speak of; not an excellent Person that I have only some remote Knowledge of, and no Interest in; but of *my Beloved*, that is entirely, unchangeably, and eternally *mine*. And this the Spouse could say, in Faith, without the least Doubt, or Hesitation, even when she had not the Joys of spiritual Sense, under the bright Shines of her Bridegroom's Royal Favour; yea, when she had provok'd him to withdraw, by her Sin, Unkindness, and Ingratitude. "Oh, as if she should say, tho' I have lost the sweet Embraces of my Bridegroom, by my own Sloth and Negligence, tho, I made sinful Excuses, and did not open to my Lord at his sweet Call; by which I justly provok'd him to withdraw, and he's gone: Yet he is *mine* still, the Relation is not *broken*, nor the Love of his Heart *changed*; and therefore, in boundless Grace, he will see me again, and my Heart shall rejoice. And mean while, tho' I mourn his Absence, yet I have a quick Remembrance of those inexpressible Glories I saw in him when I had his Presence: Yea, I can tell you what I see in him, even *now*; for as he's the same in Himself, so he has lost no Glory in my Eye." This *Beloved*, that is *mine*, is,

White and Ruddy] This may be apply'd,

First, to his *Person*, as *God Man*. He's *White:* with Regard to the *Glory of his Deity*. *Ruddy:* with Respect to the *Truth of his Humanity*. His Divine, and Human Nature, Hypostatically united, are hereby intended.

He is *White*, with Regard to the *Glory of his Deity*. The Lord Jesus Christ, the Church's Beloved, is so great a Person, that has all the immense Glories of the *Godhead*, radically in Himself. He is *God by Nature*, by *Essence*. The second Person in the Sacred Trinity, possessing co-equally, with the Father, and the Holy Ghost, the incomprehensible Perfections, the undivided Glory and Bliss, of the one Great JEHOVAH! *He thought it not Robbery to be equal with God*, Phil. 2.6. His *Father* and HE are *One*, John 10.30. His proper *Name* is, The *Mighty God*, Is. 9.6. And the LORD, JEHOVAH, *Jer.* 23.6. *Exod.* 3.14, 15. with John 8.58. Jer. 17.10. with Rev. 2.23. Thus he is White. White, and *Black*, stand oppos'd*, as Darkness*, and *Light*. And God is said to be *Light*, without *Darkness*, 1 John 1.5. And to be, The *Father of Lights*, Jam. 1.17. To shew, that he hath all Glories, originally, and independently, in his own infinite Being; and is the Author of all Light, both in Nature, Grace, and Glory, unto all the Creatures that have it. And to set forth, The Unchangeableness of his infinite Glory, he is declar'd to be, without *Variableness*, or *Shadow of Turning*. Which is doubtless spoken by Way of Allusion to that bright Luminary, the Sun in the Firmament. Which glorious Creature, being a pure Body of Light, by divine Appointment, casting his Rays upon the Moon and Stars, communicates Light to all those lesser Glories; and so, in some Sense, may be said to be, The *Father* of them. But this bright Creature, however glorious it may be, is not without *Change*. It moves from East to West, from North to South; and as it turns, casts the Shadow *variously*. But the infinite glory of *Jehovah*, is absolutely *unchangeable:* He is without *Variableness,* or

Shadow of Turning. Thus *Light*, or *Whiteness*, is put for *Glory*; and when apply'd to *God*, for *infinite* Glory. As when our Lord was transfigur'd in the Mount, it's said, *His Face did shine as the Sun, and his Raiment was* white *as the* Light. Because the *Glory* of his *Divinity*, did then cast its Rays upon, and thro' his *Human Nature*; as a Specimen of that *Glory* he now wears in Heaven, and in which he'll *shine*, as Judge of Quick and Dead, at his next Appearing and Kingdom, *Mat.* 17.2. with *Luke* 9.27, 28. &c. Thus the Church's Beloved, is *White*, in Regard of the *Glory of his Deity.*—And had he, in this Respect, been *only* White, he had never been *our Beloved*. God in the abstracted Glory of his infinite Essence, *dwelleth in Light, that is inaccessible,* 1. Tim. 6.16. It had been impossible for the highest Creatures, much more for sinful ones, to have enjoy'd any immediate Familiarity, with a God of infinite Glory.—But, oh, Behold! the Spouse's *Beloved*, is not only *White*, but

Ruddy. An immediate Relation to God, and converse with him, were Glories too high for the Creatures to have a Participation of. The most capacious of them all, would have been utterly incapable of those Heights: They peculiarly belong to the three glorious *Persons*, in the One infinite *Essence* of *Jehovah*. And therefore when GOD, the glorious GOD, held a Counsel in *Himself*, before Time began, among the ever-blessed *Three*, about the Display of his infinite Goodness, Grace, and Mercy towards *Creatures*, the Works of his Hands, and resolv'd to go forth into *Creature-Converse:* The *Man Christ Jesus*, the Project of infinite Wisdom, the Provision of infinite Grace, was *brought forth*, in those everlasting Counsels, as the great *Medium* in, and thro' which it was to be held; both in Nature, Grace, and Glory. For, lo, The eternal *Son of God* was verily *Fore-ordained* to take *our Nature* into personal Union with *Himself;* and in that Nature, to sustain and execute the Office of *Mediator*, both interposing, and attoning; to answer all the Ends of *Jehovah's* Glory, towards all the Creatures, thro' Time, and to Eternity. And as God the Father, in his eternal Decrees, and everlasting Covenant, *Prepared* Him a *Body*, i.e., a *Human Nature:* So God the Son, did then engage in the same everlasting Covenant, to take it in the *Fulness of Time*. Whereupon, God the Father, taking his great *Word*, look'd upon it as if *done*; and from thenceforth, *reputed him* as the *great Mediator*, and *transacted* with him as such. And thus he speaks of himself, as so brought forth, before any of the Works of Nature existed, *Prov.* 8.22, *&c. The* LORD *possessed me in the Beginning of his Way, before his Works of Old. I was set up from everlasting, from the Beginning, or ever* *the Earth was. When there were no Depths, I was brought forth: when there were no Fountains abounding with Water. Before the Mountains were settled; before the Hills, was I brought forth; While as yet he had not made the Earth, nor the Fields, nor the highest Part of the Dust of the World. When he prepared the Heavens, I was there: when he set a Compass upon the Face of the Depth. When he establish'd the Clouds above: when he strengthned the Fountains of the Deep: when he gave to the Sea his Decree; that the Waters should not pass his Commandment: when he appointed the Foundations of the Earth: Then was I by him, as one brought up with him: and I was daily his Delight, rejoicing always before him; rejoicing in the habitable Part of his Earth, and my Delights were with the Sons of Men.*

And as the Mediator was set up from everlasting in God's Covenant; so he was spoken of as the *Man*, all along throughout the Old Testament Times, in all those Prophecies and Promises which related to his *future Incarnation*. From whence the Faith of the Saints in that Day, look'd for the *Messiah* to come; as we now, look to him as already come. They *saw* the *Promises afar off*, were *perswaded* of 'em, and *embraced* 'em: And so *dy'd in Faith*, not having receiv'd the *Fulfilment* of 'em, or the *Things* promised. And those realizing Views of 'em they had by Faith, tho' at a great Distance, had such a mighty Influence upon their Souls, that it wean'd them from this World, and set them on the most earnest *seeking of an Heavenly Country; confessing* that they were *Strangers, and Pilgrims on the Earth,* Heb. 11.13. &c. And as they *look'd* for the *Messiah,* the great Saviour, to appear in their Nature in the Fulness of Time, so they earnestly *long'd* for it. Thus *Abraham*, rejoiced to *see* Christ's *Day*; he *saw it*, and was glad, *John* 3.56. And thus the Spouse, with the greatest Ardour of Affection, breathes out her vehement Desires, after her Beloved's coming in the Flesh: *O! that thou wast as my Brother that sucked the Breasts of my Mother: when I should find thee without, I would kiss thee, yea, I should not be despised,* Song 8.1. She saw what a Glory it would be, to have her Lord cloth'd with Flesh, with her Nature; and what a Foundation, this wou'd lay for her greatest Familiarity with him, without exposing her to Contempt, by Reason of the Lowness of her Person and Circumstance; when once her low Nature, was exalted into personal Union with the Son of God. That then she might have all that Familiarity with *God* in her *own Nature*, which her longing Soul desir'd, without being despised: and therefore she breathes after this happy Day, with an *O! that thou wast as my Brother,* &c. And as she saw, the Glory of her Bridegroom, as *God-Man*, in those divine

Declarations, Prophecies, and Promises concerning him, and were perswaded, that even then, he was the *Man*, by Covenant-Constitution; (as he pass'd by that Name in those Times: *Psal.* 80.17.) So that at the Time *appointed* of the Father, he would actually assume her Nature, and in that Nature actually espouse her Cause, and openly espouse her Person, and raise her up to the Heights of that Marriage-Glory with Himself at the End of Time; which in infinite Wisdom, Grace and Faithfulness, were unalterably settled before Time began. And therefore, she puts in his *Human Nature*, in the Description she gives of the Glory of his *Person*, under this Character of, *Ruddy*. And that this Word, *Ruddy*, doth set forth the *Human Nature*, in the Person of Christ, may appear, in that he is stiled, The last *Adam*, 1 Cor. 15.45. And this Word, *Adam*, being as the Learned observe, deriv'd of a Word that signifieth, *Red*, or, *Red Earth*; as it was apply'd to the *first Man*, who was of the *Earth, earthy*; it was expressive of his *Original*, as *formed of the Dust of the Ground*. And as it is apply'd to the *second Man*, who is the *Lord from Heaven*, it denotes the *Truth* of his *Human Nature*; or, his having taken the *same Nature* with *ours,* into Union with his divine *Person*. Not a *like* Nature, that Bears some Semblance only, but a Nature that is *specifically* the *same*. Thus *Heb.* 2.14. *Forasmuch then as the Children are Partakers of Flesh and Blood, he also Himself likewise took Part of the* same. Oh, this glorious Mystery, of the Incarnation of the Son of God; in which he appears, both *White* and *Ruddy!* This is such a *Mixture,* that renders him the most beautiful Person, in both Worlds, to the Eye of Faith. I say, *Mixture:* Not that the divine, and human Natures in the Person of Christ, were in the least wise *mixed*, by way of *Confusion.* The *Divine Nature*, by assuming the Human, sustain'd no *Change:* Nor was the *Human*, by that Assumption, *absorpt*, swallow'd up, or lost any of its essential Properties: But both these Natures, so vastly different, are closely *join'd* in *Christ*. So that tho' they remain *Two*, entire, distinct *Natures*, yet in *Him*, they make but *one Person* for ever. And as this glorious Variety of Natures, resplendently shines in the Unity of our *Immanuel's* Person; He is the endless *Wonder* of Men and Angels! *Jehovah's* WONDER! *Psal.* 89.5. i.e., Of *Jehovah's* contriving, and effecting; in which the infinite Depths of his Wisdom and Grace, illustriously shine forth, to be admir'd, ador'd, and prais'd by all the Saints and Angels, to the endless Ages of Eternity! Well may his *Name* be called, *Wonderful*, Is. 9.6. Since his *Person* is *so*. And well might the Spouse admire, and commend her Beloved, as *White and Ruddy*. For had he not been *Ruddy*, in regard of the *Human Nature*, he could never have been the *Church's Bridegroom:* His Glory as *God*, in an Abstract Consideration, was too *high*, for *him* to bear such a near Relation unto *her*. And if his Human Nature, had not been personally united to his *Divine*, in regard of which, he's *White*, he had not been a Person *great enough*, to have been the *Head*, and *Husband* of his *Church*, and consequently thereupon, the *Saviour* of his *Body*. But as he's *White and Ruddy*, he is every Way fitted to sustain this great *Relation*, and to answer all the great *Ends* of it. Again,

White and Ruddy] This may be apply'd, *Secondly*. To his *Human Nature*. He is *White*, in regard of the *Purity* of his Human Nature, and of the Whole of his Obedience therein: And *Ruddy* with respect to his *Sufferings*.

He is *White*, in regard of the *Purity* of his Human Nature, and the Whole of his Obedience therein; as it denotes absolute Freedom from *Sin*, both in its Guil, and Stain. And that *White*, in Scripture, is put for *Purity*, in this respect, appears, Rev. 7.14. with 1 John 1.7. *These are they which came out of great Tribulation, and have washed their Robes, and made them* white *in the Blood of the Lamb. And the blood of Jesus Christ his Son, cleanseth us from all Sin*. And as Freedom from all *Sin*, is set forth, by *White*; so it may be fitly apply'd to the *Human Nature* of Jesus Christ. And this Purity regards, 1. His *spotless Conception* and *Birth*. And, 2. The *Whole of his Life*, form the first Moment his Mother, *Mary*, brought him forth, until that last, in which he resign'd up his Spirit into the Hands of *God*, his *Father*.

Our Lord was *spotless* in his *Conception*, and *Birth*. The Creature, *Man*, when he first came out of his Maker's Hand, had a perfect *Whiteness*, or *Purity* of Nature. But upon *Sin's* Entrance, he instantly became *Red*, in regard, both of Guilt, and Defilement. And all the Posterity of *Adam*, even to a *Man*, that descend from him by ordinary Generation, share with him therein: They bear his corrupt, as well as his natural Image. The *first Man*, who was of the *Earth, Earthy*; both stood, and fell for *Himself,* and his whole *Posterity*, unto whom he was both a *natural*, and *federal Head*, by Divine Appointment. And therefore, *As is the Earthy, such are they also, that are Earthy:* i.e., His Offspring, that descend from him in the ordinary Way; because they belong to his *Covenant*; and therefore, share with him in his *Guilt*, and *Pollution*. And as such, they are utterly *undone*; even the *Elect of God*, themselves, by *Nature*, as related to the first *Adam*, and a broken *Law*, are in a *lost State*. And as for the *Non Elect*, they are irrecoverably *lost* in the *Fall*. When *they fell*, they had *none* to *help them up*; because they had no special Relation to *Christ*, the second *Adam*. But *Two* are *better* than *One*, Eccles. 4.9. Even those Two I have been speaking of, *Christ*, and the *Elect*; who were inseperably join'd together, as *Bridegroom* and *Bride*, in God's everlasting Covenant. For when *they*, the *Elect fell*, there was *One* to *help them up;* even their dear *Lord Jesus*, that *Mighty One*, on whom the Father laid their *Help*, Psal. 89.19. Whose Love and Power engag'd by Covenant, were stronger, infinitely stronger than all their Enemies, to subdue *Them*, and to save his *Own*, from the deepest Misery, to the highest Glory. And to bring about the Redemption of God's Chosen, the Bride of Christ, and raise her up to that open Marriage-Glory, which was anciently settled upon her, in the secret Purposes, Counsels, and Covenant of *Jehovah*, before the World was; The Son of God was ordained to take her Nature, to effect this great Work therein. For as She had ruin'd herself by Sin, and ran deep in Dept to God's Law of Justice; and He being the Person appointed to save Her from Sin, to pay her Debts, and set her free; it was necessary that *He* should take Part of the same *Nature* that sinned; that so he might represent *her Person*, and stand in *her Room*. And it was likewise necessary, that *his Nature* should be *pure*, to answer all the great Ends of *God,* in the Incarnation of his *Son*. It was a Question put, *Job* 14.4. *Who can bring* a clean Thing *out of an* unclean? and resolv'd in the Negative: *Not One*. Which was incontestably true of all created Power. For none of all the Creatures, could bring a pure Stream out of an impure Fountain, a pure Piece, out of a corrupt Mass. But what was utterly impossible to a *Finite* Arm, was possible to an *Infinite, Almighty* Agent: and gloriously *effected*, in the pure Conception, and spotless Birth of *Jesus*. The Original Promise of the *Messiah*, was, That he should be the *Seed of the Woman;* and that this Seed of the Woman, should *bruise the Serpent's Head,* Gen. 3.15. But, that the *Child Jesus*, whose Body was form'd of the Substance of his Mother *Mary*, who was a *Woman* in the same common *Condition* with the *rest* of *Adam's* Posterity, should yet be born of her *without Sin*, as he was, (and as it was necessary for him to be, in order to his Bruising of the Serpent's Head, *i.e.*, Destroying of the Devil, and his Works,) is such a *Display* of Divine Power and Grace, that justly challenges the eternal *Admiration* of saved Men, and of glorious, confirmed Angels. For this was, as I may so say, The laying the Foundation of his *Fitness* to be the *Saviour* of sinful Men, and the *Head* of glorious Angels: Had he not been *pure*, he had been *incapable* of either. And therefore, of the Incarnation of Christ, we may well say, *What hath God wrought!* And to effect this Wonder, it was the

Contrivance of infinite Wisdom, the Provision of infinite Grace, That the *Man Christ Jesus*, should be conceiv'd in the Womb of a *Virgin*, and born of One, that had never *known Man:* By the Almighty Influence of the *Holy Ghost,* the Third Person in God, *over-shadowing her* by his own *infinite Power*, thereby Forming the sacred *Body* of our *Lord*, which was *fearfully* and *wonderfully made*. Thus in Prophecy and Promise, it was long before predicted, *Behold, a* Virgin *shall* conceive, *and* bring forth *a Son, and they shall call his Name* Immanuel, Isa. 7.14. And thus it was in the Accomplishment, Mat. 1.18. *&c. Now the* Birth *of Jesus Christ, was on this wise: When as his Mother* Mary *was espoused to* Joseph, *before they came together, she was found* with Child *of the* Holy Ghost. *And he* knew her not, *till she had* brought forth *her First-born Son, and he called his Name,* JESUS. And hence it was, that the Human Nature of our Lord, tho' made of the *Seed* of *Abraham*, and of *David*, (his Body being formed of the *Substance* of the *Virgin*, who was lineally descended from them) did nevertheless escape that *Pollution* of Nature, which in the ordinary Way of Generation, taints all Flesh. For This, of his *miraculous Conception*, is given as the Reason of his *spotless Purity*, Luke 1.35. *And the Angel answer'd and said unto her,* The Holy Ghost *shall come upon thee, and the* Power of the Highest *shall overshadow thee: Therefore also that* Holy Thing *which shall be born of Thee, shall be called the Son of God*. His Human Nature, is here said to be *Holy*; because Form'd by the immediate Operation of the *Holy Ghost*. And tis' said to be a *Thing*, not a *Person*; because this *entire Nature*, consisting of a true Body, and a reasonable Soul, did not in Christ, constitute a *Person*, as it doth in *us*. The Divine Person of the Son of God, did indeed assume the *Human Nature*, (that individual Part of it prepared for him of his Father) but not an *Human Person,* into Union with *Himself*. No; the *Human Nature* in Christ, from the first Moment of its Formation, had no Subsistence of its *own*; but was personally united to the *Son of God*; so that the Divine and Human Nature in *Him*, made but *One Person*: And therefore, by a Communication of Properties, the *Child Jesus*, born of the *Virgin*, was called the *Son of God:* as it follows in this Text. And herein lay the glorious Mystery of his Incarnation; and hence it is that his Name is properly call'd *Immanuel, God with Us*, God in our Nature. And as the Divine Person of the Son of God, did assume the Nature of Man, into the strictest Union with himself; so he did it, with a special Regard to the Seed of *Abraham*.

'tis true, he had the same Nature, *specifically*, that *Adam* had, who was the common Fountain of the *Human Kind:* And therefore, his Genealogy is trac'd up as high as *Adam*, Luke 3.38. But then it is to be taken *naturally*, and not *federally*. He had the same *Nature* with *Adam*, but in such an extraordinary *Way*, that he never belong'd to *Adam's Covenant*; and so could not be a Partaker with *him* in *his* Guilt and Defilement. But as he *voluntarily* assum'd the Nature of *Man*, and as such, did not *necessarily* descend from *Adam*; so he took the *same*, with a special Eye to his *People:* That therein he might represent *them*; that he might live, die, rise, and live for evermore, to save *them* from everlasting Misery, to eternal Glory. And as he took the Human Nature, with a special Eye to the Good of his People; so with a peculiar Regard to the *Covenant* made with *Abraham*, Gen. 17.7. *And I will establish my* Covenant *between me and thee, and thy Seed after thee, in their Generations; to be a God unto thee, and to thy Seed after thee.* And hence it was, that he sprang of the *Jewish* Race, who were *literally* of the Seed of *Abraham: to confirm the Truth of God unto the Fathers*, and secure the Fulfilment of those Promises, which literally respected the Body of the *Jews* as such. And as the spiritual Seed of *Abraham*, respected the Elect of God among the *Gentiles,* as well as *Jews*; so he would have some of the *Gentile Race*, for his Progenitors, and reckon'd in his Genealogy: Because some of the *Gentiles* were to have the special, saving Benefit of his Incarnation. And as the Substance of *Abraham's* Covenant, was, That God would be *His God*, and the *God of his Seed*, in an everlasting Covenant; or make over himself to *them*, as their eternal ALL: So the Divine Person of our Lord, assum'd the Nature of the *Seed* of *Abraham*, i.e., his *spiritual* Seed; that in, and thro' *Him*, all the *Promises*, in their full Extent, and Latitude of Glory, might have a perfect *Establishment*, and full *Accomplishment*; to the *Glory of God by us*, 2 Cor. 1.20. Thus we are told, Heb. 2.16. *For verily he took not on Him the Nature of Angels; but he took on Him the* Seed *of* Abraham. Who this *Seed* were, we are told in the Context, Ver. 14. they are said to be *Children*; that is, such that were given him in the everlasting Covenant, as his *Seed* and *Offspring*, of whom he was constituted the *everlasting Father. Forasmuch then, as the* Children *are Partakers of Flesh and Blood; he Himself likewise took Part of the same.* And Ver. 17. they are call'd his *Brethren*, that is, such that stand in a special Relation to God by *adopting Grace*; among whom, he is the *First-born:* And that as such, are made *Heirs of God*, and *joynt Heirs* with *Him. Wherefore in all Things, it behoved him to be made like unto his* Brethren. He became like *them*, in every Thing but *Sin:* He took their *Nature*, in all its sinless *Infirmities*, that so he might make *them* like *Him*, in all his heavenly

Glories. He took it indeed, in all its natural *Weakness*, but yet, in its sinless *Purity*; being conceiv'd, and born for *them*, without a Spot of *Sin*.

Again, our Lord, was not only *White*, in his spotless Conception, and Birth; but he was so, likewise, in the *Whole of his Life. He did* no Sin, *neither was* Guile *found in his* Mouth, 1 Pet. 2.22. And the eternal Son of God, took the Nature of the Seed of *Abraham*, into personal Union with himself; so in this his assumed Nature, he took their *Law place.* They were under the Law, as *Creatures*, and as such, ow'd a Debt of perfect *Obedience* to its *Precept:* And had broke the Law, as *Sinners*, and as such, ow'd a Debt of *Suffering* its *Penalty.* And, alas! by Sin, they became *Insolvent.* By this, they had render'd themselves utterly incapable of yielding a perfect Obedience to the righteous Precept of God's holy Law, which was due from them: Nor could they make Satisfaction to Divine Justice for their Offence, by enduring its just Penalty. And both these Debts must be *paid*, or the Bride of Christ, could never *enjoy* the Person, the Glory of her Bridegroom; nor yet with him, *see* the Face of his, and her Father, in that beatifick Vision of his Glory, that was anciently settled upon her, as standing in such a near Relation to her Lord and Husband. And she having *nothing to pay*, and so *deep a Debt*, her Bridegroom, must lay out his *infinite Riches*, his own *vast Treasures,* to cancel *her Scores*; or lose her for ever in the Fall. And such was his great Love, aye, and his Faithfulness too, that he resolv'd to *set her free.* For this Poverty of hers, was long ago fore-view'd by him: He *knew*, even from everlasting, that she would *deal very treacherously*, and be justly call'd, a *Transgressor from the Womb.* And then, in his mighty Love, he became her *Surety*, (as *Judah* for *Benjamin*, Genesis 43.9) and entered into a solemn Engagement with GOD the great Creditor, that in the Fulness of Time, he would pay her Debts, and bring her again out of the Ruins of the Fall, and set her before the *Father's Face* for ever, as an Object of his eternal Complacency; to answer all the Ends of *his Love* towards her. For it was a Design of the Father's Love, to bring her to *Glory*; as well as it was the gracious Engagement of the *Son*, to set her before *his Face*, whatever it cost him. And therefore, upon the Bottom of those Counsels, and Covenant-Transactions, which pass'd between the Father and the Son, before the World was, when the appointed Time came, *God sent forth his Son, made of a Woman, made under the Law,* Gal. 4.4. The *Father* sent him; the *Son* came. The *Father*, in his great Love, gave him to be Incarnate, and to be under the Law for us: The *Son*, in unchangeable Grace, and infinite Faithfulness, takes our Nature, and Law-place too: *To redeem them that were under the Law, that we might receive the Adoption of Sons*, Ver. 5. and consequently thereupon, the *Inheritance* of *Sons*, both here in Grace, and hereafter in Glory. And being made under the Law, he fulfils all its Precepts: To work out a compleat, justifying Righteousness, an everlasting glorious Robe, for all those *many Sons* which are to be brought to *Glory*; in which they now do, and shall for ever stand before God, with the highest Acceptance. For *by the Obedience of One,* Lord Jesus, these *many* are made *righteous*, Rom. 5.19. And tho' our Lord was spotless in his Nature, and in that Obedience he yielded to the Law; yet was he, by way of Eminence, *a Man of Sorrows, and acquainted with Grief,* Isa. 53.3. in all which he *did no Sin*, but was perfectly conformable to the holy, righteous *Law of God*, both as to the *negative*, and *positive* Part of Obedience, or, with respect unto what is *forbidden*, and *commanded*. He always *did the Things* which *pleased the Father*, John 8.29. He did 'em perfectly, universally, and perpetually, from the first Moment of his Birth, to the last of his Life. So that the flaming Holiness of God, his strict Justice, and pure Law, could find no *Fault* with his Obedience, but was infinitely *well pleased* therewith; and in it, with all them for whom it was performed: *The* LORD *is* well-pleased *for* his Righteousness Sake, Isa. 42.21. So *white* is the Church's *Beloved!* so *pure* in his Nature, and so *spotless* in the Whole of his active Obedience, that she might well, in the Views hereof, say, *My Beloved, is white!*—And as she view'd him in the Whiteness of his Person, and of his active Obedience, by which he paid that vast Debt of universal Conformity to God's Law, which she ow'd, on which account he was an amiable Object in her Eye; so, further, to set forth his infinite Suitableness to her Case, as a *Sinner*, and his incomparable Excellency, as a *Saviour*, she adds, and

Ruddy. This respects his *Sufferings*. Oh astonishing Mixture, *White and Ruddy!* What must this *sinless* One, *suffer!* this *spotless* Lamb, *die!* Yet thus it was: *It behoved* Christ *to* suffer, Luke 24.46. His Bride had sinn'd, and was under the Sentence of Death; and die she must, if He had not dy'd for her, in her Room. Sin and Suffering go together: *She* had *sinn'd*; and *He* would *suffer*. Such was his *boundless Love!* And that *Red*, or *Ruddy*, signifies *Sufferings*; see *Isa.* 63.2, 3. *Wherefore art thou* Red *in thine Apparel, and thy Garments like him that treadeth in the Wine fat? I have trodden the Wine-Press alone, and of the People there was none with me: for I will tread 'em in mine Anger, and trample 'em in my Fury, and their Blood shall be sprinkled upon my Garments, and I will stain all my Raiment. For the Day of Vengeance is in mine Heart, and the Year of my*

Redeemed is come. These Words, represent, 1. The Triumphs of Christ's Cross. And, 2. The Triumphs of his Throne: Or, his redeeming his People, both by Price and Power. He first redeems 'em by his *Blood*; and *tramples down* their Enemies, by being *overcome.* By the *Death of his Cross*, he overcame Sin, the Law, Death and Hell: *He spoiled Principalities and Powers, triumphing over them in it,* Col. 2.13, 14, 15. In his *Death*, on his *Cross*, or in *Himself* thereby. And then, in the Virtue of his God-like Blood, his Meritorious Death, he redeems his People by the *Power* of his Arm; and *destroys* all their Enemies by his just *Vengeance*, when the Year of his Redeemed is come. 'twas *thro' Death*, he deliver'd his *Children*, and destroy'd *him* that had the *Power* of Death, *Heb.* 2.14, 15. And the Deliverance of his People, and the Destruction of their Enemies thereby, was Part of that *Joy* that was *set before him*, for which he *endur'd the Cross*, Heb. 12.2. And therefore when the Hour of his Sufferings was come, he takes a View of the Fruit thereof, to encourage him to go thro' them. By comparing himself, as having all his People, and all their Salvation in him, unto a *Corn of Wheat: Except*, says he, it be cast into the *Ground* and *die*, it *abideth alone:* but if it *die*, it bringeth forth *much Fruit,* John 12.24. And, *now*, says he, *is the Judgment of this World: now shall the Prince of this World be cast out. And I, if I be lifted up from the Earth, will draw all Men unto me. This he spake signifying what Death he should die*, Ver. 31, 32, 33. 'tis as it he should say, "My *Children* are all in *Me*, and the Whole of *their* Life and Salvation, depends upon *my Death*; and if I don't *die*, I must *abide* in Heaven *alone:* but if I *die*, I'll conquer *Death*, and *rise again* with them *all* in *myself*, and raise *them up* to Glory with me, as the *Fruit*, the glorious *Crop* of my Sufferings. And therefore *Death*, even the Death of the *Cross*, shall not separate between *Me*, and *Mine*; I'll go thro' it: And, *now* shall the *Prince of this World* be *cast out. Now*, by my *Death*, I'll save *Mine*, and destroy their *Enemies. If I be lifted up, I'll draw all Men unto me*; first in Grace, and then in Glory. And therefore, I'll set my Face as a *Flint*, and go thro' my deepest Sufferings, for the Glory of my *Father*, the Salvation of my *Chosen*, and the Destruction of their *Enemies.*" And the *Sufferings of Christ*, the Church's *Beloved*, on which account he's stiled, *Ruddy*, may be referr'd to these three Heads: 1. The *Imputation of Sin.* 2. The *Malediction of the Law.* And, 3. The *Execution of the Law's Sentence.*

1. He was *Ruddy*, with respect to the *Imputation of Sin. Sin,* is of a *Red*, or *bloody Colour*, it bespeaks *Death* to that Soul, wherever it is found: *The Soul that* sinneth, *shall* die, *Ezek.* 18.4. *Die* he must; either in his *own*

Person, as bearing his *own Sins* upon him; or in the Person of his *Surety*, as standing in *his Stead*. And therefore, when the Lord sets forth the Sins of his People, in their aggravated Guilt, and Desert of Punishment, he compares 'em to *Scarlet*, and *Crimson: Tho they be as* Scarlet, Red *like* Crimson, *yet shall they be White as Snow, and as Wooll*, Isa. 1.18. That is, by an Application of pardoning Grace, thro' the Blood of Christ, which cleanseth from all Sin. But Sin, in its own Nature, is *Red*, and makes the Person *so*, wherever it is judicially charged. The Elect of God, themselves, in the Fall, were *Red* by Sin, *Red* by the Declaration of Divine Vengeance, in the Curse of the Law, and wou'd have been for ever *Red* under the fierce Wrath of God, and his fiery Indignation; had he not been *in Christ, reconciling them unto himself,* not imputing *unto* them *their* Trespasses, 2 Cor. 5.19. And God, in order to his *Non-imputation* of Sins to his *People*, did *impute* all their Sins to his dear *Son.* Thus *Isa.* 53.6. *All* we *like Sheep have gone astray: we have turned every One to his own Way, and the* LORD *hath laid on* Him *the* Iniquity *of* us all. God the Father, in infinite Grace to us, took all the Iniquities of his Chosen, and bundled 'em up, as it were, into one *Iniquity*, one huge Mass of *Sin*, which he laid upon his own *Son*. The LORD hath *laid*, or made to *meet*, on *Him*, the *Iniquity* of *us all*. As, in the Type, *all the Iniquities and Transgressions* of God's People *Israel*, in *all their Sins,* were *put*, or *laid*, upon the *Head* of the *Scapegoat,* at the Day of Atonement: So were *all the Sins* of all that shall be *saved,* at once *laid*, or made to *meet* upon *Christ*, at that great *atoning Day,* when our Great High Priest offer'd up *Himself*, that one Great Sacrifice, once for all, to satisfy Divine Justice, and make Peace between God and Us, or to make God and his People, for ever at *One.* And this laying of Sin upon Christ, was by *Imputation:* As *2 Cor.* 5.21. *He hath made* Him *to be* Sin for us, *who knew no Sin; that we might be made the Righteousness of God in Him.* God the Father made Christ *Sin for us*, or made Him *our Sin*, by transferring, or carrying over *our Sin* unto *Him*. He put *Him* in *our Place*, that *we* might be put in *His*. He made Him *Sin*; that we might be made *Righteousness*. Sin for *us*, or *our Sin*; that we might be made *his Righteousness*, or the *Righteousness of God in Him.* Which consisted in that complete Obedience, which He, who was God and Man in one Person, yielded to the Divine Law. It was his *Human Nature* only, that was capable of *obeying*; but as that Nature was personally united to the *Son of God*; so his *Obedience*, was the Obedience of the *Person*; and was properly stiled, *the Righteousness of God*, as having a Divine Glory upon it. As his *Blood*, on the same Account, is called the *Blood of God*, Acts 20.28.

And, by the Way, Oh! the transcendent Excellency of this glorious Robe, which our Lord wrought out to be the justifying Righteousness of his People! it has, not only the utmost Perfections of a Creature in it, but the Rays of infinite Glory also, Resplendently shining therein! Oh, Who would chuse to dress himself up in a Creature-Righteousness, were it ever so *perfect*; much less in the *filthy Rags* of a Sinner's Obedience, to stand in before a God of infinite Glory; when there is such a beauteous Garment, such a transcendent, glorious *Robe* provided, to clothe every naked Soul, that desires to be found in it! I am sure, none but those, who have no Eye of Faith, to behold its superlative Excellency, its infinite Glory!

Well, Christ was made sin for us, to take away our Unrighteousness; that we might be made Righteousness, even the Righteousness of God in Him. And God's People are made so by *Imputation*, Rom. 4.6. *Even as* David *also describeth the Blessedness of the Man unto whom God* imputeth *Righteousness without Works.* For, in a Law-Sense, or by his own Obedience to the Law, *There is none* Righteous, *no not one*, Chap. 3.10. And as God's People are made *Righteousness* by *Imputation*; So, in the same *Sense*, Christ was made *Sin*. For, in no other Sense, than that of Imputation, could *He* be made Sin, who *knew no Sin*, either by Inhesion or Commission. He who knew no Sin, was made Sin for *us*; that *we* (who knew no Righteousness) might be made the Righteousness of *God in Him*. Oh the glorious Exchange! The Riches of Divine Grace display'd herein, will be the eternal Admiration of all the saved Ones! Oh how beautiful is Christ, to the Eye of his Sinful Spouse, *as Ruddy*, in this first Head of his Sufferings; while, in condescending Grace, his White, his Glorious *Self,* stoops down to be made *Sin for Her!*

2. Our Lord was *Ruddy* with respect to the *Law's Malediction*. This was consequent upon the former. The Father having imputed Sin, the Sin of his People, the original Debtors, unto Christ their great Surety: His holy Law, found Sin upon him; and thundred out all its *Curses* against him: It *anathemiz'd* him to the utmost. Thus, *Gal.* 3.13. *Christ hath redeemed us from the Curse of the Law, being made a* Curse *for* us: *for it is written*, Cursed *is every one that hangeth on a Tree.* Stand amaz'd, Oh Heaven and Earth, at this: What, *God blessed for ever,* made a *Curse*, an Execration for such *vile Wretches*, who had justly *deserved* it! Was ever *Love* like *this?* Oh Heaven-astonishing, Earth-amazing, and Hell-confounding *Love?* "Lord,

let us *know* more of this *Love of Christ*, which *passeth Knowledge!* Our dear *Jesus*, What wouldst thou endure *our Curse*, that we might enjoy *thy Blessedness!* Oh let this Love *constrain us* to give up ourselves to *Thee*, to be entirely *Thine*, who in this wondrous Instance, hast shewn thyself to be so entirely *Ours!*"

3. Our Lord was *Ruddy*, with respect to the *Execution of the Law's Sentence*. Thou shalt *die*, die the *Death*, saith the Law of God; since thou'rt become a *Surety* for those *Strangers* to God, which have *deserv'd it*, thou shalt *smart* for it. Thus it brandish'd its flaming Sword, against our dear Lord Jesus. And, *Awake, O Sword, says* strict Justice, *against my Shepherd, and against the Man that is my Fellow, saith the LORD of Hosts: Smite the Shepherd, and the Sheep shall be scatter'd, and I will turn mine Hand, upon the little Ones*, Zech. 13.7. This was the Language of God's strict Justice, when it found Sin, the Sin of the straying Sheep, upon Christ, the great Shepherd: "*Awake, O Sword:* O Divine Justice, with all thy Rigours; O Law of God, with all thy Curses: *Against my Shepherd*, who engag'd from everlasting to die for his sinful Sheep. *And against the Man that is my Fellow, saith the LORD of Hosts: Smite the Shepherd,* spare him not a Jot; if he will save his *Sheep*, let him *die* for it. Smite *the Man that is my Fellow:* Strike him to the very *Soul*, till thy Sword is *satiate* with his Blood. Thou hast here an adequate Object to deal with, the eternal Son of God, clothed with Human Nature, yea, with all the Sins of his Sheep. Therefore smite him deep, take thy Fill, he's an infinite Person, able to pay thee all thy Due. *Saith the LORD of Hosts:* Let all the Hosts of Earth and Hell combine against him. Let Sin, Curse, Men, Devils, Darkness, Death and Grave beset him round, and strike him through with their barbed Arrows. And *I will* smite him, *I'll bruise him:* Mine Hand shall be upon him. None of the combined Powers of Darkness, can fetch Blows *deep enough* to satisfy for Sin. And therefore *I'll* smite him: *I'll* let out my flaming Wrath, and fiery Indignation upon him, even into his very Soul; and make him feel the infinite Terrors of a Sin-revenging God: The Poison whereof shall drink up his Spirits, while he stands *alone*, (the *Sheep* being *scatter'd*) as the *Mark* of my Arrows, as the *Butt* of all my just Vengeance. And then, Behold, being fully satisfy'd by the Shepherd's Death, *I will turn mine Hand*, in a Way of Grace and Life upon his Sheep, those *little Ones*." Thus did the Law, and Justice of God, set themselves in Battle-Aray against Christ, when for us he was made Sin, and a Curse.

And now, if ever, the Bride of Christ wou'd have been *separate* from him, when he must *die the Death for her* (*such* a Death, that none but *himself* could sustain) had not his Love, Power, and Faithfulness been equally *infinite!* But having lov'd her into Oneness with Himself from Everlasting, he resolv'd, in the same unchangeable Grace, that *Nothing* should separate her from him. And having anciently engag'd as her *Surety,* to pay her Debts, *Faithfulness was the Girdle of his Reins;* he did not *repent,* nor *turn away back* from his Engagements, when he was call'd upon to pay her Scores; and therefore, travelling in the Goodness of his Strength, he resolves to go thro' Death for her. And,

Thus he went forth into the *Garden,* where the Law and Justice of God arrested him, *Joh.* 18.1. *Her Sin* began in a *Garden,* and so did *his Sufferings.* 'twas *here,* the approaching Storm of Divine Vengeance began to drop down upon him; which made his *Soul exceeding sorrowful, even unto Death,* Mat. 26.38. 'twas *here,* the Father gave the *Cup of Wrath,* into his Hand; which fill'd him with *sore Amazement,* Mark 14.33. 'twas *here,* he began to *sip* of that Cup of Indignation, which he was shortly to *drink off,* which cost him such an *Agony,* that he *sweat,* as it were *great Drops of Blood, falling down to the Ground,* Luke 22.44. *Here,* he began his *Conflict* with divine Vengeance, and to taste of that amazing Cup of Wrath, which made him in his innocent Human Nature, shrink, and with the greatest Earnestness, cry to his *Father,* That, if it was *possible, the Cup might pass from him:* That is, If it had been *possible* that God could have been *glorify'd,* and his People *saved,* he pray'd that the *Cup might pass from him;* if *Not,* with the greatest Resignation, he bow'd his *Human Will,* to the *Divine. O my Father,* says he, *if this Cup may* not pass from Me, *except I drink it,* Thy Will be done, *Mat.* 26.42. And then he takes the Cup into his Hand, with infinite Resolution to drink it up: *The Cup which my Father giveth me to drink,* shall I not drink it? *John* 18.11.

And after this Agony in the Garden, *Jesus knowing all Things that should come upon him, goes forth,* in the highest Love and Duty to his *Father*; and in the greatest Grace and Faithfulness to his *People*; and meets those *Officers* of the *chief Priests,* who with *wicked Hands* did take him. And thus he addresses them, *Whom seek ye?* They answer'd him, *Jesus of Nazareth. Jesus saith unto them, I am He. As soon therefore, and he had said unto them, I am He, they went backward, and fell to the Ground.* He let out such a Ray of his infinite Glory upon 'em in those Words, that they could not *stand* before it. To shew, how *feeble* all their Strength was, and how *impossible* it was for 'em, with all their Force, to *take him*, if he had not freely resign'd himself *up* to their wicked Hands. And also to shew, that it was as easy to *him*, to dash 'em into *Hell* in a Moment, with one Word of his Mouth, as it was to cast them to the *Earth.* That so their Sin, in Taking him, might be the more exceedingly aggravated, after their having had such a convincing *Proof* of his being the *Son of God.* And had they not been *Judicially hardned*, they could never, after this, have stretch'd forth their *Hands* to *touch the Lord's Anointed.* But Jesus knowing that his Hour was come, and that the Scriptures must be fulfill'd, which had predicted his Sufferings; He withdrew the Display of his divine Glory, and suffers them to rise from the Earth, and renew their Attempt to take him. When, looking upon 'em as the *Messengers of God's Law and Justice,* as well as the *Offices of the chief Priests*, he again says, *Whom seek ye?* They reply, *Jesus of* Nazareth. *Jesus answer'd, I have told you that I am He. If ye seek me, let These go their Way.* Thus he surrender'd himself up to *their wicked Hands*; and thereby, into the *Hands* of God's *righteous Law*, and *strict Justice*, to endure all that Vengeance that was due for the Sins of his People, that so they might be deliver'd from the Wrath to come. If ye seek *Me,* let *These* go their Way; *q.d.* [*quaque die* "every day" = daily]. If *I* must *suffer,* let *Mine* go *free.* If *I* must *die,* let *These live.* I give my Self to answer all that Law and Justice can demand; Take ME, and let *Mine* escape: Take the *Surety,* and let the *Debtor go,* John 18.3, *&c. Then the Band, and the Captain, and the Officers of the Jews,* (who had been conducted by *Judas,* to his Master, whom he betray'd with a Kiss) *took Jesus, and bound him and led him away to* Annas, *and to* Caiaphas, *into the Palace of the High Priest,* Ver. 12, 13, 15. Where they *mock'd him, smote him,* and *blasphem'd him,* Luke 22.63, 64, 65. Where he *endur'd the Contradiction of Sinners against himself.* While they *agreed* to bear *false Witness* against him, and could *not* agree, as to the *Matter of Charge,* Mark 14.56, *&c. But Jesus held his Peace, and answer'd Nothing.* Until the High Priest asked him, *Art thou the Christ, the Son of the Blessed? And Jesus said, I am: and ye shall see the Son of Man sitting on the right Hand of Power, and coming in the Clouds of Heaven. Then the High Priest rent his Clothes, and saith, What need we any further Witnesses? Ye have heard the Blasphemy: What think ye? And they all condemn'd him to be guilty of Death.* Then they *bound him,* and deliver'd him to *Pilate,* vehemently *accus'd him,* and instantly requir'd that he should be *crucify'd,* Chap. 15.1, *&c. But Jesus yet answered* Nothing. Because, tho' *guiltless* in *himself,* and as he stood at *Pilate's* Bar, yet he stood for *those* that were *guilty*, at the *Bar of divine Justice*, and were *there* charg'd with *their Crimes*; and therefore he *submits* to the Sentence of that inferior Court; when he was brought there, *as a Lamb to the Slaughter, he open'd not his Mouth*. And when *Pilate*, convinc'd of his Innocence, and of their unjust Rage, sought in vain, to *release him;* he *scourged Jesus,* and *deliver'd him to be crucify'd*, Ver. 15. *Then the Soldiers led away Jesus into the common Hall, where, calling together the whole Band, they cloth'd him with a purple Robe, platted a Crown of Thorns, which they set on his Head, and put a Reed in his right Hand. Then they began to salute him, Hail King of the* Jews. *They smote him, spit upon him,* and in Mockery, *bowing their Knees, worship'd him,* Ver. 16, &c. Oh, Infinite Condescension! Wou'd the *Lord of Glory*, be thus mock'd, smote, and spit upon, for such vile Worms as *We!* Wou'd HE, who was the Adoration of *Angels*, for *Us* be thus scorn'd by the vilest of *Men!* Would HE, whose Right it was to wear a *Crown of Glory*, for *Us* endure a *Crown of Thorns* to be set upon his Head! Would HE, that sway'd the *Sceptre* of Heaven and Earth, suffer a *Reed*, a *feeble* Reed, to be put into his *Right Hand!* Oh, Infinite *Grace* to *Us!* Oh, Infinite *Patience* in *Him!* Oh, Infinite *Forbearance* to those his *Enemies!* Had he not been the *strong God*, he could never have *endur'd* such *Indignities!*

And when they had *mock'd him*, they led him away to be *crucify'd*, to *Golgotha*, the *Place of a Scull*, an unclean Place. For there he was to die, because, tho' Purity it self, both created and uncreated, join'd in One, yet he had all our Uncleanness upon him: And was therefore to suffer *without* the *Gate* of *Jerusalem*; that City which had a typical Holiness in it, God having chosen it to put his Name there. As the *Bodies of those Beasts, which were offered for Sin, whose Blood was brought into the Sanctuary, by the High Priest, were burnt without the Camp,* where God dwelt, *Heb.* 13.11. Thus was he separated from God's typical People, and holy City, and brought into the Place of a Scull, where they crucify'd him, between *two Thieves*, as if *He* was the Chief of Malefactors. thus *was He number'd with Transgressors*. And here the last Scene of his Sufferings began.

Now the Rage of Earth, the Fury of Hell, and the Wrath of Heaven, were at once let *loose* upon him. They which *pass'd by, wagg'd their Heads at him;* the *High Priests mock'd him; the Thieves*, on either Side of him, *revil'd him*. And all the Powers of Hell unchain'd, vented their Fury upon him. As it was the *Hour* of his *Sufferings*, so it was the *Hour* of his Enemies *Triumph*; it was *their Hour*, and the *Power of Darkness. Many Bulls, strong*

Bulls of Bashan, *beset him* round. The *Assembly of the Wicked enclos'd him,* Psal. 22.12,—16. And Satan, that roaring *Lion*, with all his Legions of Devils, gaping upon him with their *Mouths*, would have swallow'd him up, Ver, 21. *He sought for comforters, but found none,* Psal. 69.20. No; his *Friends* forsook him; and his *Enemies* with the utmost Rage and Cruelty, triumph'd over him. He had not so much as the least Dram of Comfort from any of the Creatures. Not so much as the Light of the Sun; but there was *Darkness over the Earth, from the sixth Hour, until the Ninth*, Mark 15.33. And what was yet more, GOD hid his Face from him, and pour'd out upon him the Floods of his Indignation, even all that flaming Wrath, which was the just Desert of all that innumerable Multitude, for whom he suffer'd. Which made him cry out, *My god, my God, why hast thou forsaken me?* Ver. 34. Oh, What did our Lord endure! What exquisite Agonies in his *Body!* What unutterable, inconceivable Torments in his *Soul*, while he hung upon the Cross, in his *Dereliction-Hour!* He then endur'd our *Hell*; even all that fiery Vengeance, that we must have borne in Hell for *ever*. Oh, What a Cup of Wrath, did his capacious Soul drink off, even to the Bottom! For being an infinite Person, the Sufferings of his Human Nature, had an infinite Merit in them; and therefore at *one Draught*, HE could drink up all that Wrath, which would have been *endless to us!* And this he did when on the *Cross:* For lo, he cry'd out, *It is Finished!* The Sufferings of his Soul were finish'd, and then he *bow'd the Head*, and *gave up the Ghost*. He yielded his Spirit into the Hands of his Father, and his Body unto Death and the Grace, *John* 19.30. But Oh, What a Sight was this, to the wondring Angels! To see the *Lord of Glory* thus *suffer!* The *Prince of Life*, thus *die!* And now, the Law's Sentence was fully *executed*, and divine Justice fully *satisfy'd*. The Law call'd for the *Death* of the *Sinner*; and it had the *Death* of the Saviour! Justice call'd for the Sinner's *Blood;* the Saviour presents his *own!* Thus the Church's *Beloved*, is *Ruddy!* And, Oh, how beautiful is He, as such, in her Eye! Since in *his Death*, is *her Life!*

Thirdly. The Spouse's *Beloved,* is *White and Ruddy*, in regard to his *Victory* over his Enemies, and his *Vengeance* against them.

We have seen the Lord of Life, for us, under the Domination of *Death*, and the *Grave:* But it was *impossible for him, to be holden of them*, Acts 2.24. For having given such a full Price into the Hands of divine Justice, by his own bloody Sufferings, and meritorious Death; it was just with God, to set him *free:* And therefore, God the *Father* rais'd him from Death to *Life*, to *die no more*. And thereby, did openly acquit, and discharge him, in the

Name and Room of his *People*, whose *Surety* He was, and whose Debt of Sufferings, he had fully *paid*, by the invaluable Price of his own *Blood*. For as he was *deliver'd for our Offences, so he was rais'd again for our Justification*, Rom. 4.25. And He, having given his own Life, an infinite Ransom for his Spouse; It was a righteous Thing with God, that *she*, also, should be delivered. And accordingly she was, mystically rais'd up *in Him*, from under all Guilt, Wrath, and Death, to *endless Life with Him*, Eph. 2.5, 6. *Even when we were dead in Sins, hath* Quickned us together with Christ: *And hath* raised us up together. In which *mystical* Salvation of the Spouse, the *exceeding Riches of Grace*, and the Glory of *satisfy'd Justice*, did brightly *shine*; and herein a most firm Basis was laid, for all the vast Superstructure, of her *personal* Salvation, from Sin, Satan, Death and Grave, which shall on Day stand upon it: Wherein the *exceeding Riches* of divine *Grace*, will shine *gloriously*, to the endless Ages of *Eternity*.

And as God the Father rais'd Christ from the Dead, victorious over all his Enemies: So, *Christ*, also, rais'd Himself. He had *Power*, as the Son of God, to *lay down* his Human *Life*, and to *take it again*, John 10.10. And, says he to the *Jews, Destroy this Temple,* (i.e., Of his Body) *and in three Days, I will raise it up*, Chap. 2.19. And as, in his mighty Strength, he rose from the Grave, a triumphant *Conqueror* over *his*, and his *Peoples Enemies*; and so was *White*, in his *Victory* over them; so likewise, he was *Ruddy* in his *Vengeance* against them: He rose in Triumph, the Triumph of his having conquer'd them by the Price of his Death, to *trample 'em down in Fury*, by the Power of his Life.

And accordingly, Having conquer'd all the Enemies of his Spouse, he *ascended up on high,* to his, and her Father, *and led Captivity captive*, Eph. 4.8. Or, *dragg'd* all the Powers of Darkness, (which had led her captive) as it were at his *Chariot Wheels*. As was the Custom of the *Roman* Conquerors, (to which this seems to allude) in the utmost Triumph, to *drag* those they overcame in Battle, at their *Chariot Wheels*. So, when *God,* the Mediator, went *up with a Shout, the* LORD *with the Sound of a Trumpet*, Ps. 47.5. amidst those *Chariots of God*, which were sent to attend the LORD *of Hosts, mighty in Battle*, on his triumphant Return to his Palace Royal in Heaven; *he led Capitivity captive. Having spoiled Principalities and Powers, he,* in the utmost Triumph, *made a Shew of them openly,* Col. 2.15. amongst all his magnificent Retinue, those Hosts of glorious Angels, who were sent to attend their LORD, to shout his Victories, and proclaim his State. Oh, the bright Triumphs of that Day, when these Heralds of the King of Glory demanded Entrance for him; or call'd to their Fellow Angels, in the Royal Court, to be in Readiness to raise their Shouts, and with the highest Acclamations, welcome him Home! *Psal.* 24.7. *Lift up your Heads, O ye Gates, and be ye lift up, ye everlasting Doors, and the King of Glory shall come in.* This was the Voice of these Harbingers of this victorious Prince. Which, to make way for a further Proclamation of the Glory of his State, and wonderful Atchievements, was thus answer'd from within, *Who is this King of Glory?* To which they reply, *The* LORD *strong and mighty, the* LORD *mighty in Battle,* ver. 8. "The mighty GOD! Who, in the Human Nature, has fought single-handed, with all the Powers of Darkness, and gain'd a complete, and eternal Victory over them!" And therefore, *Lift up your Heads, O ye Gates, even lift them up, ye everlasting Doors, and the King of Glory shall come in,* ver. 9. And then again, they're answer'd, *Who is this King of Glory?* q.d. Tell us more of his Royalty, 'tis a delightful Theme; Who is HE, that comes up in such State? To which they again reply, *The* LORD *of* HOSTS, *He is the* KING *of* GLORY! Ver. 10. 'tis He, that is GOD by Nature, JEHOVAH, the LORD of HOSTS; who now comes up triumphant in the *Human Nature,* as Lord and Head of *Angels:* Yea, of all the *Creatures* in Heaven, Earth and Hell: It is the KING of GLORY! Tis HE, that has *all Glory,* originally, and independently, in, and of Himself, as *God.* That had *all Glory* anciently settled upon his Person as *God-Man,* the Great *Head* over all Persons and Things. And that now, as the great *Saviour,* is deservedly, to be crown'd with *all Glory;* and that, as such, is to be the Author, Giver, and Maintainer of *all Glory,* to saved Men, and standing Angels; and tremendous *Judge* of wicked Men and Devils.' To which no further Reply is made. No; He *enters triumphant!* All the glorify'd Saints, all the bright Angels and Arch-angels, *Welcom'd* this King of Glory to his Majestick Throne, with the highest Acclamations of Joy, the greatest Reverence, and most profound Adoration! Yea, his *Father welcomes* him; and sets him down with Him in *his Throne,* Heb. 12.2. He was so great a Person, as the *eternal Son,* of the *eternal Father,* that he *thought it not Robbery to be equal with God:* And yet he *made himself of no Reputation, and took upon him the Form of a Servant, and was made in the Likeness of Men: And being found in Fashion as a Man, he humbled himself, and became obedient unto Death, even the Death of the Cross. Wherefore, God highly exalted him, and gave him a Name which is above every Name: That at the Name of Jesus every Knee should bow, of Things in Heaven, of Things in Earth, and Things under the Earth; And that every*

Tongue should confess, that Jesus Christ is Lord, to the Glory of God the Father, Phil. 2.6, *&c.* Thus highly was he exalted, upon his Ascension to Heaven. The Father, bid him *sit at his Right Hand,* until he made his *Enemies* his *Footstool,* Ps. 110.1. Yea, he then *put all Things,* Authoritatively, *under his Feet.* And as he had a strong *Rod,* a mighty Sceptre of Government given him, to *dash* all his Enemies *in Pieces, like a Potter's Vessel*; So, this LORD at God's right Hand, *strikes thro' Kings,* even all Powers whatsoever that oppose him, *in the Day of his Wrath,* Ps. 2.9. and 110.5. Thus, the Spouse's *Beloved,* is *White,* in his glorious *Victories* over all His, and Her Enemies; and *Ruddy,* in his authoritative, and executive *Vengeance* against them in his Resurrection, Ascension, and Session at God's Right Hand. Again,

Fourthly. The Spous's Beloved, is White and Ruddy, in his heavenly Glory.

He is *White,* in that personal, and relative *Glory,* He now wears in Heaven, as the great *Head* of the Church; and *Ruddy,* as the exalted *Saviour.* God the Father, not only put all Things under Christ's Feet, *i.e.,* all his Enemies; and gave him to be the *Head over all Things to the Church,* Eph. 1.22. That is, a monarchial Head, or an Head of Government, over all Creatures and Things, for the Good of his Church: But he is also, the Head *of* the Church, *Col.* 1.18. *And he is the Head of the Body, the Church.* And he is so, 1. In regard of *Representation.* 2. In regard of *Government.* And 3. With respect to *Communication.*

1. Our Lord is the Head of the Church in regard of *Representation.*

When Christ ascended to Glory, he did not go, as a single Person, for himself, alone, but as the *Representative* of his People, Heb. 6.20. *Whither the* Forerunner, *is for us entred.* Our *Great High Priest, entred within the Vail, into Heaven itself, with his own Blood,* as the *Forerunner* of his People, to prepare, and take up *Places* for all the Heirs of Glory: And he likewise entred for us, as *Representing* all the *Persons* of his People, mystically in *Himself.* As the *High Priest* under the Law, entred into the Presence of God, as the *Representative* of the People, bearing all the *Names* of the *Twelve Tribes* upon his *Breastplate, and Ephod,* for a Memorial before the LORD continually; and likewise all their *Services,* as HOLINESS TO JEHOVAH, by that Plate of pure Gold, with this Inscription, which he wore upon his Head, *Exod.* 28. So, *Christ,* our Gospel *High Priest,* entred into Heaven for his People, and *now appears in the Presence of God for us,* Heb. 9.24. Representing us in his own Perfections, and Glory. The Law's

High Priest, indeed *stood* continually, when he entred into the Presence of God, not being permitted to *sit down*; because the great Sacrifice was not then offer'd, and so his Work of sacrificing not done. But our Gospel High Priest, when he went into Glory, *sat down*, for *ever* sat down, as having completely finish'd that great Work of Atonement, which the Father gave him to do. Nor does he sit there, *alone*. No, all *His* sit there, mystically *in Him*. As, *Eph.* 2.6. *And hath raised us up together, and made* us sit together, *in Heavenly Places* in Christ Jesus. And this complete *mystical* Salvation, secures all that complete *personal* Salvation, which the saved of the Lord shall one Day enjoy. Thus Christ is the Head of the Church, in regard of *Representation*.

2. He is the Head of the Church, in regard of *Government*. When Christ ascended to Glory, God the Father, not only made him King of Nations, and gave him a monarchial Headship over all Things, *To* (or *for* the Good of) his Church; and as such, an *Iron Rod*, to dash in Pieces all that oppose him; But he also made him King *of* the Church, and set him as such, upon his holy Hill of *Zion*; to Save, and Rule his People, by the sweet, and powerful *Septre of his Grace*, Psal. 2.6. and 110.3. Our *Melchisedec* is to his Church, *first King of Righteousness, and after that also, King of* Salem, *King of Peace*, Heb. 7.2. He's *King of Righteousness*, as he *fulfill'd* all Righteousness by his own great Obedience; as he brought this *in*, to the Presence of the Father, with the highest Acceptance, to be the *everlasting Righteousness* of his People, which he *grants* unto 'em, as their bright Array: As he *dispenses* all Righteousness *for 'em*, by subduing all their Enemies, and securing unto them, all their Privileges: And as he *works* all Righteousness *in*, and *by* them. And, he's *King of Peace*, as he *made Peace* for his People, by the *Blood of his Cross*; which was the Covenant-Foundation of his Regal Glory; and as he *dispenses* Peace from his *Throne*. All Peace, Pardon, Grace, Life and Glory, this King of Peace, dispenses from his Throne, unto all the happy Subjects of his Reign, both in this World, and that which is to come. And as such a *King*, that has done, doth, and will do so for his *People*, he now *sits in Heaven*. Thus Christ is the Head of the Church, in regard of *Government*. And

3. Our Lord is the Head of the Church, with respect to *Communication. He is the Head of the Body of the Church*. He stands, spiritually, in as near a Relation to the *Church*, as the Head, naturally, doth to its own *Body*. And as the *Head*, in Nature, communicates animal Spirits, for Sense and Motion, to all the *Members*; So, the Lord Jesus Christ, as *Head of Influence*,

communicates Life to all the *Members of his Body*; and is the Cause of all their Motion. *I live;* says the Apostle, *yet not I, but Christ lives in me,* Gal. 2.20. As the Members of the Body natural, are the *Fulness* of the Head, and *live* from it: So, the Members of the Body Mystical, are the *Fulness* of Christ the Head, who *filleth all in all*, Eph. 1.23. That is, all his Members, with Life, in all the Kinds, and Degrees of it. As Christ is the Head of the Church, so, it *pleased the Father, that in Him, all Fulness should dwell*; both of Nature, Grace, and Glory, *Col.* 1.19. As the Fulness of Light in the Sun, or of Water in the Sea: To be *communicated* to his Members, in all those various Measures, which boundless Love, and infinite Wisdom had ordain'd. And therefore the Apostle *John* speaking of Christ's Glory, as full of Grace and Truth, says, for himself, and all the Saints, *Of his Fulness have all we received, and Grace for Grace*, John 1.14.—16. Thus it is here in Grace, and thus it will be hereafter in Glory. And even *now*, Christ wears in Heaven, the Glory of *this* his Headship, both in its *personal*, and *relative Branches*. As the Sun, hath one *Glory*, peculiar to *itself*, as it is a complete *Body of Light*; and another, as it *communicates* Light, or is appointed to be the *communicative Fountain* of it, to all the Lesser Luminaries. So Christ, as the Head of the Church, hath both a *personal* and *relative* Glory. On which Account he's *White*, and exceeding beautiful in the Eye of his Spouse.

And as he's *White*, in his *heavenly Glory*, as the great *Head* of the Church; So, he's also *Ruddy*, as the exalted *Saviour*. For tho' he is not *now* under the Dominion of Death, nor shall it have any *more* Dominion over Him, *Rom.* 6.9. Yet he wears in Heaven, the *Glory* of his *Crucifixion*; and appears as the *Lamb*, that was *once slain,* Rev. 5.6. *And I beheld, and lo, in the midst of the Throne, and of the four Beasts, and in the midst of the Elders stood a* Lamb, *as it had been* slain, *having seven Horns, and seven Eyes, which are the seven Spirits of God sent forth into all the Earth.* The exalted Saviour, is here beheld by his Servant *John*, in his heavenly Glory, in the midst of the *Throne*, as a *Lamb* that had been *slain*. And tho' he's here view'd, *standing*, There *stood a Lamb*, &c. Yet this don't in the least thwart those other Scriptures, where he is said to *sit*, or be *set down*. Because, the Phrase of his being *set down*, denotes, his having *finish'd* that Part of his priestly Work, which he was to perform here *below*, in offering up Himself, as the great Sacrifice of Atonement; and his having entred into *Heaven* with his own Blood, to the full Satisfaction of divine Justice; whereupon the Father glorify'd him to the utmost, as having sav'd his

People by his meritorious Death on the Cross, and gave him all Fulness of Power, to save them by his Life on the Throne. But this, of his *Standing*, sets out, His *Readiness* to save his People, by the Execution of that Part of his *priestly Office*, which he performs now, *above*; in presenting his own Person, Blood, and Righteousness for his People, before the Face of his Father; and in the Virtue thereof, making continual Intercession for them; as also, His *Readiness* to exert the Fulness of his *Kingly Power*, for their *complete Salvation*. And so, there is a perfect harmony between these, seeming, contrary Phrases, of his *sitting*, and *standing*, as both are apply'd to the *Glory of his Throne* in Heaven. Does he *stand* as a *Lamb?* 'tis *As*, it had been *slain*; That Work *finish'd*, and in that Regard *set down:* As a *High Priest?* 'tis *As*, having *offer'd* his one *great Sacrifice*; and now, only, in the Virtue thereof, making *Intercession on his Throne.* And thus it was long ago foretold of him, *And He shall be a Priest upon his Throne*, Zech 6.13. And, says the Apostle, *We have such an High Priest, who is set on the Right Hand of the Throne of the Majesty in the Heavens,* Heb. 8.1. And so here, The Lamb as it had been slain, standing in the midst of the Throne, is set forth as having *seven Horns*, and *seven Eyes:* viz. A Perfection of Power, and a Perfection of Knowledge and Wisdom, to manage all the Affairs of his Kingdom, founded in his Sacrifice, to save his People, and destroy his Enemies; by his Spirit, (with which he is immeasurably fill'd) in his seven-fold Operations, sent forth into all the Earth. Thus the once slain Lamb, upon his Glory-Throne in Heaven, is *White* and *Ruddy*, and the great *Head* of the Church, and the exalted *Saviour!* Once more,   *Fifthly.* The Church's *Beloved*, is *White* and *Ruddy*, with respect to the described *Glory* of his *next Appearance.* He'll come again, in the brightest *Glory*, as the Church's *Bridegroom:* And in the most flaming *Wrath*, as the tremendous *Judge* of wicked Men, and Devils.

When our Lord *appears the second Time, without Sin, unto* the compleat *Salvation* of his People; he'll come in his *own Glory,* in the *Glory of his Father*, and in the *Glory of his holy Angels*; to marry his Bride openly, in the Face of all the Creatures. Thus, *Mat.* 25.10. it's said, *And while they went to buy, the Bridegroom came, and they that were ready, went in with him to the Marriage, and the Door was shut.* By the *Bride-groom* here, our Lord intends *Himself:* By his *Coming*, His next, glorious *Appearance:* By those that were *ready*, His *Bride:* By their *going in with him to the Marriage*, His *taking her*, into the open *Marriage Glory with himself.* And by those that went to *buy Oil*; those *Nominal* Christians, who only had a *Lamp* of Profession, and were destitute of the *Holy Spirit*, and his *Grace* in their Hearts. And by the *Door being shut* upon them, that it will be utterly *impossible* for *Graceless Souls*, to have the least Participation of *Glory*. This will be the sad Case of all Unbelievers in that Day, who have no spiritual Acquaintance with Christ, in his Person and Grace, by special Faith, in this. But have only prided themselves in their apprehended Purity, by a bare Profession of his Name, attended with some imperfect Moral Performances of their own; as if this was enough to recommend 'em to the Bridegroom's Favour, and a Dress sufficient to stand in before the King of Glory. When, alas, such Souls, having gone after *other Lovers*, than *Christ*, and being destitute of the Wedding Garment of *his Righteousness*; will be found *Filthy*, and utterly *Speechless*, and cast out, *Declaratively*, from Christ's visible Church, in that Day, as having had no Right to have had a Place therein, in this. And thence also, *Authoritatively,* having all their Sins bound upon 'em by the Curses of the Law, shall be cast out, into *outer Darkness:* Or, as unclean, among the Vessels of Wrath, unto whom is *reserved, the Blackness of Darkness for ever*. But as for those *Virgin Souls*, who have had the *Faith of God's Elect*; and from thence, a Discovery of the transcendent *Glory of Christ*, in his Person, Love, Blood and Righteousness; to the attracting their *Souls* into earnest Desires after Him, and an entire Resignation to him, as their Lord and Husband; and from thence have yielded Obedience to him, in all Holy Conversation, and Gospel-Profession: These, as having been secretly *espoused* to Christ here in *Grace*, shall be openly *married* unto him in *Glory*. Then that Prayer of our Lord, John 17.20. &c. shall be fully answer'd, and what was foretold therein, fully accomplish'd, *Neither pray I for these alone, but for them also which shall believe on Me thro' their Word: That they all may be one, as thou Father art in Me, and I in Thee; that they also may be one in us: That the World may believe that thou hast sent Me. And that Glory which thou gavest Me, I have given them: That they may be One, even as We are One. I in them, and thou in Me, that they may be made perfect in One, and that the World may know that thou hast sent Me, and hast loved them as thou hast loved Me.* Then all God's Chosen, that have been enabled to believe in Jesus, shall be openly one with him; or appear in the Glory of their Marriage-Union, and Relation to him; as the Father, and He were One, in the Settlement of all this Glory upon them. Then Christ the Bridegroom, and the Church his Bride, will have such a Glory put upon them, in this their mutual Relation to each other, upon the Bottom of God's everlasting Love unto them, that will fill the World with Amazement. When Christ, the Bridegroom, *appears in Glory*; the Church, the Bride, shall likewise *appear with him.*—The last View the World had of *Christ*, was, as Hanging on the *Cross*, and laid in a *Tomb*. They saw him in the Depth of his Humiliation; disbeliev'd his *Messiahship*, despised, and rejected him. But when he comes again, they shall see him in his *Glory*. They shall see that *same Jesus* whom they crucified, risen, exalted into Glory, and sitting on the Right Hand of Power, as the awful *Judge* of Quick and Dead. Yea, they shall see him, as the glorify'd *Head, Husband,* and *Saviour* of his Church; and then they shall *believe* that the *Father sent him.* Not *believe*, and be *saved:* But *believe*, and be *confounded.* These *Despisers*, shall then *See, Wonder;* and *Perish* for despising the sent Saviour, Acts 13.41. And, as to their amazing Terror, they shall see that *Jesus*, whom they once despised, and thought they had made an End of, as a poor, sorry Man, come again, in all his risen Glory; in his personal Glory, as God-Man, and in his Bridegroom-Glory, as Head, and Saviour of the Church: So likewise, they shall see the *Church*, the Bride, the Saved of the Lord, that had followed the Lamb whithersoever he went, and come up out of great Tribulations; with her Resurrection-Body, exactly comform'd to Christ's glorious Body, and her white Robes of Glory, her Bridal Garments on, advand'd to sit with Him on His Throne; or into the open Glory of Union to her Royal Bridegroom's Person, and Communion with him in all his Kingly Glory: He having completely sav'd her, and openly given her, a Participation of all that Glory which the Father gave to Him. And then the World shall *know*, to their everlasting Confusion, that the Father has *lover Her*, even as He *loved Him.* That as he loved Christ, so, as to make Him the Bridegroom of the Church; so he loved her, to make her his Bride. That as he loved Christ, as Man, into the highest Union, and Communion with himself in Glory; so he loved the Church, his Bride, into a joynt Participation of that, his inconceivable, Bliss. Then all their unbelieving *Cavils* at Distinguishing *Grace*, towards a Remnant in Christ, will be for ever *silenced*; when they behold such a Distinguishing *Glory*, put upon those, who by Nature, were no better than themselves. They'll then be fully convinc'd that nothing less than eternal Love, in Father, Son, and Spirit, in absolute Election, particular Redemption, and special Vocation; could be Foundation strong enough, to bear the vast Superstructure of that Great Salvation of God's People, which they shall then see laid upon it. Then *every Mouth will be stopped, and all the World become Guilty before God.* 'twill then be fully *known*, that Man's *Destruc-*

tion was entirely of *himself*; and his *Salvation*, only of the LORD. That those which *perish*, have destroy'd themselves by *Sin*; and those which are *saved*, are saved alone by God's *Free Grace:* When they thus *appear with Christ*, in the *Glory* of their Marriage Relation to him. Oh the Glory of that bright Day, when the *Marriage of the Lamb*, shall be *come!* Rev. 19.7. With what a transcendent Brightness, will the Lamb shine upon his Throne, when he has all that Glory given him, which he was worthy of, as once slain on the Cross! And how splendid will his Bride appear, when all that Glory is put upon her, which was purchas'd by his Blood! How glorious will the Lamb's Love then appear in his Bride's Eye, in giving her such Life, thro' his own Death! Since she had never had the Enjoyment of her Bridegroom on the Throne, if he had not been for her, the Lamb slain on the Cross! And how inconceivably great will the Joy of that Day be, when Christ, the *Beloved*, presents his Spouse unto *himself*, a *glorious Church*, *not having Spot, or Wrinkle, or any such Thing!* And how glorious will be the Lamb's Praises; when all the innumerable Multitude of saved Men, together with all the bright Hosts of glorious Angels, shall in joynt Hallelujahs, give him the Honour that is due unto his Name! But the Glory of Christ, at his next appearing, is too great to be either conceiv'd, or exprest in all its refulgent Rays! And as he'll appear *white*, as the *Bridegroom* of his Church: So also,

    Ruddy, as the tremendous *Judge* of wicked Men, and Devils. When our *Lord Jesus Christ is revealed from Heaven with his mighty Angels,* 'twill be *in flaming Fire, to take Vengeance on them that know not God, and that obey not the Gospel: Who* shall then *be punished with everlasting Destruction from the Presence of the Lord, and from the Glory of his Power*, 2 Thes. 1.7, 8, 9. Oh, this awful Day of the *Lamb's Wrath!* How terrible will it be unto the *Lamb's Enemies!* In vain they'll *cry to the Rocks and Mountains to fall upon them, to hide 'em from the Face of him that sits on the Throne, and from the Wrath of the Lamb; when this great Day of his Wrath is come,* wherein none of 'em *shall be able to stand*, Rev. 6.16, 17. As for all those Enemies of Christ, and his People, that shall be found alive at his Coming; in Righteousness he'll judge 'em, make War against them, prevail over 'em, and destroy 'em. As *Rev.* 19.12, &c. Where he's represented on a *White Horse*, as a victorious Warrior, to denote his *Victory* over them: With *Eyes like a Flame of Fire*, to shew his *Vengeance* against them: And with a *Vesture dipt in Blood*; as *treading them down*, in the *Wine-press of the Fierceness and Wrath of Almighty God. And I saw the Beast,* (saith the Apostle *John*) *and the Kings of the Earth, and their Armies gathered together to make War against him that sat on the Horse, and against his Army,* Ver. 19. *And the Beast was taken, and with him the false Prophet, which wrought Miracles before him, with which he deceived them that had received the Mark of the Beast, and that worship'd his Image. These were both cast alive into a Lake of Fire burning with Brimstone,* Ver. 20 *And the Remnant were slain with the Sword of him that sat upon the Horse, which Sword proceeded out of his Mouth: and all the Fowls were filled with their Flesh,* Ver. 21. This will be the dreadful End of all those Antichristian Powers, which shall be found in Rebellion, and open Hostility against Christ, at his next Appearing. And as for those his Enemies, who shall be so desperately hardned, as to *Compass the Camp of the Saints about, and the beloved City: Fire shall come down from God out of Heaven, and devour them. And the Devil that deceiv'd 'em,* shall be *cast into the Lake of Fire and Brimstone, where the Beast and the false Prophet* were, *and shall be tormented Day and Night for ever and ever,* Ch. 20.9, 10. Thus Christ will be the Judge of the *quick;* or of those his Enemies which shall be found *alive* at his Appearing and Kingdom. And then follows the Great, and General Judgment of all the wicked *dead.*

As for those of *Christ's,* which were *dead,* they shall be *rais'd* at his *Coming,* 1 Cor. 15.23. to endless Life, and Glory with him, by Virtue of their Union to him, who is the *Resurrection and the Life;* and of that conquest he made for them over Death and the Grave, when he died for them, and rose again. And the *living* Saints shall be *changed,* immortaliz'd in a *Moment,* and *caught up together* with the raised Saints, to *meet the Lord in the Air*; 1 Cor. 15.51. *1 Thess.* 4.17. and so shall come with him. For when he comes again, *The Dead in Christ shall rise first,* and *all the Saints* be brought *with him,* 1 Thess. 4.16. and 3.13. And be advanc'd to sit with him on his Throne, as Assessers in the awful Judgment of wicked Men, and Devils. *To him that overcometh* (saith our Lord) *will I grant to sit with me on my Throne,* Rev. 3.21. And, *know ye not* (says the Apostle) *that the Saints shall judge the World?* And that *We shall judge Angels?* 1 Cor. 6.2, 3.

And in order to this awful Judgment, Christ, the tremendous Judge on his Great White Throne, will utter his Almighty Voice, and summons all the wicked dead, to stand before God. He'll call their Spirits, from their infernal Prison, to take their Bodies, rais'd by a Word of his Mouth, from all their various Graves, or Places, where they've been reposited: To receive a just Judgment, according to their Works. And lo, they must obey, and stand before his Throne *for* Judgment! Tho' most terrible this will be to the ungodly, who shall know, that they can never stand *in* the Judgment, or be acquitted in Judgment. Oh, how glad would the wicked be, to have their Carcasses for ever lie in Rottenness, and Putrifaction! But as their Bodies have been Partners with their Souls in Sin; so must they be Partakers with them in Punishment. Sinc e it is a righteous thing with God, to recompense Tribulation to them that knew him not, and that obey'd not the Gospel; but oppos'd Christ, and troubled the Saints: They must come forth to Judgment, to take their Trial, and receive their Sentence. And as this will be a most terrible Day, to wicked Men; so likewise, to the fallen Angels. *?The Devils believe, and tremble,* as being *reserv'd in Chains of Darkness, to the Judgment of this great Day.* When they must stand before Christ, their tremendous Judge, to receive all that just Judgment, and fiery Indignation, which is due unto them, for all their Sins against God, and Man, and especially for that Opposition they have made against Christ and His, from their first Apostacy, to their final Sentence; when they shall be shut up for ever, in the bottomless Pit, of remediless Torment. Oh this *Judgment Day!* well may it, by way of Emphasis, be call'd, The *Great Day!* For so it will be indeed; when all the Wicked, both Men, and Devils, shall stand before God, to receive the just Reward of all their evil Deeds! And of this Great, and General Judgment, the Apostle *John,* had a Fore-view, *Rev.* 20.11, 12, 13, 14, 15. *And I saw a Great White Throne, and Him that sat on it, from whose Face the Earth and the Heaven fled away, and there was found no Place for them. And I saw the Dead, small and great, stand before God; and the Books were opened: and another Book was opened, which is the Book of Life: and the Dead were judged out of those Things which were written in the Books, according to their Works. And the Sea gave up the Dead which were in it, and Death and Hell deliver'd up the Dead which were in them: and they were judged every Man, according to their Works. And Death and Hell were cast into the Lake of Fire: This is the second Death. And whosoever was not found written in the Book of Life, were cast into the Lake of Fire.* Oh, what a dreadful Day will this be unto all Unbelievers, when all their Works shall be try'd, and cast, and their Persons too, as standing upon that Bottom, by the pure Law, and strict Justice of God! None shall escape the fiery Vengeance of God in that Day, but those who are found in Christ, whose Names were written in the Book of Life, To these on his *Right Hand*, Christ will say, *Come ye blessed of my Father, inherit the Kingdom prepared for you from the Foundation of the World.*

For I was an hungred, and ye gave me Meat, &c. *Mat.* 25.34, &c. But unto those on his *Left Hand,* he'll say, *Depart from me, ye cursed, into everlasting Fire, prepared for the Devil and his Angels. For I was an hungred, and ye gave me no Meat,* &c. Ver. 41, &c. *And these shall go away into everlasting Punishment: But the Righteous into Life* eternal Ver.46. Thus *Ruddy,* in flaming *Wrath,* will *Christ appear,* as the tremendous *Judge* of wicked Men and Devils. And since his Judgment will be *just,* and his Vengeance *righteous:* For the Vindication of God's Honour in judging and destroying his Enemies, for the Fulfilment of his Threatnings against them, and for the Accomplishment of his Promises to his People, in pleading their Cause, and subduing all their Enemies under their Feet: He is exceeding lovely in the Eye of his Spouse, as *Ruddy* in this Regard. For which she'll sing his Praises, when He has destroy'd all His, and her Enemies; as she's said to do, upon the Lamb's Destruction of the Whore of *Babylon,* Rev. 19.1, 2, 3. *And after these Things, I heard a great Voice of much People in Heaven, saying, Allelujah; Salvation, and Glory, and Honour, and Power unto the Lord our God: For true and righteous are his Judgments; for he hath judged the great Whore, which did corrupt the Earth with her Fornication, and hath avenged the Blood of his Servants at her Hand. And again they said, Allelujah.*

Thus Christ, the Church's *beloved,* is *White* and *Ruddy: White,* in the *Glory* of his *Divinity:* and *Ruddy,* in the *Truth* of his *Humanity. White,* in the *Purity* of his *Human Nature;* in his spotless Conception, and Birth, and in the Whole of his Life: and *Ruddy,* in the *Greatness* of his *Sufferings. White,* in his *Victory* over his *Enemies:* and *Ruddy,* in his just *Vengeance* against them; in his Resurrection, Ascension, and Session at God's Right Hand. *White,* in his heavenly *Glory,* as the *Head* of the Church, both in its personal and relative Branches: and *Ruddy,* as the exalted *Saviour.* And *White,* in his *glorious Appearing,* as the Church's *Bridegroom,* to save her completely from all her Enemies, and marry her openly unto Himself in Glory: and *Ruddy,* as the tremendous *Judge* of wicked Men and Devils. From all which, put together, it appears, that *Christ's Beauty, is incomparably Great!* And that the Spouse might well say, *My Beloved, is White and Ruddy!* To which, She justly adds,

The Chiefest among Ten Thousand] A *certain* Number, is here put for an *uncertain:* And Christ is said to be the *Chiefest* among Ten Thousand, to set forth *His* super excellent Glory, above *all* the Creatures, in *both* Worlds. In that *Song of Loves,* concerning Christ, and the Church, the

Heavenly Bridegroom, and his Bride, this King of Glory, and the Queen at his Right Hand. *Ps.* 45. the *Psalmist* begins it, with the Commendation of His Beauty, Ver. 2. *Thou art fairer than the Children of Men*, &c. Not fairer than some of the Children of Men in *particular*; as *some* among them, are fairer than *others:* But fairer than the Children of Men in *general*. Fairer than the *fairest* of them, fairer than *All* of 'em, put together, *superlatively Fair!* All those Glories, Beauties, and Excellencies, which are *disperst* among the Sons of Men, and shine, as so many *scatter'd* Beams, among all their innumerable Multitude; *meet* together in *His* Sun-like Face; and are infinitely Outshone, by *His* incomparable Brightness! And as He's fairer than the Sons of Men on *Earth*; so, fairer than the Sons of Men in *Heaven*, fairer than the perfect Saints above! Yea, fairer than the glorious Angels! For *who in the Heavens can be compared unto the* LORD? (this LORD, the Mediator?) *Who among the Sons of the Mighty can be likened unto the* LORD, *Ps.* 89.6. As the Circumference-Lines, *meet* in their *Center*, and the scatter'd *Beams*, in the Sun's *Body*; so all created Excellencies *meet* in *Christ*, as in their Center, Source, and Origin. There they shine, with the most bright refulgent Glory; and thence they cast their Rays, upon all the Creatures in both Worlds. Do *Creatures* shine, like twinkling *Stars?* *Christ* is the *Sun*, which casts *all* their starry Lustre! And as all *created* Excellencies, meet in Christ; so, *uncreated*, likewise! He who is fairer than the Children of Men; to whom none in the Heavens may be compar'd, none among the Sons of the Mighty, likened; is *God by Nature*, the LORD, JEHOVAH! God and Man, in one Person! And as such, the Church's *Beloved*. And therefore he must needs be, *the Chiefest among Ten Thousand!* He is so, in Himself; and he is so in Her Esteem. What Glories meet not in so *Great a Beloved!* And what *Great Things* can he not, and will he not do for his *Spouse*; whom he has made *One* with him, and *loves as Himself! Unto you therefore that believe*, says the Apostle, *He is precious*, 1 Pet. 2.7. Christ is precious in Himself, and precious to his People. All Glories meet in him universally, perfectly, and perpetually. He's Beauty, without Deformity: Light, without Darkness: Joy, without Sorrow: and Life, without an End! Oh, this *precious* JESUS! what a ravishing Object is HE, to those Souls, who have an *Eye* to see his *incomparable Glory!* None but *blind Souls*, dote upon *Creature Excellencies*; those *Glow worm Glories*, sparkling in the Night of Nature's Ignorance. No; they, which have an Eye of Faith, to *see Jesus*; have beheld in *Him*, such a transcendent Brightness, that puts out the Light of all *Creature-Beauties*, and makes 'em appear, when compar'd with *His*, to be but mere *Blackness*. They have seen such a super-excelling Glory in Christ, that attracts their whole Soul after him; and makes 'em say, with the greatest Languishment when they want him, and with the greatest Delight when they enjoy him, *None but Christ! None but Christ! So precious is He, unto them which Believe!*

And as Christ is Beauty in *Himself*; so he has it for his *Spouse*. The Beauty of other Husbands, can neither be accounted, nor communicated to a deformed Bride. But Christ, makes His Spouse comely, in His Beauty, *Her Beauty perfect*, thro' *His Comeliness*, which *He puts upon her*, Ezek. 16.14. He makes Her Pure, in His Purity; Righteous, in His Obedience; Clean, in His Blood; White, in His Victories; Acceptable, in His Acceptableness; Wise, in His Wisdom; Strong, in His Strength; and every way Glorious, in and with Himself: By taking *Her* up, into an Interest *in*, and Participation *of* all *His Glory!* And in this Regard also, He is to Her, *The Chiefest among Ten Thousand!* None like *Christ*, this *Precious Jesus*, to his *Spouse*, in Heaven or in Earth! He's Precious in his Person, as the Head and Husband of the Church; and Precious in his Office, as the alone Saviour of the Body. His Personal Glories, are Immense! His Riches, Unsearchable! His Love, Boundless! His Compassions, Deep! His Faithfulness, Great! His Wisdom, Infinite! And his Power, Almighty! And His Salvation, is Full, Free, and Eternal! And, in a Word, *He is, what HE is!* And what he is in *Himself*, That he is to his *Spouse!* He is in Himself, an Incomprehensible, Eternal *Fulness* of all Life and Glory! And he is unto *Her*, a Communicative *Fountain* of all Life and Glory, thro' all Times, and unto all Eternity! And therefore, Well might the Spouse say, *My Beloved is White and Ruddy: The Chiefest among Ten Thousand!* Thus much, as to the *General* Description the Spouse gives of her *Beloved*, in this tenth Verse of the fifth Chapter of *Solomon's* Song. I come, now,

To take a little Notice of that *Particular* Enumeration of his Beauties, which She gives in the following Verses. In which I shall endeavour all possible Brevity.

Ver. 11. *His Head is as the most fine Gold, his Locks are bushy, and black as a Raven.*

His Head is as the most fine gold:] The *Head*, in Nature, is the most *ex-cellent* Part of the Body; the Seat of Knowledge and Wisdom, which doth influence, and govern the Whole. And by the *Head* of Christ, as I humbly conceive, we may apprehend, 1. The *Godhead* of Christ: which is the most *excellent* Nature in him, and fits him for the Office of Mediator, and the Discharge thereof; by sustaining his human Nature, and directing, and influencing all the Actions thereof. 2. His *Constitution*, as *Mediator* between God and Man, may be hereby intended: This being the first, and principle *Cause*, whence all his Mediatory Performances flow. And, 3. His *Government* of the *Church*, and of all *Creatures*, and *Things*. And in that Christ's Head, is compar'd unto *Gold, fine* Gold, the *most* fine Gold; it denotes the super-excellent *Glory, Permanency, Unsefulness, and Profitableness*, of his Divinity, his Mediatorship, and his Mediatory Government. And *in Him*, in all Respects, *are hid, all the* Treasures *of Wisdom and Knowledge.*

His Locks are bushy, and black as a Raven] *Locks*, in Nature, are an *Ornament* to the Head, and have all their Growth, and Nourishment, immediately from it. And by the Locks of Christ, as I conceive, we may understand, 1. His *Counsels*, his *Purposes*, all those innumerable, well-order'd *Thoughts of his Heart, which stand fast to all Generations:* As the Multiplicity of well-set *Hairs*, deeply rooted in the *Head*. And, 2. His *Providences*, or the *Execution* of his Purposes, according to the Order of his Counsels, which are *visible* unto others: As so many well-set *Hairs*, fully *grown*, from their respective Roots in the Head. And as well-set Hair, fully grown, is an *Ornament* to the Head; so the eternal Counsels of Jesus Christ, and his working all Things in Providence, according thereunto; are a great *Ornament* to Him, as God, as Mediator, and as King and Governor: While he appears hereby, to be *Great in Counsel, and Mighty in Work.* And in that his Locks are said to be *bushy, and black as a Raven:* It denotes, 1. The *Innumerableness* of his Purposes, and Providences. 2. The *Mysteriousness*, and *Depth* of both. And, 3. The *Native Vigour*, and *perfect Strength*, of his Pardon, Willing, and Working. His Purposes, and his Providences, like *bushy* Hairs, are *beautiful,* and *innumerable.* As *Ps.* 139.17, 18. *How precious are thy* Thoughts *unto me, O God! how* Great *is the* Sum *of them! If I should count them, they are more in* Number *than the* Sand. And *Psalm* 40 5. Many, O LORD *my God, are thy wonderful* Works *which thou hast done, and thy* Thoughts *which are to us-ward: they cannot be reckon'd up in Order unto thee: if I would declare and speak of them, they are more than can be* numbred. And as they're Numberless; so, *Mysterious*, and very *deep.* Tere is the most excellent *Order* in both, his Counsels, and Providences; but they are so curiously *interwoven* thro' each other, that 'tis hard to *discern* the Order in which they stand. As 'tis to *discern* the Order of *bushy Hair*, (so as to say, *this* comes from *that Root*, and *that* from *another*) by reason of their *Interweavings.* And therefore the Apostle admires the mysterious Depths of Divine Counsels, and Providences, in their wonderful Interweavings, according to the manifold Wisdom of God, *Rom.* 11.33. *O the* Depth *of the Riches both of the* Wisdom and Knowledge *of God!* how Unsearchable *are his* Judgments, *and his* Ways *past* finding out!—Again, Christ's *Locks* being said to be *bushy*, and *black as a Raven:* Denotes, the *native Vigour*, and *perfect Strength* of his Person, Willing, and Working. *Bushy, black Hair*, in Nature, denotes *Vigour*, and *Strength of Youth*; as *thin, gray Hair, Decay thro' Age.* And as here apply'd to *Christ*, it denotes *His* Unchangeableness, or, his being *Jesus Christ the same, Yesterday, to Day, and for Ever:* that there neither *is*, nor *can* be any Decay in Him, *Heb.* 13.8. And tho' *He*, when coming to *Judgment*, is sometimes represented with *Hair, white as Wooll*; as *Rev.* 1.14. yet this bespeaks no *Decay in Him*; but only sets forth his Eternity *past*, or his being the *Ancient of Days*; which renders him fit for a *Judge.* As *black Hair*, sets forth the *Perfection* of his Strength, and *Unchangeableness* of his Glory, thro' Time and to Eternity to *come*; which renders him lovely as a *Bridegroom.* For the Spouse, in describing the Glory of her Beloved, not only tells us what he then was, but what he now is, and ever will be: She had such a *Beloved*, that Millions of *Ages*, could make no *Change*, or *Alteration* in! And as his *Person* is the same; so his *Counsels*, and his *Providences* don't decay. Christ's *Hairs,* never fall *off* his Head, nor *lose* their Glory. His Purposes *stand fast*; and the Execution of 'em, in Providences, *never fail:* Nor do either *lose* their Beauty, but both have an *unchangeable* Glory in them.

Ver. 12. *His Eyes are as the Eyes of Doves, by the Rivers of Waters, washed with Milk, and fitly set.*

His Eyes are as the Eyes of Doves,] The *Eye*, in Nature, is the *Organ* of *Sight.* And by Christ's *Eyes*, we may understand, His *Omniscience.* As, Psal. 94.9. *He that formed the* Eye, *shall not* He *see?* And *Heb.* 4.13. *All Things are naked, and opened unto the* Eyes of Him *with whom we have to do.* And, *Prov.* 15.3. *The* Eyes *of the* LORD *are in every Place, beholding the Evil, and the Good.* And with his all-seeing *Eye*, he *searcheth the Hearts, and trieth the Reins*, Rev. 2.23. And these Eyes of his, towards his *Own*, are as *Doves* Eyes: That is, pure, piercing, loving, chaste. They are so *pure*, that they *cannot behold Iniquity*, (i.e., with Approbation) *Hab.* 1.13. And therefore he'll destroy it utterly in, and for his Spouse. They are so *piercing*, that they perfectly *see all Things*, in all the Creatures, which tend, either to her Damage, or Benefit. And therefore he'll defend her from Evil, supply her with Good, and over-rule all Things for her Advantage, *Rom.* 8.28. And the Omniscient Eyes of Christ, towards his Spouse, are *Loving, Gracious* Eyes; full of Kindness, Tenderness, and Compassion. And his *Eyes* being upon her in a Way of Love, Grace and Mercy, in all her Wants, and under all her Distresses; 'tis hence his *Ears* are open to her Cry, and she finds Grace in his Sight, *Psal.* 34.15. *Gen.* 6.8. Again, The Eyes of Christ towards his Spouse, are *Chaste.* He always looks upon his *own Dove*, with a *full Eye*, of infinite, free, distinguishing Love and Favour; and never casts the least *Glance* of this his Eye, in his Bridegroom-Delights and Compassions, upon *any*, but his *own Bride.* He calls her, *Hephzibah*; his *Delight* is *in her*, Isa. 62.4. He delights in her Person, he delights in Communion with her, in *manifesting himself unto her*, as he *doth not unto the World*, John 14.19, 20, 21. He *rests in his Love* towards her, *rejoyceth* over her with *Singing*, employs his *Almightiness* to save her, and doth her *Good* with his *whole Heart*, and with his *whole Soul*, Zeph. 3.17. Jer. 32.41.

By the Rivers of Waters washed with Milk] As the Eyes of Doves are beautiful, and clean: So, 'tis observ'd of 'em, That they delight to bathe themselves in Rivers, Springs, and Fountains of *pure Water*; when they appear most clean, and beautiful. And by *Christ's* Dove-like Eyes, being said to be, *By the Rivers of Waters, washed with Milk*, we may understand His *Penetrating*, or *Diving* into those infinite *Depths*, those full, free, eternal *Rivers* of Grace, Life, and Glory that are in God's *Heart*, his *Counsels*, his *Covenant*, and *Promises* for his People; as he has made over *Himself*, in all his *Persons*, and in all his *Perfections*, to be *their* GOD. These are call'd *Wells of Salvation*, Isa. 12.3. *Therefore with Joy shall ye draw Water out of the* Wells of Salvation. *Therefore: Wherefore?* Why, Because *God* is the *God of his People*, the *God of* their Salvation, yea, *God their Salvation*, as having made over Himself, as the Great JEHOVAH, in all his Persons, and Perfections, to be their Salvation: Therefore they may draw *Water* out of these *Wells of Salvation:* These deep, inexhaustible, ever-flowing Wells, which spring up, in the Earnest of the Spirit, the begun, and advancing Life of Grace in this World; and will rise to overlook Floods of perfect Life and Glory in the World to come. And thus, the infinite Fulness of the Spirit, and Grace of God, for the Supply of the Church, is set forth by a *River*, Psalm

46.4. *There is a* River, *the Streams whereof shall make glad the City of God. And there,* says the Prophet, *will the glorious* LORD *be unto us, a Place of broad* Rivers *and* Streams, *Isa.* 33.21. *And I,* saith the Lord, *will open* Rivers *in high Places,* Chap. 41.18. These are *Rivers* of Grace, Peace, Life and Glory, *opened* for poor Sinners, by virtue of Christ's being lifted up, on the *Cross,* and lifted up, on the *throne;* in these *high Places,* are these *Rivers of Grace* open'd. And *by* these Rivers of Waters, rivers of Grace, provided for his Spouse, are the Dovelike Eyes of Christ, continually. In these he *bathes,* as it were, in every gracious *Look* he casts upon *her,* whereby he manifests, and communicates all Grace to her. And whenever, in his Providence, for her Unkindness, there appears the least *Anger* in his Eyes towards her; it endureth but for a *Moment:* They presently appear *mild,* and *gracious;* being *wash'd,* as it were, with *Milk,* or with the *milky Streams* of rich, free, super-abounding *Grace.*

And fitly set.] Eyes, that stand not too far *in* the Head, nor too far *out* of it, are *fitly set:* And *so* are *Christ's.* His Omniscience, by virtue of the personal Union of his Divine, and Human Nature, is *fitly set,* to look upon his own Dove, and for Her to converse with, and delight in. His Eyes, as Mediator, her beloved Lord, and Saviour, stand not too far *inward,* towards the Perfections of the *Godhead;* to prevent his looking with Grace and Favour upon *Her:* Nor too far *outward,* towards the *Creatures,* so as to cast the same Rays of Grace upon *others,* which he does upon Her. But they are *fitly set;* to look upon *Her,* as One in the same *Nature* with him, as One in the nearest *Relation* to him, as One that is his special *Charge,* and peculiar *Care.* His Eyes, as in Office to save her, are immeasurably fill'd with Grace, and Compassion towards her. He has an immeasurable Fulness of the *Spirit of Grace,* that Heavenly *Dove,* dwelling *in* him, and resting *upon* him; and from thence he casts the Rays of his *Grace,* in his *Dove-like* Eyes upon *Her.* And as they are *fitly set,* to compassionate her *in* all her Miseries, and to comfort her *under* all her Distresses; so likewise, to save her *out* of all her Troubles. They are not pitying Eyes, which can afford *no* Relief; but they are powerful, gracious Eyes, which bring *all* Salvation to her. Thus *Exod.* 3.7, 8. *I have surely* seen *the Affliction of my People which are in* Egypt, (or, I have *seen,* I have *seen:* to denote the Quickness of his Sight, and Strength of his Love) *and I am come* down *to deliver them.* The *Sight of her* Misery, *engageth his* Mercy, Power, and Faithfulness for her Deliverance: So *fitly,* are the Eyes of Christ *set,* to look upon his own Dove!

Ver. 13. *His Cheeks are as a Bed of Spices, as sweet Flowers: his Lips like Lilies, dropping sweet-smelling Myrrh.*

His Cheeks are as a Bed of Spices, as sweet Flowers:] The *Cheeks* in Nature, when they are full, and comely, are a special Part of the Beauty of the *Face*. And by the *Cheeks* of Christ, we may understand, those *Manifestations* he makes of *Himself* to his Spouse, either in Grace, or Providence. And in that they are compar'd to a *Garden-Bed*, which is *higher* than the other Parts of it: It denotes, the *Fulness*, or *Height* of their Glory. And as they are likened to a *Bed of Spices*; and to *sweet Flowers:* It shews, their exceeding *Beauty*, and *Fragrancy*, to delight the spiritual Senses of his Spouse. And as the Cheeks are such a Part of the Face, which may be *seen*, when the full Countenance is *not beheld:* So by the *Cheeks* of Christ, may be intended, those *lesser* Manifestations he makes of Himself to his Spouse; which, in Comparison of those that are more *full*, are but as it were, a *side Look* of his Face. As also, that *all* the Manifestations he makes of Himself to her, in this World; if compar'd with that full Vision of him, she shall have in the World to come, are no more than a Glimpse, a *side Look* of his Glory. And in that these Cheeks of Christ, are said to be a *Bed of Spices, as sweet Flowers:* it informs us, that those imperfect Discoveries of his Glory, which his Spouse is favour'd with in this World, and the least Glances thereof, are exceeding *beautiful, fragrant,* and *delightful*, to her spiritual Senses. And 'tis as if she should say, "My *Beloved*, is such a *Bundle of Sweetness*, such a *Mass of Beauty*; that if I get but the least *Glance* of his sweet, his glorious Face, my Soul is *ravish'd* with the utmost Delight! And if the least Glimpse of Him, here *below*, thus fills me with all kinds of Pleasure; What inconceivable Glories must be in his Person! and what inconceivable Joys will fill my Heart, when I shall *see him as he is!* When I shall be blest with the full, immediate, and endless Vision of his Glory *above'!* Thus the Apostle *Paul*, 1. Cor. 13.12. *Now we see thro' a* Glass darkly; *but then* Face to Face. And, says the Apostle *Peter, Whom having not* seen, *ye love, in whom, tho' now ye* see him not, *yet believing, ye rejoice with Joy unspeakable and full of Glory*, 1 Pet. 1.8. The Spouse of Christ, even now, in New Testament-Times, has not yet *seen* the full Glory of her *Beloved's Face*; tho' his *Cheeks*, a Side-Look of him here by Faith, is sufficient to fill her with *Joy unspeakable, and full of Glory*. But the full Vision of his infinite glory, to her eternal Ravishment with his Person, and full Conformity to his Image, is reserv'd for the World to come. Then she shall *see his Face*, or *see him as he is*, to her inconceivable Joy, and endless Wonder. Mean while, *His Cheeks are as a Bed of Spices! as sweet Flowers!* And,

His Lips like Lilies, dropping sweet smelling Myrrh] The *Lips*, in Nature, are the *Organs* of *Speech*, the Instruments by which Words are utter'd: and in Scripture Phrase, are frequently put for the *Speech* itself, or for the Words spoken. As *Prov.*10.21. *The* Lips (i.e., the *Words*) *of the Righteous feed many*. And so, by the *Lips* of Christ, we may understand, the *Words* of his Mouth. And as the *Lips* are put for the Words spoken; so, for the *Manner* of speaking, *Prov.* 16.21. *The Wise in Heart, shall be called prudent, and the* Sweetness *of the* Lips *increaseth Learning*. Where, by *Sweetness of the Lips*, we must understand, not only the Excellency of the *Matter* spoken, but chiefly, the *Manner* of speaking it: Or, the apt, grateful Expression of excellent Matter, whereby it's render'd sweet to the Hearer, and fit to convey Instruction. And thus, *a Word* fitly spoken, *is like Apples of Gold, in Pictures of Silver,* Prov. 25.11. And if we take the Lips of Christ, in this Sense, for his *Manner* of speaking: Then it shews, His *Fitness*, or inward *Ability* to speak *well*, or to speak excellent *Things, excellently*, seasonably, and gratefully. And in this respect, *Christ's Lips*, have a *Sweetness* in 'em, that infinitely *exceeds* all others. Put *all* the Sweetness together, that ever flow'd from the whole Creation, from the Tongue of Men, or of Angels; and compar'd with *His*, it's no more than a *Drop* to an immense *Ocean! Grace*, in its immeasurable *Fulness*, is *pour'd* into *His Lips,* Psa. 45.2. And, *the Lord* GOD, says he, *has given me the* Tongue of the Learner, *that I might know how to* speak a Word in Season *to him that is weary*, Isa. 50.4. And as he has an Ability to *speak*, and to speak *well*; so he speaks such Words of Grace, so graciously, so plentifully, so seasonably, so powerfully, and so sweetly to his Spouse; that she may well say of him, *His Lips are like Lilies, dropping sweet smelling Myrrh!* His Lips are like *Lilies*, for their Purity, Beauty, and Fragrancy. Like *dropping* Lilies, which communicate their own Sweetness: Like Lilies dropping *Myrrh, sweet smelling Myrrh*; which is most odoriferous in itself, and refreshing to the Senses. The Droppings of Christ's Lips, the Words of his Mouth, even all of 'em, have an infinite Sweetness, an Almighty Efficacy in *themselves*; and they are unspeakably quickning, and delightful to his *Spouse*. They are Life-giving Words: Yea, *The Words of eternal Life*; by which eternal Life, is both granted, and communicated to her, *John* 6.68. And therefore, they must needs be exceeding precious, and refreshing to her; as she here says, *His Lips are like Lilies, dropping sweet smelling Myrrh.*

Ver. 14. *His Hands are as Gold-Rings set with the Beryl: his Belly is as bright Ivory overlaid with Sapphires.*

His Hands are as Gold-Rings set with the Beryl:] *Hands*, are the *Instruments* of *Action*. And are sometimes put for the *Ability* of Working: As *Ps.* 115.4. *Their* Idols *are Silver and Gold, the Work of Men's* Hands. And also, for the *Skill* of working, *Isaiah* 45.9. *Shall the* Clay *say to him that fashioneth it, What* maketh thou? *or thy* Work, *He hath* no Hands? That is, no Skill, or Artifice in working. And *Hands* are likewise put, for the *Works* themselves perform'd by 'em: As *Prov.* 12.14. *The Recompense of a Man's* Hands *shall be rendred unto him:* i.e., of the *Works* of his Hands. And all these, are to be understood, by the *Hands of Christ*: vis. His *Ability* of working, His *Skill*, or *Artifice* in working, and the *Works* themselves, which he performs. As for his *Ability* of working; He has *all Power* radically in Himself, as *God:* or rather, *is* all Power, the *Lord Almighty*, Rev. 1.8. And as *Mediator, all Power* in Heaven and in Earth, is given to him of his Father, *Mat.* 28.18. As for his *Skill* in working; He is *Wisdom* itself, *Prov.* 8.12. *I* Wisdom *dwell with Prudence, and find out Knowledge of witty Inventions.* And, *Mat.* 11.19. Wisdom *is justify'd of her Children*; i.e., *Christ* is justify'd of his People; tho' despis'd, and reproach'd of his Enemies. And as for his *Works* perform'd; they are of equal *Extent* with God the Father's, *John* 5.17. *My* Father worketh *hitherto, and* I work. As he is One in *Essence* with God the Father, and with God the Holy Ghost; so he is One in *working:* In all the Works, both of Nature, Grace, and Glory. And further, As these Hands of Christ, his able, skilful Works, are commended by the Spouse, as the Hands of her *Bridegroom*, her *Beloved*; so it may peculiarly refer to the Works, which he performs for her, and towards her, as *such*. And as she compares these his Hands, to *Gold-Rings:* It denotes, their Beauty, Purity, Preciousness, and enriching Nature. The Hands of others, are *adorn'd* with Gold-Rings: But Christ's Hands, have such a *native* Beauty, Purity, Preciousness, Richness and Glory in them; that nothing without *themselves*, can *add* any Lustre to them. *Gold*, is one of the greatest Excellencies in Nature: But what's all the purest, brightest Gold in the Universe, the most artfully wrought; if compar'd with the *Hands*, the *Works of Christ*, in which the *Glory* of the *Godhead* shines! The

Spouse says, they are *as* Gold-Rings, to note their *native* Excellency; but not to restrain their *super-excellent* Glory. And as these Hands of Christ, are infinitely precious and excellent in themselves; so they're infinitely rich and beautiful in the Eye of his Spouse; as the Rays of infinite Glory, resplendently shine herein. Oh, what a ravishing transporting Sight, are these Hands of Christ, to his Spouse, while she views what he hath done, doth do, and will yet do for her as Her Bridegroom! Again, As the Hands of Christ are compar'd to Gold-Rings, for the Excellency of their *Matter:* So, as I conceive, it may likewise respect their *Form.* Gold is excellent, and Rings of Gold, are *round*, and enclose the Fingers on which they're put: And so the precious *Hands of Christ*, gloriously *enclose* his *People. As the Mountains are* round about *Jerusalem*, so the LORD is round about his People, *from henceforth even for ever,* Ps. 125.2. And a *Ring* was to be put on the Prodigal's *Hand*, upon his Return to his Father's House, *Luke* 15.22. to shew that God's *eternal Love*, is put upon the Soul, to the *View*, And upon the *Hand* of its *Faith*, when it's enabled to turn from Sin and Satan, unto God, as to its own Father in Christ. And this Love is compar'd to a *Ring*; because of its endless *Round:* As it encircles the Chosen of God, from Eternity, before Time began, thro' Time, and to Eternity, on Time's backside, in one unbroken, everlasting *Round.* And as this Ring respects the Love of *God*, in all his *Persons*; so particularly, the Love of *Christ*, the Church's *Bridegroom*. And this Love of His, as manifested in his *Works.* And with these *Hands of Love*, as with *Gold Rings*, doth he gloriously *enclose her:* By which her Time Safety, and her eternal Salvation is secur'd, *John* 10.28. *I give unto them* eternal Life, *and they shall never perish, neither shall any pluck them out of* my Hand. And as the Hands of Christ are compar'd to Gold Rings, *set with the Beryl:* It may note, either, 1. The *Variety* of their Glory and Preciousness, and the *Curiousness* of their Art. Or, 2. that the Spouse of Christ stands *herein*, and has a *Fixation* in his *Hands.* The *Beryl*, is a *precious Stone:* One of those set in *Aaron's* Breastplate, on which the Names of the Twelve Tribes were engraven: Which, in the Mystery and Glory of it, was to shew, that the Chosen of God in all their Individuals, stand as so many *Jewels* upon the Heart of Christ, and as such, are borne by Him continually, for a Memorial before the Father. And as they stand on his *Heart*; so on his *Hands. Set me*, says the Spouse, as a *Seal* upon *thine Arm*, Song. 8.6. She wanted to be set there evidentially, as he had done it really. Thus, *Isaiah* 49.16. *Behold*, says he, I have *graven thee* upon the *Palms of my Hands, Zion*, the Church, that thought her Lord had forgotten her; receives this Answer from her glorious Bridegroom, I have *graven thee* upon the *Palms of my Hands.* And he here tells her, He had graven her upon the Palms of his Hands, to comfort her under all her Fears, least he had *forgotten* her, or should *forget* her in his Works. And 'tis as if he should say, "How can *that* be, my *Love?* How can I *forget thee*, when thou art so deeply *interested* in mine *Heart*, and *engraven* on my *Hands?* Take an Instance in that which is most familiar to thee: Consider the Bowels of a tender *Mother* towards her *sucking Child.* What think'st *thou?* Can she *forget it?* Such a Monster in Nature, is *rarely* found: But it's *possible*, that Creature-Love, wound up to the greatest Height of Tenderness, may fail; she *may* forget. But *my Love* to *thee* is infinite, my Compassions *fail not*; and therefore tho' Creatures may forget, and Nature turn Topsy-Turvy: *Yet will not I forget thee,* Ver. 15. And if the Compassions of a tender Mother, towards her sucking Babe, should not *fail*; yet she mayn't be always *present* with it, and have it *before* her, to see its Wants, or hear its Cries; and so she *may* forget it, in *some* Moments of its Need. But I am *ever* present with *thee*, and thou art *always before me*; I wear thee upon my Hands. For, Behold, I have *graven thee* upon the *Palms of my Hands.* So that I never stretch forth my Hands, to do any of my Great *Works*, but I therein see thy *Name*, regard thy *Good*, and interest *thee*, in all the *Productions* they bring forth." Thus the *Spouse* of Christ, stands as a bright *Jewel,* with her *Name engraven* on his *Hands*; in all his *Works*, which are *Honourable, and Glorious:* Or, his *Hands*, which are as *Gold Rings*, are thus *set with the Beryl*!

His Belly is as bright Ivory, overlaid with Sapphires] *Belly*, in Scripture, is sometimes put for the *Heart*; As, Joh. 7.38. *Out of his* Belly *shall flow Rivers of living Water.* And that *Belly*, is here put for the Heart; is evident, from what follows, Ver. 39. *This spake he of the* Spirit, *which they that Believe on Him should receive.* And 'tis in the *Heart* of a Believer, that the *Spirit* of Christ dwells. And His constant abiding there, as a Fountain of Grace, is the Cause of all those gracious Flows, which proceed out of a Believer's Mouth. 'Tis out of this *Abundance* of his *Heart*, that his *Mouth* speaketh. And thus *Job* 32.19, 20. *My* Belly *is as Wine that hath no Vent, it's ready to burst like new Bottles. I will* speak, *that I may be refreshed.* *Belly*, here likewise, is put for the *Heart*, the Fulness of Matter therein, and the inward Workings thereof: And therefore *Elihu*, resolves to vent it by the *Mouth*, to *speak*, that he may be eased. And thus, the *Belly* of Christ, is to be taken for his *Heart*. The Heart is the Seat of Love and Tenderness. And strong Love in the Heart, working towards a beloved Object, under Misery, produceth Mercy, and Compassion; which is called *Bowels*, the *Sounding* of the Bowels, or the *Heart's making a Noise*. As *Jer*. 4.9. *My* Bowels, *my* Bowels, *I am pained at my very* Heart, *my* Heart *maketh a Noise in me*. And thus, by the *Belly* of Christ, we are to understand, His *Love, Mercy,* and *Bowels of Compassion* towards his Spouse, in all her Wants, and Miseries. And as in the former Part of the Verse, she had spoken of his *Hands*, i.e., his *Works:* So, in this, she speaks of his *Heart*, the *Fountain* whence they flow, the *Cause* of those *Effects*. And the Love, Mercy, and Tenderness of his Heart, she commends; by comparing it unto *Ivory, bright* Ivory; for its *Purity*, and *Beauty*. The Love, Mercy, and Bowels of Christ, being without the least *Spot* of Impurity; and of *transcendent* Beauty. And they must needs be so; since, as *Man,* he's *spotless*, as *God*, infinitely *pure*, and as *God-Man, incomparably* Beautiful, and *Immensely* Glorious. And as is his *Person*, so is his *Love*. The Bowels of Christ, are truly *Human*, and yet truly *Divine*. For as the Divine, and Human Natures, are closely *join'd* in his Great Person: So the *One* Love of Christ, the Church's Bridegroom, hath *all* Perfections in it, both created and uncreated; and shines forth with an *infinite* Beauty, an *incomprehensible* Glory! And this glorious Heart of Christ, his Spouse *has*. She describes him as her *Own*; and all his Excellencies, as deeply *interested* in them. And therefore *His Belly*, which is as *bright Ivory*, must needs be a most glorious Sight to *Her:* While she views his *Inwards*, the Greatness of his Love, he Depth of his Mercy, the Strength of his Compassions, working towards her, under all her Sins, Miseries and Distresses; and infinitely sufficient for her compleat Deliverance! Especially, since his Belly, which is as bright Ivory, is *overlaid with Sapphires!* The *Sapphire* is a *Precious Stone*, of a *blue* Colour, shining with *golden* Sparkles. Thus, *Exod*. 24.10. *And they saw the God of* Israel: *and there was under his Feet as it were the paved Work of a* Sapphire-Stone, *and as it were the Body of* Heaven *in its* Clearness: That is, *Blue* and *Shining*. And as *Blue*, is a Colour in Nature, which is least subject to *Change:* So the bright Belly of Christ, being overlaid with *Sapphires*, may denote in general, his *Unchangeableness:* Or, That his Love is *Unchangeable*; his Mercy *Everlasting*; and his Compassions *Never-failing*. And in Particular, The *Unchangeableness* of all his *Grace*, as *overlaid* with His *Covenant-Engagements*, and *faithful Promises*. The Love, Mercy, and Bowels of Christ, are unchangeable in their own *Nature*; and further are, and appear so to his Spouse, as thus *overlaid*, Heb. 6.17, 18. *Wherein God willing more abundantly to shew unto the Heirs of Promise, the* Immutability *of his* Counsel, *confirmed it by an* Oath. *That by* two immutable Things, *in which it was impossible for God to lie, we might have a strong Consolation, who have fled for Refuge to lay hold on the Hope set before us.* The Spouse of Christ, has a strong Consolation, in her fleeing for Refuge to lay hold on Him, and all his Grace, the Hope set before her, as the infinite *Love of his Heart*, is overlaid with his *Word and Oath:* Wherein, it is *impossible* for *Him,* who is *God,* to *lie.* He had *betroth'd* her to Himself in *Righteousness, in Judgment, in Loving-Kindness, and in Mercies: Yea, and in* Faithfulness too; and she *shall know the* LORD, *Hos.* 2.19, 20. The highest Communion-Love, is secur'd in Union Love, thus *engag'd,* or thus *overlaid,* Is. 54.8, 9, 10. *With* everlasting Kindness *will I have Mercy on thee, saith the* LORD *thy Redeemer. For this is as the Waters of* Noah *unto Me: For as I have* sworn *that the Waters of* Noah *should no more go over the Earth; so have I* sworn *that I would not be wroth with thee, nor rebuke thee.* And oh, what a lovely, joyful, transporting Sight is it to the Spouse of Christ, to see all the Love of her Bridegroom's Heart, *overlaid* with all his Covenant Engagements for her, and faithful Promises to her; as so many rich, unchangeable, sparkling *Gems!* Whereby, she has his glorious Heart *now,* and is secur'd of it *unchangeably,* and for *ever!* Since his *Belly,* as *bright Ivory,* is thus *overlaid with Sapphires!*

Ver. 15. *His Legs are as Pillars of Marble, set upon Sockets of fine Gold: his Countenance is as Lebanon, excellent as the Cedars.*

His Legs are as Pillars of Marble, set upon Sockets of fine Gold:] *Legs,* in the Body natural, are the *Support* thereof. And *Pillars,* the *Legs* of a Building, *sustain* the Structure, and *bear* its Weight. To which, the Allusion seems to be here. And so, by the *Legs* of Christ, we are to understand, His infinite Ability to *sustain* the Church; and that fit, full, actual *Support,* which He affords to it, both in Nature, Grace, and Glory; as the whole Fabrick thereof is *built* upon him, and the whole Weight of it *borne* by him. And these mighty *Legs* of His, by which he supports the Church, in Providence, in Grace, and in Glory, are compar'd unto *Pillars of Marble:* For their *Costliness, Art, Beauty, and Durableness.* That Support, Christ affords to his Church, tho' it be to Her, all of the freest *Grace,* yet it cost the Father, and Him *dear*; even no less than the immense *Riches,* the infinite *Treasures* of the *Godhead,* laid out in the meritorious *Death of Jesus:* That so he might *rise again*, to *sustain* his Church, in all that Life and Glory design'd for her. In which, as he fitly and firmly *bears her Weight;* the Project, and Product of infinite Wisdom *shines:* And the *Support* afforded, with an infinite Variety of *Beauties* and *Glories*. Which, for *Duration*, lasts thro' all *Time*, and unto all *Eternity*. 'Tis *Christ*, which *builds the Temple of the* LORD, and *He* that *bears the Glory,* Zech. 6.13. He *builds* his *Church* upon *Himself*, the *Rock of Ages*; and bears her up in Glory, without the least *Shake*, notwithstanding all the Cunning, and violent Assaults of the *Gates of Hell*, in its Power, and Policy against it, *Mat.* 16.18. The whole Glory of the Church, as it flows from him, so it's borne by him, and shall everlastingly be given to him. Again, his *Legs*, are not only commended, as *Pillars of Marble*, but also, as set upon *Sockets of fine Gold*: That is, upon the pure, glorious, unalterable *Decrees* of Heaven. These are the *Basis*, upon which all the Support Christ affords to his Church, is *founded:* Upon these it stands *firm*, to all the Ends of the Father's Grace, in her complete Salvation. Thus, *John* 5.19. *The* Son *can do nothing of* Himself, *but what he seeth the* Father *do: For what Things soever* He *doth, these also doth the* Son *likewise*. All the mediatory Works of *Christ*, and so this, of his *bearing* the Church, and *sustaining* all her Glory; and *founded* upon what the *Father* did, in his absolute *Settlements*, and unalterable *Decrees* concerning them. And so his mighty *Legs*, stand *firm*, and *immoveable*, upon these *Sockets of fine Gold,* to which they're fitted, with the utmost Exactness. Oh, the *Glory* of Christ's mighty Legs! What Support can they not, and will they not, afford to his Church, both here and hereafter, since he can *uphold all Things*, with a *Word!* Heb. 1.3. And this *Word of his Power*, stands immoveably fixt upon the absolute *Will of his Father*; which he came down from Heaven on purpose to fulfil! *John* 6.38. Oh, how infinitely *able* are the mighty Legs of Christ, to *bear* the greatest Weights! to bear up his Church, under all her Burdens, from sinking into Death; yea, to bear her up to perfect Life, and endless Glory; as these *Legs* of His, stand firmly *fixt* upon the unalterable *Decrees* of Heaven! Well might the Spouse, in the Views of her eternal Security hereby, from endless Death to endless Life, admire the Glory of her *Beloved*, as having *Legs* like *Pillars of Marble*, thus *set upon Sockets of fine Gold*.

   His Countenance is as Lebanon, *excellent as the Cedars*.] The *Countenance*, in Scripture, is put for the whole *Personage*, or, a full View of the *Person*, in all his Parts. As, 2 *Sam.* 23.21. *And he slew an* Egyptian, a goodly Man. A Man of *Countenance*: As the Word is. Who is call'd *a*

Man of Stature, 1 Chron.11.23. Which shews, that his *Countenance*, is put, for the comely *Appearance* of his whole Person. And if taken in this Sense, then by the *Countenance* of Christ, we must understand, The complete Glory of his *Person*, in the beautiful Symmetry, or comely Proportion of all his *Parts*. The Spouse had been describing her *Beloved*, from *Head* to *Foot*; and how takes a View of him in his *entire Glory*, as her perfect *Head*, her complete *Saviour*; and says of Him, as such, *His Countenance is as* Lebanon, *excellent as the Cedars!* Again, *Countenance*, in Scripture, is put for the *Face*, or, a View of the whole *Face*. As, 2 *Cor*. 3.7. *The Children of* Israel *could not stedfastly behold the* Face *of Moses, for the Glory of his* Countenance. It's evident, that *Countenance* is here put for the *Face*; and the Glory of *Moses's Countenance*, for the Brightness that was upon his *Face*, when he had been in the Mount with God. Which was so resplendent, that the Children of *Israel* could not *look* upon his Face, but were *afraid* to come nigh him. As, *Exod*. 34.29, 30. And as the Word is frequently us'd in this Sense; So by the *Countenance* of Christ, we may understand, The whole Glory of his entire *Face*; or, those *full Manifestations of Himself*, which he makes to his Spouse, when she has the most *comprehensive Views* of his Glory. She had describ'd the Glory of his *Cheeks*, (those *lesser* Manifestations of Himself, when she had but as it were, a *side Look* of his Face) by comparing them to a *Bed of Spices*, and to *sweet Flowers*: as having a *Height*, and *Fulness* of Glory and Fragrancy, proportionable to *Themselves*, Ver. 13. And here, she describes the Glory of his *Face*, (or, the most *full* Manifestation of Himself, that He ever makes, and she is favour'd with) and says of it, *His Countenance is as* Lebanon, *excellent as the Cedars!* Thus the most bright *extraordinary* Displays of divine Glory, the Lord made to his People of Old, were call'd *seeing of his Face*; when compar'd with those they *commonly* enjoy'd; which were but as it were, a *side Look* of his Brightness. As, Numb. 12.6, 7, 8. *If there be a Prophet among you, I the* LORD, *will make my self known to Him in a Vision, and will speak unto Him in a Dream. My Servant* Moses *is not so*—(*i.e.*, Not an *ordinary* Prophet, and *ordinarily* favour'd: But) With Him *I will speak Mouth to Mouth, even apparently, and the* Similitude *of the* LORD *shall* He behold. And, *Exod*. 33.11. it is said, *The* LORD *spake unto* Moses Face to Face, *as a Man speaketh unto a Friend*. And yet the *brightest* Discoveries of the Glory of the Lord, that the Old Testament Saints *had*; when compar'd with those *transcendent* Displays, which New Testament Saints *are favour'd with*; were but a *side Look* of him, a *vailed* Discovery of his Glory.

But we all with open Face *beholding as in a Glass, the Glory of the Lord, are changed into the same Image, from Glory to Glory, even as by the Spirit of the Lord,* 2 Cor. 3.18. 'tis a full, open-fac'd *View* of the Glory of Christ, which his Spouse has now under the *Gospel*; when compar'd with that she had under the *legal* Dispensation. And yet, the brightest Discoveries she has ever yet had, or *can* have in this World, are still but a *side Look* of him; when compar'd with that *transcendent* Display of his Glory, which she *shall* have in the World to come. Christ has such a *Countenance*, such a *Face*, that will take up *Eternity it self*, to *behold the immense Glories of it*! But even now, his Spouse at Times, sees so much of the Glory of his Face, or has such an open-fac'd View of him, suitable to the *present State*; that strikes her with equal Transports of Wonder, Love and Joy; and enables her to say of him to others, as the Spouse here, to the Daughters of *Jerusalem: His Countenance is as* Lebanon, *excellent as the Cedars! Lebanon*, was a most fruitful, beautiful, fragrant Mountain in the Land of *Canaan*, Deut. 3.15. Judg. 3.3. And therefore, the Glory, Fruitfulness, and Fragrancy promis'd to the *Church*, is set forth by it. As, *Is.* 35.2. It (i.e., the Church, who by Reason of Sin, had been as a Wilderness) *shall* blossom *abundantly*, and *rejoice even with Joy and Singing: the* Glory of Lebanon *shall be given unto it.* And Hos. 14.5, 6. *I will be as the Dew unto* Israel*: he shall grow as the City, and cast forth his Roots as* Lebanon. *His Branches shall spread, and his Beauty shall be as the Olive-tree, and his Smell as* Lebanon. And as this was a most excellent *Mount:* So the most excellent Things are compar'd to it, or set forth by it. As, The *Glory of the Church*: And, here, The *Glory of Christ*: *His Countenance is as* Lebanon. As *Lebanon* was a most stately, beautiful Mount to the Eye, abounding with refreshing Sweetness: So, and much more, is the *Countenance* of Christ, a most glorious, beautiful Prospect to the Eye of his Spouse, which affords her all Manner of Delights: So that while she beholds him, she lives amidst Glory and Sweetness, to their utmost Heights! His Countenance is said to be, as Lebanon; because *that* was one of the greatest Beauties, and Excellencies in *Nature*. But what are all the Glories and Perfections of Nature put *together*, what low, inconsiderable *Things*, yea, what empty *Nothings*; when compar'd with *His*, who is the GOD of Nature, Grace, and Glory! How is *Lebanon* itself, *Out-shone*, by the ravishing Beauties, the infinite Glories of *Christ's Countenance!* So that, whatever Soul would know what *Christ is*, in his own Glory and Sweetness; must have intimate Acquaintance with *Himself.* There being nothing short of *Communion with Christ*, that can acquaint a Soul, with what He *is*; or with the inexpressible Glories, and Sweetnesses which are in *Him*, and enjoy'd by that *Soul*, that has Fellowship with him. Because, tho' all the Excellencies in *Nature*, are summon'd together, to set forth *Christ's*; yet they fall far short of describing them as they *are*. And needs they *must,* since *finite*, and *limited Beauties*, can never fully set forth his *infinite*, and *immense Glories*, in their native Height, and proper Altitude! So that those who would know what the Glory, and Sweetness of Christ's Countenance *is*; must *come and see!* And they'll soon say, from their own Experience, *It is as* Lebanon! They'll compare it to the greatest Excellencies in *Nature*; and find in it, such transcendent *Glories*, which can never be exprest by *Words!* And as the Spouse describes her Beloved's Countenance, by the Glory of *Lebanon*; So she adds, *Excellent as the Cedars!* The *Cedars*, were beautiful, ever green Trees, incorruptible in their Nature, and excellent in their Stature. And the most choice of 'em grew, in Abundance, in Mount *Lebanon*, *1 Kings* 5.6. Which for their Excellency, are call'd, The *Trees of the* LORD, *Ps*. 104.16. *The* Trees of the LORD *are full of Sap: the Cedars of* Lebanon, *which* He *hath planted*. And Mount *Lebanon*, as thus richly, and plenteously adorn'd with *Cedars*, for its Beauty and Glory, was call'd, The *Garden of God*, Ezek. 31.8. And the tall *Cedars* thereof, with their full, and beautiful Branches, had a Majestick *Glory* in them. On which Account, the Majesty of *Kings,* was resembled by them. As, *Ezek*. 17.3, 12. And the Majestick *Glory* of the Church, in her abundant Fruitfulness; is set forth by the *shaking of Lebanon*, i.e., by the Majestick shaking of the Trees that grew thereon, *Ps*. 72.16. *There shall be an handful of Corn in the Earth upon the top of the Mountains; the Fruit thereof shall* shake *like* Lebanon. And as the *Countenance of Christ,* is said to be *excellent as the Cedars:* It denotes, The Height, Fulness, Beauty, Majesty, Unchangeableness and Eternity of *his Glory*. Was Mount *Lebanon*, in the Glory of its choice *Cedars*, a most stately, beautiful *Sight?* Much more *si*, is the *Countenance of Christ*, in whom the *Fulness of the Godhead dwells Bodily!* His Countenance, is *Excellent* as the Cedars of *Lebanon,* in Nature; as the Cedars of *Lebanon*, or the Church, in Grace; and as the Cedars of *Lebanon*, or the Church, in Glory! And infinitely *over-tops* them all! All *their Glory* is deriv'd from him, meets in him, and shines in *his Countenance,* with the brightest Refulgency: Yea, is infinitely *out-shone*, by his *immense* and *all surpassing Glory!* And therefore the Spouse might well say, (and say the utmost she could, by way of Comparison) *His*

Countenance is as Lebanon, *excellent as the Cedars!* And, Oh, *Happy They*, who are *blest* with a *Prospect* thereof!

Ver. 16. *His Mouth is most sweet: Yea, he is altogether lovely. This is my Beloved, and this is my Friend, O ye Daughters of* Jerusalem.

His Mouth is most sweet:] The Spouse had compar'd her Beloved's *Lips*, unto *Lillies, dropping sweet-smelling Myrrh*, Ver. 13. by which the precious *Words* of his Mouth are intended. And here she commends his *Mouth*; not by comparing it to this or that particular *Sweet*; or *Degree* of Sweetness, but by calling it *most sweet*, or, *Sweetnesses*, as the Word is. She says, It is *Sweetness*, in the Abstract. *Sweetnesses* in the Plural: Because Sweetness, in its *Perfection,* Sweetness, in all its *Kinds*, is *summed up therein*, as in its proper Element, and Height of Glory. And by the *Mouth* of Christ, here, as it stands distinguish'd from his *Lips*, Ver. 13. I understand, the *Kisses* of his Mouth; or the most sweet, and sensible *Manifestations* of his Love, in the powerful *Application* of the Declarations, and Promises of his Grace. His *Lips* drop those precious *Words*, which are the Matter of his Spouse's Consolation; and his *Mouth* applies it to Her in particular, and seals it as it were with a sweet, and powerful *Kiss:* While he brings home the precious Promises to her Heart, with the greatest *Sweetness*, the most glorious *Power*, and the highest *Evidence* of *her* Interest, in all *his* Grace. And for these *Kisses* of Christ's *Mouth*, the Spouse earnestly long'd, Ch. 1.2. *Let him* kiss *me with the* Kisses *of his* Mouth: *For thy* Love *is better than* Wine. *Kisses*, especially in the Conjugal Relation, are Expressions and Tokens of mutual *Love*. And so the *Kisses* of Christ's Mouth, respect those special *Manifestations of his Love*, which his *own Spouse,* and none but *she*, is favour'd with. And therefore, when she prays for these sweet Kisses, she gives this as a Reason: For *thy* Love *is better than Wine*. That is, thy *Love*, manifested in the *Kisses of thy Mouth*, is better to me, than the most exhilarating *Wine*, to the drooping Spirits. And of this *Mouth* of Christ, the Spouse says, It is *sweet, most sweet!* or *Sweetness, Sweetnesses!* Oh, None know the *Sweetness* of Christ's Mouth, but his own Spouse, who enjoys it! Others *hear* of Christ's Sweetness: and that's *all*. For they *know* nothing of it experimentally. They neither *see* his Glory, nor *enjoy* him as their *Own*. Nor are they ever favour'd with *one Kiss* of his *sweet Mouth.* No; Christ manifests his Love to *none* by the sweet Kisses of his *Mouth*; but to those who are entirely and eternally interested in the infinite Love of his *Heart*. And *these*, when *thus* favour'd, find his *Mouth* to be *most sweet* indeed! All in Christ is *sweet,* yea, *Sweetness* itself. And his Spouse knows it to be *so*; which makes him the *Chiefest of Ten Thousand* in Her Eye, even when she ha'n't immediate *Communion* with him. But when she lives at his *Mouth*, and finds all the Sweetnesses in *Christ*, to be her *own*, for her present Enjoyment, and endless Solace; while the Sweetness of his *Heart*, vents itself upon her by the Sweetness of his *Mouth*, to the utmost Delight of her spiritual Sense: Then she lives in *Sweetness*, in *Sweetnesses* inexpressible! Oh what is it, to have one of the *Kisses* of Christ's *Mouth!* To have one Moment's *Communion* with him in his boundless *Love*, his infinite *Sweetness*, shed abroad in the *Heart*, by the *Holy Ghost*, thro' the *Word of Promise:* Witnessing to the Soul, its particular *Interest* therein, and *sealing it up* to the Day of *Redemption!* 'Tis a *Joy*, that hath never *entred into the Heart* of the *natural Man*, to conceive of ! that *Strangers intermeddle not with!* And if the Mouth of Christ be so *sweet*, here in *Grace*, what will it be in *Glory!* If now and then a Moment's Communion with him, be so *sweet* to his Spouse here *below:* How will she be immers'd in *Sweetness*, and overwhelm'd with *Pleasures*, when the full *Tides* of his *Love*, shall eternally flow out upon her, to that *Fullness of Joy*, those *Rivers of Pleasures,* which are at his *Right Hand for evermore!* Mean while, she finds so much *Sweetness* in his *Mouth*, at Times, that enables her to say, from blessed Experience, as here, *His Mouth is most sweet!* To which she adds,

Yea, He is altogether lovely] The Spouse had been describing the Glories of her *Beloved*, in his particular *Parts*, by resembling them to the *chiefest* Beauties, the *greatest* Excellencies in *Nature*; and likewise summed up the *Whole,* general Glory of his *Person*, and Majestick *Appearance*; and said of this his *Countenance*, it is as *Lebanon*, excellent as the *Cedars!* And now, in this Verse, both in this, and the former Clause, she gives over describing her *Beloved* by *Creature-Beauties* and *Excellencies*; they being *all* much too low, to set *Him* forth, in his own *native* Worth, and *transcendent* Glory; and betakes herself to the infinite *Glories* of her Beloved's *Person,* to tell what HE is: *His Mouth is most sweet: Yea, He is altogether lovely!* q.d. If ye would know what my *Beloved* is; you must take up his Excellencies, in their *own* Light. In the former Clause, *His Mouth is most sweet*, She declares the Nature, and Glory of intimate *Communion* with him in *Love*; and says of it, It is *Sweetnesses*, the Element of Sweetness, of *Sweetnesses!* And in this, She declares the Glory of his *Person*, in the comprehensive *Fulness*, of its incomprehensible *Greatness:* Yea, HE is *altogether lovely!* or, *all Desires!* as the Word is. And this being brought in with a *yea*; intimates a Kind of *Dissatisfaction*, which she found in the *Description* she had given of him; as being much too *low*, to set forth *His* Unsearchable Glory. Concerning which, his Spouse did, doth, and ever will find herself under a Necessity, when she has said all she can, still to add a *yea!* to it. And it likewise sets forth, that vast *Esteem* she had of *Him*, and of his infinite *Excellencies*. So that *His Glory*, being the most delightful Theme she cou'd dwell on; she begins *again* with it, when she had done as it were, with a *yea!* HE is *altogether lovely!* And 'tis as if she should say, "I have told you what my *Beloved* is, both in Particular, and in General; and have set forth His Excellencies, by a Choice Variety of the Chief of Nature's Beauties: But don't think I have describ'd him *fully*, have said *All* that can be said of him, or have told you what he is in *Himself*. No; There's such an infinite Variety of Beauties in *Him*, such an Immensity, and Eternity of all Glories; that it would be endless for *me*, either to enumerate, or describe them! And therefore, I cast all the Particulars I have mention'd into one Sum Total; and say of *Him, yea*, HE *is altogether lovely!*" She began her Discourse, with a General Description of his Glory, Ver. 10. *My Beloved is White and Ruddy, the Chiefest among Ten Thousand!* And so she here closes it, with a *yea*, HE *is altogether lovely!* Which shews, That as He is the *Sum* of all Blessedness in *Himself:* So the *Center* of *Her Soul*, the Sum of *Her Delights*, yea, of *all Delights!* As She here expressly says, *He is all Desires!* That is, all Things that are truly *desirable*, meet in *Him*, universally, unchangeably, essentially, and eternally! And 'tis as if she should say, "Stretch your Thoughts to the utmost Extent of all that's *desirable,* in Persons or Things, in all Worlds, in all Times, and unto all Eternity: And this. *My Beloved is!* He *is all Desire!* He *is* them all, substantially, and essentially! He is *all* of them, universally, unchangeably, and eternally! Yea, let all, even the most enlarged Saints on *Earth*, and the more capacious Saints in *Heaven*, with all the Hosts of *Angels*, in their bright *Understandings*; stretch their Thoughts to the utmost Extent, of all they can possibly *desire*, both particularly, and universally, for present, and future, even to an endless Eternity: And this, *my Beloved is!* He *is all Desires! All Beauties*, in their vast variety, perpetually *meet*, and radiantly *shine*, in all their bright *Lustre*, in the one, unchangeable, and eternal *Glory* of *His Great Person!*" And as He is All Desires, *Relatively,* with respect to the *Creatures*, as all, that all the most excellent of them can possibly desire, in all States, at all Times, and unto all Eternity, to fill 'em with all Pleasures; Meets in His One, All-comprehending, and Eternal Glory: So he is, All Desires, *Absolutely:* That is, *All* that can be *desired*, either by *God*, Angels, or Men, meets in *Him!* Such are the infinite *Perfections* of his *Glorious Person*, that he is GOD's *Delight! My Soul*, says he, *Delighteth in him,* Isa. 42.1. The *Soul* of *God the Father*, if I may so say, finds all its *Desires*, complacently *fill'd*, to an Infinity, and Eternity of *Delight*; with the immense, unchangeable, and endless *Glories* of his *own Son!* And therefore the Spouse might well *glory* in this *her Beloved*; since he is such a *Great Person*, of such boundless, and immense Glories; that he is the *Beloved*, ever, of GOD *Himself! HE is ALL Desire!* What could she say more? Had she employ'd her Tongue to an eternal Space, as she will do, in commending, and adoring his Excellencies; might not all be summ'd up in this one Word, HE is *all Desire!* And as she thus winds up her *Discourse*, and *herself* thereby, into the *infinite Glory* of her *Beloved's Person*; so it shews, that the longer Souls are acquainted with *Christ;* the greater *Esteem* they have of Him. the Excellencies of a *Creature*, yea, of *all* of 'em put together, may be soon *founded*; and those who were once their *Admirers*, may quickly want *Matter*, either to *maintain*, or *increase* their Admiration. But the *Glories of Christ*, are a *bottomless Ocean*, that can never be *fathom'd;* a *boundless Sea*, that can never be *sail'd over*; an *infinite Height*, that can never be *reach'd*; and an *Eternal Length*, that can never be *ended!* And as, in their full Variety, and entire Beauty, they'll always abide the *same*, in His unchangeable *Person:* So they'll always appear *new* to his *Spouse*, and admit of new *Displays* to all *finite Minds*; by reason of their *Immensity*, in His *infinite Person!* Whereby he'll *satiate* all his Saints, and Angels with the *Vision of his Face*, to an *endless Eternity!* And so transport 'em with *new Delights*, under the *new*, and *increasing Displays* of his infinite Glory; as to attract them in their different *Spheres*, and according to their distinct *Relations*, unto *Himself for ever*; and make it thereby, impossible for them to *lose their Bliss*, by casting an *Eye* from off HIM, or so much as a single *Thought* from off his *immense Glories*; to an *eternal Space!* And the nearer the Saints come to *Perfection*, the deeper they dive into, and the more intensely they delight in the *personal Glories* of *Christ*. Thus *Eph.* 4.13. *Till we all come in the Unity of the Faith, and of the* Knowledge *of the* Son of God, *unto a* Perfect Man, *unto the Measure of the Stature of the Fulness of Christ.* The Happiness of Christ's *Spouse*, in the Height of perfect Glory; will consist in the *Knowledge* of her *Beloved*, in his *Personal Excellencies*, as the *Son of God*, or in a perfect *Discerning* of him, and eternal *Communion* with him, in all his *Immense Glories*, as the *Son of God!* When to endless Ages, to his eternal Honour, and to her eternal Joy in him, and Endearment to him, she'll say of him, as here, HE *is altogether lovely!* or, *all Desires!* To which she gladly subjoins,

This is my Beloved, and this is my Friend, O Daughters of Jerusalem!] Here she exults, and glories in *Her Beloved: This! This is* HE! And as she had begun with Interest in his Person and Glory: *My Beloved,* &c. so she ends: *This is my Beloved.* And 'tis as if she should say, "I ha'n't been describing the Glory of some excellent Person, that I have no Relation *to*, nor Interest *in:* But of One, that is entirely, and eternally *Mine! This is my Beloved!* One that I have the nearest Union *to*, and Communion *with*; One that is infinitely *lovely* in *Himself*, that infinitely *loves Me*, and that *I* entirely *love*, with the utmost Intention, the highest Affection of my *Soul!*" And as this excellent Person, is my *Beloved*; so likewise, *this is my Friend?* As if she should say, "By my Sin, Unkindness, and Ingratitude, I have justly provok'd my *Beloved* to withdraw from me for a Moment, which fills my Soul with Pain. But as he is *my Friend*, he'll return to me again. He'll put up, and pardon all my Provocations. For, *Who is a God like* him, *that pardoneth Iniquity, that passeth by the Transgression of the Remnant of his Heritage, because he delighteth in Mercy!* Mic. 7.18. Such is the boundless Compassion, the infinite, and unchangeable *Love* of this *my Friend*; that he'll yet *command his loving Kindness*, and say, concerning me, notwithstanding all my Sinfulness, *Go yet, love a Woman (beloved of her Friend, yet an Adultress) according to the Love of the* LORD *toward the Children of* Israel, *who look to other Gods, and love Flagons of Wine,* Hos. 3.1.*This*, that is, *my Friend, loves at all Times,* Prov. 17.17. There's nothing past, present, or to come, has *separated*, can, or ever shall be able to *separate* Me, from His invariable everlasting *Love*, Rom. 8.38, 39. In which my compleat Deliverance from all Misery, to all Glory, is eternally secur'd! How *blessed* then and *I*, in *this my Beloved*, in *this my Friend! O Daughters of* Jerusalem!"

And as upon the Whole, she thus pathetically addresses the Daughters of *Jerusalem:* It denotes, as, the inexpressible *Glories* of Her *Beloved*, and her transcendent *Happiness* in Him; so likewise, that ardent *Desire* she had, after *their* further *Knowledge* of him, and *Acquaintance* with him. And 'tis as if she should say, "O Daughters of *Jerusalem*, look upon my *Beloved*, until you're *enamour'd* with his infinite Glory! Look upon his *fair Face*, yea, upon this *all fair,* this *altogether lovely* One; until you're *ravish'd* with his incomparable Beauty, and struck with the highest Admiration of his incomprehensible Glory! Look upon him, in the Loveliness of all his *Parts*, and in the beautiful Symmetry of the *Whole*; and *see* whether ye can find such *another Beloved,* in *both Worlds!* You that have known *somewhat* of his Worth; rest not in what you've already *seen*; but press *forward* after the fullest *Knowledge* of his unbounded *Excellencies*; till your Souls are *fir'd* with Love to him, and Longings after him, and resolve to *seek him with me?"*

And as the attracting of *their Souls* after him, was one great *End* she had in View, in the wonderful Description she gave them, of her *Beloved's Glory*; so this End of hers, was happily *attain'd*. As, in the first Verse of the next chapter: Where they Reply:

Song 6.1. *Whither is thy Beloved gone, O thou fairest among Women? Whither is thy Beloved turn'd aside? that* We *may* seek him with thee. They say not now, *what* is *thy Beloved,* more than *another Beloved?* But being fully convinc'd of his *transcendent* Excellency, and *enflam'd* with Love to him, by a further Display of his infinite Glory; they say, *Whither is thy Beloved Gone? Whither is thy Beloved turn'd aside? that* We *may* seek him with thee. And the Intenseness of their Love to him, and the Earnestness of their Desires after him, appears in their doubling the Question: *Whither* is He *gone? Whither* is He t*urn'd aside?* q.d. "No *Difficulties* shall stop our *Pursuit* after Him, *we'll seek Him with thee,* until we *find Him,* whom *thy Soul loves,* whom *our Souls admire:* Yea, HIM, who is the *Wonder, Love,* and *Joy*, both of *Heaven* and *Earth!"* And, Oh *happy Souls!* who are thus *drawn to Christ,* by omnipotent *Grace,* as the *Sum* of all their *Happiness,* and *Center* of their *Bliss*; under the *Reports* they hear of his immense, unchangeable, and eternal *Glories!*

Thus, Sir, as enabled, I have gone over this *Description* the *Spouse* gives of her *Beloved:* And leave it with the eternal *Spirit*; who can give you a Display of *Christ's glory,* even by the *Lispings of a Babe:* To the attracting of your Soul into the strongest *Desires* after him, and the nearest *Coalition* with him; to your *present Felicity,* and *endless Glory!*—I subscribe myself,

Sir, Yours, &c.

A. D.

F I N I S.

A
TREATISE
ON
JUSTIFICATION:
SHEWING

The Matter, Manner, Time, and effects of it.

By the REVEREND

Mr. THOMAS DUTTON,

Late Minister in LONDON, and Author of the Discourse
on the NEW-BIRTH, and RELIGIOUS LETTERS.

It is God that justifieth.   Rom. viii.33.

THE THIRD EDITION.

GLASGOW:

Printed by WILLIAM SMITH,
For ARCHIBALD COUBROUGH, Bookseller; and
Sold at his Shop, above the Cross.
==================
MDCCLXXVIII.

ADVERTISEMENT.

THE scripture doctrine of the free justification of guilty sinners, thro' the meritorious obedience and imputed righteousness of the adorable Redeemer, received by faith, as it is of the utmost importance in itself, so it has ever been one of the received articles of all the reformed churches, and is still held, by all true protestants, as one of the most essential doctrines of Christianity. It has always been the delightful theme of every orthodox and evangelical minister; and constantly yields the most solid comfort to every sincere Christian.

Though there have been many useful and elaborate Treatises written upon the point, by divines of distinguished abilities, there is yet room for more, as the subject is inexhaustible.

The small tract now offered to the public, needs no recommendation: the worthy author of it was well known; and the performance, when read, will sufficiently recommend itself, and has already done so, to such as have perused it.

The author's plan in the discourse is shortly this;—To consider the doctrine of the justification of a sinner, in the sight of God, in the MATTER of it, *viz.* the complete *obedience* of Jesus Christ, exclusive of all works of the creature;—in the MANNER of it, as, with respect to God, it is by *imputation*, and with respect to ourselves, by *faith;*—in the TIME of it, as it respects the whole *body* of the *elect*, and every individual person of God's *chosen;*—and in the EFFECTS of it, with respect to the SOUL, as it regards its *peace*, its *state*, and its *obedience*.

In this edition, the Treatise is divided into distinct Sections, agreeable to the above plan: and to each Section there is prefixed a scripture text, suitable to the respective branches of the discourse. With a preface and introduction, giving some account of the Author, and the work.

The editor makes no apology for the present publication: he has been warmly importuned to it; and the scarceness of the book, with the easy terms on which it is now offered, (not being the one half of the former price); the interesting nature of the subject; and the clear and distinct manner in which it is handled, will, he hopes, sufficiently excuse the attempt.

THE
PREFACE.

*A*MONG *the many peculiar and interesting doctrines in the Christian system, necessary to be properly understood, there is none of greater importance than the doctrine of the justification of guilty sinners. As right notions of this important point, is of the utmost consequences to fallen men; so the scriptures of truth exhibit the most full and distinct view thereof: there we are told that guilty men are only justified in the sight of God, by having the finished righteousness of the blessed Jesus, consisting in his active and passive obedience, freely imputed, exclusive of all good works of the creature, and received by faith.*

This is not only the scripture doctrine of justification, but also the doctrine of all our reformed churches; and was of such great account with our protestant reformers, that Luther said of it, "That the church either stood or fell, as this doctrine was maintained, or rejected."

The Rev. Mr. DUTTON, *author of the following Treatise, on the important doctrine of Justification, was also the author of some other Tracts. We have seen his discourse concerning the* NEW BIRTH, *and his* LETTERS *on religious subjects. In these he has given uncontested proofs of his pious disposition, and thorough acquaintance with the inspired oracles of divine truth: and it is evident, in the whole of his performances, he has studied more the edification of such of his readers, as love truth in its native dress, when stript of every human embellishment, than to gratify their vain curiosity with a flow of words which the wisdom of man teacheth.*

In the following Treatise on Justification, he has endeavoured to exhibit to his readers, a scriptural view of his subject, in the words of the Holy Ghost, comparing spiritual things with spiritual: and, undervaluing the censure of captious and ill-natured critics, who itch more after elegant diction and well turned periods, than substantial truth, he has conveyed his sentiments in language easy, intelligible, and scriptural.—And the discourse is not only doctrinal, but practical; for, while the author discovers himself to have a clear knowledge of his subject, he also displays an experimental acquaintance with the power of religion, in pointing out the comfort of saving faith, in the atonement of Christ, and its salutary influence on the renewed heart.

*The plan of his discourse is plain and comprehensive. He endeavours to give his readers a distinct view of the complete atonement of our Lord Jesus Christ, as the alone justifying righteousness of guilty sinners. This he views in both its branches, consisting in his active and passive obedience. His active obedience, which lies in his full and perfect conformity to the whole divine law, without the least failure, either of parts or degrees of obedience, every way answerable to the dignity of his divine person as God-man.**—In his* passive *obedience, which consists in his giving complete satisfaction for sin, by suffering, in the human nature, all that wrath, threatened by the law, as due to elect sinners, as their surety, and enduring the infinite execution of the curse upon him in his death, to the full compensation of all the injuries done to an infinite God, by all the sins of an elect world.*[†]*—This our author proves by the most conclusive arguments, to be the alone righteousness, by which elect sinners are justified in the sight of God, exclusive of all foreseen good works, or any qualifications in the creature, previous to their justification, all such being quite insufficient to recommend a sinner to the favour of God, and have no part in that righteousness whereby the sinner is justified.*

As nothing is of greater importance, or can give more satisfaction to the real saint, than to be instructed with regard to the nature of the justifying righteousness of the Lord Jesus Christ, and how this righteousness becomes his; so, the author of the following Treatise beautifully illustrates this interesting point, from the infallible oracles of divine truth, and shews it to be by imputation *on God's part;*[‡] For he hath made him to be sin, [viz. *by imputation*] for us, who knew no sin, that we might be made the righteousness of God in him, [viz. *by justification and imputation:*]—*and by* believing *on our part.* *Here our author illustrates the nature of saving faith, shews how it acts, and what are its proper objects.*

With regard to the time of justification, our author views this both as immanent and transient; immanent, as an act of God's will, and consequently from eternity; God was in Christ reconciling the world to himself: *transient, as an act which passes upon the whole body of the elect at once, in Christ, their representative, and on every individual of God's elect, when the soul is first enabled to believe in Christ.*[†]

Matth. v. 17, 18
†Gal. iii.13. Eph. v.2
‡Rom iv.6.2 Cor. v.21
*Rom. x.10, and iv.16, iii.22
†Rom i.17. iii.22, 26. iv.5. x.10 andActs xiii.39.

As nothing can be more desirable, or yield more real comfort to the true Christian, than to be acquainted with the satisfactory evidences of his being justified, the author has accordingly shewn, in this Treatise, the effects *of justification, as it respects the soul's peace, its state, and obedience.—He has, on this part of his discourse, endeavoured, in the most scriptural manner, to specify the difference between the peace of a justified soul, and that false peace of an unjustified sinner.*

The author, before he concludes his excellent discourse, propounds a particular objection against the scheme of doctrine laid down and illustrated, which he answers with the greatest evidence and clearness, and shews the absurdity and falsehood of it in the clearest point of view, though stated with a specious appearance of truth.—The discourse is concluded with a variety of very important and useful instructions, natively deduced from the doctrine, admirably well calculated to gladden the hearts of sincere Christians, as well as for the instruction of the ignorant.

Upon the whole, it will be allowed, that the subject-matter of this excellent discourse, is at once comprehensive, glorious, and delightful, and of all others, of the utmost importance; and that right notions of this important article, the justification of a sinner by the blood and righteousness of Christ, tend, through divine grace, to yield the most solid comfort and real joy to every true Christian. It must also be granted, that no knowledge is of equal importance with that of knowing Christ, and the way of salvation through his imputed righteousness. Ignorance of this cardinal doctrine of our holy religion, is joined in scripture with not-submission *to it; and all such, in the issue, must be miserable souls indeed, who are found* ignorant of Christ's righteousness, and go about to establish a righteousness of their own, not submitting themselves unto the righteousness of Christ, Rom. x.3.

To promote these important ends, the instruction of the ignorant, as well as the establishment and consolation of the people of God, no doubt, the intention of the pious author in composing and publishing this discourse. The manner *in which the subject is handled, is concise, clear, and scriptural; and it is hoped will be found well calculated, through the divine blessing, to answer the great ends just now mentioned, which, there is no reason to doubt, have already, in some good measure, been attained by its publication.*

That they may be farther promoted by this new edition, and that the knowledge of Christ, and the way of salvation through him, may be diffused through the world, is the sincere desire of those concerned in the publication of it.

GLASGOW, Oct.
24th, 1777.

A

Treatise on Justification.

←–←

ISAIAH xlv.26.
In the Lord shall the seed of Israel be justified.

INTRODUCTION.

THE scriptures of truth are the great treasury of divine knowledge; for therein, among many other precious truths, the righteousness of Christ is not only revealed, but brought near to guilty sinners. The blessed gospel brings the most joyful tidings to the children of men: and as there is no other robe in which fallen men can stand accepted, before God, but the Redeemer's justifying righteousness, this is therein said to be *unto, and upon all that believe.* This garment of Christ's everlasting righteousness, the gospel presents as the alone ground of that eternal salvation we enjoy by him; and is every way sufficient for us both to live on, and to die in.

IN the *justification* of a sinner, in the sight of God, I shall consider four things principally. As, 1. The *Matter* of it. 2. The *Manner* of it. 3. The *Time* of it. And, 4. The *Effect* of it, with respect to the soul. And then, 5. In the last place shall add something by way of *Use*. I shall consider each of these in the order laid down.

✠✠

S E C T. I.

Of the MATTER *of Justification.*

JER. xxiii.6.

This is the name whereby he shall be called,
THE LORD OUR RIGHTEOUSNESS.

THE *matter* of *justification*, or the *matter* of that *righteousness*, whereby a sinner is made *Righteous* in the sight of God, is first to be considered: and this, according to *the scriptures of truth*, is the complete *obedience of Jesus Christ*, exclusive of all the creature's *works*, whether before, or after its regeneration by the Spirit of God. The complete obedience of Jesus Christ, to the divine law, hath two branches, which are commonly styled, his *active* and *passive obedience;* which consist, in his fulfilling all the law's requirements, and enduring all its penalties. The righteousness which God's law requires, hath two parts, *viz.* a negative part, and a positive part. The negative part of righteousness, consists, in abstaining from, or the *not* doing of those things which the law *forbids*. And the positive part of righteousness, consists, in the *doing* of those things which the law *requires*. And *Sin is the transgression of the law*, in both these respects; on which account, the law's penalty, becomes righteously due to every transgressor. And these two parts 0f the law's righteousness, though they may be distinguished, yet cannot be divided. For, whoever wants that conformity to the law, which it requires, is likewise a transgressor of it, in doing what it forbids; and whoever doth what the law forbids, wants that conformity to its precepts, which the law requires, so that they cannot be *divided*; but yet they may be *distinguished*. And the transgressor of the law, is an unrighteous person, in the eye of the law, in both these respects. And answerably, it was necessary that the righteousness of Christ should consist of two parts. As,

 1. His *active* obedience, to answer to the *positive* part of the law's righteousness. And this consists, in that perfect, universal, and perpetual obedience, which he yielded to the requirements of God's holy law, both internally and externally, in heart, in lip, and in life, from his birth to his

death. Whereby he gave the law its due, even all that obedience, which its extensive precepts demanded; and so fulfilled it, as to the positive part of its righteousness. For being *made of a woman, he was made under the law,* Gal. iv.4. And *what things soever the law saith, it saith to them who are under the law,* Rom. iii.19. Christ was under the law, and what things soever it saith, in its requirements, it said to him; and he yielded a perfect obedience thereto, on purpose to fulfil it. Thus he says of himself, Mat. v. 17. *Think not that I am come to destroy the law or the prophets: I came not to destroy, but to fulfil.* And chap. iii. ver. 15. *Thus it becometh us to fulfil all righteousness. And he that sent me is with me,* (says our Lord;) *the Father hath not left me alone: for I do always those things that please him,* John viii.29. He did *all* the things which God's law required; he did them *perfectly;* he did them *constantly,* or always did them, in such a manner, that God the Father was *well pleased* with his obedience. By this, he satisfied the law's requirements, and gave it *all* that it demanded: Yea, let me say, he gave it *more* than it could demand. All that the law demanded, as it was given out to *Adam,* and in him, to all his *posterity,* was no more than the perfect obedience of the creature that was under it. And this Christ yielded in his human nature; not for all *Adam's race,* but for all his *own,* whom he represented. And the obedience Christ yielded in his human nature, that nature being personally united to his divine, was the obedience of his person; and so had an infinite worth, and glory in it; whereby he gave the law *more* than it could demand. As was foretold of him, Isa. xlii.21. *The* LORD *is well pleased for his righteousness sake; he will magnify the law, and make it honourable.* Oh how was the divine law magnified, by so great a person's being made under it! How honourable was it made by his great obedience! Let me say, the law could not have been so magnified, nor have had so much honour given it, by the most perfect obedience of *all* the creatures, to eternity, as it had by the obedience of this *one* Lord Jesus! If sin had never entered, the creatures would have obeyed the law, *perfectly,* and *perpetually.* But their obedience could have risen no higher than their beings, which were but *finite;* and so the law could have had but a finite honour. But the person of Christ being infinite, his obedience was such; and so the law had an infinite honour given it. O the transcendent glory of Christ's obedience! And how *well pleased* was *the Lord* for this *his righteousness sake!* How well pleased was he *with* this righteousness! And for this righteousness *sake,* how well pleased was he, with all *those* for whom it was wrought out. For, as our Lord, yielded a complete obedience to all the precepts of the moral law, whereby he wrought out a perfect righteousness, so he did it, not for *himself*, but for *us*. As he was born for us, so he was made under the law for us, and obeyed it for us; and thereby he wrought out a righteousness for us. He needed it not for himself, no; it was to cover his naked children. All mankind had a perfect robe of moral righteousness, in their representative-head, Adam, while he stood in the state of innocence. But upon his first sin, they lost it, and became naked; and as such, were exposed to the wrath of a sin-revenging God. And this was the case of the elect of God, as well as others, as they stood related to the first Adam, and considered in the fall. But these being of old *ordained to eternal life*, it was necessary, that they should be completely righteous, that so the law, and justice of God, might not oppose their enjoyment of eternal salvation. And in order to make them so, Christ, the second Adam, obeys the law perfectly for them, in such a manner, as they, by reason of sin, were utterly incapable of. Whereby he wrought out for them a righteousness, that was every way as large, and spotless, as that which they had in their first head, Adam, before his fall: yea, in such a manner, as to make them a righteousness, that is every way answerable to his own superior glory, as the second Adam, *the Lord from heaven*; and to their transcendent relation unto him, their heavenly head, as such. The first Adam's righteousness, was a bright garment, that was every way fitted, to make creatures stand before God, with acceptance, in the enjoyment of Eden's bliss, or the natural happiness of an earthly paradisaical state; but the second Adam's righteousness, is an outshining, glorious robe, that is every way fitted, to make all those who are clothed with it, to stand before the face of God, or in his immediate presence, with the highest acceptance, in the enjoyment of the *heavenly* paradise, or *third heaven's* glory. The finite glory of the first Adam's righteousness, was changeable in itself, and might be lost; and accordingly it was: but the infinite glory of the righteousness of the second Adam, is absolutely unchangeable in itself, can never fade, or be lost, but endureth for ever. It is a *durable*, an *everlasting righteousness*, that will abide the same, in all the immense glories of it, through all the successive ages of time, and to the endless ages of eternity. *Riches and honour are with me,* says our Lord; *yea, durable riches and righteousness,* Prov. viii.18. And, Isa. li.6. *Lift up your eyes to the heavens,* says he; *and look upon the earth beneath: for the heavens shall vanish away like smoke, and the earth shall wax old as a garment, and they that dwell therein, shall die in like manner: but my salvation shall be for ever,* (here is salvation in *this* righteousness, and there is none in any other) *and my righteousness shall not be abolished.* How well, then, are they drest, who are cloathed with this glorious, unchangeable, everlasting robe! And how miserably apparelled are those wretched souls, who seek to adorn themselves with the *filthy rags* of their own *righteousness*; which can never make any foul righteous in the sight of God! For, *as by one man's disobedience, many were made sinners; so by the obedience of one, shall many be made righteous,* Rom. v.19. As by the *disobedience of one* man, Adam, *many,* [i.e., all his *natural posterity,*] *were made sinners*; so, by the *obedience of one, Lord Jesus Christ, shall many* [i.e., all his *spiritual seed,*] *be made righteous.* But thus much shall suffice, as to the first branch of Christ's obedience, or his active obedience to the law's requirements; whereby he makes all his *positively* righteous, to the utmost perfection, and highest glory, in the eye of the holy law, and strict justice of God.

2. The *passive* obedience of Jesus Christ, is another part of his righteousness, which was absolutely necessary to make us completely righteous in the sight of God, with respect to the *negative* part of the law's righteousness; which, as was said, consists, in the not doing of those things which the law forbids. And as we were transgressors of the law, we had done those things which were forbidden by the law; and on this account, justly deserved its penalty. And therefore it was necessary, in order to set us free from guilt, condemnation, and wrath, that he should be *made a sin-offering,* and *a curse for us,* and *die* in our stead; which, in infinite grace, he submitted to. And in these sufferings of his, his passive obedience consisted: he *became obedient unto death, even the death of the cross,* Phil. ii.8. *He was made sin for us,* 2. Cir. v.21.; and *a curse for us,* Gal. iii.13.; and *died* in our stead, 1 Pet. iii.18. And being an infinite person, he was able by *himself,* the sacrifice of himself, *to purge away our sins,* to overcome the curse, to endure all that wrath which was due to us, till he had drank off that bitter cup, even to the hast drop of it; and, then, the law and justice of God, being fully satisfied, he was judicially *raised from the dead:* God, the great creditor, set him free, when he sent an *angel from heaven,* as the messenger of justice, to *roll away the stone from the door of the sepulchre:* for, as he had *made peace by his blood,* so God, as *the God of peace, brought him again from the dead, through the blood of the everlasting covenant;* and thereby did openly acquit him, as the great representative of his people, in their name and room. For, as *he was delivered for our offences, so he was raised again for our justification,* Rom. iv.25. And thus by his passive

obedience, he made us completely righteous in the sight of God, and in the eye of his holy law, with respect to the *negative* part of its righteousness, or the not doing of those things, which it forbids; and as spotless, as if sin had never entered. *He loved us, and washed us from our sins in his own blood,* Rev. i.5. *His blood cleanseth us from all sin,* 1 John i.7. And hence we are said to be *justified by his blood,* Rom. v.9.; and to *have redemption through his blood, even the forgiveness of sins, according to the riches of* the Father's *grace,* Eph. i.7.

Inasmuch as the law and justice of God, being fully satisfied by his blood, here was a way opened, in which the exceeding riches of divine grace might be extended unto us, in the forgiveness of all our sins, with honour to all the divine perfections. In *this,* God can be *just* in *forgiving of sins,* 1 John i.9. And, with reverence be it spoken, God could not forgive sin without a satisfaction to his law and justice, to the injury of his infinite holiness, his unchangeable truth, and strict justice. No; the glory of infinite grace, and boundless mercy, might not be advanced, to the eclipsing of any of the divine perfections. If it had been possible, that all the perfections of God could have been glorified, in the salvation of sinners, without the blood of Christ's cross, he had never given up the darling of his soul, unto the stroke of his justice. But it was not *possible*; and therefore *the cup might not pass from him, without his drinking it.*—The kings of the earth, indeed, to shew their royal *grace,* do sometimes *pardon* malefactors, who are justly *condemned* by the laws of the kingdom; and herein it is true, the *clemency* of the prince is displayed, but still, the *law* suffers, and prince's *honour* too, in relation to it. And this, because it is impossible for them to find out an *expedient,* whereby the law's *penalty* might be endured, and the *life* of the transgressor saved. But this kind of proceeding was altogether incompatible with the honour of the divine Lawgiver, and with the dignity of his righteous law. And therefore his infinite wisdom interposed, and found out a way to punish sin, and yet to *save* the sinner, to the harmonious glory of all his attributes. And this is the *great salvation,* we have by *Christ's cross*. By the cross of Christ, we are for ever delivered from all that wrath that was due to us on account of our sin; and that in such a way, which makes us *spotless* creatures in the eye of the law; so that it hath nothing to charge us with, as washed in Christ's blood, nor can thunder out any of its curses against us. For, being *washed* in this *fountain,* we are *white as snow;* yea, *whiter than the snow,* Psal. li.7. and have a *negative* righteousness, as large as all the prohibitions of God's extensive law. And this is an unspeakable privilege unto us, who are sinners, as considered in ourselves.

But then, if this *negative* righteousness, which we have by the *passive* obedience of our Lord, whereby we are freed from the law's *curse*, was all the righteousness we had, we should not be completely righteous, with respect to the law's requirements, or the *positive* part of the law's righteousness; and so could not have a right to the *blessings* thereof: and therefore, the *active* obedience of our Lord, or that perfect obedience which he yielded to the law's requirements, through the whole course of his life, is an *essential* part of his righteousness, which was absolutely necessary to make us perfectly *righteous,* and so fully *blest*, according to the utmost latitude of the law. It is this that makes us positively righteous: yea, it is this that I look upon to be, in the most strict and proper sense, his *righteousness.* It is this that makes us beautiful, glorious creatures, in the eye of God, and of his holy law; as beautiful and bright, as righteous Adam was, in his paradisaical state; yea, transcendently more beautiful and glorious: for, as was said, that great obedience, which our Lord yielded to the divine law, was every way answerable to the transcendent dignity of his person, as God-man; and so must needs have a transcendency of glory in it, infinitely beyond what was possible to be found in the most perfect obedience of all the creatures. Does the law *require* us to love the Lord our God with all our heart, soul, and strength? Does it require us *always*, thus to do? We are just *such* in Christ, as it requires us to be; and have such a conformity thereto, that it can find no fault with, but every way approves of, and is satisfied with. Yea, such a conformity, that not only pays the law its *due*, and whatever it can demand of the most perfect creatures; but that hath a *redundancy*, an overplus, or *more* than enough in it. So that in this righteousness of Christ, we are not only made perfectly righteous, in a law-sense, according to the glory of the first Adam's state; but superlatively righteous, every way answerable to the superior dignity of the new Adam's person, and the transcendent glory of his heavenly state. And we being foreordained to a participation hereof, it was necessary that we should have such a righteousness, that would fit us to stand for ever in the presence of Jehovah, with the highest acceptance, as the objects of his eternal complacency.

Thus it appears, that the *active* and *passive* obedience of our Lord, or both these *branches* of his righteousness, were absolutely necessary, to make us completely *righteous* in the sight of God, and of his holy law. And though these two parts of his obedience cannot be *divided*, yet they may be *distinguished:* divided they cannot be, inasmuch as that soul, who is *washed from sin in his blood,* or by his passive obedience, is also made *righteous* by his active obedience; and whoever is made righteous by his active obedience, is likewise made *spotless* by his blood. On which account, the blessedness of a justified state is sometimes expressed by one *part* of his righteousness, and sometimes by the *other.* But though they cannot be *divided,* yet they may, and must be *distinguished:* forasmuch as by his *passive* obedience, we are more properly *discharged* from *guilt,* and *freed* from the *curse;* and by his *active* obedience, we are more properly made *righteous,* and inherit the *blessing.* And both these *parts* of our Lord's obedience, make up that *one righteousness* of his, whereby we are *justified* in the sight of God; or, which is the *matter* of a sinner's justification before God.

And as the complete *obedience* of Christ, in both its *parts,* is the *matter* of *justification,* or of the justifying righteousness of a sinner before God; so it stands *alone,* a *such,* in its own comprehensive glory, exclusive of all the creature's *works,* whether before, or after its regeneration by the Spirit of God. As, Rom. iv.6. *Even as David also describeth the blessedness of the man unto whom God imputeth righteousness without works.* This righteousness, which is here said to be withuot works, is the obedience of Jesus Christ; which is the justifying righteousness of a sinner; and is so *complete* in itself, that nothing can be *added* to it, to make it more so. All the *works* of the creature, since the *fall,* are *imperfect;* and therefore, utterly *unfit* to be its justifying righteousness before God, either in whole, or in part. It is impossible, that an *imperfect* obedience can make the person that performs it *perfectly* righteous; and such is the infinite purity of God's nature, and the strictness of his justice, that he can accept of nothing for *righteousness,* that is not perfectly conformed to the *rule* of it, in his holy *law.* And therefore our own obedience cannot be the *whole* of our righteousness before God: nor can it be any *part* of it; because, that which is *wholly* imperfect, can be no *part* of perfection.

The best moral performances, that a person is capable of, while in an *unregenerate* state, fall far short of that perfect *righteousness* which the law requires; and therefore cannot be pleasing unto God, and accepted by him as such; and so they cannot make the person acceptable in his sight, that performs them. Whence it is, that *they that are in the flesh,* (or in a state of unregeneracy) *cannot please God,* Rom. viii.8. *For without faith it is impossible to please him,* Heb. xi.6. The chief *end* of every natural man, in doing good works, is to make himself *righteous* in the sight of God; and as he brings his own righteousness to make him *accepted*, which falls so far short of what God's law *requires*, it is impossible that he should be *pleasing* to him, or *justified* by him. So that the works of the creature, while in an unregenerate state, can be no part of that righteousness, which makes a sinner just in the sight of God.

And as for those *works* of the creature, which are done after it is *born* from above, though they are indeed pleasing, and acceptable unto God, by Christ, in point of filial *obedience*, yet not in point of justifying *righteousness:* nor doth such a soul perform them for that *end*. No; the soul that is born again, that has faith in Jesus, brings nothing for its *acceptance* with God, and *justification* in his sight, but the *righteousness* of Christ: and with *this* God the Father is so well pleased, as it answers the glorious perfections of his nature, and all the requirements of his holy law, that he cannot but accept such a soul; and pronounce it righteous, to the utmost perfection, in that glorious righteousness its faith lays hold of, and pleads before him. Thus its *person* is accepted: and where God accepts the person, he accepts the *works* of that person; as Gen. iv.4. *And the* LORD *had respect unto Abel, and to his offering*. First to Abel's *person*, and then to his *offering*. And the reason why God had respect unto him, and to his offering, was because he had *faith* in the *Messiah*, who was to come; and looked for all his acceptance with God, in *Christ*, the promised *seed*. As, Heb. xi.4. *By faith Abel offered unto God a more excellent sacrifice than Cain*. His *faith* brought *Christ*, typified out in that offering, for the acceptance of his *person*, in point of *Righteousness*, with God; and that *sacrifice*, to be accepted by Christ, in point of filial *obedience:* and so both found the highest acceptance with God. And thus all the good works of the newborn, being done in faith, are acceptable unto God, by Christ, but not in point of righteousness; nor do they perform them for that end. The good works of a *regenerate* person are indeed of a more excellent *kind*, than can possibly be performed by any natural man; inasmuch as they spring from a principle of true love to God in the heart, have an higher conformity to the perfect rule of his holy law, and the end of them is the glory of God in Christ. But yet, they are not without *sin*; they have much imperfection in them, and need washing in the blood of Christ, in order to their acceptance with God, in point of obedience. And being thus imperfect in themselves, they can be no part of that perfect righteousness, which is the matter of a sinner's justification in the sight of God.

Thus it appears, that all the *works* of the creature, both in a regenerate, as well as in an unregenerate state, are altogether *unfit* to be the *Matter* of its *righteousness* before God; and therefore must needs stand excluded from being any *part* thereof.

Besides, it was not becoming the infinite wisdom of Jehovah, to *appoint* any other obedience, for a justifying righteousness, than that which is absolutely perfect, which his holy law can approve of, and his strict justice accept; and accordingly, he hath *appointed* no other. And on this account also, all the *works* of the creature, stand excluded from being any part of its justifying righteousness. As they are altogether unfit, in themselves, to be the matter of it; so they were never *appointed* for this end. No; God hath *appointed* the obedience of his Son, to be the only justifying righteousness of a sinner; and this, as was said, is so complete in itself, that nothing can be added to it, to make its glory more full.

It is impossible, that our *imperfect* obedience should make Christ's more *perfect:* yea, was ours absolutely *perfect*, yet could it add no *perfection* to his. Christ's righteousness, has all perfections in it, both created and uncreated! And what can be added to that which is infinite? and such is the glory of Christ's righteousness! Would it not then be a disgrace to this full, this glorious robe, to tack any part of the creature's obedience to it, was it ever so *perfect?* How much more then is it so, to join our *imperfect* obedience, the filthy rags of a sinner's righteousness, to the spotless obedience, the infinitely glorious righteousness of the Son of God! Would it not be a disgrace to the creature-*sun*, to pretend to set a *candle* by its bright body, to make its light more *glorious?* Much more is it so to Christ, *the sun of righteousness*, to pretend to join the dim *light* of our obedience with his, as if this could add to its infinite *glory!* No, no; let Christ stand *alone*, in that exalted sphere, where his Father has placed him, and for ever shine forth in the peculiar glory of his own great name, THE LORD OUR RIGHTEOUSNESS! while all the innumerable multitude of the saved ones, for ever bow down, with the deepest adoration; rejoicing to be made perfectly glorious, and everlastingly blessed, by the resplendent rays of his infinite brightness cast upon them! while wondering angels assist the joy, and join the praise, to the endless ages of a blest eternity!

But stay, my soul, thou art in the body; and must wait a while, for the glory of that bright day, when, in heavenly raptures, and endless praises, thou wilt sing the *Lamb's new song*; proclaiming him *worthy* to have all the *glory* of thy *salvation*, who has *loved thee, and washed thee from thy sins in his own blood*; and made thee splendidly glorious, by the refulgent rays of his own infinite righteousness! which he hath cast upon thee, and with which he surrounds thee! And mean while, though thou art overspread with sin, death, and darkness, in thy self; yet lift up thy head, rejoice in thy Saviour, and praise the LORD THY RIGHTEOUSNESS, to the utmost of thy present ability, and thy little strength; and humbly make thy *boast* in him all the *day* long; even all this short space of thy mortal life, until the days of eternity come on; and *then*, thou shalt *see him as he is*, and praise him as thou wouldest, in those heights of glory and bliss, which are yet unknown! in that mount of vision, from whence thou shalt never come down!—But, to return from this digression.

The obedience of Christ, as the justifying righteousness of a sinner, being so *perfect* in itself, that nothing can be *added* to it, by any of the creature's *obedience*, to make its *glory* more full; yea, so perfect, that the highest obedience of a creature, were it possible that it could be joined with it, would be but a *disgrace* to its infinite glory: what saint then is there, that would desire to be found in any other righteousness, for his justifying dress before God? I am sure, to a man of them, they are all of Job's mind, who, *though he were prefect, yet would not know his soul; but despise his life,* Job ix.21. He saw such a transcendent glory in his Redeemer's righteousness, that though his own were perfect, he would not know his soul; that is, he would not approve of his own obedience, as his justifying dress before God; but would despise his life, or those, his supposed, perfect works, to which the law's promise of life is annexed'; and chuse to be found in Christ's righteousness, for all his acceptance with God; that so he might enjoy that superior life, glory, and blessedness, which are only to be had in and through Christ. And of this mind was the apostle Paul, Phil. iii.7, 8, 9. He counted all his birth-privileges, and his legal performances, both before, and after his regeneration, to be *but loss and dung, for the excellency of the knowledge of Christ;* that so he might *be found in him,* and *his righteousness*, not having on his *own*. And all the saints are of this mind; they are such *that rejoice in Christ Jesus, and have no confidence in the flesh*; As, verse 3.

And as the complete obedience of Jesus Christ, is the matter of a sinner's justification before God, exclusive of all its own works; so, all along, throughout the whole *gospel*, it stands *opposed* to *the works of the law*, or our own *obedience* to the law; this alone, having the broad seal of heaven, the stamp of divine authority upon it for this end. And had it not been thus, there could have been no salvation for any one soul. And therefore the apostle Paul, when he professeth himself not to be *ashamed of the gospel of Christ;* because *it is the power of God unto salvation,* Rom. i.16. gives the righteousness of Christ, as the reason of all that salvation, which this powerful gospel brings to poor sinners, verse 17. *For therein* [i.e., in the gospel] *is the righteousness of God revealed from faith to faith.*

This righteousness, which is here spoken of, is the righteousness of Jesus Christ; and it is styled, *the righteousness of God;* 1. Because, it was of God the Father's contriving, for the justification and salvation of his people. 2. Of his appointing for that end. 3. Of his revealing. And, 4. Of his accepting.—Again, it is styled, *the righteousness of God;* because the Lord Jesus Christ, the person who wrought it out, is God equal with the Father, and has all the essential perfections of the *Godhead* in him.

And thus, in all respects, it denotes, the glory and excellency of this righteousness, and the sufficiency of it, for the justification of a sinner. Thus, chap. iii.20, 21. *Therefore by the deeds of the law there shall no flesh be justified in his sight; for, by the law is the knowledge of sin.* In this verse, all the creature's obedience, stands for ever excluded, as its justifying righteousness before God; and therefore, if there had not been a better righteousness provided, there could have been no salvation for one sinner. But, in the next verse, the salvation of God revealed in the glorious gospel, is brought in with an adversative, a *but.* But *now the righteousness of God without the law is manifested; being witnessed by the law and the prophets.*

This righteousness is said to be *manifested,* and *now* to be manifested; that is, by the blessed *gospel,* and the dispensation thereof, which *brought life and immortality to light,* thereby, for poor sinners. And this righteousness of God, is said to be *without the law;* that is, without our *obedience* to the law. But though, as if the apostle should say, this righteousness of God, by which a sinner is justified and saved, is altogether *without* the law, the *works* of the law, or the creatures *obedience* to it; yet is not the *law,* hereby, set aside, or made void, but completely *fulfilled.* It is such a *righteousness,* that though it is not *of* the law, nor of the law's bringing to *light;* yet now it is manifested by the *gospel,* the *law approves* of it, as that which answers all its demands, and satisfies it to the full. The law bears *witness* of it as current coin, that pays it all its due, even to a mighty overplus. And therefore, when free-grace justifies a sinner, in this righteousness, that person is pronounced righteous, as a doer of the law; for none but *the doers of the law* can be *justified,* Rom. ii.13. And as none can keep the *law* in their own persons, and so cannot be justified by their own *obedience*; so those who are justified in *Christ's, the righteousness of the law*, is said to be *fulfilled* in them, Rom. viii.4.

And as this righteousness of God, manifested by the gospel, is *witnessed* to *by the law*, as being every way such that it requires; so likewise, it is no new, strange thing, that was never heard of in the world, before the gospel, as a *dispensation*, entered; for it is *witnessed by the prophets*. Thus it was foretold, what the language of all that are Christ's should be, as they came up in the successive ages of time; who, one by one, even every one for themselves, should say, *In the* LORD *have I righteousness,* Isa. xlv.24. And thus the Lord himself speaks concerning his people, chap. liv.17. *No weapon that is formed against thee shall prosper; and every tongue that shall rise against thee in judgment, shalt thou condemn. This is the heritage of the servants of the* LORD, *and their righteousness is of me, saith the* LORD. thus, Isa. xlvi.12, 13. *Hearken unto me, ye stout-hearted, that are far from righteousness. I bring near my righteousness; and my salvation shall not tarry.* And, thus it was predicted, concerning the *Messiah*, as his peculiar work, *to finish transgression, to make an end of sin, to make reconciliation for iniquity, and to bring in everlasting righteousness,* Dan. ix.24. And, to mention no more, *This is his name whereby he shall be called,* THE LORD OUR RIGHTEOUSNESS, Jer. xxiii.6.—Thus the righteousness of God (the complete obedience of Jesus Christ) without the law (or exclusive of all the creature's works) being manifested, by the gospel, is witnessed by the law and the prophets, as the only justifying righteousness of a sinner before God.—And so much for the first thing proposed, *viz.* the *matter of justification*.

❀❀❀❀❀❀❀❀❀❀❀❀❀❀❀❀❀❀❀❀❀❀❀❀❀❀❀❀❀❀❀

S E C T. II.

Of the MANNER *of Justification.*

Rom. iv.6. i.17. x.10.

God imputeth righteousness without works.—The righteousness of God is
revealed from faith to faith.—With the heart man believeth unto
righteousness.

THE *manner* of *justification* is likewise to be considered. And this is
twofold; and has respect, 1. Unto God. And, 2. Unto ourselves.

I. With respect unto God, the *manner* of the *justification* of a sinner is
by *imputation.* And this stands, in God's *reckoning*, or *accounting*, and
pronouncing of a sinner righteous, in the *righteousness* of his Son. And thus
it stands opposed to a person's being righteous by *inhesion*, and by his own
performances, as Adam was before the fall. The law of God requires perfect
righteousness, both in heart and life, in the creature that would be justified
by it; and it can justify such an one, and no other. But since the fall, neither
Adam, nor any of his *posterity*, were legally righteous in themselves; and so
could not be justified by their own righteousness. For, in this sense, *there*
is none righteous, [*i.e.*, legally righteous in themselves, and by their own
performances] *no not one*, Rom. iii.10. And *therefore by the deeds of the*
law, no flesh can be justified in the sight of God, ver. 20. *All have sinned,*
and come short of the glory of God, ver. 23.; and so are shut up under the
curse of his righteous law, and bound over to his wrath, in the sentence
thereof; and so there is no life for a sinner by the law: it cannot justify, but
must condemn an unrighteous person. But the gospel reveals a righteousness of God's providing;* wherein a sinner may be perfectly righteous in the
eye of his holy law and strict justice; and accordingly justified and saved
unto life eternal. And this, as was said, is the righteousness of Christ, which
God the Father *reckons*, or *imputes* to a poor sinner as its *own.* He puts, or

---

*Rom. i.16, 17.

placeth, Christ's righteousness to the *sinner's* account; as he put, or placed, his sin unto Christ's score: As 2 Cor. v. 21. *For he hath made him to be sin for us, who knew no sin; that we might be made the righteousness of God in him.* Christ knew no sin, either by inhesion, or commission; and yet God the Father put, or placed, the sins of his people to his account, *imputed* them unto him, and so made him sin for us; that so we, who know no righteousness, might be made the righteousness of God in him, by having his righteousness put, or placed, to us as ours, and we pronounced righteous therein; even perfectly so, merely by *imputation.* And as it was a righteous thing with God, to impute the sins of his people unto Christ, because of his voluntary undertaking for them, as their *Surety,* in the everlasting covenant, to take their debts upon himself, and pay them to the full; so likewise, it is a just, and equitable thing with God, to *impute* the righteousness of his Son to his people; because it was performed by him for them, as their *representative,* in their room and stead: and accordingly, he doth impute it unto them, and thereby make them just, and pronounce them righteous in his sight. And this is the only way, whereby a sinner can be made righteous before God, *viz.* by his imputing a complete righteousness to it, which the soul itself puts not so much as the least finger to the performance of; but is wholly wrought out for it by another. As Rom. iv.6. *Even as David also describeth the blessedness of the man unto whom God* IMPUTETH *righteousness without works.*

And as God *imputes* the righteousness of his Son to poor sinners, that have none in, or of themselves, and can be *just* in justifying them in this way; inasmuch as this righteousness is such an one, that every way answers the perfect purity of his nature, and righteous law, and was wrought out on purpose for them; so, in justifying a sinner in this way, he displays the *exceeding riches of his grace.* It was free grace that *contrived* and *appointed* this righteousness for a sinner; free grace that *accepted* of it for him, when performed; and it is free grace that *imputes* it to him, puts it upon him, or makes him *righteous* therein. Hence we are said to be *justified freely by his grace, through the redemption that is in Christ Jesus*, Rom. iii.24. And to *have redemption through his blood, the forgiveness of sins* (which is one part of justification) *according to the riches of his grace*, Eph. i.7.

The *matter* of justification, or of the justifying righteousness of a sinner before God, as was before observed, is the righteousness of Christ, or of his active and passive obedience; and the *manner* of God's justifying a sinner, by the imputation of this righteousness, regards both. God *imputes* the *passive* obedience of Christ unto the soul, or his being *obedient unto death, even the death of the cross*; whereby he satisfied justice, and thereby discharges it from all *guilt*, and freely forgives all its *sins*. And he likewise *imputes* his *active* obedience, or the obedience of Christ's life, to the soul; whereby he *makes*, and *declares* it to be *righteous* in his sight: And in both respects, there is the most bright display of *the exceeding riches of his grace*. And therefore the righteousness of Christ, by which a sinner is justified, is said to be a *gift*, a *free* gift, and a gift by *grace:* As Rom. v. 15, 16, 17. *But not as the offence, so also is the free gift. For if through the offence of one, many be dead; much more the grace of God, and the gift of grace, which is by one man, Jesus Christ, hath abounded unto many. And not as it was by one that sinned, so is the gift: for the judgment was by one to condemnation; but the free gift is of many offences unto justification: for, if by one man's offence, death reigned by one; much more they which receive abundance of grace, and of the gift of righteousness, shall reign in life by one, Jesus Christ.*—Thus the manner of a sinner's justification, with respect unto God, is by imputation, or the imputation of Christ's righteousness to him, by God the Father, of the freest grace. And,

II. With respect unto *us*, the *manner* of *justification* is by *faith*. And here I shall shew, briefly, 1. What kind of faith, justifying faith is. 2. How this faith acts towards its proper objects. And, 3. How, or in what respects, the justification of a sinner is by faith. I shall begin to shew,

1*st*, What *kind* of faith, justifying faith is. And in order hereto, shall observe, 1. What it is *not*. And, 2. What it *is*. And,

1. Justifying faith, is not a mere *historical* faith, or a bare assent to the truth of Christ's coming into the world to be the Saviour of men, of his dying for sinners, of his rising from the grave, and of his coming again at the last day, to be the Judge of quick and dead. This is no more than the *devils* have, who *believe and tremble*; and no more than what thousands may have, where the gospel comes, and yet *die in their sins*, and perish for ever. But,

2. Justifying faith, is a *special* faith, that is peculiar to *God's elect*; and therefore styled, *the faith of God's elect*, Tit. i.1. And though this faith is called *common faith*, ver. 4.; yet this phrase denotes no more, than that it is common to all the elect of God; and is not to be understood, as if it was common to others, together with them. It is likewise styled *precious faith*, 2 Pet. i.1. *To them that have obtained like precious faith with us.* And it is said to be a *gift* of God's free grace, to the saved ones, Eph. ii.8. That same

free grace, that gives them *salvation,* as *the end of their faith*, gives them *faith* as a *means* to that end. This gift of justifying faith, springs out of the grace of election; and therefore it is said, Acts xiii.48. *As many as were ordained to eternal life, believed.* And to denote the speciality of its kind, it is said to be *the faith of the operation of God, who raised Christ from the dead,* Col. ii.12. And to be effected by the *exceeding greatness of God's power, which he wrought in Christ, when he raised him from the dead,* Eph. i.19. 20. But thus much as to the *kind* of justifying faith. I come to shew,

2*dly*, How this faith *acts* towards its proper *objects.* The objects of justifying faith are, the person of *Christ* in his death and resurrection, his blood and righteousness; and *God* the Father, in and through him, as justifying the ungodly. Christ is the *immediate* object, and God in him the *ultimate* object of this justifying faith. And how it acts towards these its objects, I am now to shew. But before I speak of its *acts*, I would just give a hint of it as it is a *principle:* for, as in nature, there must be life, before motion; so it is in grace.

Justifying faith, then, as it is a *principle*, grows not in nature's garden, is not brought into the world with us, nor acquired by human endeavours; but is wrought in the soul, by the almighty energy of the Spirit of God, at the time of regeneration. And hence, the grace of faith is reckoned up among the rest, as the *fruit of the Spirit*, Gal. v. 22. When I say the principle of faith is wrought in the soul, by the *Spirit* of God, I intend thereby, *his* immediate *efficiency* therein; and not to exclude the *Father* and the *Son*, from this great work. No; all the three persons in God, have a joint *efficiency* in the work of faith; and accordingly, it is ascribed to them all: sometimes to the *Father*, sometimes to the *Son*, and sometimes to the *Spirit*; because all have a joint hand therein. The *Father* works it by Christ, *Christ* works it from the Father, and the *Spirit* works it from both. For, when the appointed time comes, that a vessel of mercy is to be filled with the life of grace; God the *Father*, the great *husbandman, cuts* the soul *off from the wild olive tree*, its old stock, the first Adam, and the old *covenant*, and ingrafts into Christ, the second Adam, the *good olive tree*; and thereby brings it under the new *covenant*, and gives it a new *life*, the life of grace, from Christ, its new and living root. And *Christ*, at the same instant *apprehends*, or lays hold on the soul, and secretly unites himself to it; and hereby communicates the *spirit* of grace, and the spiritual *life* of grace unto it, out of his own fulness. And the holy *Spirit* of God, at the same moment, being sent from the Father and the Son, takes possession of the soul for Christ, to form his image in it; and instantaneously gives it the *life* of grace, or a *principle* of every grace, and so, in particular, of this grace of *faith*, by his own immediate *efficiency*. Thus this grace of faith, as a *principle*, is created in the soul, by *Father*, *Son,* and *Spirit*; and, with respect to each of the *sacred three*, is a work of *almightiness*. But as the holy *Spirit* is the immediate efficient hereof, so, as I said, this principle of faith is wrought in the soul, by *his* almighty energy. And this principle of faith, wrought in the soul, is a spiritual *ability* to know *Christ*, and *God* in him, to have communion with him, to receive all *grace* from him, and to give all glory to him.

Hence, in its *acts*, as it is a *Christ* discerning faith, a *soul* transforming faith, an *heart* purifying faith; so it is a *working* faith, *it worketh by love:* I unites the soul to the objects beheld; it makes *Christ*, and *God* in him, *precious* to the soul; it makes his promises precious, his ordinances precious, his commandments precious, his people precious; and enables the soul to lay out itself for the glory of God, in all holy obedience: and while it thus walks in *wisdom's ways*, it finds them *all to be pleasantness, and all her paths peace.* But as I am not to speak of the acts of faith comprehensively but only of those, which are peculiar to it, as *justifying*; I shall pass over those of its acts, whereby it is more properly called, uniting faith, sanctifying faith, and working faith; and shall attend to the proper acts of *justifying* faith: for in these it *worketh not* at all.

Thus having hinted, how the *principle* of faith is wrought in the soul, and that it is a spiritual *ability* to know, and obey God in Christ; I come now to speak of the *acts* of this principle, as it is styled *justifying* faith; or to shew, how justifying faith *acts* towards *Christ*, and *God* in him, its proper *objects*.

And in order to the actings of faith towards these its objects, there must be first a *revelation* of them. The *principle* of faith, as I have said, is a spiritual ability to know and obey Christ, and God in him; and the *actings* of this *principle*, towards its *objects*, differ from it, just as the *actions* of the *eye*, in *seeing* an *object*, differ from its *power* of sight; and as the *action* of the *hand*, in *receiving* a *gift*, differs from its *power* of reception. And as the *eye,* in nature, though it be ever so good, cannot *discern* an object, unless it is presented before it, in *light*, the proper *medium*, whereby it may be beheld; so, neither can the *eye* of faith see Christ, unless he is *revealed* to it, by his Spirit in his word. And as the *hand*, in nature, cannot *receive* a *gift*, unless it is exhibited to it; so neither can the *hand* of faith, *receive* Christ, unless he is *held forth* thereto, and *put into it* by his Spirit and word.

And therefore, says our Lord, speaking of the *holy Ghost, he shall glorify me; for he shall receive of mine, and shall shew it unto you,* John xvi.14.

And further, in order to the *revelation* of Christ, (for I begin with Christ, because he is the *immediate* object of faith) the holy Spirit of God, having wrought the principle of faith, discovers to the soul, its own miserable and wretched state by nature; as being under the guilt and power of sin, the curse of God's law, and the due desert of his eternal vengeance. And this he does, by bringing the law home to the conscience, in its purity and spirituality; as it requires perfect, universal, and perpetual obedience, in heart, lip, and life; and denounceth wrath and death upon every transgressor, for the least failure herein. Whereupon, the soul receives a full conviction of its present misery, and of its utter inability to help, or deliver itself from it; and so it dies unto all hope of life by the law. And having such a clear discerning by faith, of the depth of its misery, as it never before had, nor could have imagined, it cries out, as being in the greatest distress, *What must I do to be saved?*

And now, the soul being *sick*, has a sensible *need* of the *physician*. And being hereby *prepared* for the revelation of Christ, the holy Spirit *reveals* him to the soul, and sets him before the *eye* of its faith, in all his fullness, as the great Saviour, as every way suitable to its case, as a miserable sinner. And hereby he makes such an alluring display of his glory to it, that attracts the whole soul after him. And as he presents the excellency of Christ to the eye of faith, so he convinces the soul of the absolute necessity of *looking* unto him alone, for all its salvation. As it is the command of God, that a perishing sinner, made sensible of its misery, should *believe on the name of his Son Jesus Christ*; and as it is the declaration of heaven, *that there is salvation in no other*, either person, or thing, nor in any other way, than by *faith* in him; whereupon, the soul seeing the misery and damnation that will inevitably be the lot of all unbelievers, and the happiness and salvation of all those who are enabled to believe in Christ; it attempts to put forth an *act* of faith on him; for itself, being emboldened herein by the *command* of God, and encouraged hereto by the indefinite *promises* of the gospel. And though the soul feels its utter *inability* to put forth an *act* of faith on Christ, for itself, by reason of those weights which are upon it, those innumerable sins and fears which drag it downward towards despair; yet it is enabled so to do, by the *exceeding greatness of God's power, according to the working,* the energy, or the present exerting *of his mighty power, which he wrought in Christ, when he raised him from the dead, and set him at his own right-hand*, &c. Eph. i.19, 20. And as the soul is enabled to act faith upon *Christ*; so it is upon him, as presented in some *promise*, or declaration of the *gospel*. For, as the *Spirit* is the revealing *agent*, and *Christ* the revealed *object*; so the *gospel*, in the hand of the Spirit, is the revealing *light*; in which faith's *object*, being presented, it *acts* towards him as such, according to the degree of the revelation made, and assistance afforded, by that sovereign Lord, who, as he worketh herein, *divideth to every man severally as he will.*

And by the way, this shews the woful ignorance of those persons, who think *faith* is a light matter; and from thence are apt to say, What! must we do nothing to be saved, but just *believe?* This is an easy thing indeed. But, ah! miserable souls, how wretched is their case who thus argue! This shews them to be yet *in the gall of bitterness, and in the bonds of iniquity*; that they never knew what the pangs of the new-birth, nor soul-plunges were: that they never experienced what it is, for a soul to have the guilt of sin charged home upon the conscience, to have the curses of the law roaring out against it, and to be stript naked of all self-righteousness and strength; and, in such a case and time, to be called to put forth an act of faith on Christ for itself; and that they never knew, what power is requisite, to enable a soul so to do. Will any say it is an easy thing to *believe?* Aye, say I, so it is, with such a *faith* that thousands have, and yet *perish*. With such a *faith*, by which the soul shelters itself under the false *refuges* of its own apprehended righteousness and strength; while it *wears its own garment*, and *eats its own bread*, i.e., works for life, or thinks to live upon its own earnings; while it only makes mention of Christ, and would be *called by his name,* a Christian*, to take away* its *reproach*, Isa. iv.1. It is an easy thing to *believe*, with such a *faith*, that can only stand in a *calm*; but is it an *easy* thing to *believe* in a *storm?* When the storm of God's apprehended *wrath* beats vehemently against the soul; then for it, in the face of the *tempest,* to put forth an *act* of faith on Christ for *itself*, is this an *easy* thing? If it is an *easy* thing for a *dead* man to *act*; then it is an *easy* thing for an *unregenerate, unquickened* soul, to put forth an *act* of saving faith upon Christ. If it is an *easy* thing for a creature, in the utmost *weakness*, to perform *mighty acts*; then, is it an *easy* thing, even for the new-born soul, in all its felt *weakness*, to put forth an *act* of *faith* on Christ for itself, in the depth of its distress, which is such a *mighty* performance? No; this is a thing, quite out of the reach of all *creature-power*. It is indeed *easy* for a soul, that has a *principle* of saving faith wrought in it, to put forth an *act* of faith on Christ, when the *power of God* enables it thereunto; as *easy* as it is to *breathe*, when respiration is *free*; as *easy* as it is for the eye to *see* a presented object, when it has a perfection of *light*, and a plentitude of *visive* sprits; and as *easy* as it is for the hand to *receive* a gift that is put into it; and for the foot to *walk* unto any designed point of the compass, when both have a fullness of *life* and *spirits* for those motions: but otherwise, to put forth an act of faith, is quite out of the reach of the creature's ability. But to go on.

It is a most certain truth, that nothing less than *omnipotence* is required to enable a soul to put forth an act of faith on Christ, according to the degree of the revelation of him made unto it. If any thing less than almightiness could work faith, the power that enables a soul to believe would never have been so aggrandized, as here, in this *Ephesian* text it is; where it is said to be, *his, i.e.*, God's power; the *greatness* of his power; and the *exceeding* greatness of his power; and that souls believe, according to his *mighty* power, and to the *working* of his mighty power, *which he wrought in Christ, when he raised him from the dead, and set him at his own right-hand in the heavenly places,* &c.

Our Lord, by the almighty power of God, had a *double* resurrection from the dead; and so have his people, in conformity to him. He had first a resurrection of his soul, from under all that guilt, wrath, and death which he endured for us; when the sufferings of his soul being *finished*, and divine justice, in that regard, satisfied, the joys of his Father's favour, and of his being the God of peace, both to him and his, broke out upon his spirit, like the sun from under an eclipse, and raised him up to that life of joy, in which he cried out, *It is finished!* Whereupon he *commended* his triumphant *Spirit* into the *hands* of his *Father, bowed the head, and gave up the Ghost.*—And again, he had a resurrection of his *body*, from under the dominion of death and the grave; when, in his whole person, he was openly discharged from all the debts which his people owed, and which he had taken upon himself to pay; and as having done it, was publicly justified, and entered upon endless life and glory, in their room and stead.—Thus *Christ*, by the power of God, had a *double* resurrection; and so have his *people:* for, by virtue of their union with him, they have a conformity to him.

They have first a resurrection of their *souls*; when, by the mighty power of God, they are raised up from under all guilt, wrath, and death in the conscience, unto *faith* in Jesus; whereby they receive a full discharge from all sin, a right and title to endless life and glory, and enter into the present life of a joyful persuasion thereof; which is the first fruit of that full harvest of joy and glory, reserved for them, when they shall enter into life eternal.—And again, they shall have a resurrection of their *bodies*, at Christ's second coming; they shall be openly discharged from all sin, and publicly pronounced righteous; and as such, called to *inherit the kingdom which* is *prepared* for them.—Thus the resurrection of Christ's people, in general, bears an analogy with his; and in particular the resurrection of their *souls*, when first raised up unto *faith* in him, as dying for their sins, *and raised again for* their *justification*; and is effected by the same *mighty power of God, which he wrought in Christ, when he raised him from the dead*; according to that proportion, which was requisite to raise the hand and the members.

And as the first *actings* of faith, in the *same* soul, pass under various descriptions; such as, *looking unto Jesus, coming* unto Christ, *seeing* unto him, the *city of refuge, running into his name, as a strong tower, committing* the soul into his *hands*, and *trusting* in his *name*, for life and salvation; so the first *actings* of faith, in *different* souls, may in some measure *vary*, while, as was said, they believe according to the *measure* of the revelation of Christ, made unto them, and to the *degree* of assistance afforded them; and yet in the main, they all *agree*, and may be summed up in this, *viz*. The soul's believing on Christ, for itself, for all life and salvation. Some souls have clearer views of Christ, and are enabled to believer on him more strongly, and others are more weak in faith: but yet all believe truly, that have a *discerning* of Christ, as the only Saviour, and *trust* in him alone, for all their salvation.

There were *six cities* appointed, under the *Jewish* state, to be *refuge cities*; whither the *man-slayer* might flee, and be safe: all which typified out that fullness of refuge and safety, that there is in our one Lord Jesus for perishing sinners, that flee unto him by faith, as the hope set before them in the gospel. And as the *man-slayer*, being to *haste* for his life unto one of *the cities of refuge*, was ordered to flee unto that city which was *nearest* to him; so it is the duty and privilege of poor sinners, when they see their miserable condition, to *haste* immediately unto *Christ*, the great *Saviour*; and unto *that* in Christ, which they have the clearest *discerning* of, and so in that regard, is the *nearest* unto them; as being a suitable *relief* for that part of their *misery*, which most sensibly *effects* them.—And thus some souls, being most sensibly touched with the guilt and filth of *sin*, have a more clear revelation of the *blood of Christ*, in its excellency and suitableness, to *cleanse from all sin*, and are enabled to haste unto *this*, as the immediate *refuge* set before *them*.—Other souls are more sensible of their misery, as *naked* creatures, and have a more clear discovery of Christ, as a suitable, glorious remedy, in regard to his *righteousness*; and these are enabled to run into his name, THE LORD OUR RIGHTEOUSNESS, as the *refuge* that is *next*, or most immediate unto *them*.—And others, who have a more *general* sense of their misery, have a more *general* revelation of Christ's excellency; and are enabled to flee unto him for *refuge*, as a complete *Saviour*, that is every way suitable to *their* case. And though the distinct *actings* of faith on Christ, in all these, *vary*; yet in the main they *agree*, inasmuch as it is one *Christ*, that is believed on for justification and life. They all flee unto Christ for *refuge*, and so are all *safe*; though one flees unto him under one consideration, and another under another, according to that revelation they have of him, as suitable to their case. For, though the soul's first actings of faith on Christ, may more peculiarly respect some *one* of his distinct excellencies, than the rest, yet *all* are implied: faith acts towards a *whole* Christ; and those of his excellencies, which were not at first so distinctly viewed, and *acted*, towards by the soul, are afterwards more fully *discovered*, and particularly dealt with.—Thus in *general*, justifying faith *acts* towards *Christ* its *object*.

But more *particularly*; the holy Spirit of God, as the *Spirit of wisdom and revelation*, reveals the *blood* of Christ to a sin-burdened soul, in its infinite all-sufficiency to cleanse from all sin, in some one or other promise or declaration of the gospel; and enables the soul to *act* faith therein. Thus Rom. iii.25. *Whom God hath set forth to be a propitiation, through faith in his blood.* And the particular *actings* of justifying faith, towards Christ, with regard to his blood, are, 1. A *discerning* of its all sufficiency to take away sin. 2. An *approving* of it as such. And, 3. An entire *dependance* upon it, and recourse unto it, for all pardon and peace with God. All which are comprehended in that phrase, *Faith in his blood.*

The soul that *acts* faith in Christ's *blood*, as on the one hand it *discerns* the infinite *all-sufficiency* thereof, to cleanse it from all sin; so, on the other, it sees an utter *insufficiency* in every thing else, in all its prayers, tears, sufferings, &c. to take away the least *sin*, or in the least-wise to remove, either the guilt or stain of any of its transgressions.

And as such a soul *approves* of the blood of Christ, as sufficient in itself to take away sin, and as it is appointed of God for this end; so, it *disapproves* of the pretended efficacy of every thing else for this purpose.

Again, as such a soul has an entire *dependence* upon the precious *blood* of Christ, for all its pardon and peace with God, and as it has an utter *independence* upon every thing else, either to procure its pardon, or make its peace; so, it would not, for a world, *substitute* any thing of its own, either doings or sufferings, in the room of Christ's *blood*, or *join* them together with it; because it sees, that nothing else can take away *sin*; and also, because it would not derogate from the honour of the Redeemer's *blood:* no; the soul that acts faith in Christ's blood, falls down and adores the *Redeemer*, in the infinite all-sufficiency of his great *sacrifice*, and depends upon this alone, for its justification from all sin, in the sight of God. Faith will give none of the glory, that is due to Christ's *blood*, as it cleanseth from all sin, to any thing done or suffered by the *creature*; but sets the crown upon the Redeemer's head, and proclaims the *lamb worthy to have all the glory of washing his people from their sins in his own blood*, Rev. i.5.— Thus justifying faith *acts* towards Christ, its *object*, with regard to his *passive* obedience, his *blood*, according to the revealed efficacy thereof, for a full discharge from all sin.

Again, the Spirit of Christ reveals to the soul, in and by the gospel, his *active* obedience, his *righteousness*, strictly so called; and faith *acts* towards it accordingly. Thus, Rom. i.17. this *righteousness of God* is said to be *revealed from faith to faith*. As the righteousness of Christ is *externally* revealed in the gospel, which is the doctrine of faith; so likewise, it is *internally* revealed by his Spirit to the soul; or set before the eye of its faith, in some one or other word of the gospel, shining in upon the heart in the light of the Holy Ghost. Christ is said to be *made of God unto us righteousness, as well as redemption*, 1. Cor. i.30. As he is made redemption to us, both by price and power for the forgiveness of all our sins, and for our deliverance from all enemies; so he is made righteousness to us, for the justification of our persons in the sight of God; or, for the making us positively righteous before God, to the utmost perfection: whereupon we are declared righteous, have now a title to, and shall, ere long, inherit eternal life. So likewise, it is said, that Christ was *made sin for us, that we might be made the righteousness of God in him*, 2 Cor. v. 21. And that it is *by the obedience of one, that many shall be made righteous*, Rom. v.19. And when the Spirit of Christ takes the righteousness of Christ, and shews it to the soul, in these *words*, or in any other *word* of the gospel, he makes such a *revelation* of it to the mind, that it never before saw.

The soul had wont to think, that that righteousness, whereby it might find acceptance with God, and be justified before him, was something either *in*, or *done* by itself. If it had any sight of the need of Christ's blood, to cleanse it from sin; (as some sight of this, a natural man is capable of, though not of that saving sight of it, which is peculiar to the new-born, upon the Spirit's revelation;) yet still the soul thought, that it must endeavour to make itself *righteous* in the sight of God, by its own *obedience*; and that for this end it must do good works. But when the Spirit shews the righteousness of Christ, to the faith of any soul, it is quite of another mind. Now, the soul sees, that that righteousness, which alone can make a sinner just before God, is only *in the* LORD; *i.e.*, in the Lord Jesus, as the representing head of his people. It sees, that CHRIST is *made unto us righteousness*; that it is in HIM *we are made the righteousness of God*; and that, it is by HIS *obedience, that many shall be made righteous*. And as by this revelation of the Spirit, the soul sees the righteousness of Christ, in its reality, and also in its beauty, fullness, excellency, and glory; so, by faith, it *acts* towards it for justification. As this righteousness is *revealed to faith*; so faith *acts* towards this *righteousness*, or towards *Christ*, with regard to his *righteousness;* 1. By *looking* unto it. 2. By *receiving*, or embracing of it. And, 3. By *depending* upon this alone, for its only justifying righteousness before God.

As the righteousness of Christ is revealed, in the gospel, unto all nations for the obedience of faith; and revealed, by the Spirit, unto all those who have faith wrought in their hearts: so faith *acts* towards this *righteousness*, by *submitting* to it. As is plainly implied, in what is asserted concerning unbelievers, that *they, being ignorant of God's righteousness, go about to establish their own righteousness, and have not submitted* themselves unto *the righteousness of God*, Rom. x.3. If this is the character of an unbeliever, that he is such an one, that doth not *submit* to this righteousness of God; then the character of a believer must be just the *reverse*; and the soul that *acts* faith, in submitting to this righteousness, *looks* unto this alone, for its justification in the sight of God.

As poor sinners are called to *look unto Jesus* alone, for all that fullness of *salvation* that is in him; so, in particular, they are called to look unto him, as THE LORD OUR RIGHTEOUSNESS; and that when they are far from righteousness, or have none at all of their own to recommend them to God: As, Isa. xlv. 22. *Look unto me, and be ye saved, all the ends of the earth.* And, chap. xlvi.12, 13. *Hearken unto me, ye stout-hearted, that are far from righteousness: I bring near my righteousness.* It is as if the Lord should say,

"Hear ye stout-hearted souls, that, in the pride of your spirits, have refused subjection to my righteousness, and have gone about making yourselves righteous, by the works of your hands, which yet leave you in a state that is far from righteousness; I bring near my righteousness, I have a righteousness for you, that you never thought of; a complete glorious robe, of my own working out, in which there is a fullness of salvation for you: look therefore, upon this *my* righteousness, and be ye saved." And accordingly, the soul that believeth, *looks* away from all its own righteousness, as being fully convinced of the vanity of looking for salvation from thence; and *looks* unto the Redeemer's righteousness, and to that alone, as being infinitely sufficient to justify and save it. And the language of such a soul, when it comes unto Christ for justification of life, is the same with that of the church, Jer. iii. 23. *Truly in vain is salvation hoped for from the hills, and from the multitude of mountains*; (from the works of our own hands, which were once high as mountains, in our esteem, for security) *Truly in the* LORD *our God is the salvation of Israel.* And thus, Hos. xiv.3. *Ashur shall not save us, we will not ride upon horses, neither will we say any more to the work of our hands, Ye are our gods*; (our deliverers, to whom we look for salvation) *For in thee the fatherless find mercy:* it is as if they should say, we are such miserable souls, that cannot save ourselves, and have none to provide us either bread or *clothing*, in a spiritual respect; but thou hast *all* we want: we come to thee therefore, in our starving, *naked* condition; and *look* to thee, for that bread, that *clothing* which thou hast provided; for in thee we shall find all the mercy we can want, unto eternal life.—Thus, a poor soul, when stript *naked* of all its own *righteousness, looks* by faith unto Christ's, as its only justifying robe. And the eye of a believer is *single* towards Christ, in this respect; it does not look partly to *Christ*, and partly to its own *works*, to make it righteous in the sight of God. No, Christ commends his spouse, as having *doves eyes*, Song. iv.1. that look *singly* unto *him*, her glorious *Mate*, for that royal robe of his, that *wedding-garment*, which can only fit her to stand with him, in the heights of glory, before the face of God, with the highest acceptance.

Again, justifying faith *acts* towards *Christ*, its *object*, with regard to his *righteousness*, by *receiving* or embracing of it. This righteousness is styled *a gift*, Rom. v.17. And accordingly, the hand of faith *receives* it, as a gift of the Father's free love, to a naked sinner, to make it completely righteous in his sight: for, in *giving* Christ to the soul, he gives him in all his *fullness*, and so in *this*, of his glorious *righteousness*, which is infinitely full for its *justification*. And faith *receives* Christ, as God *gives* him; it *receives Christ Jesus the Lord,* as the Father's *gift*, in all his fullness, in all his glories, and so in this, of his being its complete *righteousness* before God; and as such it *walks* in him, in all its approaches to the Father, as the saints are exhorted to do, Col. ii.6. As faith's eye *looks* unto this righteousness; so faith's hand *receives* it: it brings nothing to *buy* this righteousness with; nor yet doth it bring any thing to *join* with it; but merely *receives* it, in the fullness of its glory, and freeness of its bestowment.

As this righteousness is a royal *grant* from the throne, to *array* the *bride* of Christ, and so every believer, who, in itself, is a naked creature; so the soul by faith *receives* it, and *puts* it on, as it were: *It puts on the Lord Jesus* as its righteousness before God, enwraps itself herein, and adorns itself herewith; and hereby *makes itself ready for the marriage of the Lamb.* And in this spotless, beauteous, glorious robe, it will appear to be made ready indeed, for the enjoyment of the marriage-glory, with its royal Bridegroom, when that happy day comes on,. Rev. xix.8. An *unbeliever,* as he has no *eye* of faith, no spiritual ability to *see* Christ's righteousness; so he has no *hand* of faith, or spiritual ability to *receive* it. No; the *eye* of the natural man *looks* to his own works, to make him righteous: these he admires, bows down to, and idolatrously sets up in the room of Christ's righteousness. And as for his *hand*, it is a *working* hand, not a *receiving* hand; it *works* for righteousness, not *receives* righteousness. The natural man is too proud to be beholding to free-grace, for a righteousness before God, that is all of mere *gift*, and of another's working out; this he *understands* not, this he *approves* not, to this he *submits* not. But to a *believer*, O what a glorious sight is the righteousness of Christ, in his eye, as it is the Father's free *gift*, for the justification of a sinner! And, with what gladness doth the hand of faith *receive* and embrace this gift of righteousness!

And as the soul, by faith, looks to and receives this righteousness; so it *depends* upon this alone, for its justification before God. And therefore, the apostle gives this description of believers, that they are such *that rejoice in Christ Jesus, and have no confidence in the flesh*, Phil. iii.3. As they have no confidence in the *flesh*, in their external privileges, or legal performance, as their righteousness before God; so they have all their confidence in *Christ*, and his righteousness, for their complete justification in God's sight. Here they *confide*, on this they *depend*; and knowing the fullness, glory, and excellency of this righteousness, appointed of God for such a glorious end, they do it with joy. They rejoice in Christ Jesus, as having an exuberant fullness of justification, life, and glory in him; even above what perfect Adam was capable of in innocency. And as the apostle *here* describes believers in general; so, in the succeeding *verse*, he gives us an account of himself in particular, with regard to his *distrusting* every thing of his own, and his entire *confidence* in Christ, or the *actings* of his faith towards him, in respect to his righteousness.

Verse 4. *Though I might also have confidence in the flesh, if any other man thinketh that he hath whereof he might trust in flesh, I more.* It is as if he should say, "I have as much of external privilege, and legal performance, as any of you all; and if these things would stand me in any stead, for my righteousness before God, I might trust in them as much as any man, nay, more."

And then he proceeds, verses 5, 6. to give a particular enumeration of his privileges and performances; *Circumcised the eight day,* says he; *of the stock of Israel, of the tribe of Benjamin, an Hebrew of the Hebrews; as touching the law a Pharisee; concerning zeal, persecuting the church; touching the righteousness which is in the law, blameless.* It is as if he should say, "Come, you *Jews*, who *rest in the law, and make your boast of God*, and see if I am a *whit* behind you, in any of your *birth,* or *church* privileges, and *legal* performances, in which you vainly trust; or rather, whether I have not *more* of those things, than many of you can pretend to.—Are you *Hebrews*, of the seed of *Abraham*, whom God chose to be his peculiar people? *So am I.* Yea, an *Hebrew* of the *Hebrews*; I am so, both by father's and mother's side; which many of you cannot say.—Are you *of the stock of Israel,* who as a prince with God, prevailed with him for the blessing? *So am I.* And I can tell you of what *tribe* too, I am of *the tribe of Benjamin*; when many of you cannot reckon up your *genealogy*.—Were you *circumcised? So was I.* And that at *the eight day* too, the precise time appointed by God; which many of you cannot say.—Have you been observers of the *law? So have I. As touching the law, a Pharisee; of the strictest sect:* and *profited more in the Jews religion, than many of mine equals*, who profest themselves to be *Pharisees*, of the same *sect* with me.— Have you been strenuous *maintainers* of the *Jewish religion*, and *opposers* of all you judged innovations, and destructive of the rites and ceremonies thereof? *So have I.* I was no cold half-hearted professor, that cared not what men believed, or practiced in religious matters; but was so *exceedingly zealous of the traditions of the fathers,* that in this my blind *zeal*, I even *persecuted the church of God, and verily thought I ought to do many things contrary to the name of Jesus of Nazareth*; because I judged that *Jesus*, and his *followers*, taught and practiced things contrary to the law of *Moses*, and the religion *established* by God himself. *And being exceedingly mad against them, I breathed out threatenings and slaughter, haled men and women to prison; some I compelled to blaspheme, and others I persecuted even to strange cities*; so that in this regard, I was as great an *hero* as any of you all, and perhaps there is not a man among you, that has been so great a zealot as myself; *concerning zeal persecuting the church:*—And as for *the righteousness which is the law,* take it in the most comprehensive sense, which our doctors have given of it, *I was blameless.* None could charge me with an unrighteous action, with any want of conformity to, or transgression of the law of God, according to that sense of it given by the *Rabbins*; I have been a person of a spotless conversation, of an unblemished character, *touching the righteousness which is in the law, blameless.*"

Thus he drew his own picture to the *life*, and presented it to them, in all the beautiful features of his privileges and performances, while he remained an *unbeliever*. "And now, you *Jews*, as if he should say, who are fond of your own *righteousness*, and trust in this for your acceptance with God, what think you of such a man as I? Do not you think *my* righteousness was large enough to cover me all over, and to render me acceptable unto God? If any man of you all *think he hath whereof he might trust in the flesh, I more.* Surely I had righteousness enough to *vie* with you all, and to *outstript* many of *you*. But come now, you *self-righteous* creatures, and I will tell you how little *worth* all your own *righteousness* is, in point of *acceptance* with God. I once thought, as you now do, that I had righteousness sufficient to justify me in the sight of God; but come I will tell you my *experience*, how insufficient I saw the best righteousness of a fallen creature to be, what little account I made of all my *own* righteousness; and what great account I made of *Christ's*, when *God revealed his Son in me*, and wrought faith in my heart. You have seen me *exalting* myself to the greatest altitude of that *pharisaical* perfection, I had while an *unbeliever*; and now you shall see me, as a *believer, laying* my *self*, and all my *own* righteousness, down at the *feet* of Jesus; shrinking into the dust, under a sense of all my own nothingness and vileness, before this Lord of glory, who is THE LORD MY RIGHTEOUSNESS; upon whom only I now *depend*, and in whom alone I now rejoice." And so he turns the tables, and begins his discourse in the next verses, with an adversative, a *but*.

Verse 7. But *what things were gain to me, those I counted loss for Christ.* "And now, as if he should say, you poor souls, that seek to be justified by your works, see how vain a thing it is to trust in your own *righteousness*, which cannot endure the fiery inquisition of the holy *law*, and strict *justice* of God. See how it fared with me, when God brought home his law in its *spirituality* to my conscience; I soon found that none of my external privileges, and *figleaf* performances, could screen me from the storm of his avenging *wrath*. I then saw, that all my *goods*, I had been laying up for many years, and thought they would have *gained* me eternal life, were but mere *loss*; that these counterfits would never pass for current coin; and that if I *trusted* to these, I must *lose* my soul for ever; and therefore, when my judgment was set right, I *counted* them *loss*. And as God shewed me the insufficiency of my *own* righteousness, so likewise the all-sufficiency of *Christ's.* I then saw, that *Christ* was the only *gain*, that it was his *righteousness* alone that could *deliver* me *from death*, and give me life; yea, I saw such a super-excellent glory in Christ's righteousness, that did infinitely exceed my *own*, had it been ever so perfect; and that I must *part* with my own, if ever I *had* Christ's, and therefore, I freely cast all my own righteousness *overboard*, and *counted* it *loss for Christ*, that glorious *object*, and those immense treasures of *gain*, I should have in *his* righteousness. I *parted* with my own *righteousness*, indeed, in point of *dependence*; but then it was for a *better:* I *cast* away all my falsely supposed *gain*, and counted it *loss for Christ*; when once I saw the real, the infinite *gain*, of that glorious *object*, which I then *received* and *embraced*. Therefore, be convinced, you ignorant souls, who would *establish* your own *righteousness*, that it cannot stand you in any stead, and that if ever you are saved, you must have a better; that you must have a righteousness that *exceeds the righteousness of the Scribes and Pharisees, or in no case you can enter into the kingdom of heaven.* Thus, as if he should say, I have told you, what little *account* I made of all my *pharisaical* righteousness, and what an high *value* I had of *Christ's*, in the day when God wrought *faith* in my heart; *I count it loss for Christ.* And as I then *did* count it, so I now *do*; Christ has lost no *glory* in my *eye*. I will take all my *pharisaical* righteousness, while an *unbeliever*, and add to it all the righteousness I have wrought, since I *believed* in *Jesus*, and since I was an *apostle* of the *Lamb*, who *have laboured more abundantly than they all*; and tell you even now, what little *account* I make of all these things put together; and what an high *esteem*, at this time, I have of *Christ*, as my *justifying* dress before God."

Verse 8, 9. *Yea, doubtless, and I count all things, but loss, for the excellency of the knowledge of Christ Jesus my Lord; for whom I have suffered the loss of all things, and do count them but dung, that I may win Christ, and be found in him, not having mine own righteousness, which is of the law; but that which is through the faith of Christ, the righteousness which is of God by faith.* "I put all things together, all my own *righteousness,* while a *Pharisee,* and since an *apostle,* and tell you, *I count all things but loss for Christ;* for the *knowledge of Christ,* for *the excellency of the knowledge of Christ Jesus my Lord*; that glorious *object* my faith now *deals* with, that anointed *Saviour,* whom I *adore,* as the Lord MY RIGHTEOUS-NESS, in whom is all my *salvation: For him I have suffered the loss of all things, and do count them but dung that I may win Christ.* I *lose* all, to *win* all; or rather, I lose an *all* that is *nothing,* and worse than nothing, to gain immense *treasures,* and infinite *fullness,* a mass of unbounded *sweetness,* and an eternity of *life* and *glory.* I joyfully part with *all,* for *one Christ*; the Father's *Christ* is infinitely *enough* for me. I cast away all my own *blemished* performances, for the *spotless* beauty of my lovely *Lord*; and *count them but dung that I may win Christ, and be found in him.* Oh! it is in *Christ,* not in *myself,* that I would be *found,* at the awful day of judgment. It is, as *not having on mine own righteousness, which is of the law*; I dare *trust* in none of my own *obedience* to God's law, which I love and serve, as my *righteousness* before God; nor would I be found in this garment, when I appear before him: *but as having on that righteousness which is through the faith of Christ, the righteousness which is of God by faith.* That *righteousness* which Christ has wrought out, which God hath appointed for the justification of a sinner, which faith sees, and receives: it is this *righteousness,* I would be *found* in; it is upon this alone I *depend* for justification before God, and eternal glory with him."

Thus this great apostle gave an account of the actings of his faith towards Christ, with regard to his righteousness for justification. And, as all that are justified have the same *faith*; so it *acts,* in like manner, towards the righteousness of Christ for justification of life. It is this righteousness *justifying faith looks* to; it is *this* it *receives* and *embraces*; and upon *this* alone it *depends.* For, as all believers debase their *own* righteousness; so they exalt *Christ's:* they set the crown upon *his* head, and will for ever give him the *glory* of all their *justification* before God. As they give his *blood* all the *glory* of *cleansing* them from *sin*; so they give his *righteousness* all the *glory* of their *acceptance* with God. And thus justifying faith *acts* towards *Christ* its *object.*

In the next place, I would shew briefly, how justifying faith *acts* towards *God* its *object.* And this, in short, is the soul's *looking* unto *God,* as *justifying,* through the blood and righteousness of his Son; and *expecting* all its justification from him, only upon the account of what Christ has done and suffered. And in order hereto, the blessed Spirit makes a revelation of *God* to the soul, as *justifying* a poor sinner, of the freest *grace,* and yet according to the strictest justice, through the *blood* and *righteousness* of Christ; and enables the soul to *look* unto God, as so justifying for itself, even when it sees nothing but ungodliness in it; and to *receive* the justifying sentence of God pronounced in the word of the gospel, concerning the soul, which believes in Jesus, with respect both to the *forgiveness* of its sins, and *acceptation* of its person; and this, merely upon the truth and faithfulness of that God, who makes the declaration.

From whence, as the soul receives that present justification given it by the gospel, into its own conscience; so it *expects* the open promulgation of this sentence, or that open justification, which shall be given it at the day of judgment, in the face of men and angels, when it shall be pronounced, *Blessed of the Father,* and called, as such, to *inherit the kingdom prepared for it, from the foundation of the world.* And as the soul that thus acts faith, sees it an impossible thing, that God should justify a sinner in any other way, than by his free grace, through the blood and righteousness of Christ; and so *looks* to him as justifying, only in this way, for its own justification and salvation; so it likewise herein regards the *glory* of God. Such a soul brings nothing with it, but *Christ,* for all its *acceptance* with God; nor dare plead any thing, as a moving *cause* of its justification and salvation, but God's free *grace;* nor doth it bring any thing of its own, to procure the divine favour; because it would not eclipse the *glory* of free grace. No; as faith *looks* for, *receives,* and *expects* justification and life, from the God of all grace, through Christ; so it gives the whole *glory* hereof to him.

Thus, as through the blood and righteousness of Christ, God is declared to be *just,* in his being *the justifier of him that believes in Jesus,* Rom. iii.26: and, in this way, to justify a sinner *freely by his grace,* Tit. iii.3.: so faith *receives* this justifying sentence, proclaiming in the gospel, and brought home by the Spirit to the soul; and gives all the *glory* of justification, both as to *forgiveness* and *acceptation,* to the free *grace* of God, from whence alone it is received. And therefore the apostle, in the triumph of faith, challenges all the enemies of God's people, to bring in their accusations, if they have ought to say against them, with a *Who shall lay any thing to the charge of God's elect?* And nullifies them all, with this one word, *It is God that justifies*, Rom. viii.33. And we are *justified*, says he, *freely by his grace*, chap. iii.24. As we have *the forgiveness of sins, through* Christ's *blood, according to the riches of his grace;* so, by the same grace, he *hath made us accepted in the beloved*, Eph. i.6, 7.—Thus, having shewn how justifying faith *acts* towards Christ, its *immediate*, and God in, and through him, its *ultimate object*, I proceed to the next thing proposed; which was,

3*dly*, To shew *how*, or in what respects, the justification of a sinner is by *faith*.† When the scripture speaks of being justified by faith, in some places, it is to be taken *objectively*, and not *subjectively*; or, for *Christ*, the *object* of faith, and not for the *grace* of faith, inherent in, and acted by the soul. As, where it is said, Rom. iv.5. *But to him that worketh not, but believeth on him that justifieth the ungodly, his faith is counted for righteousness.* The word *faith* here, which is said to be counted for righteousness, is not to be understood of the *act* of faith, but of *Christ* the *object* of faith; for the act of faith is not imputed for righteousness, but that which faith lays hold of, *i.e.*, the obedience of Christ, which is the object about which the act of faith is conversant. And thus, verse 3. it is said, *Abraham believed God, and it was counted unto him for righteousness.** Where *Christ* must necessarily be understood by the *it*, that was counted unto him for righteousness. As is plain from the three last verses of the chapter; where it is said, *Now it was not written for his sake alone, that it was imputed unto him; but for us also, to whom it shall be imputed, if we believe on him that raised up Jesus our Lord from the dead; who was*

---

†"Faith justifies a sinner in the sight of God, not because of those other graces, which do always accompany it, or of good works, that are the fruits of it, Gal. iii.11.; nor as if the grace of faith, or any act thereof, were imputed to him for justification, Rom. iv.5.; but only as it is an instrument, by which he receiveth and applieth Christ and his righteousness, John i.12." Larger Cat. Q. 73.

*It is exceeding observable, that it is not said, Abraham left his country, quitted his idolatry, abandoned his relations, or that he offered his son, and it was imputed to him for righteousness; but that Abraham believed God, and IT *was counted to him for righteousness*. Gen. xv.6.; which shews the peculiar dignity and excellency of faith. It is as singularly fitted and suited to take hold of Christ, and his righteousness, as a beggar's hand to receive an alms.

delivered for our offences, and raised again for our justification. Since it was the same *it* that was imputed unto *Abraham*, that shall be imputed unto *us*; hence it appears, that it was not the *act* of *Abraham's* faith that was imputed unto *him* for righteousness; because it is not the *act* of his faith that is imputed unto us. But it was the *object* that his faith looked to, the complete obedience of a crucified and risen *Jesus*, that was imputed unto him for righteousness; and that shall be imputed unto *us*, if we, having the same faith that he had, believe as he did, in Christ for justification, and in God as justifying in, and through him. For, it is *by the obedience of* this *one*, that *Abraham*, and all true *believers*, from the beginning of the world to the end thereof, even all the *many* that shall be saved, are *made righteous*, as chap. v.19. But, as to be justified by *faith*, in *this sense*, is the same as to be justified by the *righteousness* of Christ, and so respects the *matter* of justification, which I have spoken of under the first general; so I shall pass it here, where I am treating of the *manner* of justification, which, with respect to ourselves, is by *faith*, as *subjectively* and not *objectively* taken: and I shall attend to the manner of justification by *faith*, as *inherent* in, and *acted* by the soul; or shew how, or in what respect, the justification of a sinner is thus by faith. And,

1. It is by *faith*, as it stands opposed to *works*. As saith the apostle, Rom. iii.28. *Therefore we conclude, that a man is justified by faith, without the deeds of the law.* The justification of a sinner is by faith *alone*, not by faith and works *together;* but by faith, *exclusive* of all works, both before and after faith is wrought in the soul. Works done before faith can have no influence into justification; since *by the deeds of the law, no flesh can be justified in* God's *sight.* And works done after believing, are done for no such end, as to make the person righteous before God; nor do they add a whit to his justification in his sight. So that it is by faith *alone* that a sinner enters into a justified state. Thus, Rom. iv.5. *To him that worketh not, but* BELIEVETH *on him that justifieth the ungodly, his faith is counted for righteousness.* It is, as if he should say, that is a justified man, that doth no good *works*, nothing at all to obtain it; but *believeth* on *Christ*, for complete pardon, righteousness, and life; and on *God*, as justifying, only in and through him, even the *ungodly.* For, as God in justifying as sinner, through the blood and righteousness of Christ, considers that soul as in itself *ungodly*; so the soul, when it acts faith for justification, sees nothing in itself but *ungodliness:* and under this consideration, of its being a *sinner* and *ungodly*, looks out of itself, unto *Christ*, and unto *God* in him, for all its

justification and salvation.——Thus the justification of a sinner is by faith alone; *i.e.*, by *faith*, without *works*. And the apostle gives the reasons of it, Rom. iv.16. *Therefore it is of faith, that it might be by grace, to the end the promise might be sure to all the seed.* It is of *faith, i.e.*, of faith *alone*; (empty-handed faith, that doth nothing at all for justification, but merely receives it as a free gift) that it might be by *grace*; that God's free grace might have the whole glory of justification; and all creature boasting be for ever excluded.—And it is likewise thus of faith, that the promise might be *sure* to all the seed. If the promise of justification and life, had in the least depended upon the good works of the creature, it could never have been sure; but as it stands wholly upon grace, absolute grace, and is merely received by faith alone, so it stands *sure*, inviolably sure to all the *seed*, to all the heirs of promise, through all time, and unto all eternity.—Thus the justification of a sinner is by faith, as it stands opposed to works, as to the *manner* of it; or the manner of the soul's possessing Christ's righteousness.

2. It is by *faith*, as faith is that grace which is *appointed* of God, to *receive* justification and life from him. Thus Mark xvi.15, 16. *Go ye into all the world, and preach the gospel to every creature. He that believeth, shall be saved; but he that believeth not, shall be damned.* And John iii.36. *He that believeth on the Son, hath everlasting life: and he that believeth not the Son, shall not see life; but the wrath of God abideth on him.* And *we*, saith the apostle, *have believed in Jesus Christ, that we might be justified by the faith of Christ*; and this we did, says he, as *knowing that a man is not justified by the works of the law, but by the faith of Jesus Christ;* or, as knowing that faith is that grace, which God hath *appointed* to receive justification, Gal. ii.16. Again,

3. The justification of a sinner is by *faith*, as God *imputes* the righteousness of his Son, and *declares* the imputation thereof, in his *word*, unto every *believer*, for his complete *justification*. Thus the righteousness of Christ is said to be *unto, and upon all them that believe, without difference*, Rom. iii.22. *And by him all that believe, are* (declared to be) *justified from all things, from which they could not be justified by the law of Moses*, Acts xiii.39. There is not a believer in the world, that looks to, receives, and depends upon the righteousness of Christ alone, for justification before God, but God imputes it to him, and justifies him, completely therein: For it is unto, and upon all them that believe, without difference. One believer is not *more*, and another *less* justified; because, though there may be a great deal of difference between the *faith* of one and of another, in respect of

degree; yet all that have faith of the right *kind*, as they *receive* the same *righteousness*, the righteousness of Christ, for their whole and entire righteousness before God; so he *imputes* it to them, as such, and completely justifies them all equally, and alike therein. They are all, in this respect, *complete in Christ*; so complete, that nothing can be added to it, to make their justification more *full*, Col. ii.10. And as all believers are *completely* justified in Christ, by the free-grace, and according to the strict justice of God; so in him they are *everlastingly* justified. They *stand* immoveably, unchangeably, and eternally in the *grace* of justification, Rom. v.2. *They are so passed from death to life, that they shall never come into condemnation*, John, v.14. Though in themselves they are sinners, both by nature and practice; yet, as God doth not impute their sins, but the righteousness of his Son to them, for their complete justification; so they have life, everlasting life, in this respect.—But as I shall have occasion to speak more fully of *this*, under the next head; so I shall add no more here.—And thus much shall suffice for the second general, the *manner* of justification, as with respect unto *God*, it is by *imputation*; and with respect to *ourselves*, by *faith*.

❊∞∞❊∞∞❊∞∞❊∞∞❊∞∞❊∞∞❊∞∞❊∞∞❊∞∞❊∞∞❊

S E C T. III.

Of the TIME *of Justification.*

Rom. iv.25. iii.26. 1 Tim. iii.16.

He was delivered for our offences, and raised again for our justification.—
God is just, and the justifier of him that believeth in Jesus.—God was
justified in the Spirit.

THE next thing proposed to be considered, was, The *time* of justification.
As justification is God's act, so it is to be considered, either as
immanent, or *transient*, and timed accordingly.

1. As *immanent*, or an act of God's will, that always abideth the same
in his divine mind, from eternity to eternity: and so it was from *everlasting*;
as 2 Cor. v. 19. *God was in Christ*, (who can tell how early? Surely he was
in him, by his eternal counsel, will, and covenant) *reconciling the world*
unto himself, not imputing their trespasses unto them.

2. The act of justification is to be considered as *transient*; or, as it is an
act of God that passeth upon the creature in *time.** And as such, admits of
a two-fold consideration.

(1.) As Passing upon the whole *body* of the *elect* together, and at once,
in *Christ* their *head* and *representative.* And so the *time* of it was when
Christ, our Surety, made full *payment* of all the debts of his people, and
received a full *acquittance*, or a full and open discharge, in their *name* and
room. For, he *was delivered for our offences, and raised again for our*
justification, Rom. iv.25. As he died, as a *public* person, for our sins; so, as
a *public* person, he was raised again for our justification. When God the
Father *raised* him from the *dead*, he thereby did openly *discharge* him from
all our sins, which before lay upon him; and in *his* discharge, *we* were
discharged likewise. *He* was discharged for *us*, and *we* were discharged in

---

*"Though, from eternity, God decreed to justify all the elect; yet they are not
actually justified, until the Holy Spirit doth, in due time, apply Christ, and his
righteousness, unto them, 1 Pet. i.2, 19, 20. Rom. viii.30. Gal. ii.16. Tit. iii.4, 5, 6,
7." Conf. chap. xi.4.

him, as he was our great *representative*. And thus the apostle sounds his triumphant challenge, to all the enemies of God's people, to bring ought against them, if they can, Rom. viii.33, 34. *Who shall lay any thing to the charge of God's elect? It is God that justifieth. Who is he that condemneth? It is Christ that died; yea, rather, that is risen again.* As the *act* of God *justifying*, gives *being* to, and is the *foundation* of our *justification*; so, he first *sounds* his triumph *here*, and answers all the charges which might be brought with this, *It is God that justifieth:* and then he proceeds, *It is Christ that died; yea, rather, that is risen again.* So that, by Christ's *death* and *resurrection*, and at the *time* thereof, the whole *body* of the *elect*, as such, had a full *discharge*, a complete *justification*, in *Christ* their *Head.** But,

(2.) Justification, as a *transient* act, is to be considered, as passing upon every individual *person* of God's chosen; and so the *time* of it is, when the soul is first enabled to *believe in Jesus. For, with the heart man believeth unto righteousness*, Rom. x.10. And God is *just, and the justifier of him that believeth in Jesus,* chap. iii.26. For, notwithstanding the *secret* state of an elect person God-ward, before *believing*, is a state of *peace* and favour, as he has a *secret* interest in God's justifying *act*, and in Christ's full *discharge*; yet his *open* state, as in *himself*, related to old Adam, and the *first* covenant, is a state of law-charge, and so of wrath and condemnation. He is *of the works of the law*, and as a law-breaker, is under the *curse*; as *the wrath of God,* in his holy, righteous law, *is revealed from heaven against all unrighteousness of men.* He is in the same common state with all the children of Adam, of whom it is said, *there is none righteous, no not one;* and so, a child *of wrath by nature, even as others.* And there is no way, appointed of God, whereby he can pass from this *open* state of *wrath*, and *condemnation* by the law, into an *open* state of *justification* by grace, but by

---

*Jesus Christ being once justified himself, Isa. l.8. 1 Tim. iii.16.; so all his people are justified in him; and God is just in doing so, Rom. iii.26. Christ died as a public representative for the iniquities of his people, Isa. liii.11.; and the sacrifice and oblation he offered up was of a sweet-smelling savour unto God; Eph. v.2. And therefore, Jehovah declares, that he is not only *well-pleased for his righteousness sake*, Isa. xlii.21.; but that he is *near to justify him*, Isa. l.8.; yea, that he is *justified in the Spirit,* 1 Tim. iii.16.: and consequently Christ's resurrection, ascension, session at his Father's right hand, intercession for his people, and having all judgment committed to him, is an evidence that all his people are virtually justified in him as their head, and shall all rise and reign with him in due time.

faith in Christ: for *he that believeth on the Son, hath everlasting life,* the life of *justification; and he that believeth not the Son, shall not see life, but the wrath of God abideth on him,* John iii.36. So that, according to the *declaration* of God, in his *word,* by which he will *judge* all men at the last day, no person is in a *justified* state, but he that *believeth* in Jesus. And therefore, the *time* of justification, as applied to a particular *person,* or as God's justifying *act,* passeth upon a sinner, in the declaration of his *word,* and is brought home to the *conscience,* is when the soul *believes;* or, when being warned of its misery, and acquainted with its remedy, it first flees for refuge, from the wrath to come, to lay hold upon Christ, the hope set before it. And in this sense, *all that believe,* and none but they, *are justified from all things, from which they could not be justified by the law of Moses.*

❇ ∞∞∞∞ ❇ ∞∞∞∞ ❇ ∞∞∞∞ ❇ ∞∞∞∞ ❇ ∞∞∞∞ ❇ ∞∞∞∞ ❇

S E C T. IV.

Of the EFFECT *of Justification.*

Rom. v.1. iv.7. 2 Cor. v.14.

Being justified, by faith we have peace with God, through our Lord Jesus
Christ.—Blessed are they whose iniquities are forgiven.—The love of
Christ, who died for us, constraineth us to live unto him.

THE next thing I am to consider, is, the *effect* of *justification* with respect
to the soul. And this is three-fold; and has respect, 1. Unto the soul's
peace. 2. Unto its state. 3. Unto its obedience, To each of these, a little
in order. And,

 1. The *effect* of *justification,* to a justified soul, is *peace.* As Rom. v.1.
Therefore, being justified, by faith we have peace with God, through our
Lord Jesus Christ. As Christ, by his death, made peace with God for poor
sinners, and as God the Father declared himself to be *the God of peace,*
when he *brought again from the dead the Lord Jesus, that great Shepherd*
of the sheep, through the blood of the everlasting covenant; so this complete
and everlasting peace, is declared, and particularly applied to the soul, by
the blessed Spirit of God, when it is enabled to believe in Christ for
justification. Peace with God was the legacy our departing Lord left with his
people, which was confirmed by the death of the testator. Thus, John xiv.27.
Peace, says he, *I leave with you; my peace I give unto you: let not your*
heart be troubled, neither let it be afraid. It is as if he should say, "My dear
disciple, I am just a going to leave you, just upon the point of finishing all
that work which the Father gave me to do in the world, for your salvation:
but when I depart, I will leave *peace* with you, *my* peace; that peace with
God, I shall make by the blood of my cross, I *give* unto you. I do not give
it *partially, conditionally*, and *precariously*; I do not give and take, as the
world doth; but my peace I give unto you *wholly, absolutely,* and *irrevers-*
ibly: therefore, *let not your heart be troubled, neither let it be afraid.* Do not
be troubled that I am going to leave you, as to my bodily presence; for, *it*
is expedient for you, that I go away: I go to prepare a place for you. When,
as your High-Priest, I have done the work of making peace for you on earth,

I have still another work to do for you in heaven; I must carry my peace-making blood, into *the holiest of all*, and sprinkle it before the face of God; and so *reconcile* that holy place, and make room for you to come thither; or thereby, *prepare* those mansions, those abiding places in glory, which are appointed for you. And therefore, *let not your heart be troubled*, since my departure from you is so much for your advantage; *neither let it be afraid*, for as I *made* peace for you, by my death on the cross, so I will *maintain* it for you, by my life on the throne: you need not be afraid that there should be any after-breach between God and you, nor fear the least flaw being made in that peace with God, which I give unto you." And as this complete and everlasting peace with God, was made by Christ, and is given to his people; so it is applied, by the blessed Spirit, to every believer in particular; as our Lord promised, in the preceeding verse: *But*, says he, *the Comforter, which is the Holy Ghost, whom the Father will send in my name, he shall teach you all things, and bring all things to your rememberance, whatsoever I have said unto you.* As this verse stands *connected* with the *former*, we may take the scope of our Lord's words thus; "Though I am going to leave you, *I will not leave you comfortless; I leave peace with you, I give peace to you*; and I will give you the *Comforter, whom the Father will send in my name*, to open this peace to your understandings, to apply it to your hearts, and bring it to your rememberance, to your unspeakable joy, while passing through a world of trials." And accordingly, when the Spirit of God has revealed the obedience of Christ to the soul, and enabled it to act faith thereon, for justification, he applies the blood of Christ to that soul, by bearing witness to it, of its own particular *interest* in the death of Jesus, and in that *peace* with God, made by his blood; and hereby gives it *peace* of conscience; even *true, solid, lasting peace*, that will abide through *life*, through *death*, at *judgment*, and to *eternity*.† And this peace, is peculiar to a *justified* soul, and a proper *effect* of *justification*.

---

†Though our author here very strongly affirms the permanency of that peace which a justified person has with God, through the blood of Christ; yet he is not to be understood, as asserting, that the peace of a justified person is never interrupted in a present life, which is very frequently the case, through the prevailancy of the remains of inherent corruption, especially with exercised Christians: he only means, that it is such a peace as the grounds and foundation of it cannot be utterly taken away, being Christ's legacy bequeathed to them; because he rests in his love, and *his gifts* and *callings are without repentance.*

An *unjustified* soul, indeed, may have some kind of *peace* of conscience, while he works for life, goes about to establish his own righteousness, and quiets his conscience with his own obedience, either present, or resolved on for the future. But this is a *false* peace; conscience is but lulled asleep, and not truly pacified: *as many as are of the works of the law*, that work to make themselves righteous before God, *are under the curse*, Gal. iii.10.; and therefore must be wicked persons in God's account: and *there is no peace to the wicked, saith my God*, Isa. lvii.21. *The way of peace they have not known*, Rom. iii.17. They may cry. *Peace, peace* to themselves; but *sudden destruction* shall come upon them. This miserable, delusive *peace*, cannot stand the test of God's holy law and strict justice, nor abide the storms of his indignation, which shall come down *upon every soul of man that doth evil,* that is in an unrighteous, unjustified state. The storm of God's wrath, that will meet such a soul at death, will sweep away all this false peace; and nothing but terrors will then surround it. Conscience, that was once lulled asleep, by a false apprehension of the creature's *goodness*, as if sufficient to make its *peace* with God, will then awake, and, like an enraged lion, gnaw and torment the soul for ever; when, upon the fullest *conviction*, though too late for all *remedy*, it shall see, that nothing could *make* peace with God, for a sinner, nor *give* peace to it, but the *blood and righteousness* of Christ. And thus the poor soul, being stript *naked* of all its own righteousness and peace, that *hiding-place*, whither it had fled for shelter, that *refuge of lies*, with which it had been deceived, shall stand exposed to all the curses of God's righteous *law*, and the amazing storm of his vindictive wrath, which shall break-forth upon it thereby, and *drown* it in eternal *perdition*. For, the *waters* of God's indignation, *shall overflow the hiding-place* of a sinner's own righteousness, *and sweep away the refuge of lies*, its false peace, built thereupon, and drive away the naked soul, like an irresistible *torment,* into the bottomless *gulf* of remediless *torment*, Isa. xxviii.17, 18.

But he that *believeth* on *Christ*, the *foundation, God has laid in Zion, shall never be confounded*, verse 10. with 1 Pet. ii.6. He that hath *Christ* for all his righteousness and peace, hath such a *righteousness,* such a *peace*, that shall *abide* for ever. That man, that is *justified* by faith, is a *perfect* man, an *upright* man, in God's account; and concerning him, the Psalmist says, *Mark the perfect man, and behold the upright; for the end of that man is peace,* Psalm xxxvii.37. And as it is the happiness of the righteous man to *enter into peace*, when he dies, Isa. lvii.7.; so is it his privilege to have peace while he lives, and that even in the midst of *tribulation*; in the midst of outward *troubles*, he hath inward peace, John xvi.33.

As for that *false* peace, which the *wicked* have in this world, as it shall perish at last, so it is often broken now, by the flashes of God's *law* in the conscience; which are as many earnests of that approaching storm of his fiery *indignation*, which shall quickly overtake them. And, alas! for these miserable souls, when under pressing afflictions, how are they like the *troubled sea, that cannot rest, whose waters cast up mire and dirt?*—But as for the *righteous* man, he hath *peace*, even in the most trying circumstances; such peace, that the world can neither give, nor take, nor yet can understand. That *peace of God*, that *keeps his heart and mind, through Christ Jesus, passeth all the understanding* of the natural man, Phil. iv.7. A justified soul, having his *feet*, his faith, *shod with the preparation of the gospel of peace,* having *peace with God, through Jesus Christ*, is well prepared to pass securely through a *thorny* world. Such as one may safely tread upon all the briers of the wilderness, without fear of danger, since his *shoes* are like *iron and brass*, that will even turn a *thorn*, Eph. vi.15. Deut. xxxiii.25.—And, in a word, there is nothing can *hurt* that soul, who, being *justified* by faith, has *peace* with God, neither in this world, nor that to come. So great is the privilege of that *peace*, which is the *effect* of *justification!* Again,

2. The *effect* of *justification*, with respect to the soul, may be considered, with regard to its *state*. And the state of a *justified* soul, is a state of *blessedness*. As soon as ever the soul is enabled to believe in Christ, for justification, and in God, as justifying in and through him, it passes *from death unto life*, John, v.24. It is delivered from the *curse* of the law, and all the *blessings*, both of the law and gospel come upon it. As *Christ has redeemed* it *from the curse of the law; so the blessing of Abraham, comes upon it through faith*, Gal. iii.13, 14. And thus the apostle, speaking of a *justified* state, Rom. iv.5. calls it a state of *blessedness*, verses 6, 7, 8. *Even as David also describeth the blessedness of the man, unto whom God imputeth righteousness without works, saying, Blessed are they whose iniquities are forgiven, and whose sins are covered. Blessed is the man to whom the Lord will not impute sin:* and verse 9. *Cometh this blessedness then upon the circumcision only, or upon the uncircumcision also?*—Thus it appears, that a *justified* state, is a state of *blessedness*.

The state of an *unjustified* soul is a state of *wrath*; and such an one is under the *curse* wherever he is, or whatever he does: as Deut. xxviii.16, 17,

18, 19. The Lord has not only threatened to curse him, by sending upon him *vexation and rebuke*, as verse 20.; but even to *curse his blessings* his outward enjoyments, as Mal. ii.2.

But, on the contrary, a *justified* soul is *blessed* in all conditions; his enjoyments are *blessings* to him, and so are his afflictions. *All things are his*, whether comforts or crosses, life or death; *all work together for his good,* and *turn to his salvation,* 1 Cor. iii.22. Rom. viii.28. His very *sufferings* are *gifts* of divine favour, Phil. i.29. And he has reason to *rejoice* even when he *falls into divers temptations*; because of that present and eternal advantage he shall reap thereby, and that peculiar *blessedness*, which attends him therein, James i.2,—12. *A justified* soul passes on from *blessing* to *blessing*, in every changing providence; for every *change* opens to him a new scene of *blessedness*, to make his enjoyments thereof more full. He is *blessed* in prosperity, and *blessed* in adversity; and God over-rules both for his present and eternal advantage, and especially his *afflictions*, to increase his grace, and prepare him for his crown: so that his short-lived *afflictions*, are but *light*; since, as God works upon *him* by them, they *work for him, a far more exceeding, and eternal weight of glory,* 2 Cor. iv.17. A justified soul has a right to all *blessedness* now; and shall have the full enjoyment of all *blessedness* hereafter. As he is now delivered from the *curse*, and fully *blest*, even in those very *afflictions* which, in their own nature, are the fruits of the *curse*; so, when God has wrought all that good for him, which was designed by them, he shall be delivered from the very *being* of these grieving things. There shall be no grieving briar, nor pricking thorn, no sin, sorrow, nor death, to disturb that rest, or destroy that life of *blessedness*, which is reserved for him in the state of glory, in the vision of God and of the Lamb for ever: as Rev. xxi.4. *And God shall wipe away all tears from their eyes; and there shall be no more death, neither sorrow, nor crying; neither shall there be any pain: for the former things are passed away.—And there shall be no more curse; but the throne of God and of the Lamb shall be in it; and his servants shall serve him. And they shall see his face; and his Name shall be in their foreheads. And there shall be no night there; and they need no candle, neither light of the sun; for the Lord God giveth them light: and they shall reign for ever and ever,* chap. xxii.3, 4, 5.

Thus the justified ones, as they are *blest* at all times, shall be *blest* to all eternity. And to acquaint them with their state of blessedness, to comfort their hearts under their present troubles, and in the expectation of their future bliss, the Lord bid the prophet, *say unto the righteous,* that *it shall be* *well with him,* Isa. iii.10. It shall be *well* with him in *life; well* with him at *death*; *well* with him at *judgment*; and it shall be *well* with him for *ever.*—It shall be *well* with him in *life*; for, *blessed is the man that trusteth in the* LORD, *and whose hope the* LORD *is*, Jer. xvii.7, 8.—It shall be *well* with him at *death*; for, *blessed are the dead that die in the* LORD, Rev. xiv.13.—It shall be *well* with him at *judgment*; for then he shall be openly pronounced *blessed*; and as such admitted into endless life, or into the inconceivable *blessedness* of *eternal life*; and so it shall be *well* with him for *ever*, Mat. xxv.34,—46.——Thus *blessed* is the righteous man! Thus *well* shall it be with him! *But wo unto the wicked; for it shall be ill with him:* his state, in all respect, is just the reverse. How distinguishing then is the favour, how great the privilege of that *blessedness* of *state,* which is the *effect* of *justification!** But,

---

*The privileges and benefits of these persons, who have the Lord to be their righteousness, are very many.—They are not only pardoned, but justified; and their pardon is not only a fruit of mercy, but an act of justice; God is Just in justifying, Rom. iii.25, 26.—The justified persons are redeemed from the curse, by Christ's being made a curse for them, Gal. iii.13.—These who are interested in Christ's righteousness, are delivered from wrath: because he was delivered up to sufferings and death, Rom. viii.32. he can deliver from wrath, 1 Thess. i.10.—These who are clothed with Christ's righteousness, have a sure and permanent state of justification; *There is no condemnation to them*, Rom. viii.1.—Justified persons have a sure and firm standing in the grace and favour of God, Rom. v.2.—These to whom Christ is made righteousness, do also receive the holy Spirit, Tit. iii.5, 6.—The prayers of justified persons are acceptable to, and powerful with God, because the Spirit encourages them to, and assists them in prayer, Prov. xv.8. *The prayer of the upright is God's delight. The Spirit also helpeth our infirmities with groanings which cannot be uttered,* Rom. viii.26.—All the outward and temporal mercies of justified persons are heightened and sweetened to them, by the spring from whence they flow, and they have a new relish. *He delivered me,* says David, *because he delighted in me,* Psalm xviii.19. *In love to my soul,* says Hezekiah, *he hath delivered me from the pit of corruption, having cast all my sins behind his back,* Isa. xxxviii.17.—Justified persons enjoy their temporal favours by God's promise, Heb. xi.9.; and have a spiritual right to them by the death of Christ, *who is the heir of all things,* Heb. i.2.—All the afflictions of justified persons *work for their good,* Rom. viii.28. They are often allayed and mitigated, Ezra ix.13.; they spring from God's care of them, Heb. xii.6, 7.; they are medicinal to them, Isa. i.25.; they are purifying to them, Heb. xii.10, 11.; they are but short and momentary, 2 Cor. 4, 17.—Death

3. In the last place, I am to consider, the *effect* of *justification*, as it respects the soul's *obedience*. And as a *justified* soul is saved from wrath, and has peace with God, as it is redeemed from the curse, and brought into a state of blessedness; so it is delivered from *servile,* and enabled to yield *filial* obedience. *It is no more a servant, but a Son*; and obeys its Father, as *an heir of God through Christ,* Gal. iv.7. As a *dear child*, it becomes a *follower of God, and walks in love, as Christ also has loved it, and given himself for it,* Eph. v.1, 2. *The love of God shed abroad in the heart* of a poor sinner, *justified* by his grace, forms its own image there, and enables the soul to *love* God again, who has *first loved* it; and to shew this love, in *keeping his commandments,* Rom. v.5. 1 John iv.19. and v.3. *The love of Christ constrains it, to live unto him, who died for it, and rose again for our justification,* 2 Cor. v.14, 15.

An *unjustified* soul, as it is under the servitude of the law, so it is acted by *the spirit of bondage*; and all its obedience to God, springs from a slavish *fear* of his *wrath*; and the main *end* thereof is self-preservation and deliverance. And therefore, notwithstanding all that *fair shew,* which it makes *in the flesh,* all its *legal* obedience which looks so specious in its own and others eyes, God will call it *an empty vine, that brings* forth no *fruit* unto *him,* but all unto *itself,* Hos. x.1.

But it is quite otherwise with a *justified* soul; such an one is *under grace,* and is acted by *the Spirit of adoption,* which gives him glorious freedom, and abundant liberty to worship and serve God, as his own Father in Christ, from a principle of *love* and *gratitude*, for that great love manifested to him, and that full salvation bestowed upon him; and the main *end* of his obedience is to *glorify* his Father which is in heaven. And thus

---

to justified persons, who are clothed with Christ's righteousness, is of great advantage; it is theirs, 1 Cor. iii.22. and to them *great gain,* Phil. i.21.—Justified persons have a blessed and glorious resurrection secured to them in Christ their head; for, as they *die in the Lord,* Rom. xiv.8.; so they shall be made *alive in Christ* 1 Cor. xv.21, 22. and *raised up unto eternal life,* John vi.54.—In a word, justified persons will stand assoiled and acquit at the last day, because the Judge is their friend, Acts xvii.31. Isa. lviii.11. and the kindly intimation will be issued forth, *Come, ye blessed of my Father, inherit the kingdom prepared for you, from the foundation of the world,* Matth. xxv.34.—O how many are the privileges and inconceivably great the blessedness of those who are interested in the finished righteousness of the adorable Redeemer!

the *justified* soul, in his obedience, *brings forth fruit unto God:* as saith the apostle, Rom. vii.4. *Wherefore, my brethren, ye also are become dead to the law by the body of Christ, that ye should be married unto another, even to him who is raised from the dead, that we should bring forth fruit unto God.* To *bring froth fruit unto God,* is such a proper *effect* of justification, that it is impossible it should be found in an *unjustified* soul. And therefore the apostle sets forth the deliverance of the *justified* ones, from the bondage of the *law*, as a covenant of works, and so from *servile obedience* to it, by a woman's being *freed from the law of her husband, when he is dead*; and their new obligation to gospel-obedience, or to serve the *law* of God *in the newness of the Spirit*, by the loosed woman's being *married to another man*, verses 2, 3. As is evident by his applying, verse 4. what he had said in the former: *Wherefore my brethren, ye also are become dead to the law by the body of Christ*; q.d. You are delivered from the bondage and servitude of the law, by Christ's fulfilling its requirements for you, and enduring its penalties; by which the law is become *dead* to *you*, and you to *it*. The *law*, as it is a covenant of works, that requires doing for life, and threatens death upon disobedience, has no more obedience to require of *you*, nor you to yield to *it*, than a *dead* man has to require of her that was formerly his *wife*; nor than *she* has to yield to him that was formerly her *husband*, when once the relation is broken. And then follows, *That ye might be married to another, even to him who is raised from the dead, that we might bring forth fruit unto God*; q.d. You were thus *freed* from the *law*, that you might be *married* unto *Christ*, as risen from the dead; that you might be one, everlastingly one with him, your living head: and so being completely justified, in and through him, you might share with him, in the power of his endless life; and under the plenitude of his life and blessedness, be richly influenced *to bring forth fruit unto God.*

Thus the *justified* ones are fruitful in *new* obedience: as they *now* regard the *glory* of that God that has justified them, as the *end* of all their *obedience*; so they receive his *law*, from their *husband*, Christ, as the *rule* of it, and love it as such, exceedingly; and thus *serving the law of God, in the newness of the Spirit, and not in the oldness of the letter*, or in the grace of the *gospel*, and not in the terror of the *law*, they *bring forth fruit unto God,* verse 6.

And, by the way, I look upon this, to be the discriminating *difference* between a *regenerate* and an *unregenerate* soul. The one obeys as a *slave*; and mainly regards his own *safety* therein; the other obeys as a *Son*, and the *glory* of God is the chief *end* of his *obedience:* or, the one lives unto *himself*, brings forth fruit unto *himself*; the other lives unto *God*, and brings forth fruit unto *him*. Thus, Rom. xiv.7. *For none of us liveth to himself*, [*i.e.*, none of us who have the life of justification bestowed on us, and the life of sanctification, or the new-creature life wrought in us] *and no man* [*i.e.*, none of us] *dieth to himself: But whether we live, we live unto the Lord; or whether we die, we die unto the Lord: whether we live therefore or die, we are the Lord's.* And thus, when he had said of himself, and the rest of the saints, whom he stiles, *they which live*, [*i.e.*, a life of justification, and a life of sanctification, as the effect of Christ's death and resurrection] that *the love of Christ constrained them, that they should not henceforth live unto themselves,* in their conversation, *but unto him who died for them, and rose again,* 2 Cor. v.14, 15. he adds, verse 16. *Wherefore henceforth know we no man after the flesh*; that is, we *approve* of no man, as a *living* man, as a man in *Christ*, a *justified* and *sanctified* man, after the *flesh*, or the *first* life: *Yea,* says he, *though we have known Christ after the flesh, yet now henceforth know we him no more*; q.d. We do not converse with Christ now, as we once did in the days of his flesh; but as risen from the dead to a new *life* and glory: and those who are *risen* with Christ, live a new *life* unto God, by virtue of his *resurrection*; and these are the men we *know* and approve of, as living, believing, justified, and sanctified men. As it follows, verse 17. *Therefore if any man be in Christ,* [*i.e.*, a believer in him, and so a justified man] *he is a new creature*; [*i.e.*, a sanctified man, that lives a new life unto God] *old things are past away; behold, all things are become new.* With such an one, *old dependances* for life, *old enjoyments*, and *old ends* in obedience, are past away; and all things are become *new*: his dependance for life upon Christ, and God in him, are *new*; his enjoyments of God, Christ, his people, word, and ordinances, are *new*; and his life unto God, in obedience, is *new*; or what he never experienced before he was created a new in Christ Jesus.—Thus it appears, that *new* obedience, the soul's living unto *God*, or bringing forth fruit unto *him*, is proper unto a *justified* and *regenerate* man, and demonstrative of his *justified* state, and of his being *a new creature*; since all *unjustified unregenerate* souls live unto *themselves*. But, to go on.

     As new *obedience* is a proper *effect* of *justification*, and properly belongs to the justified soul, so his privilege, as such, is exceeding great; in that all his works are *accepted*. Those who are washed from their sins in Christ's blood, and clothed with his righteousness, are *made kings and priests unto God, to offer up spiritual sacrifices, acceptable to God by Jesus Christ,* Rev. i.5, 6. with 1 Pet. ii.5. *The grace of God, which bringeth salvation,* efficaciously *teacheth* the saved ones, *that denying ungodliness and worldly lusts,* they *should live soberly, righteously, and godly, in this present world,* Tit. ii.12. They *maintain good works, for necessary uses, that they may be profitable* unto others, and that they themselves, *may not be unfruitful,* Tit. iii.8, 14.; and chiefly, that thereby they might *glorify God;* to which they are exhorted, Phil. i.27. *Only let your conversation be as it becometh the gospel of Christ:* q.d. You saints, have nothing else to do in the world, but to live unto God, to glorify him, by a conversation becoming the gospel of Christ; which declares your complete justification, and secures your eternal salvation.—Thus the saints are exhorted to *do* good works, and thus they *perform* them. And all their service is *acceptable* to God, in point of *filial* obedience, though not in point of *justifying* righteousness. As for this end, they do not perform good works; so, blessed be God, for this end they do not need them. No; they have a complete justifying righteousness, wrought out by Christ, a glorious robe, which they themselves have no hand in, nor put the least finger to prepare; and are so completely justified in Christ, that nothing can be added to it, to make their justification more *full.* But though none of their good works go to the stock of their *justification;* yet all of them go to the treasure of their filial *obedience;* and are *acceptable* to God, by Jesus Christ, and shall be openly *rewarded* at his next appearing. And both the *acceptableness* of the saints service to God, and the *advantage* they themselves shall reap thereby, are proposed to them, as encouragements to be abundant and constant in the performance of good works.

Thus, Heb. xiii.15, 16. *By him therefore let us offer the sacrifice of praise to God continually; that is, the fruit of our lips, giving thanks to his name. But to do good, and to communicate forget not, for with such sacrifices God is well-pleased.—And he that in these things serveth Christ, is acceptable to God,* Rom. xiv.18.; that is, in point of *obedience.* And therefore the apostle, for himself, and in the name of the rest of the apostles, *beseecheth* the saints, the brethren, whose persons were already *made accepted in the Beloved,* in point of *righteousness* before God, and *exhorts them by the Lord Jesus, that as* they had *received of* them *how they ought to walk, and to please God,* i.e., in point of obedience, so they *would abound more and more,* 1 Thess. iv.1.: q.d. Since the good works, the filial *obedience* of you *justified* ones, are so *acceptable* by Christ unto God your

Father; see that you labour to be abundant and constant therein. And as the *acceptableness* of the saints to God, is proposed as an encouragement to their filial obedience; so likewise the *advantage* which they themselves shall reap thereby.

As, 1 Cor. xv.58, 59. *Wherefore, my beloved brethren, be stedfast, unmoveable, always abounding in the work of the Lord; forasmuch as ye know that your labour is not in vain in the Lord.* No; those whose *persons* are accepted in Christ, and their *obedience* accepted through him, shall have all their good works *rewarded*, by the same *grace,* that enabled them to the performance thereof. These shall find, that *in keeping* God's *commandments there is great reward*, Psalm xix.11.

The service of God carries its own reward in it now; that peace of conscience, that joy in the Holy Ghost, that life of the divine favour, that honour God puts upon his people, in his appearances for them, and those fore-tastes of glory, they are favoured with, while walking with him, in the *obedience* of children, are a *reward* so great, that none can either know or enjoy, but those who are brought into *the glorious liberty of the sons of God.* But, O the exceeding greatness of that *reward*, that is reserved for them in the day of Christ! As all their services are now accepted; so they shall then appear to be so, by their being openly *rewarded*.

There is none of their service, though so small as the giving *of a cup of cold water to a disciple, in the name of a disciple,* that *shall in any wise lose its reward,* Mat. x. 41, 42. All their obedience, both in heart and life, shall *be found unto praise, honour, and glory, at the appearing of Jesus Christ,* 1 Pet. i.7. *And all the churches shall know,* saith our Lord, *that I am he that searcheth the reins and hearts; and I will give unto every one of you according to your works*, Rev. ii.23. *To him that overcometh,* says he, *will I grant to sit with me in my throne, as I also overcame and am set down with my Father in his throne,* chap. iii.21. *And behold, I come quickly, and my reward is with me; to give every man according as his works shall be,* chap. xxii.12.

And, in short, the chief design of our Lord, in what he ordered his servant John, to write to the Asiatick churches, where he commends their obedience, and reproves what was wanted therein, was, to stir them up to a *zealous* performance of good *works*; and the *motive* he used hereto was, that the *crown* of glory which he would give unto them, as the *reward* of their obedience, at his appearing and kingdom; which, in greatness, should be proportioned, according to the *degree* of their *services* done for him in the present state.

He acquaints them with those special *favours*, those particular *honours* which he had in reserve for those of his *servants*, who had most distinguished themselves in his *service*. And hence will arise all those different degrees of *glory*, in which the saints shall shine, *at the resurrection of the just*. They will all be bright and glorious, and *shine as the stars for ever and ever;* and yet *as one star differeth from another star in glory, so shall it be in the resurrection of the dead,* 1 Cor. xv.41, 42. As the *stars* now shine with different *glories*, so shall the *saints* then: for those who have *done* and *suffered* most for Christ, in this life, shall have an higher sphere of *glory*, and shine with a superior *brightness* in the life to come.

And while the saints, with Moses, have *respect unto this recompence of the reward*, their *filial* obedience is quickened thereby. *Wherefore we labour*, says the apostle, *that whether present or absent we may be accepted of him,* 2 Cor. v.9. They did not labour to be *accepted*, in point of *righteousness* before God; for so they already had an acceptance in Christ so full, that none of their labours could add any thing to it. But they laboured to be *accepted*, with regard to their *obedience*; or, they laboured in the whole of their conversation to *walk worthy of the Lord unto all pleasing*; i.e., to walk worthy of their high *relation* to him, those great *favours* they enjoyed from him, and that eternal *interest* they had in him, unto all *pleasing*; or, unto all *acceptable* obedience here, and to the open *acceptation* thereof, in the day of Christ.

And the earnestness of their souls herein, the apostle sets forth by *running of a race, for a prize, or crown,* 1 Cor. ix.24, 25. *Know ye not that they which run in a race, run all, but one obtaineth the prize? So run that ye may obtain. And every man that striveth for the mastery, is temperate in all things: now they do it to obtain a corruptible crown, but we an incorruptible.* And as the *prize*, fore-viewed, quickens the saints in the *race*; so that *crown of righteousness* they shall receive, when their *course is finished*, will be a rich and abundant *reward* of all their labours; in which the glory of God's free grace, and the greatness of its provision, for these favourites of heaven, shall for ever shine forth. *Then, they which feared the Lord,* that *speak often one to another*, (whose thoughts, words, and works for God, he graciously regarded, and accepted here) shall be openly *rewarded*, and appear to be *his*, by that bright glory he will put upon them, in the day when he *makes up his jewels.* When the *wicked*, to their utmost *horror*, and everlasting *confusion, shall return and discern between the righteous and the wicked, between him that serveth God, and him that serveth him not*, Mal. iii.16, 17, 18.—It being the peculiar privilege of the *justified* ones, to have all their *obedience*, thus *accepted* and *rewarded:* so that, though the good *works* of the saints do not go to the stock of their justifying *righteousness*; yet as they go to the treasure of their filial *obedience*, which is so *acceptable* to God, and shall be so *rewarded* by him, there is encouragement enough for them, to have an universal and constant regard unto all God's *commandments.—The effect of righteousness shall be peace, quietness, and assurance for ever*, Isaiah xxxii.17.

Thus I have considered, the doctrine of *justification*, or the justification of a sinner in the sight of God,—in the *matter* of it, *i.e.*, the complete *obedience* of Jesus Christ, exclusive of all the *works* of the creature;—in the *manner* of it, as with respect unto God, it is by *imputation*, and with respect to ourselves, by *faith;*—in the *time* of it, as it respects the whole *body* of the *elect*, and every individual *person* of God's *chosen;*—and in the *effects* of it, with respect to the *soul*, as it regards its *peace*, its *state*, and its *obedience.*—And what I have briefly said hereon, I take to be the *scripture* doctrine of *justification*; and that which our *protestant* reformers earnestly *contended* for, at the time of their first *reformation* from *popery*, as the main *basis* on which it was founded. And this doctrine of justification, by the free-grace of God, through the righteousness of Christ, received by faith alone, was of such great account with Luther, that he said of it, "The church either stood or fell, as this was maintained or rejected."

❧✳∞≺≻∞✳❧✳✳∞≺≻∞✳❧✳✳∞≺≻∞✳❧✳✳∞≺≻∞✳❧

S E C T. V.

An OBJECTION, urged against the preceding Scripture-Doctrine of *Justification*, answered.

JAMES ii.21.
Was not Abraham our father justified by works, when he had offered his son Isaac upon the altar?

B UT against what has been said, some may object, thus:

Object. "The justification of a sinner is not by *faith* alone, but by *works* also, as is plainly implied in that *text*, 1 John iii.7. *He that doth righteousness, is righteous, even as he is righteous.* And fully exprest, James ii.24. *Ye see then how that by works a man is justified, and not by faith only.*" To which I answer,

Answ. That the truth laid down, of justification by faith alone, is not in the least shaken by this *objection*, founded upon these *texts*, we shall now evince.

As to the first, *He that doth righteousness, is righteous:* it is not to be understood, as if that person was righteous, by his *doing* of righteousness; but that by his *doing* of righteousness, it was manifested that he was a *righteous* person. And therefore the apostle begins the verse, with a *let no man deceive you;* q.d. Do not take every man for a *righteous* man, a *justified* man in the sight of God, that may pretend thereto; but look into his *conversation*, and see whether his *faith* in Christ for *justification*, produceth fruits of *righteousness* in his life: if not, you may depend upon it, that he is not a righteous man; if he is an unrighteous man, in the general course of his *conversation*, he is certainly such an one, that is not righteous by *imputation:* for, *he that doth righteousness, is righteous*; i.e., he is *so* to begin with, before his doing of righteousness; even *perfectly* so, *as He,* [*i.e.,* Christ] *is righteous*; the perfect obedience of Jesus Christ, being imputed to him, for his complete justification before God. And whoever is thus righteous by *imputation*, is likewise righteous by *impartation*, as having a principle of righteousness *imparted* to him, and *inherent* in him; and from thence he is righteous in his *conversation*. And by his thus doing of righteousness, in his conversation before *men,* it may be fully *known,* that he is such an one, that is under imputed righteousness of Christ, for his justification before *God:* and therefore, verse 10. he says, *In this the children of God are manifest, and the children of the devil: whosoever doth not righteousness, is not of God, neither he that loveth not his brother.* He doth not say, he that doth not righteousness, is not of God, *because* he doth it not, as if the not doing of it, made him to be not of God; but by his not doing of righteousness, it is *manifest*, or made to appear, that he is not of God. And thus we are to understand him, verse 7. where, by *he that doth righteousness, is righteous*, we are to apprehend, that a righteous person's doing of righteousness, is only *evidential*, and not *constitutive*, of him as such. And so this *text*, implies no contradiction against the doctrine of a sinner's justification before God, by *faith* alone. And,

As to the other *text*, that *by works a man is justified, and not by faith only:* though justification by *works* be fully exprest, yet it is another *kind* of justification that is here spoken of, than *that,* by *faith*, which I have asserted; and so, is no contradiction to it: the apostle Paul saith, Rom. iii.28. *That by faith a man is justified, and not by the deeds of the law*; and the apostle James here, *that by works a man is justified, and not by faith only*. And though there is a seeming contradiction between them in *terms*; yet there is really none in *sense*. Because the apostle Paul speaks of the *justification* of a sinner before *God*, or his real state of justification, Godward, which is by faith alone; and the apostle James of the *apparency* of the *truth* of his faith, and *so* of his justified state before God, by his good *works* before men; by which only it can be *known* to them. So that while one asserts *real* justification before *God*, to be by *faith* alone; and the other, *apparent* justification before *men*, to be by good *works*, flowing from faith; there is no contradiction, but a glorious harmony between them. Inasmuch as that *faith*, by which a sinner is justified before God, will certainly be productive of good *works*; which *evidence* a state of *justification* before men.

And that the apostle Paul did speak of a state of real justification before *God*, when he asserts it to be by *faith*, without the deeds of the law, is evident, verse 20. where he likewise excludes the deeds of the law, from having any hand in the justification of a sinner; and what kind of justification he intends, he expresseth by those words, *in his sight. Therefore by the deeds of the law there shall no flesh be justified* IN HIS SIGHT; or, before God.

And as for the apostle James, it is evident, that he spake of a state of justification before *men*, or an apparent state of justification before them, when he asserts it to be by *works*, and not by faith only: for, verse 18. he says, *Yea, a man may say, thou hast faith, and I have works:* To which he replies, *Shew me thy faith* WITHOUT *thy works, and I will shew thee my faith* BY *my works.* As he professeth to *shew* his *faith*, and so his *justification* by his *works*, it is plain, that he intends an apparent, or manifestative justification before *men*, when he asserts it to be by *works*. And this will further appear, by the instance he gives of Abraham's justification hereby, verses 21, 22. *Was not Abraham our Father justified by works, when he had offered Isaac his Son upon the altar? Seest thou how faith wrought with his works, and by works was faith made perfect?* By the word *made* here, we are to understand, *manifested*; i.e., that by his works, his faith was manifested to be *perfect*; or of that perfect *kind*, to which the promise of justification is annexed. For the word *made* in this *text*, is to be understood just in the same sense as it is, 2 Cor. xii.9. *My strength is made perfect in weakness.* As from *this* text, we are not to think that the weakness of the creature can add any *perfection* to the almighty *power* of God in *itself,* but only in its *manifestation,* as thereby the *power* of God appears to be *perfect,* or stands forth to be *beheld* in its own *almightiness*; so, neither from the *other* are we to apprehend, that Abraham's works did add any *perfection* to his *faith* in *itself,* but only in its *manifestation*; as thereby his *faith* appeared to be *perfect,* or stood forth to be *beheld* by men, in its own *perfection*; as being of that very *kind* which receives *justification* from God, and accompanies the *salvation* of the soul: as it follows, verse 23. *And the scripture was fulfilled which saith, Abraham believed God, and it was imputed unto him for righteousness; and he was called the friend of God.* In the former part of this verse, Abraham's justification before *God,* is plainly asserted to be by *faith, he believed God,* and IT [*i.e.,* the obedience of Christ, which his faith saw in the promise] *was imputed unto him for righteousness.* And then, in the latter part of the verse, his justification before *men* is plainly implied to be by *works*; inasmuch as his faith, so worked by love, in obedience to God's commands, that *he was called the friend of God.* And thus the apostle James, when he speaks of Abraham's justification before *God,* asserts it to be by *faith,* as much as Paul; and when he speaks of it by *works,* he intends that only which he had before *men.* And in this sense, the apostle Paul asserts justification by *works,* as much as James, Rom. iv.2. *For, if Abraham was justified by works, he hath whereof to glory, but not before God.* This *if* here is not to be taken for an *interrogation,* a question, whether he was or not; but for a *concession,* a grant that he was. And therefore, follows, *he hath whereof to glory; but* (where?) *not before God.* No, no, says the apostle; had he been justified by *works,* before *God,* he would have had whereof to *glory* before *God*; but since his justification by *works,* extended only to *men,* his *glorying* was *there* limited; and all *boasting,* both from *him,* and his *seed,* is for ever *excluded, by the law of faith,* chap. iii.27.: that is, by the *doctrine* of faith, the *gospel*; which reveals the *obedience* of Christ to be the only justifying *righteousness* of a sinner before God, as it is *imputed* to him, of the freest *grace*, and *received* by *faith* alone.*

---

*Besides what has been so pertinently advanced above, in answer to the objection urged against the free justification of guilty sinners, by the imputation of the complete obedience and finished righteousness of the divine Redeemer, received by faith, exclusive of all works done by the creature, as attention to the following particulars will throw some farther light thereon, and fully evince, that there is no contradiction between the apostle Paul in affirming, *That God imputeth righteousness without works,* &c. Rom. iv.5, 6.; and the apostle James, saying, *Ye see then, how that by works a man is justified, and not by faith only*, James ii.24.

In order to illustrate this we must carefully distinguish between the several sorts of persons that Paul and James had to do with.—Paul's discourse is bent proud self-righteous *justiciaries*, who thought to build up a righteousness of their own, by which they designed both to adorn themselves in the eye of God's holiness, and to secure themselves from the sword of his justice: and therefore Paul teacheth, that no righteousness of man can weigh in God's balance, or is pleadable at the bar of justice. *We are all as an unclean thing, and our righteousness is but as filthy rags. By the deeds of the law shall no flesh living be justified*, Rom. iii.20, 21. But James hath to do with boasting and self-deceiving *hypocrites*, who pretends to faith, but it is a barren, idle, dead faith. They say they had faith, but they had no works, James ii.14.; they could not shew, or evidence their faith, because they had no works: and therefore his design was, to shame, confound, and silence these hypocrites, and to demonstrate, that they had no true faith at all, but did grasp a lye, and hug an idol of their own, instead of true faith.—Paul treats of faith, as it respects *Christ's righteousness*, and as it builds and is acted only on this before God. But James speaks of faith, as it is to come forth, and to be demonstrated before *men*—The justification that James speaks of is not a justification of the *person*, but of the *faith* of Abraham, of his sincerity and integrity, Gen. xx.12. But the justification that Paul treats of, in the justification of the *ungodly person,* by the imputation of Christ's righteousness, Rom. iv.5, 6.—Paul treats of the *causes* of justification, he searches after the springs of it, *viz.* Christ's righteousness, and faith as receiving it: but James speaks of the *effects* of justification. A man whose person is justified before God will certainly justify his faith and sincerity before men, by works of righteousness.—Paul speaks of the justification of a *sinner;* James treats of the approbation of a *believer.* Paul discourses of the *righteousness* that must justify, *viz.* the righteousness of Christ; James treats of the *faith* that must evidence a person justified, of what kind it must be, *viz.* not an idle, lazy, but an operative faith. Paul speaks of justification before *God*, Rom. iii.20, 21.; James treats of justification before *men*, James ii.18. *Shew me thy faith*; that is, prove it, if thou canst, to be a

Thus I have endeavoured to answer the objection made against this doctrine, I before laid down, by opening the *texts* on which it was founded; and I have been the larger herein, in order to set *them*, and the *truth*, in a clear light.

---

right faith, if it bring not forth good works.

Moreover, that the apostle James doth not speak of a *proper* justification of the parson of a man before God, by works, might be made evident by several arguments.—The proper justification of a man is from *sins* that he hath been guilty of; not for *works of righteousness* which he hath wrought: good works are not shewed before God's tribunal; but iniquities are *covered*, Psalm xxxii.1, 2.— Nothing will properly justify a person, but what is *commensurate* to the divine law, and will *satisfy* the justice of God: but no obedience of ours can do this; nothing but the finished righteousness of Christ: therefore we cannot be justified by our works; the man that is justified, is μή ἐργαζόμενος, *he that worketh not*, Rom. iv.5.— Nothing will properly justify us, but what justified *Jesus Christ*; he could not be justified, except he had fulfilled the precept of the law, and endured the curse also in his death: therefore we cannot be justified by our works; if we could, then would Christ have died in vain.—In a proper justification, we are justified *before God*, Rom. iii.20, 21. But our own good works cannot be imputed unto us for a righteousness before God, because he sees so many faults, blemishes, and defects in them.—Our best works need a *pardon*; and therefore cannot be our righteousness to justify us: that which needs forgiveness, and really deserves punishment, can never earn a reward, and be accepted for a justifying righteousness.—If we could be justified by our works, we should justify *ourselves*; but it is *God's act*, and not our to justify, Rom. viii.33. *It is God that justifieth.*—In true justification, we *receive* a righteousness and an atonement, Rom. v.11, 17. But our works cannot make an atonement for us, or be a righteousness to us.

S E C T. VI.

The INSUFFICIENCY of legal obedience to the justification of a Sinner.

Rom. iii.20.
By the deeds of the law, there shall no flesh be justified in his sight.

AND now, to shew the *impossibility* of a sinner's being *justified* before God, by the *works* of the law, or by his own obedience to the law, I shall take a little notice, what it is that God, by his *law*, requires of man; and also, for what *end* the law was given. And,

First, God, by his *law*, requires of every man *perfect obedience*; which is his duty to perform, although he cannot do it. As all men are creatures of God's *making*, and were all at once made representatively, in their natural head Adam; so in him, as their covenant head, they were creatures of God's *governing*; when he gave him the fundamental *law* of nature, commanding him to eat of the trees of the garden, with a particular prohibition of the tree of knowledge of good and evil, Gen. ii.16, 17. *And the* LORD *God commanded the man, saying, Of every tree of the garden thou mayst freely eat: But of the tree of knowledge of good and evil, thou shalt not eat of it; for in the day thou eatest thereof, thou shalt surely die.* And it was meet that God should govern the creature he had made both for his own *glory*, and the creature's *good:* for, as God's manifestative *glory* was concerned in his creature's obedience; so it was the *happiness* of the creature to serve its Creator, and in this way to enjoy him. God is so great, so good, and so glorious a Being, that it is the happiness of the angels in heaven to be subject to his commands; and so it was of man in paradise, to be subject to this law given him: in which, though the threatening of dead, upon his disobedience, be only *expressed*; yet the promise of life, or the continuation of that blissful state he was then in possession of, for himself and his seed, upon his obedience, was *implied.*—And this original *law* did summarily contain all the *ten words* given at *mount Sinai*, or the substance of the moral *law*, delivered in the *ten commandments*, by the LORD's audible voice from heaven; and wrote by him, in the *two tables of stone*, when he gave his *law*, in this peculiar manner unto *Israel*. And when this moral *law*, in the original *form* of it, was first given to Adam, and in him to all *mankind*, his heart was perfectly conformed thereto; and he, and so they in him, had *power* to have kept it; and it would have been his, and their *happiness*, so to have done.

But he, being a *mutable* creature, and left to the freedom of his own *will*, soon hearkened to the temptations of *Satan*, cast off his loyalty to his *Maker* and Sovereign *Lord*, and yielded subjection to the *prince of darkness*, in obeying his *dictates*, and eating of the forbidden *fruit*. In doing which, he for *himself*, and his whole *posterity*, broke the whole *law* at once. From whence, the *penalty*, or threatening, became righteously due to him and them, as the just reward of his *disobedience*, whereby *many were made sinners: and so death passed upon all men in him, in whom all had sinned*, Rom. v.12, 19.

And as soon as Adam had sinned, and *we* in him, there was thenceforth no *life* to be had for a fallen creature, by its own *obedience* to the law: because the *law* being once *broken*, Adam and every one of his *race*, were looked upon in the eye of the law, as *transgressors*; and therefore the righteous *law*, could do nothing to *justify* a *sinner*; it became *weak*, in this regard, through our *flesh*, or corrupt nature, Rom. viii.3. But all the power it had, considered as *broken*, was to thunder out curse and wrath, against every soul of man that had done evil.

And besides the *guilt* of the first transgression, on which account Adam, and all his *posterity*, were at once laid under the curse; from which they could never deliver themselves, and so no life for them by a broken *law*, which bound them over to punishment; besides this, I say, there was an universal *pollution* of nature, that overspread the soul of Adam, the *curse* taking hold upon him in the very *instant* of his disobedience. The threatening was, *In the day thou eatest thereof, thou shalt surely die;* or, *in dying thou shalt die.* In which was contained *death* spiritual, temporal, and eternal, as the just *wages of sin.* And the *first* of these was instantly executed upon him: in that very day, hour, and moment, in which he *sinned*, he *died*, in his soul, or spirit, with regard to that life of holiness, and perfect conformity to the law, which before he was possessed of: and thereby he lost all his *power* to fulfil the law, or to yield such an obedience as the holy law of God requires, or can accept. The law *requires* perfect obedience, and can *accept* of no less; and Adam having lost all his moral *rectitude*, he was utterly incapable to *fulfil* the law. And as it was with Adam in this regard, on account of his *first* sin, so it is with every one of his *descendants*, that proceed from him by ordinary generation: as they became *guilty* in *his* first transgression, so coming into the world, in *union* to him, as their covenant-head, standing together with him, under the same broken *law*, they become *filthy* likewise; the contagion of sin overspreads the whole soul, as soon as ever it informs the body. And thus every child of Adam, being *shapen in iniquity, and conceived in sin*, comes forth into this world a *sinner*, with a defiled nature, a *carnal mind*, or corrupt soul, *which is not subject to the law of God, neither indeed can be*, Psalm li.5. Rom. viii.7.

And that *infants* are born *sinners*, appears from Rom. v.14.; where the apostle, proving that sin was in the world, before the giving of the law at *mount Sinai*, in that *death reigned from Adam to Moses*, gives the *death* of *infants* as an instance of their being *sinners*. *Nevertheless*, says he, *death reigned from Adam to Moses, even over them that had not sinned after the similitude of Adam's transgression:* that is, over *infants*, who were not capable of sinning *actually*, as Adam did; but they being *guilty* in him, and *filthy* from him, the law of God finds them *sinners*, and so *death, the wages of sin*, seized upon them.

Thus we are sinners by *nature*, before we are so by *practice:* and *none can bring a clean thing out of an unclean; no not one*, Job xiv.4. There can be no pure *obedience* yielded to God's holy law, such as it requires, by *filthy, abominable man*. And as *Adam*, upon his first sin, became *guilty*, and *we* in him; and as *he* instantly thereupon became *filthy*, and *we* as soon as we have a being; so there can be no *life* for a fallen creature, by the works of the law. For, *first*, he has already *broken* the law, and so is under the *curse*. And, *secondly*, he has lost his *power* to obey it; and so cannot obtain the *blessing*. And therefore, when Adam had sinned, *The* LORD *God drove out the man from the garden of Eden, and placed cherubims and a flaming sword, that turned every way to keep the way of the tree of life*, Gen. iii.24. This did signify to him, and to all his posterity, that now he had broken the law, there was no life for them by their own obedience; or that it was impossible that fallen man, should have life by his obedience to the law, as Adam was to have had in *Paradise*; and that whoever should attempt it that way, must be inevitably destroyed by the *flaming-sword* of God's justice, *which turned every way*, towards every one of the commandments, which man had broken, to keep the sinner from life by the law. And therefore, the apostle says, That as many as in vain, attempt to obtain life by the law, are under the *curse*, Gal. iii.10. *For as many as are of the works of the law, are under the curse: for it is written, Cursed is every one that continueth not in all things written in the book of the law, to do them.*

Thus there is no life for a fallen creature by the works of the law; because he has lost his *power* to yield such an obedience as the law requires. For, the eternal law of God *requires* the same perfect, perpetual obedience, now man is *fallen*, and has lost his *strength*, as it did when he was *upright*, and had *power* to perform it, and that *righteously* too. Because, when the law was first given to Adam, and in him to all *mankind*, he had *power* to have kept it; and though man, by sin, has lost his power to *obey*, yet God has not lost his power to *command*. And therefore, every man that cometh into this world, notwithstanding his being born a *sinner*, and previously under the *curse,* is bound to yield a perfect *obedience* to God's holy law, in thought, word, and deed; in heart, lip, and life, from his birth, to his death, without the least failure, or wry step; and upon default hereof, he righteously falls under the *condemnation* of the law, and the fiery indignation of a sin-revenging God; which must be born, either by *himself* or his *Surety*, as, blessed be God, it hath been by the *Surety, Christ*, for all that shall be *saved*. And as for those that *perish*, they must bear the weight of their own *sins*, and of God's inexpressible *wrath*, breaking forth upon them, through the curses of a broken law, in the torments of hell for ever.

And this shews the great misery, and cruel bondage we are in by nature, by reason of *sin*, as being under the *law*, which is the *ministration of death*, 2 Cor. iii.7. It *commands* duty, and that *righteously*, but can give no *strength*; and this was shadowed forth by the *bondage* the children of *Israel* were in, in *Egypt*, under *Pharoah*, and his cruel *task-masters*; who commanded the *full tale of brick, and yet afforded no straw.* And it was an *unrighteous* thing in *them*, thus to command the *Israelites*, and then to *beat* them for the non-performance of that, which they never had *ability* to do; yet, as was said, it is a *righteous* thing with God, according to his law, to command perfect *obedience* of *fallen* man, and to curse him to *death,* upon default hereof; because he once had power to have yielded it, and by his own sin deprived himself hereof. But however righteous it is, (as those that perish shall one day own, *When every mouth shall be stoped, and all the world become guilty before God,* Rom. iii.19.) yet the misery of man by reason hereof, is exceeding great. And,

Secondly, To *shew* this, *viz.* the misery of man, by sin, as being under the exacting and condemning law, and so the need he had of a Saviour, was one great *end* of the *giving* of the *law* at *mount Sinai. For, until the law,* says the apostle, *Sin was in the world; but sin is not* IMPUTED *when there is no law,* Rom. v.13. How is that? Why, it is not to be understood, as it *God* did not *impute* it; for that *he* did, is evident, in that he inflicted the punishment thereof, the wages due to it; *death: for death reigned from Adam to Moses,* as in the next verse. But the meaning is, that during that tract of time, from Adam to Moses, the consciences of men were grown in a great measure *secure*, and not having that just sense they ought to have had of the law's severity, (as it was given out to Adam, and to *them* in him) they did not do their office, in condemning for sin. When they did evil, they did not *impute sin* unto *themselves*; or, at least, not in such a manner as they ought, or was agreeable to the strictness of the holy law; and therefore it amounted to little more, nay, no more, in the phrase of the Holy Ghost, than a *non-imputation* of it. And therefore God would have his law come forth in a new edition, with the tremendous Majesty, and amazing terror of a GOD, *glorious in* HOLINESS; *when he came down on mount Sinai, in flaming fire, with thunders, and lightenings, and a great earthquake; and the voice of a trumpet, sounding exceeding loud,* to summons the people to hear the voice of their Creator, GOD, in his holy law, which he summed up, and gave in ten words, or the *ten commandments,* Exod. xix.16, &c. and xx.1. &c. Whereupon *the people removed, and stood afar off;* as struck with the amazing *purity* of God's *nature*, displayed in his holy *law*; while he appeared as *a consuming fire,* to shew his just vengeance against all *law*-breakers: and they being *guilty*, and *self*-condemned, began to see their need of a *Mediator*; and said to Moses, (the *typical* one) *Speak thou with us, and we will hear; but let not God speak with us, lest we die,* verses 18, 19.— Thus *the law entered that the offence might abound; that sin by the commandment might become exceeding sinful*; or appear to be sinful sin indeed, Rom. v.20. and vii.13.

The *end* of the *law's* being *given* on *mount Sinai*, to *fallen* man, was not that he should obey it for *life*; but that, by the apparent straightness of the *rule*, the crookedness of his *ways* might be *manifest*; and that by the strict purity of his holy *law*, now drawn out in all its beautiful lineaments, the defilement of man's *nature*, and the odiousness of his *features*, in his disconformity thereto, might appear: and that by this *law*, in the hand of the Spirit, which was at first *ordained unto life*, but now by *sin*, become *the ministration of death*, the sinner might be *killed*, as to all hopes of life therefrom, *the offence thereby abounding in his sight unto death;* that so by *this* he might be prepared to receive the *free gift* of life in Christ, and the superabounding *grace* of God, *reigning through righteousness, unto eternal life* by him.

Again, the *Sinai* law was *given*, that *Christ* might be made *under* it, to fulfil its *requirements*, and suffer its *penalties* for his people; to make them *righteous* by *his obedience* to it, or the *active* obedience of his *life*, and to redeem them from the curse of it by his *passive* obedience, or his meritorious *death*. And that thus *fulfilling* it, he might become *the end of* it *for righteousness* unto them, and for ever deliver them from it, as it is a covenant of works; that so from *him*, their Saviour-King, they might receive this royal *law*, as a *rule* of life, to square their obedience by; which is designed to glorify God, and not to obtain salvation from: and thus in love, *Serve it, in the newness of the Spirit, and not in the oldness of the letter*, Rom. v.19. Gal. iii.13. with chap. iv.4, 5. Rom. x.4. 1 Cor. ix.21. Rom. vii.6.

Thus it appears, that the *law* was given for ends *subservient* to the *gospel:* and not to *oppose* and *destroy* the gospel. For which end the corrupt nature of man doth perversely use it, in endeavouring to *obey* it for *righteousness* unto *life*, when there can be no life had thereby. Not but that the promise of *life*, upon the creature's *obedience*, is contained in the *law*; as the threatening of *death* on his disobedience: *For Moses describeth the righteousness which is of the law, that the man that doth those things, shall live by them;* as the apostle declares, Rom. x.5. But then the *sinner* has already broken the law, and lost his *power* to fulfil it; and on both accounts, it is impossible for *him* to obtain *life* by it: and to *attempt* the same, is a *God*-dishonouring, and a *soul*-destroying thing. The soul that seeks life by the law, *dishonours* God, in that it does its utmost to *oppose* the great *design* of his infinite wisdom and grace, in saving sinners by his Son: and it *destroys* itself, in seeking the *blessing* in such a way, wherein it is impossible to be had; and whereby it must inevitably fall under the *curse*. And such a soul, in *doing* for life, runs quite counter to God's way of *believing* for life: and *he that believeth not the Son*, (living and dying in that state) *shall not see life; but the wrath of God abideth on him*, John iii.36. which will sink him into the abyss of unutterable and eternal torment. But it may be said,

"You talk of *doing* for *life*, and *trusting* to our own obedience for *acceptance* with God, and that this is a *soul*-destroying thing: But who is there that goes about it? Do not all that profess the name of *Christ*, believe that he died to *save* mankind? But we must not from thence sit *still*, and do nothing *ourselves*; we must do what we *can*, and what we cannot *do*, Christ will make up by his merit, and God will *forgive* us our sins."

And so the person that makes this objection, would not be thought to *seek life by the works of the law*; but is for salvation in a *mixed* way, partly by *works*, and partly by *grace*. But as no such thing can be, for grace and works, in the point of *salvation*, can no more *mix* than *iron and clay*; so the person that seeks life at *all*, by his own works, will be found to seek it *wholly* by the works of the law, if what Paul says is true, Rom. xi.6. *And if by grace, then it is no more of works; otherwise grace is no more grace: but if it be of works, then is it no more grace; otherwise work is no more work.* It must be *wholly* of works, or *wholly* of grace. And therefore every man must stand either on the side of *works*, or on the side of *grace*. And as it is God's way to save sinners alone by his *free grace;* so every soul that shall be saved, is made willing to be saved in *this* way. And that soul that is not willing to have salvation alone by God's *free grace* in Christ, without the least regard to his own *works*, in point of *acceptance*, must for ever go without it. And as for that soul, whoever he be, that adheres, in the least, to his own *works*, he will be found to be *of* the works of the law; and as such, must inevitably fall under the *curse*; for he, adhering to the *law*, chooses to stand at its *bar*; and *that* requiring of him perfect *obedience*, which he cannot perform, (although it is his duty) it will *curse* him to death for the want of it. Such a soul, in attempting to do *any* thing for life, tacitly says, that he is able to keep the *whole* law; and so out of his own mouth will be *judged* and *condemned* for the non-performance of it.

Little do souls know, what a dreadful *task* they undertake, when they go about *working for life*, and to *establish their own righteousness*. They reject the great, full, and free *salvation* of God in the *gospel,* and bind themselves over to the *condemnation* of a broken *law*, and to the fiery *indignation* of a sin-revenging God; and will find it a most *fearful thing to fall* into his *hands*. And whoever thou art, soul, that art for *doing* for life, thou wilt find *enough* to do; for no less than to fulfil the *whole* law doth God *require* of thee thereby. But it may be further said;

"Why, then, we may even *throw* away the *law*, cast off *subjection* to it, and live as we *list*."

But, hold, man; thou art *under* the law, and canst not so easily deliver thyself from its *yoke*. It bids thee *do*, and do *perfectly:* and though thou canst not yield such an obedience as it requires, yet thou art indispensably bound to do what thou *canst*; (yea, and infinitely more than is in thy power to perform) and thou oughtest to do thy utmost, as a *creature*, in point of *obedience* to God, thy Creator and Preserver. And he will regard the acts of thy moral righteousness; and, in the bounties of his providence, *reward* thy obedience, with good things, in this present life. So that, in this respect, thou wilt not serve an hard master: For *whatsoever good thing any man doth, the same shall he receive of the Lord, whether he be bond or free,* Eph. iv.8. And hence there is *encouragement* enough for *fallen* man, to use his utmost *diligence* to do what God requires of him in his *law*. But if he would be *saved,* he must seek salvation in another *way*; even in that way wherein God has declared it may be had.

For, if a sinful creature, will obey the *law*, with an eye to make himself *righteous* in the sight of God, and to obtain eternal *life* thereby; as this was not God's *end* in giving the *law* to fallen man, so he will say to such an one, *Who hath required these things at your hands?* And cast all his *obedience* as *dung*, and abominable *filth*, into his face, to his everlasting *shame* and utter *confusion:* for, in point of *righteousness* before God, nothing less than perfect *obedience* can be *accepted*; which a fallen creature cannot perform: and God having *appointed* the *obedience* of his Son, to be the only justifying *righteousness* of a sinner; if a sinful creature sets aside the *perfect* obedience of Christ, by introducing his own *imperfect* obedience in the stead thereof; or presents his own *filthy rags*; to join with Christ's spotless, glorious *robe,* in order to obtain *life* by the *works* of his own hands, when God had declared, that it is only to be had by his *free gift*; it is a most daring affront to the *grace* of God in the *gospel,* and to the *justice* of God in the *law*. And the *condemnation* of such a soul, will be exceedingly more aggravated, and his *punishment* more intollerable, that thus adheres to the *law*, under the promulgation of the *gospel*, than that of the *heathens* who perish, not having heard of the *Name* of Christ. And thus it is a dreadful thing, for a poor sinner, to attempt to *do* any thing himself, that so he may *inherit eternal* life. For, if *he will enter into life* that way, he must *keep all the commandments*, in heart, lip, and life, without the least failure continually, which he can never *do*; and so runs himself upon the flaming Sword of God's *justice*, in his fiery *law*; and dying in that state, he must *suddenly be destroyed, and that without remedy.* But again, it may be said;

"If there is no such thing, as life to be had for a fallen creature, by its own obedience to the law, then it is made void."

I answer, with the apostle, *Do we then make void the law through faith? God forbid: yea, we establish the law,* Rom. iii.31. It is *those* destroy the *law*, who would put it off with their own *imperfect* obedience: for thereby, they tacitly say, that the *law* is not so strict and holy as it once was; nor so binding to the creature, either in its requirements of duty, or obligation to punishment, as it was wont to be. But as for *those* who assert, that the law of God is an eternal rule of righteousness, and that it indispensibly requires of every man that is under it, as a covenant of works, perfect and perpetual obedience, which is the creature's duty to perform, although he cannot do it; and that upon default hereof, it righteously binds the transgressor over to punishment, and so set it *aside*, and cease to *obey* it for life; these *establish the law:* in that they, by faith, take hold of Christ's *obedience*, who has fulfilled it perfectly, and is become the *end of it for righteousness, to every one that believeth*; and in that, to all unbelievers who remain under it, they assert its equity and eternity, in requiring of them complete, and constant obedience, and binding them over to death, both in soul and body, in time and to eternity, for the non-performance thereof.

Thus, as it is the *duty* of the creature, man, to *do* whatever his Creator commands in his holy law, which yet he *cannot* do: so it appears to be utterly *impossible* for him to be *justified* by his own obedience; and the *misery* of man, with regard to the *law*, is exceeding great indeed: and therefore, the good news the *gospel* brings must needs be *glad tidings*; as it reveals pardon and life for a *sinner*, through the complete *obedience* of Jesus Christ, *imputed* to him for his justifying *righteousness* before God, which is to be received by *faith* alone.

S E C T. VII.

The C O N C L U S I O N.

ISA. xlv.24.

Surely, shall one say, In the Lord have I righteousness.

IN the last place, I shall add something by way of *use* from what has been said, as a conclusion of the whole. And,

1. Since the *justification* of a sinner is by the complete *obedience* of Jesus Christ, *imputed* to him, and received by *faith*, and produceth such great and glorious *effects*; we may hence learn, what reason we have to *admire* that infinity of *wisdom*, which shines forth in the *contrivance* of this wonder; and to adore that immensity of *grace* which is displayed in this glorious *provision* made for the favourites of heaven!* When the beloved John was favoured with a visionary light of the *the woman-bride, the*

---

*This divine righteousness of the adorable Redeemer, which is the alone ground of a guilty sinner's justification, has many ingredients in it, and peculiar excellencies appertaining to it, that should excite wonder and admiration in these who have had it imputed unto them. It is not only in itself, a full, sufficient, complete, and meritorious righteousness; but a righteousness of God's contrivance, Psal. lxxxix.19, 20. Isa. xlii.6, 7.;—of God's working out, Heb. ii.17. John xvii.4, 19, 30.;—of God's approving, Isa. xlii.21.;—of God's accepting, Eph. v.2.;—of God's revealing, Rom. i.17. iii.21.;—of God's bringing near, Heb. ix.23, 24. Isa. xliv.13.:—But it is also a righteousness by which the law is magnified, Isa. xlii.21.;—justice satisfied, Rom. viii.34. Psalm lxxxv.10.;—sin expiated, Heb. i.3. ix.26.;—transgression finished, Dan. ix.24.—wrath appeased, and deliverance from it obtained, Micah vii.18. 1 Thess. i.10.;—the curse removed, Gal. iii.13.;—the guilty assoiled, Rom. viii.33, 34.;—freedom from condemnation secured, Rom. viii.1.;—the sinner eternally saved, Isa. xlv.17.;—Heaven purchased, Heb. x.19, 20.;—God glorified, Isa. xlix.3. John xvii.4.;—Christ honoured, Isa. liii.12. Phil. ii.8, 9.;—believers adorned and exalted, Isaiah lxi.10. Psalm lxxxix.16.:—And, to crown all, it is a permanent and an everlasting righteousness, Dan. ix.24. Isaiah xlv.17.—What reason then have the redeemed ones to be filled with wonder and admiration in contemplating the finished surety-righteousness!

Lamb's wife, as *clothed with* Christ, *the Sun* of righteousness, and shining forth in the resplendent rays of her Bridegroom's glory; he says, he saw *a* WONDER, Rev. xii.1. And a wonder it is indeed; so great, that it calls for the admiration both of men and of angels. This is one of those glorious *things,* that by the gospel is revealed unto us, *Which the angels desire to look into,* 1 Pet. i.12. And while sinful men have *the forgiveness of* their *sins, through* Christ's *blood,* and the *acceptation* of their *persons,* in him *the Beloved, according to the riches of* the Father's *grace, wherein he has abounded towards* them, *in all wisdom and prudence*; it becomes then to admire, and adore the same, and to cry out, with the apostle, *O the depth of the riches, both of the wisdom and knowledge of God! How unsearchable are his judgments, and his ways past finding out!* Eph. i.6, 7, 8. Rom. xi.33. That the *obedience* of the Son of God should be made our *righteousness,* the righteousness of a *sinner,* to his complete *justification* before God, is such a *project* of infinite *wisdom,* such a *provision* of infinite *grace,* for the *salvation* of God's chosen, that it every way becomes the great JEHOVAH! And will be the endless wonder of men and angels!

2. Since the justification of a sinner is wholly by the righteousness of another, which is a *way of life above* nature, above being discovered by nature's *light,* and seen by nature's *eye,* or discovered by the light of the *law,* and discerned by natural *reason*; we may hence learn, what an absolute necessity there is of a super-natural *revelation* thereof, in order to the soul's receiving of this *righteousness,* and so of he grace of *justification* thereby. This is one of those *things* that God has *prepared* for his people, that never *entered into the heart of* the natural *man to conceive of,* which he had neither *known* nor *can* understand; and therefore deems it *foolishness,* or a foolish thing, for any to think they shall be justified by the obedience of Christ, exclusive of all their own works. But the people of God, *receive not the spirit which is of the world, but the Spirit which is of God, that they may know the things which are freely given* them *of God.* And *this,* of *the free gift of righteousness, is revealed unto* them by his *Spirit,* though it is one of those *deep things of God,* which are hidden from the *natural man*; and which are impossible to be known by any, but heaven-born souls, under a special *revelation* from above, 1 Cor. ii.6, &c.

3. Since the *justification* of a sinner is by the *obedience* of Christ alone; we may hence learn, how greatly *important* the *knowledge* thereof is! The *knowledge* of this righteousness, must needs be of the utmost *importance,* since *ignorance* of it, and *non-submission* to it, (which always go together)

leave the soul in an *unrighteous* state, Rom. ix.31, 32. and x.3. All those miserable souls, who are *ignorant* of Christ's *righteousness, go about to establish their own righteousness;* and, alas! *The bed is shorter, than that a man can stretch himself upon it, and the covering narrower, than that he can wrap himself in it,* Isa. xxviii.20. There is no true *rest* for a *sinner,* from the *works* of its own hands; no *covering* for a *naked* soul, from the *fig-leaves* of its own *righteousness,* though ever so artfully sewed together. Our Lord told his *disciples,* that *except* their *righteousness did exceed the righteousness of the Scribes and Pharisees, they should in no case enter into the kingdom of heaven,* Mat. v.20. These *Scribes and Pharisees* were the *zealous,* the *religious* men of that *age,* the strict observers of Moses's law, that trusted in *themselves,* that they were *righteous,* by their own *legal* performances, and thought to get to *heaven* by means thereof. But our Lord declares, that none shall ever come *there,* but those who have a *better* righteousness, a *righteousness* that exceeds a *pharisaical* righteousness; *i.e.,* such a righteousness, that every way answers to all the extensive require-ments of the *law,* in heart, lip, and life; and this is no other than the *righteousness* of Christ, imputed to poor *sinners,* or made *theirs* by *imputation*; in which, being completely *justified,* according to *law* and *justice,* they shall, as *righteous* persons, be admitted into the kingdom of *heaven,* or into the glory of the heavenly *state*; while all those who trust in their own *righteousness,* and think they have done *many wonderful works,* which they dare plead for acceptance with God, shall be sent away from Christ, into eternal *misery,* with a *depart from me, ye workers of iniquity,* Matth. vii.22.

And as our Lord, in this his *sermon* upon the *mount,* had been expounding the law of God, in its *spirituality,* as extending to the *heart,* as well as *life*; and asserting the necessity of *keeping* the commandments in the same extensive manner, that the law *required,* in order to make a person *righteous*; so, in the conclusion thereof, he says, *Therefore, whosoever heareth these sayings of mine, and doth them, I will liken him unto a wise man, who built his house upon a rock: and the rain descended and the floods came, and the winds blew, and beat upon that house; and it fell not, for it was founded upon a rock,* verses 24, 25. These *sayings* of our Lord, contain the *substance* of the moral *law,* and the *doing* of them unto *righteousness* before God, is by *believing*; as faith lays hold on Christ, who has *obeyed* the law perfectly, as the *representative* of his people: on which account, *they* may be said to have done, or *fulfilled,* the law unto him; his *obedience*, being *imputed* unto *them*, for their complete *justification* before God.

As the *Surety's payment*, among men, is accounted to the *debtor*, and is the same, in the eye of the *law*, and as effectual for his full *discharge*, as if he himself had paid the *debt*. And he that thus *doth* the law, or these *sayings* of Christ, he *likens* him *unto a wise man, who built his house upon a rock*. It is a piece of natural *wisdom*, to lay a good *foundation* for a stately *structure*; and the most *firm*, that any house can be built on, is that of a *rock*. And he that is spiritually *wise, wise unto salvation*, lays the whole *stress* of it, and builds all his *hope* of life, upon Christ, the *rock* of ages; in which it appears, that he is *wise* indeed: for, as in nature, a *house* that is built upon a *rock*, will stand the *storm*; so the *soul* that is built upon *Christ* shall never be *removed: the rain may descend, the floods come, and the winds beat*; afflictions, temptations, and trials of all kinds, may *beat vehemently against* that soul; but shall never *destroy* its *salvation*, nor make it *ashamed* of its *hope*. No; Christ, the *rock* of immutability, will hold it *unshaken*, in a state of *salvation*, through *life*, through *death*, at *judgment*, and *for ever*.—Such a soul *stands* as *immoveable*, in the grace of *justification* and *life*, as the *rock* itself on which it is founded: *Because I live*, saith our Lord, *ye shall live also*, John xiv.19. Christ's *life* is the life of that *soul*, that depends upon him alone, for all its justification, and eternal salvation. And therefore the *wisdom* of faith is great indeed! in that it foresees the storm, and thus provids against it.

But he, saith our Lord, *that heareth these sayings of mine, and doth them not* [*i.e.*, that *heareth* the law's *requirements*, and endeavours to *obey* the same, for *righteousness* before God, and so doth them *not;* because his obedience cannot come up to that perfection which the law requires] *shall be likened unto a foolish man, which built his house upon the sand; and the rain descended, and the floods came, and the winds blew, and beat upon that house; and it fell, and great was the fall of it,* Matth. vii.26, 27, Oh! the *folly* of that poor sinner, who lays the *stress* of his salvation, and builds his *hope* of life, upon his own righteousness! For this *sandy* foundation cannot endure the *storm*s of divine *wrath*, which shall be revealed from heaven against all unrighteousness of men; nor secure the soul from being driven away, by the tempest of God's *anger*, and the floods of his *indignation*, into the abyss of eternal *misery*. The *house fell*, that was thus built upon the *sand, and great was the fall of it!* Oh! what a miserable disappointment will it be to that soul, that *goes down to the chambers of* eternal *death, with this* *lie of his own righteousness in his right-hand*; from which he had all along hoped for eternal life! When this *way, that seemed right to him in his own eyes,* as if it would lead him to everlasting life, (by his *depending* thereon) shall *end* in eternal *death! The hope of the hypocrite* [or, of him that trusts in himself, that he is righteous, by his own external performances, when yet his heart is far from that conformity to God, which the law *requires*] *shall perish, at the giving up of the ghost. His hope* [i.e., his *salvation* hoped for] *shall* then *be cut off. He shall lean upon his house,* [i.e., his own *righteousness*, which he had raised up, in his imagination, to *shelter* him from the *storm* of divine vengeance] *but it shall not stand; he shall hold it fast, but it shall not endure,* Job viii.13, 14, 15. No; this *house* of his shall be as soon destroyed, by the storm of God's indignation, as a *spider's web* is swept down by the besom that comes against it; and the miserable soul, that trusteth herein, shall be driven away into eternal perdition.

Thus an error in the *foundation* will prove *fatal* to the building; and therefore the *knowledge of Christ,* as the alone way of a sinner's *justification* and *life,* must needs be of the highest *importance*; since no other *refuge* can stand the *storm,* but Christ, as THE LORD OUR RIGHTEOUSNESS; this glorious *hiding-place* which God has prepared for poor sinners, whither they may *run,* and be for ever *safe.* And as for *those,* who live and die in *ignorance* of, and *non-submission to* the righteousness of Christ, they will certainly *die in their sins,* and *perish* for ever. They will all be found *filthy* at the day of judgment, that have not been enabled to *believe* in Christ's *blood,* for cleansing from all sin; they will all be found *unjust,* at that awful day, that have not *believed* in the Redeemer's *righteousness,* for their justification before God; and so must remain *for ever:* for, concerning them, it will then be said, *He that is filthy, let him be filthy still; and he that is unjust, let him be unjust still; i.e.,* let him *abide* to an endless *eternity.* But,

4. Since there is but one *way* for a sinner to be *justified* before God, and that is by the *obedience* of Christ alone; this informs us, what great *folly* those persons are guilty of, who *press* poor sinners to obey the *law,* to make themselves *righteous* in the sight of God, when there is no law given that can give life unto them; and how *dangerous* it is for souls, to sit under such a ministry, that naturally *misleads* them; since, while *the blind leads the blind, both fall into the ditch. If there had been a law given that could have given life,* says the apostle, *verily righteousness should have been by the law,* Gal. iii.21. But as there is no law given, that can give life to a sinner, it is a *vain, foolish* thing, to *press* such a soul, to get a *righteousness* by his

own *performances*, which was never appointed of God, nor can be *attained* by man. No; *the scripture hath concluded all under sin, that the promise* (of life) *by faith of Jesus Christ* (as a sinner's righteousness) *might be given to them that believe*, verse 22. And those who receive it not in this *way*, shall never attain it in any *other*, but must go *without* it forever. *The labour of the foolish,* says the wise man, *wearieth every one of them, because he knoweth not how to go to the city,* Eccles. x.15. A man may labour all his *days*, to make himself *righteous* before God, by his own *performances*, and to make his *peace* with him, by his *legal* repentance, and humiliation for *sin*; and yet *lose* all his labour at *last*, and so weary himself in *vain*, being never able to reach that *city*, that eternal rest, which God has prepared for his people: because he *knoweth* not *Christ*, the only *way*, that leads thither; and so *walks* not by faith, in him, as such.

All men by nature, are ignorant of Christ's *righteousness*, as it is God's *way* of *justifying* and *saving* a sinner; and it is *dangerous* for souls to sit under such a ministry, that presseth *doing*, and persuades them their *safety* lies there, instead of *believing:* for, *how shall they believe,* saith the apostle, *in him of whom they have not heard? and how shall they hear without a preacher? And how shall they preach, except they be sent?* Rom. x.14, 15. How shall the poor souls *believe* in Christ for *justification*, when they have never *heard* of his *righteousness*, which is the proper *object* of faith? And how shall they *hear,* without a *preacher* of that gospel which declares it? And how shall they *preach* the gospel to others, who have never *seen* that salvation it reveals for sinners, by the *righteousness* of Christ themselves? How shall they declare the glory and efficacy thereof to *others*, who have never seen, nor experienced it *themselves?* And how does it appear, that they are *sent* by Christ, to preach the gospel, who neither *know*, nor *proclaim* his *righteousness,* for the *justification* of a sinner, which is such a main *doctrine* thereof?

Have we not reason to fear, that many of those who are called *ministers* of the *gospel*, are rather *preachers* of *Moses*, than of *Christ?* and that their *ministry* rather tends to lead souls to the bondage and death of the *law*, than to the liberty and life of the *gospel?* But, *how beautiful are the feet of them that preach the gospel of peace, that bring glad tidings of good things.* That publish that *peace* with God, which was made for sinners alone, by the *blood* of Christ's cross; and is possest, only by *faith* in him! That proclaim the glad tidings of those good things, which God has prepared to be enjoyed by *sinners,* through the justifying *righteousness* of his Son! And how great is the privilege of those souls, who sit under a *gospel*-ministry; since this is the *means* appointed of God, to work *faith* in them, and to bring *salvation* to them! Once more,

5. Since the *justification* of a sinner is by the *righteousness* of Christ, *imputed* to him, and received by *faith* alone; we may hence learn, how great the *obligation* of the *justified* ones is, to *live* to the *glory* of that *grace*, which has so freely and fully *justified* them, in and through Christ, unto eternal *life* by him! When the apostle had asserted the justification and salvation of God's people, both *Jews* and *Gentiles*, to be wholly of his free *mercy*, in and through Christ, Rom. xi.32. and admired the riches of his *wisdom*, which was so brightly displayed in the dispensations of his *mercy* towards them, verse 33. he thus concludes his discourse, verse 36. *For of him, and through him, and to him are all things; to whom be glory forever,* Amen. It is as if he should say, since all things, relating to the justification and salvation of God's people, are *of* him, and *through* him, it is meet that the glory of all should, by them, be given *to* him: and therefore, when he applies this doctrine of God's free mercy in Christ, to them who had obtained it, he thus addresseth them, chap. xii.1. *I beseech you therefore, brethren, by the mercies of God, that ye present your bodies a living sacrifice, holy, acceptable unto God, which is your reasonable service.* I beseech *you*, says he; *You* that have obtained *mercy; therefore,* or, since it is God's design, to *glorify* his mercy, in the salvation of sinners, that you give him the *glory* of it: *by the mercies of God*; those *mercies* of God, which you are partakers of, in the *forgiveness* of all your *sins*, and in the *justification* of your *persons; that ye present your bodies a living sacrifice, holy, acceptable unto God,* that ye continually offer up yourselves, as a whole burnt-offering, in the flames of *love*, unto him that hath *loved* you, in all holy and acceptable *obedience*, to the *glory* of that God, who has thus had *mercy* upon you; *which is your reasonable service,* for it is a most reasonable thing, or a thing for which there is the highest *reason*, that you should ever *serve* the Lord, to the *glory* of that *grace*, by which you are freely *justified*, and shall be eternally *glorified*. And thus the apostle Peter, 1 Pet. ii.9. *But ye are a chosen generation, a royal priesthood,* [who are washed from all your sins in Christ's blood, and clothed with his righteousness] *an holy nation, a peculiar people; that ye should shew forth the praises of him who hath called you out of darkness, into his marvelous light.* And, *you know,* says the apostle Paul, *how we exhorted and comforted, and charged every one of you,* [*i.e.*, of you justified, saved ones] *that*

ye would walk worthy of God, who hath called you unto his kingdom and glory, 1 Thess. ii.11, 12.

And in short, as it was God's design to get himself *glory,* in the *justification* of sinners, by the *righteousness* of Jesus Christ; so the *display* thereof, throughout the whole gospel, lays *them* under the highest *obligation* to *live* to his *praise.* Does God the *Father impute* the *obedience* of his Son to poor sinners? Did God the *Son obey,* in *life* and in *death* for them? And does God the *Spirit, reveal* and *apply* this *righteousness* to them, and enable them to *receive* the same, as a *free gift* of grace, unto their eternal *life* in glory? What thanks, what praise, is due to God, in each of his glorious persons, for this abundant grace! And let the language of the justified ones, in heart, lip, and life, in all kinds of holy *obedience,* both now, and always be, *Thanks be unto God, for the grace of* JUSTIFICATION! *for this, his unspeakable* GIFT! 2 Cor. ix.15. *Amen! Hallelujah!*

T H E   E N D.

E R R A T A.
[Editor's note: Errata have been corrected in the text.]

A P P E N D I X.*

A S no revealed truth is of greater importance to the sons of men, than the justification of a guilty sinner, through the imputed righteousness of Christ; so, there can be no inquiry more interesting than for a person to know, if they be divorced from the law, as a covenant; married to Christ, as their best husband; and clothed with the robe of his justifying righteousness, as their adorning garment. To attain some satisfaction on this important point, the conscience may be posed with the following question, as an additional improvement of the foregoing subject.

1. Did you ever come to *yourselves?* Luke xv.17.; that is, did you ever feel yourselves to be bound with the cords of guilt, laden with iniquity, and ready to sink into the bottomless pit? Men must be condemned, before they are justified; be cast down, before they are lifted up; apply the curse to themselves, before they take hold of the blessing; hear the sentence of death denounced against them by the law, before they partake of the justification of life by the gospel.—If you were never burdened, you cannot be eased; if you were never broken, you cannot be bound up; if you were never mourners, you cannot be comforted; if you never tasted the bitterness of sin, you cannot taste of the sweetness of the grace of Christ, and experience his purifying blood, and his reviving righteousness.—If you are justified, how did you come by pardon and peace? Was it by wrestling and prayer?

2. Are you *sanctified?* Justification and sanctification always go together. Where ever the blood of Christ is applied to justify, his Spirit is implanted to sanctify: they are always joined together, John xix.34. Blood and water came out of his side; blood to justify, and water to sanctify. Jesus, at the same time that he satisfied for sin, crucified our *old man*, Rom. iv.6. Those who are justified, by the sprinkling of his blood, are also redeemed from all iniquity, and consecrated to God. Where Christ washes with his blood, he likewise anoints with his Spirit.

3. Are we *adopted?* Justification is always attended with adoption. These who receive the *white stone* of justification from all their sins, have also in it the *new name*, Rev. ii.17. What is this new name, but the name of

---

*This Appendix was not in the first impression of this Book.

a child of God? Adoption is an amplification of our justification. We are no only pronounced righteous, and owned as friends; but reputed and accepted as sons and daughters; are nearly related, and greatly endeared to God.

4. Do you *love* God and Christ? It is recorded concerning Mary, *That she loved much, because much was forgiven her*, Luke vii.47. When great debts are remitted, heinous sins pardoned, deep spots and stains fetched out, this calls for the highest and most fervent love. It is said, Prov. xvii.9. *He that covereth transgression, seeketh love.* Surely then, with the greatest propriety it may be said, that God and Christ have sought our love, by *covering our sins*, Psalm xxxii.1, 2. If you give not your hearts to God, if you do not set your love on Christ, who redeems from all iniquity, it is a plain sign that you have not tasted of the grace of God, or experienced the kindness of Christ in forgiving your sins.

5. What free *access* have you to God, and what joy and delight have you in him? Are your consciences so perfectly purged from iniquity, that you dare draw nigh God with confidence and boldness? *Having therefore, brethren, boldness to enter into the holiest by the blood of Jesus,* Heb. vii.19 and x.19. Do you rejoice in God, through Christ Jesus our Lord, as having now *received the atonement?* Rom. v.11. Are you so justified in the Lord as to glory? Isa. xlv.25. *In the Lord shall all the seed of Israel be justified, and shall glory.* Is your justification matter of the greatest joy to you? *I will greatly rejoice in the Lord, my soul shall be joyful in my God; for he hath covered me with the robe of righteousness*, Isaiah lxi.10.

6. Are you employed, and do you take great pleasure and delight to *bless* and *praise* the Lord, for pardoning all your sins, and reconciling you to himself? This was David's delightful employment; *Bless the Lord, O my soul; and all that is within me bless his holy name,—who forgiveth all mine iniquities*, Psalm ciii.1, 2, 3. Justified souls will sing praises to God who heals their backslidings; and rejoice in Christ Jesus, who is their righteousness and ransom: The redeemed of the Lord shall return to *Zion with songs*, Isa. xxxv.10. Our lips were once sealed up with guilt; but now the mouths of accusers are stoped, by Christ's satisfaction: and shall not our lips then be opened, and our tongues loosed, to sing aloud of God's grace, and of Christ's righteousness?

7. Are you willing to go out of this world; to *die*, and to be with God, and Jesus Christ? Those that are justified have *peace with God*, and *rejoice in the hope of the glory of God*, Rom. v.1, 2. Though condemned sinners shall be cast away on the shores of a miserable eternity; yet justified souls

shall be landed safe in the harbour of glory, and enjoy a blessed eternity. When others pass into the prison of hell, justified persons enter into the palace of God, Matth. xxv.34, 41. When the tares are reaped for the furnace, believers are reaped for, and gathered into the garner, Matth. iii.12.—Will justified persons shun the glorious presence of God, and slavishly dread his tribunal? Will pardoned and adopted persons be afraid to go home to their Father, and be put in possession of the heavenly inheritance? Are you therefore willing to be *absent from the* body, and to be *present with the Lord*, 2 Cor. v.6, 8. Can you therefore conquer the fears of death? are you willing to leave your place on earth, to enjoy the place prepared for you in heaven? to put off the rags of mortality, that you may be clothed with the robes of glory? to quit your *earthly tabernacle,* for *the house not made with hands eternal in the heavens?* 2 Cor. v.1.

If these and the like, are your attainments, and the happy dispositions of your soul, they may be viewed as so many infallible evidences, that you have passed from death to life, are in a justified state, interested in the Redeemer's righteousness, have it imputed unto you, and shall, in due time, be honoured to *see God's face in righteousness*, Psalm xvii.15.

As these are the only *happy* persons who have the righteousness of Christ imputed to them, and are *made the righteousness of God in him*, 2 Cor. v.21.; so they are of all others the most *miserable* who have no interest therein.—Why, they are in their *natural* state, and the scripture describes all such not only to be *stout-hearted* and *far from righteousness,* Isa. xlv.12; but to be *filled with all unrighteousness*, Rom. i.29.—These who are not justified have all their *sins recorded* in God's book, Isa. lxv.6. Man's iniquity is said to be written, so as to be marked before God, Jer. ii.22.; and there is a counterpart of this record kept in the sinner's own conscience, Jer. xvii.1.—Till Christ becomes their righteousness, their souls are *shamefully naked*, Rev. iii.17. As men are poor, they are void of an inherent righteousness; and, as they *are naked*, they are destitute of an imputed righteousness. Till the righteousness of Christ is spread over the soul, the glorious image of God is not put on it.—Till they are justified, there is a *breach* between God and them. Sin hath made a breach; and this breach stands open, and we need a Mediator to stand in the gap, Psalm cvi.23. But there is none fit for this, but Jesus Christ, the living advocate, 1 John ii.1.—There is a dreadful *storm of wrath*, in the cloud of the threatenings, which hangs over the heads of guilty sinners, Psalm xi.6. This cup of indignation shall come to their lips; this storm shall fall on their souls. If God rains, the storm must needs be terrible: *I will rain*, says Jehovah, Gen. vii.4. Though, by reason of unbelief, *God's judgments are now far above, out of the sight of sinners*, Psalm x.5.; yet *their eyes shall see their destruction,* and *they shall drink of the wrath of the Almighty*, Job. xxi.20. The long and large roll of the curse will in due time fly to them, Ezek. lii.2, 3, 4.—All the sins of unjustified persons are so many *evidences* and *witnesses* against them: these evidences are preserved and kept safe; their sins are hid that they may not be lost, Hos. xiii.12. *The iniquity of Ephraim is bound up, his sin is hid.* Their iniquity is bound up, that in due time it may be bound on them; their sin is so hid, that it shall be found, brought forth, and charged on them. So many sins as men have committed, and are unpardoned, so many witnesses have they provided against the day of their trial, Jer. xiv.7. *O Lord, our iniquities testify against us.* Isa. lix.12.—Every sin deserves, and every unjustified soul will be rewarded with *eternal death*, Rom. vi.23. Death is "øþíéá the *wages of sin.* The word signifies *soldiers wages*, Luke iii.14. They who cleave to Satan as their general, who abide in his tents, fight on his side against God, shall have eternal death as wages paid them, Isaiah lix.18. and liv.15. And as there is a judgment to come, God, who seeth the provocations of all men, will be a *swift witness against them*, Matth. iii.5. And if their sins are not pardoned, but remain before God's face, and they inherit the iniquities of their whole life, they will be heirs of shame, misery, and eternal torments. Psalm xc.8. Job xiii.26. *The wicked shall be turned into hell.*

Though this is the unhappy situation of all unjustified persons, who have no interest in the Redeemer's righteousness; yet, such is the goodness of God to poor sinners, that he *brings near this righteousness* to them, Isaiah xlvi.13.; he reveals it fully to them in the gospel, for it is the *minis-tration of righteousness*, 2 Cor. v.18.: and Christ himself declares, that he is the *end of the law for righteousness to every one that believeth*, Rom. x.4; and that *his righteousness is unto and upon all that believe*, Rom. iii.22.— And all the redeemed shall glory in it, saying, *Surely, in the Lord have I righteousness and strength. In him shall all the seed of Israel be justified, and shall glory,* Isaiah xlv.24, 25. *I will greatly rejoice in the Lord, my soul shall be joyful in my God; for he hath clothed me with the garments of salvation, he hath covered me with the robe of righteousness*, Isaiah lxi.10.

F I N I S.

A

D I S C O U R S E

Concerning the

N E W - B I R T H :

To which are added

Two POEMS;

THE ONE

On Salvation in Christ, by Free-
Grace, for the Chief of Sinners:

THE OTHER

On a Believer's Safety and Duty.

With an Epistle Recommendatory,

By the Reverend

Mr. *J A C O B R O G E R S*, B.A.

L O N D O N

Printed; and Sold by JOHN OSWALD at the *Rose* and *Crown* in the *Poultry*,
near *Stocks-Market*; and EBENEZER GARDNER, *at Milton's* Head in
Grace-Church-Street. 1740.
(Price Bound one Shilling and three Pence.)

PREFACE.

Dear Reader,

*A*S *I have read over the ensuing Discourse concerning the* New-Birth, *with some Pleasure and Satisfaction to my own Soul; so I wou'd take the Liberty to recommend it likewise to thy serious and impartial Perusal. It is full of the sweet and wholesome Words of the Gospel of the Grace of God; and sets forth the Nature, Necessity, and Excellency of the* New-Birth, *in such a plain and easy Manner, (not with Words which Man's Wisdom teacheth, but which the Holy Ghost teacheth) that, methinks, by the Blessing of God, it will be found truly useful and edifying to thy Soul. The Author is well known to me, and I think it my Duty to acknowledge that I have been much strengthen'd and comforted, under God, by conversing with one, whose Communication is indeed good to the Use of Edifying, and powerfully ministers Grace to the Hearers. The Reverend Mr.* Whitefield, *and Mr.* Seward, *now with God, who both held a Correspondence with the Author, have also frequently declar'd with what Savour and Sweetness, the reading of the Author's Letters, has been accompanied to their Souls; which gives me Hopes that all who have the Taste and Spirit of those Servants of the most high God, will not only be inclin'd to read this Discourse, when it comes to their Hands, but likewise receive that spiritual Edification from it, which those Gentlemen have done from other Writings of the Author.*

'Tis certain that Books of this kind are but too too much neglected, and despis'd by the wise and prudent Men of this World, who, whatever may be their other Accomplishments, discern not the Things of the Spirit of God; but poor Soul, whosoever thou art that desirest, by the Eye of Faith, to behold the Glory of Christ, the Glory as of the only begotten of the Father full of Grace and Truth, *'tis to be hop'd thou wilt* lay aside all Malice, and all Guile, and Hypocrisies, and Envies, and all Evil-speakings, *and as* a New-born Babe, desire the sincere Milk of the Word, (*which as far as I can judge from the Scriptures of Truth, and my own Experience, is contain'd in the following Discourse) that thou may'st* grow-up *thereby into him in all Things who is the* Head of the Body *his* Church, even Christ. *Let me once more,* Dear Reader, *intreat thee fairly to weigh the Greatness and Importance of the Matter, and beg of the Lord for a spiritual Discernment of the Truths in the following Work, and for a real and powerful Application of them to thy own Heart by his Holy Spirit, without which all thy Reading will be vain and useless. May the Lord give thee his Grace here; and prepare thee for eternal Glory hereafter; which is the hearty Prayer of one of the poorest and weakest Servants of the Lord.*

JACOB ROGERS.

A
DISCOURSE

Concerning the

NEW-BIRTH.

THE Doctrine of the *New-Birth*, is a Doctrine of the Bible, clearly taught, and necessary to be known; and yet Multitudes are ignorant of it, and care not to be acquainted with it: although the Necessity of it is such, that without it, no Man can enter into the Kingdom of God; or the Glories of the heavenly State, either in the Church below, or the Church above. No, tho' an unregenerate Man, should profess Faith in Christ, as *Simon Magus* once did, and be thereupon admitted into any of the Churches of Christ here on Earth; yet could he not see *Sion's* Glory, nor enter into spiritual Fellowship with the Church, partaking of its Privileges, as it is a Kingdom of Grace, Power, Righteousness, Peace and Joy in the Holy Ghost. These Things every natural Man is a Stranger to, he understands them not, neither can he know them. 'Tis the *Pure in Heart,* or those that are born again, and those only, who have now the Blessedness of *seeing God* in his Church, or Kingdom, below; and that shall have the Vision of his Glory in his Kingdom, or Church above. And since many think the New-Birth, a strange, and unnecessary Thing, being at a Loss to know what it is, or, what it is to be born again, I shall give some Hints concerning it, in the following Method.

First, I shall shew, What the New-Birth is, or, What it is to be born again, by giving a Definition thereof.

Secondly, Endeavour to explain, and prove it from the Word of God.

Thirdly, Shew, What we may learn from this Phrase of being Born again. And

Fourthly, With some Uses, conclude the whole.

First then, The *New-Birth*, or, to be Born Again, is, a supernatural Work of the Holy Spirit of God, by the Word, upon the Soul of a Man; creating it a-new in Christ Jesus, in all the Powers and Faculties thereof; by which he produceth an abiding Principle of spiritual Life; which contains in it all Kinds of Graces, every way fitted for, and actings towards their proper Objects.

Secondly, I shall endeavour to explain, and prove this Definition of the New-Birth, from the Word of God. That it is a Work of the Holy Spirit of God, by the Word, appears plain, from what our Lord asserts, in his Discourse with *Nicodemus*, John iii. where, after he had declared the Necessity of being Born again, with a *Verily verily,* (a double Asseveration, the more to ascertain the Thing) *Except a Man be Born again, he cannot see the Kingdom of God*, Ver. 3. He further urges it, Ver. 5. and declares to *Nicodemus*, who had carnal Conceptions of it, the true Nature of the Thing, and the proper Intendment of his Speech therein; by acquainting him with the Almighty Agent of this great Work, the Divine Spirit, whose creating Efficacy, working with the Word, brings forth this spiritual Production. *Verily verily I say unto thee, except a Man be Born of Water and of the Spirit, he cannot enter into the Kingdom of God.* Hence it is fully proved, that the Spirit of God is the Author of the New-Birth, in that the Man that is Born again, is said, to be Born *of* the Spirit. As also, Ver. 8. where our Lord sets forth this Work of the Spirit on the Heart, analogously with the Wind's blowing in the Air: *The Wind* (says he) *bloweth where it lifteth, and thou hearest the Sound thereof, but canst not tell whence it cometh, and whither it goeth: so is every one that is Born of the Spirit.* From this Text we are taught, 1. That the Spirit of God is the *Author* of the New-Birth. 2. That the Operations of the Holy Ghost in this Work, are altogether *Free* and *Sovereign.* He acts herein as a *Free* and *Sovereign* Lord, in the greatest *Freedom*, without Motives from the Creature, as being under no Obligation from any of the Works of his Hands; and in the highest *Sovereignty*, while, in distinguishing Favour, he blows upon one Soul, and passeth another by. For, *as the Wind bloweth where it lifteth*, (to *this* Point, and not *that*, upon *this* Tree, House &c. and not *another*) so is every one that is Born of the Spirit. 3. That the Soul herein is *Passive* to the Spirit, before it *acts*; just as the Subjects blown upon are to the Wind, before they move. 4. That the Spirit works by an *irresistible* Power in the New-Birth; which corrupt Nature can no more *resist*, than moveable Things can *withstand* an irresistible Wind. Grace and Power herein, are so wisely mixed, that it's hard to say which of them has the Ascendant: He sweetly draws the Heart, and strongly subdues Corruption, by an irresistible Sweetness, an alluring, soul-overcoming Energy. And, 5. That the regenerating Operations of the Spirit on the Soul, are an absolute *Secret* to the natural Man, tho' he hears the Sound, the Report thereof; Yea, that the Soul itself, that hears the Spirit's Voice to its Heart, in his Word, when the Work first begins, may be greatly at a Loss to know *whence* it is that its Mind should be so wrought on, and *what* will be the Issue, until the Lord opens the Mystery to it. *Thou hearest the Sound thereof, but canst not tell whence it cometh, and whither it goeth: So is every one that is born of the Spirit.* And as the New Birth is a Work of the Spirit of God; so it is his Work, as the *holy* Spirit, or the Spirit of *Sanctification.* For it is as the Spirit is sent down from the Father, and Christ, into the Hearts of his People to *sanctify* them, that he thus operates upon them. The Spirit of God is holy in his *Nature*, yea, *Holiness* itself, as that Perfection of the Godhead, belongs to the Spirit, co-equally with the Father, and the Son. But, as I conceive, 'tis chiefly on the Account of his *Office*, as a *Sanctifier* to the People of God, that he's stiled, The *Holy Spirit.* And when he creates the *New Man* in the Soul, it is said to be in *true Holiness*, Ephes. iv.24. And all that were chosen of God the Father, in Christ, before the World was, unto eternal Life, were ordained to pass through *Sanctification of the Spirit*, as a Means to this great End, *1 Pet.* i.2.

And as the New Birth is a Work of the Holy Spirit of God; so likewise, it is a *supernatural Work*; or a Work that is wholly above his *common* Operations in the Hearts of natural Men: Yea, even above what he wrought in the Heart of perfect *Adam.* For tho' he was perfectly Holy, and all his Posterity in him, when he came out of his Maker's Hand, in the Capacity of a common Person; and so every way fitted to enjoy Communion with God, as the God of Nature, displaying his Glory in the Creatures of this lower World; yet the Begun Holiness of the Saints, communicated to them in the New-Birth, (which the Holy Ghost will perfect in its appointed Season) is of a far higher *Kind*; inasmuch as it is a preparing of them for a far higher *Glory*; to wit, the Glory of the *heavenly State:* Which consists, in Communion with God, and Conformity to him, displaying his Glory in Christ, as the God of all Grace, to be enjoyed here by Faith, and hereafter by Vision. Thus the superior Glory of the New Creation Work on the Soul, is set forth by Way of Allusion to the Old Creation, 2 Cor. iv.6. *For God, who commanded the Light to shine out of Darkness, hath shined in our Hearts, to give the Light of the Knowledge of the Glory of God, in the Face of Jesus Christ.* As the Glory of God, discovered in the Face of *Jesus Christ*, is a more transcendent *Display*, than that which at the first Creation was made in the Face of the *Creatures*; So the Light, which by a creating Voice, is produced in the Hearts of God's People, by which this is *beheld*, is of a far higher *Kind* than the first Creation Light, and every Way fitted for converse with more glorious Objects. In the old Creation, there was a perfect

Agreement between the Objects to be seen, the Eye that conversed with them, and the Light, the Medium, by which they were beheld; So in the New, on which Account, the one is resembled by the other. Yet so, that a *Transcendency* of Glory, in all respects, is still on the Side of the *New Creation*. In the *Old* Creation, the *Objects* to be seen were *Natural*; But in the *New,* they are *Supernatural*. In the *Old* Creation, the *Eye* that saw them was *Natural*, whether we respect the corporeal, or mental Eye, or the Light of Reason in *Adam's* Heart, it was no more than Natural; But it's *spiritual* Eye, that takes in *spiritual* Objects, the Eye of *Faith*, which is far more bright and clear than the Eye of *Reason*, in its greatest Perfection. In the *Old* Creation, *natural Light* was sufficient to discover *natural Objects*; but 'tis the *spiritual, supernatural Light of the Gospel*, that is the Medium by which the glorious Objects of the New Creature's Sight are *beheld*. Thus, it appears, that the *New-Birth* is a Work of the *Spirit*, the *Holy* Spirit of God, that is truly *supernatural*. But then,

Further, The New-Birth is likewise a Work of the Spirit of God, by the *Word*. Hence in that fore-quoted Text, *John* iii.5. the Man that is born again, is said to be born of *Water*; by which the *Word* of God is intended. And the Word is set forth by Water, to shew the cleansing Efficacy thereof in the Hand of the Spirit; for as Water cleanseth the Body from natural Filthiness, so doth the Word of God cleanse the Soul from spiritual Uncleanness. And as the Use the Holy Spirit makes of the Word, in the New-Birth, is in this Text, set forth by the Metaphor of Water, to shew his sanctifying Operations therein, in the *Mortification of Sin*; so, the other Part of his sanctifying Influences therein, in *quickning the Soul to a Life of Grace, by the Word*, is set forth, where it is compar'd to *a Living Seed*, as, 1 Pet. i.23. *Being born again, not of Corruptible Seed, but of Incorruptible, by the Word of God, which liveth and abideth for ever.* For, as the casting of a *living Seed* into the Earth, under the Influences of the God of Nature, working with second Causes, is productive of that Plant or Tree that was *seminally* in its self; so the *Word* of God, (and particularly the Word of the *Gospel,* as it follows, Ver. 25.) being *cast* into the Heart, under the Almighty Operations of the Spirit, is productive of *Spiritual Life, the Life of Grace,* or the *New Creature* in the Soul. And the Blessed Spirit makes Use of the Word in his Work, in a *Mediate*, or more *Immediate* Way, according to his sovereign Pleasure. Some Souls have the Word brought home to their Hearts with Almighty Power, like a Sun-beam, irradiating their dark Minds, or as a Fire, enkindling their cold Affections, thawing their frozen Hearts, yea, melting their whole Souls down, as Metal is melted in a Furnace, whereby they are prepared for, and then cast into another Form, to wit, The Form of the Word, and the Likeness of Christ. (As *Rom.* iv.17. *Ye have obeyed from the Heart that Form of Doctrine which was deliver'd you.* So it is translated; but, as some have render'd the Word, it's thus, *Ye have obeyed from the Heart that Form of Doctrine into which ye were deliver'd:* For as the melted *Metal* is cast into the *Mould*, to receive another *Form*, so the Soul, being melted down by the fiery Operations of the Spirit, in and by the Word, is cast *thereinto*, and *fashion'd* like it). And all this in an *Immediate* Way. Others again, have the same Work wrought upon 'em in a *Mediate* Way, *viz.* In reading the Word of God, or in hearing the same preach'd. God breaks in in an Instant to the Souls of some of his People, in the *reading* of his Word, with a bright Display of his Glory in Christ, by which they are *transform'd* into the same *Image*. But his more general Way of Working, in Regenerating the Soul, is by the *Preaching of the Gospel*. Hence the Gospel is set forth *as the Ministration of Life:* Not only because it is the Doctrine of Life, and Salvation for poor Sinners, thro' a Crucified, Risen, and Ascended Saviour; but also because Life is communicated to dead Souls, under the Ministry thereof, by the Spirit of God, who fills the same, and is communicated thereby, *2 Cor.* iii.6, 8. Thus the Apostle sets forth the Folly of the *Galatians*, in giving Heed to those Seducers, who labour'd to draw them off from the Gospel of Christ, and the full Salvation they had thereby, unto an Adhesion to the Works of the Law, in the Point of Justification and Acceptance with God, by putting them in Mind of their own Experience, when the Lord first wrought upon their Hearts in the New-Birth: *This only would I learn of you,* (says he) *Received ye the Spirit by the Works of the Law, or by the Hearing of Faith?* Gal. iii.2. *Faith* here, is put for the Doctrine of Faith, *i.e.,* the *Gospel*; by which the Spirit of Life from God, in his Regenerating Influences, was receiv'd; which shews the transcendent Excellency of *this* Ministry, above *that* of the Law, which is *a Ministration of Death.*

And Satan knows well enough, that 'tis God's usual Method to save Sinners by the Preaching of the Gospel; and therefore he labours to the utmost, to *blind the Minds of them which believe not, lest the Light of the glorious Gospel of Christ, who is the Image of God, should shine unto them,* 2 Cor. iv.4. And one great Way of his doing this, is by casting opprobrious Names upon the Gospel, and the Preachers thereof, thereby to prejudice Persons against it, and keep 'em from coming under so much as the Sound thereof; lest by the powerful Grace of the Gospel, they should be snatch'd, as a Prey, from his Teeth; so great is his Malice! And that *All* are not thus blinded, is owing to *distinguishing* Grace, which has undertaken for a *Remnant*, to bring them under the Sound of this despised Gospel, and to make it efficacious for the eternal Salvation of their Souls. For, *the great Trumpet shall be blown,* (the Gospel shall be preach'd) *and they shall come which were ready to perish in the Land of* Assyria, *and in the Land of* Egypt, *and shall worship the Lord in His Holy Mount at Jerusalem,* Isa. xxvii.13. Perishing Sinners, at the greatest Distance from God, shall be brought by an over-ruling *Providence* under the Sound of the *Gospel,* and by efficacious *Grace* unto *Christ* by the *Gospel, and worship the Lord in his Holy Mount at Jerusalem*; i.e., In his Gospel-church; the heavenly *Jerusalem*; which is here set forth by the Place of the Temple-worship of old. But, to return,

As the New-Birth is a supernatural Work of the Holy Spirit of God, by the Word, so it is upon the *Soul* of a Man, creating it anew in Christ Jesus, in all the Powers and Faculties thereof. That the *Soul* is the Seat of this Work, is plain, in that the New Creature form'd in it, is call'd the *Inward Man,* 2 Cor. iv.16. which is there said to be *renewed Day by Day*; because the Work of the Spirit, in Regeneration, tho' perfect in Respect of *Parts*, is yet imperfect in Respect of *Degree*, and is still upon the *Increase*, until it arrive unto *Perfection*. The New-Born Soul, in Respect of *Grace*, and the compleat Glory of Christ's Image in it, is just like a New-Born Infant in Nature, which has all the *Parts* of a Man, tho' it wants the full *Stature* of a Man; and therefore *increaseth* until it arrive unto the *Perfection* of Manhood. A Child is truly *born*, tho' not a *Man* presently; So the Soul, in Regeneration, is truly *born again*, tho' it arrives not presently at that *Perfection*, which is design'd it, and to which it tends: No, this *Inward Man*, the New-Born Soul, being renewed Day by Day, is still increasing towards Perfection, as the Body, the *Outward Man* (to which 'tis here opposed) perisheth, decreaseth, and draweth on towards its Dissolution, But,

Again, As the Work of the Spirit, in the New-Birth, is upon the Soul of a Man, so herein he *creates* it anew in Christ Jesus. That the New-Birth is a *Creation*, has been hinted already; and I shall add little more than one express Text to prove it; for, *Eph.* ii.10. The Apostle says, *We* (that is we that are sav'd by Grace, or New-Born) *are his Workmanship, created in Christ Jesus, unto good Works, which God hath before ordained that we should walk in them.* Here the New-Born are said to be *Created*, and that

Anew; for 'tis *in* Christ Jesus, i.e., In *Union* to his Person, and in *Conformity* to his Image. *Creation*, is a Making of Things out of Nothing. The old Creation was so: and the New Creation is a producing the Life, or Being of Grace, out of no pre-existent Matter in the Soul, or Goodness in the Creature which dispos'd it hereunto. Nay, so far is it from this, that every Thing in Nature, or in the Soul of Man in a natural State, opposeth it. Which makes it appear to be an *exceeding Greatness of God's Power, which is put forth herein*; as the Apostle's Phrase is, *Eph.* i.19. When God created the Heavens and the Earth, tho there was no previous Matter to work upon, yet there was nothing to resist; but in the new Creation there is much Opposition. To instance in the Creation of Natural *Light:* When God said, *Let there be Light, there was Light:* His Almighty Power went forth with his Word to produce it. And tho' there was no previous *Disposition* in the precedent Darkness, towards the Light; yet there was no Resistance therein; for natural Darkness was but a meer *Negation*, or the not being of Light. But when God commands spiritual, supernatural Light in the Soul, and instantaneously produceth the same, by the exceeding, or super-excelling Greatness of his Power; there is, not only natural Darkness in the Mind, as it notes, *No Disposition* to spiritual Light, but there is also, Moral Darkness, or the Darkness of Sin; which is an active Principle, that *resists, opposes,* and *hates* the *Light*. How great then is the Display of Divine Power in the New Creation! And what a Folly is it in sinful Man, to think, that he can make himself a New Creature? Or, that this is the Work of a finite Arm? Or, of any created Person, or Thing, whether *internal*, as any supposed Virtue of the Mind, or *external*, as the Ordinance of Baptism, or a visible turning from a vicious Course of Life? &c. Alas! 'tis not in the Power of these Things to make a new Creature, or to regenerate the Soul.

The Ordinance of *Baptism* was never instituted by Christ, to regenerate a Man, or to be a Means of the New-Birth; but for quite different Ends, whatever mistaken Notions Men may have about it. And if they trust to *this*, as their Regeneration, and never seek for, nor experience the Almighty Power of God, changing their whole Souls, and giving them a new and spiritual Life, alas! they'll *die* in *Unregeneracy*.

And as to visible *Reformation* of Life, it is good in its Place, and well would it be, if there was more of it, in Persons, Families, and Nations. But, if the Person turning from a vicious Course, or some outward Acts of Sin, which are visible to every Eye, call'd, *The Filthiness of the Flesh*, 2 Cor. vii.1. hath not, before this, had gracious Experience of the Almighty Power of the Spirit, working upon his Soul, in giving him an Holy Heart, by forming the New-Creature Life, and so furnishing of him with a spiritual Ability to turn from Sin unto God; Alas! all turning from outward Acts of Sin, unto a Performance of some Things materially good, leaves the Soul but just where it found it, *viz.* in a State of *Nature,* an *old* Creature still: For tho' the Soul turns indeed, yet 'tis not from Sin unto God, but rather from sinful Self, unto righteous Self; it ceaseth to run such Lengths as it had done in outward Acts of Sin, but runs greater Lengths in Heart-sins, the *Filthiness of the Spirit*, in idolizing its self, and its own Righteousness; by setting up its self, as the End of its Obedience, and its own Obedience, as the Matter of its Acceptance with God: Which a Man that is born again, dare not do; no, it is far otherwise with such a Soul, in its visible Reformation of Life: Such an one is made a *new Creature* to begin with, and then it puts forth Acts of the *New Life*, in *turning* from Sin unto God, both internally and externally. It turns from all Sin, as Sin, from an intense Hatred of it, as it's against God, a God of boundless Love, yea, that God which the Soul sees, has loved *it* in particular; for the Love of God shed abroad in the Heart forms its own Image there, and makes the Soul to love him again: Hence, as it hates Sin as Sin, so it turns from it unto God, setting up his Glory as the End of all its Obedience, and its own Obedience in the Place of Duty, but not in the Place of its Righteousness before God. And thus to turn from Sin unto God, none but a *New Creature* can do; because, it's a *Good Work,* and the Soul must be *created unto Good Works*, before it can walk in them, either this, or any other; as in this Text, *Eph.* ii.10. In a Word then, since the New-Birth is a Work of *Creation*; nothing less than Almightiness, or, the Omnipotent Power of *Jehovah*, can effect it. And that this Creation in Christ Jesus, is a *New* Creation, is plain, from *2 Cor.* v.17. (where it's said) *If any Man be in Christ, he is a New Creature: Old Things are past away, behold all Things are become New.* But this brings me

To shew, that this New Creation Work upon the Soul, is in all the *Powers* and *Faculties* thereof. *If any Man be in Christ* (says this Text) *he is a new Creature:* There's the *Kind* of the Work specify'd. Behold, *all Things are become new:* There's the *Extensiveness* of it, as it reaches to all the Faculties of the Soul: Not that there are new Faculties created in the Soul, but the Soul is created anew in all its Faculties.

To begin with the *Understanding:* This noble Faculty of the Soul, while a Man is in a natural State, is *Dark*, yea *Darkness* itself; without the least spiritual Knowledge of God in Christ, as the Author of Salvation; of the

Salvation itself prepared, and of the Way and Means, by, and through which it is Possessed and Enjoyed, by every saved Soul; *i.e.*, as it is, Meritoriously, by Christ alone, and Instrumentally, thro' Faith in him, without the Works of the Law, or any part of the Creature's Obedience, as a procuring Cause thereof. And thus the Apostle sets forth the vast Difference that is made in the Understandings of God's People, when they are New-Born, by *Light*, the Opposite of *Darkness*, Eph. v.8. *For ye were sometimes Darkness*, (that is while in a natural State) *but now* (when New-Born) *are ye Light in the Lord*. And thus the New-Born are said to have an *Understanding given* them to *know him that is true*, 1 John v.20. And *we know that the Son of God is come, and hath given us an Understanding that we may know him that is true*. By which is intended, that supernatural Light, which is created in the *Understanding,* at the Time of the New-Birth; which gives the Soul a spiritual Ability to know God in Christ, and his Things, in such a Manner as no *natural Man*, either doth or *can know them*, 1. Cor. ii.14.

Again, The *Will*, while in a natural State, is *opposite* to God, and to the Way of Salvation by Jesus Christ. *The carnal Mind is* therefore said to be *Enmity against God,* Rom. viii.7. And what our Lord said of the unbelieving *Jews*, is true of every natural Man; *Ye will not come unto me, that ye might have Life*, John v.40. And the Difference that is made in the Soul, when New-Born, in respect of this Faculty, is set forth by its being made *willing*. For 'tis the Father's Promise to Christ, that *his People shall be Willing in the Day of his Power*, Psal. cx.3. They're made Willing to be saved in God's Way; by his Free Grace, through his dear Son, without the Deeds of the Law.

And as to the *Conscience*, while the Soul is Unregenerate, it's wholly destitute of spiritual *Life*, and under the Dominion of *Death:* It has no true Sense of God, or Regard to him, as the God of all Grace in Christ; wherein its *spiritual* Life consisteth. And as for that Degree of *natural* Life which it hath, which consists, in some Sense of God, as the God of Nature, displaying his Glory in the Moral Law, alas, it's weak, and gives but a very imperfect Account, of what is Duty, and what not, according to the Law; for the Spirituality of the Law, is a Glory too bright for its weak Sight. Hence the Apostle *Paul*, speaking of himself, when a zealous *Pharisee, I was without the Law once,* says he, *Rom.* vii.9. Yea, says he, I was *alive* without it. What's that? Why, his Conscience had so little Sense of the Holiness of God, and of his Law, in the strict Requirements thereof, that it justified him in, or gave him Hopes of Life by his imperfect Obedience; whereas it should have condemned him, for the Imperfection thereof. As it did when it was quickened by the Spirit of God and enabled to give its Verdict according to God's Law, as it follows, *But when the Commandment came, Sin revived, and I died.* When the Commandment came, in the Spirituality thereof, as being brought home by the Spirit of God to his renewed Conscience, he died, or became a dead Man in Law: He instantly saw himself to be Law-condemned, and actually stood Conscience-condemned, even for those very Things, it formerly had justified him in, before it had a quick, and lively Sense of God's Holy Law: But now it roundly told him, that as many as are of the Works of the Law, are under the Curse; and that there was no Life for him by the Works of his own Hands, or for any fallen Creature by its own Obedience. Upon which, he at once, became a dead Man, 1. *In* Law; in that he stood both Law, and Conscience-condemned, because his Obedience was imperfect. 2. *To* the Law; in that by this Law-Discovery, of the Impossibility of his obtaining Life by the Works of his own Hands, he ceased to seek it that Way. *For I thro' the Law* (says he) *am dead to the Law, that I might live unto God,* Gal. ii.19. Hence it appears, that the Conscience in its natural State, is in a great measure senseless, of that compleat Obedience, the Law of God requires, and therefore justifies, when it should condemn.

But then further, As to that true Sense it has of the Mind of God in his Law, as it respects outward Acts; so, in the Execution of its Office, as God's Vicegerent, it registers sinful Actions, and condemns for them. And thus considered, it is said to be an *evil Conscience*; that is, a guilty, accusing, condemning Conscience. And as such, it stands prepared to depart from God. The Soul of an unregenerate Man, under the Influence of an evil Conscience, hates God, and flees from him as his greatest Enemy. And therefore the New-Born, in order to their drawing nigh to God, are said to have their *Hearts sprinkled from an evil Conscience,* Heb. x.22. that is, to have their Conscience appeased, by the *sprinkling of Christ's Blood*; that as it before condemned them as Transgressors of the Law, it now justifies them, as it receives and declares God's justifying Sentence, in and through that Jesus who died for them, and rose again. And thus the New-born, are said to have their *Consciences purged from dead Works, to serve the living God,* Heb. ix.13, 14. *For if the Blood of Bulls, and of Goats, and the Ashes of an Heifer, sprinkling the unclean, sanctifieth to the purifying of the Flesh; how much more shall the Blood of Christ, who through the eternal*

Spirit offered himself without Spot to God, purge your Conscience from dead Works, to serve the living God? Thus the Spirit's Work, in the New Birth, extends to the *Conscience*, both in quickning and purging it. But then,

Again; It likewise reacheth to the *Affections*. These, while the Soul is in a natural State, are *earthly, sensual, vile.* The Affections of an unregenerate Man, are set upon earthly Things, the Gratifications of Sense, yea, the Gratification of Sin and Satan. Hence *they that are after the Flesh,* (*i.e.*, in a State of Nature) are said to *mind the Things of the Flesh*, Rom. viii.5. that is, carnal, worldly Things: These they desire, seek, love, and rejoice in, when obtained; these they fear the want of, grieve for the Loss of, and are displeased when any way stript thereof. But, as for God, he is not in all their Thoughts, as the chief Good their Soul seeks after. Thus also they are said to be *sensual, not having the Spirit,* Jude 19. And, says the Apostle, *Tit.* iii.3. *We ourselves also were sometimes foolish,* (*i.e* when in an unregenerate State) *disobedient, deceived, serving divers Lusts and Pleasures, living in Malice and Envy, hateful, and hating one another. But* (says he) *after that the Kindness and Love of God our Saviour towards Man appeared, not by Works of Righteousness which we have done; but, according to his Mercy, he saved us by the washing of Regeneration, and renewing of the Holy Ghost; which he shed on us abundantly, through Jesus Christ our Saviour*, Ver. 4, 5, 6. Efficacious Grace *(says he)* made new Men of us; it cleansed our Souls of that Earthliness, Sensuality and Vileness, which filled our Affections; and made them Heavenly, Spiritual and Pure, by the washing of Regeneration, and the renewing of the Holy Ghost; that is, by the cleansing Efficacy of Christ's Blood, both as it respects Guilt and Filth, brought home by his Spirit in his Word, at the Time of Regeneration; and by the Life-giving Influences of the Spirit of Grace, the Holy Ghost; which he shed on us abundantly, through Jesus Christ our Saviour. And 'tis from this supernatural Change made in the Affections, that the new-born love *God* above all; and cleave to him as their *All* in *All*, their desirable *Lot* and *Portion*, both for this World, and that to come; As saith the *Psalmist, Whom have I in Heaven but Thee? and there's none on Earth that I desire beside Thee. My Strength and my Heart faileth; but God is the Strength of my Heart, and my Portion for ever,* Psal. lxxiii.25, 26. 'Tis hence they love his *Worship* and Ordinances, as, *Psal.* xxvi.8. LORD, *I have loved the Habitation of thine House, the Place where thine Honour dwelleth.* Hence also, they love his *Statutes:* An Instance of this we have in holy *David,* in the cxixth *Psalm*, throughout; where, he says, *I love thy Commandments above*

Gold, yea, above fine Gold. Therefore I esteem all thy Precepts concerning all Things to be right; and I hate every false Way, Ver. 127, 128. And 'tis so natural to the New-Born to love God's *People,* for his sake, because they belong to him, and bear his Image, that it's made a demonstrative *Evidence* of their New-Birth, *1 John* iii.14. *We know that we have passed from Death unto Life, because we love the Brethren.* Thus it is with the Affection of *Love*; and all the other Affections are regulated by it. What we love, we desire, we seek, we rejoice in the Enjoyment of. What we love, we fear the Loss of, and hate that which is destructive of it, or contrary to it. Thus, *Psal.* xcvii.10. *Ye that love the Lord, hate Evil.* Thus the Work of the Spirit, in the New-Birth, extends to all the Faculties of the Soul. But

In the next Place; The Holy Spirit, by this Work on the Soul, produceth in it an abiding *Principle* of spiritual Life. That he hereby produceth a *spiritual Principle,* appears from *John* iii.6. where our Lord says, *That which is born of the Spirit, is Spirit*; that is, it's a spiritual Principle, of a spiritual *Kind* and Nature; and so it stands opposed to *that which is born of the Flesh,* and is of a fleshly *Kind.* And that it is a Principle of *Life,* we may see, *Eph.* ii.1. *And you hath he quickned, who were dead in Trespasses and Sins.* And hence the New-Born are exhorted, to *yield themselves unto God, as those that are alive from the dead,* Rom. vi.13. And that this Principle is an *abiding* Principle, or that that will remain for ever, is evident from *1 Pet.* i.23. *Being born again, not of corruptible Seed, but of incorruptible, by the Word of God, which liveth and abideth for ever.*

The next Thing to be considered is, That this Principle of spiritual Life, produced by the Spirit in the Soul, contains in it all Kinds of Graces. And therefore the Holy Spirit, when given to regenerate the Soul, is stiled *the Spirit of Grace,* Zech. xii.10. because he is given to work all Grace in the Soul, and is the Author of it there. Hence Faith, Hope, Love, Patience, Humility, Meekness, &c. are said to be Fruits of the Spirit. As *Gal.* v.22. *But the Fruit of the Spirit is Love, Joy, Peace, Long-suffering, Gentleness, Goodness, Faith, Meekness, Temperance; against such there is no Law.* Here's a bright Train of Graces mentioned; and tho' Hope is not named among the rest of the Fruits of the Spirit, yet it is implied: For Long-suffering, which is Patience, is set on work by Hope; and on this Account it's called *Patience of Hope, 1 Thes.* i.3. and when the New-Born *abound in Hope, it's through the Power of the Holy Ghost,* Rom. xv.13. And this Variety of Graces, produced in the New-Born Soul, as they are *fitted* for, so they *act* towards their proper *Objects,* at the Time of the New-Birth.

I shall begin with the Grace of *Faith*, that being the leading Grace. And, as in Nature, a Child is first formed and quickned in the Womb, in order to its Birth and Life in this World; so in Grace, the Soul is first formed anew, and has a Principle of Life, or of every Grace given it, in order to its being brought forth into the Liberty of the Gospel, and the visible Actings of every Grace. And as a Child in Nature, from its secret Life, has a secret Motion in the Womb, before its open Life, and visible Motion in this World; so the Soul of the Regenerate, from the secret Life of Grace given it, has a secret Motion towards Christ, and God in him, antecedent to its open Life of Grace, and the visible Actings of Faith upon the Son of God; when it may be said of it, that it's born again.

For the precise Time of the New-Birth, as I take it, is, when the Soul is first brought forth from under the Darkness and Bondage of Sin, and the Law, into the marvelous Light, and glorious Liberty of the Gospel; as being enabled to act Faith on Christ, and on God in him, in the Promise, to a comfortable Persuasion, in a greater or lesser Degree, of its own Salvation by free Grace, in and thro' Christ. The Work of the Spirit, in giving the new Life, is an instantaneous Thing; but his ripening of Grace, and bringing the Soul forth into the visible Life, and Actings, thereof, is effected sooner in some Souls than in others, according to his sovereign Pleasure. When the Soul is first quicken'd, it is so surrounded with Darkness and Bondage, the Guilt of Sin, and the Terrors of God's Wrath, in the Curses of a broken Law, and so beset with Unbelief, that until Almighty Power be exerted, it cannot put forth an Act of Faith on Christ, for its own Salvation: It is afraid to come forth into the Liberty of the Gospel; it is *slow of Heart to believe*; and tho' God calls it, in its Distress, to *believe on the Lord Jesus Christ for Salvation*, to cast it self into his Arms, at the Feet of his Mercy, and to take him at his Word, in his Promise of Life in his Son, for it self in particular; yet, alas, the Soul dares not venture into the Liberty of the Gospel, but lingers under the Bondage of Sin and the Law, as *Lot* in *Sodom*; until omnipotent Grace lays hold of it, and brings it thro' the Straits of the New-Birth, to *flee* by an Act of Faith, unto *Christ, the City of Refuge*; and so to escape the fiery Vengeance of God, that will inevitably fall upon all Unbelievers, that abide under Sin and the Law; As the Angels laid Hold of *Lot's Hand, the* LORD *being merciful to him, and brought him forth, to escape for his Life to Zoar,* when *the* LORD *rained Fire and Brimstone from the* LORD *out of Heaven, and destroy'd the Cities where Lot dwelt*, Gen. xix.16. And this Folly and Slowness of Heart to *believe*, the Lord blames his People, his *Ephraim* for, *Hos.* xiii.13. *The Sorrows of a travailing Woman shall come upon him; he is an unwise Son, for he should not stay long in the Place of breaking forth of Children.* It is the Soul's Duty at God's Command, when the Pangs of the New-Birth come upon it, in Convictions of Sin, and Misery by the Law, to put forth an immediate Act of Faith upon Christ for Salvation; and thereby to come forth into the Liberty of the Gospel, thro' ten thousand Fears and Difficulties which obstruct its Passage: And it is its Folly and Sin to delay it, or to *stay long in the Place of breaking forth of Children.* But tho' it is the Soul's Duty to put forth an Act of Faith, upon Christ, the Great Saviour, and upon God as the God of Grace, in him; yet such is the Strength of Unbelief, and the Power of Temptations which oppose it, that weak Faith, finds it difficult to make Head against them, and the Soul, thro' Discouragement, lies still, as it were, and doth not exert that spiritual Ability which it has; and so *it stays in the Place of breaking forth of Children.* And never would come forth by an Act of Faith on Christ, into the Light and Liberty of Free Grace, if the *exceeding Greatness of* God's *Power, which he wrought in Christ, when he rais'd him from the Dead,* was not put forth to effect it, *Ephes.* i.19, 20.

And this he does by the Word of the Gospel, either in a Mediate, or Immediate Way. God the Father, reveals Christ, by the Spirit, in the infinite Fulness, Fitness, and Freeness of his Salvation for lost Sinners, and so, of his own Love and Grace in him, for that Soul in particular, in some or other Word of Promise; and by his omnipotent Power, sweetly allures, and draws the Soul to come forth by an Act of Faith on Christ, into that glorious Liberty, Free Grace has provided for it; while he effectually persuades the Soul of the Truth and Faithfulness of the promis'd Grace, and of the Soul's Interest in it, in particular; and enables it to take him at his Word, and so in a firm Persuasion, upon the Word of a God, that cannot lie, to come forth, in the Face of all Discouragements, into the Joy of Faith, in his everlasting Favour, and of the Soul's eternal Happiness, as being interested therein, *Gal.* i.16. *John* vi. 44, 45. *1 John* v.10, 11. *Heb.* vi.18.

As for Instance, when the Soul sees it self to be undone by Sin, and that it is utterly unable to help or relieve itself; if that Word concerning Christ be spoken to the Heart, *Heb.* vii.25. *Wherefore he is able also to save them to the uttermost, that come unto God by him,* &c. The Soul feels mighty Power, bringing it forth, in an Instant, into the Liberty and Joy of Faith, as to its own Salvation, by this All-sufficient Saviour. Or, if, when the Soul labours under the Burden of Sin, both in its Guilt and Filth, lying on the

Conscience, that Word of the Lord is applied by the Spirit, *1 John* i.7. *The Blood of Jesus Christ his Son, cleanseth us from all sin;* The Soul finds present Deliverance, and is brought forth into the Liberty of the Gospel, and the Joy of Faith, as to its own being cleansed from all its Crimson and Scarlet-dy'd Sins, and made *White in the Blood of the Lamb.*

For when the *Spirit of Grace is pour'd* out to regenerate the Soul, and has given it a new Life, it has such a Sense of Sin, in its Guilt and Defilement, as it never had before, and the Soul feels it self shut up under Sin by the Law; but this is in Order to God's having Mercy upon it, thro' the meritorious Blood of his dear Son. And therefore 'tis said, *Zech.* xiii.1. *In that Day there shall be a Fountain opened to the House of* David, *and to the Inhabitants of Jerusalem, for Sin and for Uncleanness.* And oh! what glorious Views doth the Spirit of God open now, under the Gospel, to the *House* of *David*, the People of Christ among the *Gentiles, and to the Inhabitants of Jerusalem*, of his Gospel-Church, when they are savingly convinc'd of Sin, and of the infinite Efficacy of Christ's Blood, to cleanse them from Sin, and from Uncleanness; from Sin in its Guilt, and in its Defilement! And what glorious Liberty, as the Sons of God, are they brought into thereby! For as the Soul sees, that the least Sin, even that of a *Thought*, is of too deep a Dye, to be taken out by any Thing less than the Blood of *Jesus*; so now it sees, that there is Efficacy enough in that Blood, to cleanse it from *All* Sin, even those of the greatest Size; from all its Sins, tho' like the Stars for Number, and the Mountains for Greatness! And how will *the Spirit of Grace* set open the Fountain of Christ's Blood, in its infinite Fulness of Merit, to cleanse from all Sin, to the converted *Jews*, at the latter Day, when *a Nation shall be born at once!* When *they* shall *look by Faith upon him that they have pierced,* and *mourn* for their aggravated Sins, in *killing the Prince of Life*; and yet see Efficacy enough in the infinite Merit of that *Blood*, which their Forefathers had wickedly imprecated upon themselves, and their Children, to cleanse, even *them*, their guilty Posterity, from all their deep-dy'd Sins! By which they also shall be brought forth into the glorious Liberty of the Sons of God, when this Prophecy shall be literally fulfill'd. And mean while, the *Spirit of Grace, opens* the infinite Merit of Christ's Blood, to cleanse from all Sin, to the poor *Gentiles*, at the Time of their New-Birth, to bring them forth into the Liberty of the Gospel.

Again, if a Soul in Distress has that Word of our Lord brought home to it, in the great Power of God, *John* vi.37. *Him that cometh unto me, I will in no wise cast out.* The Soul instantly believes the Truth of the Promise, with Respect unto it self in particular, That Christ will not *cast him out*, but *receive him to the Glory of God*; And so comes forth into *Joy unspeakable, and full of Glory:* Or, if that Word is brought home to the Soul, by the Spirit, *Mat.* ix.2. *Son, be of good Cheer, thy Sins be forgiven thee*; The Faith of Forgiveness of Sins, is immediately produc'd in the Soul, and it comes forth in the Joy of it, into that *Liberty wherewith Christ has made it free:* Or, if that Word is brought home by the Spirit, to any distressed Soul, *Jer.* xxxi.3. *I have lov'd thee with an everlasting Love; therefore with Loving Kindness have I drawn thee.* His Almighty Power goes forth therein, in the Moment of Application, to the producing Faith in that Soul, concerning God's everlasting Love to *him*, in particular; upon which the Soul is brought forth into Liberty and glorious Light in an Instant. Or, If the Lord says, to any fearful hearted Soul, *Fear not, for I am with thee, be not dismayed, for I am thy God,* &c. as, *Isa.* xli.10. There's Power goes forth with his Word, to dispel Fear, and Dismayings, and to produce Faith, Joy, and Liberty immediately. As when he said, in the first Creation, *Let there be Light, and there was Light.* And thus the Souls of God's Children are brought forth by his Almighty Power, when New-born Babes, from the Darkness and Bondage of Sin and Death, into the open Life of Grace, and the visible Actings of *Faith on the Son of God;* while he thus *manifests himself unto them, as he doth not unto the World*, in these, or in any other of the Life-giving Words of his Mouth, whether spoken unto them immediately by his Spirit, or mediately by the Ministry of the Gospel; or whether particular Words are brought home to the Soul, or the Salvation in the Word, in general, is open'd and apply'd: For it's all one, in this Respect, when God takes the Word into his own Hand, and brings it home to the Heart; the Work is done, Faith is given, and the Soul New-born in an Instant. And so the happy Subjects of the New-Birth, being brought forth into the open Life of Faith, are hereby prepar'd for all the After-actings and Increase hereof, until Vision takes its Place.

And tho' an Unregenerate Man understands not the Nature of spiritual Faith, nor how the Soul is brought forth into the Life of it; and therefore speaks Evil of the Things which he knows not; yet this is most certainly the Nature of Faith, or the Faith of the New-Born, to act towards, and take in the Salvation of God in Christ, reveal'd in the Gospel, for that Soul, in particular: For, as God the Father, has *chosen a Remnant* in his Son to *Eternal Life*, and God the Son *Redeem'd 'em by his Blood, out of every Nation, Kindred, Tongue and People;* so God the Spirit knows every individual Person of that (to Men) numberless Number, and *applies* this great Salvation unto every one of *them*, in particular. And the quicken'd Soul can't find Ease from those Pangs which gird it about, when the New-Birth approaches, in a general Faith, that Christ dy'd for Mankind; (which is no more than *All* may have where the Gospel comes, and yet perish; yea, is no more than what the Devils have) but it must have a particular Application of Christ's Death unto it *self*, and a special Faith given; And accordingly it has, when it comes forth into the open *Life of Faith on the Son of God,* and is enabled to say, *He loved me, and gave himself for me,* Gal. ii.20.

For Faith, as the Apostle says, *Heb.* i.1. *Is the Substance of Things hoped for, and the Evidence of Things not seen.* It gives a substantial *Being,* or Existence in the Soul, to the Things of Christ, and Salvation by Free Grace, as reveal'd by the Spirit in the Promise, which can't be *seen* by the Eye of Sense, or natural Reason; and is the Soul's demonstrative *Evidence* of the Reality and Certainty of those Things, which it yet has not the Enjoyment of, but hopes for. And now, having hinted the time of the New Birth, how Faith is wrought, and the Soul brought forth thereby, into the Liberty of the Gospel, I shall go on to shew the *Fitness* of this Grace of *Faith*, in the Souls of the Regenerate, to act towards its proper *Objects*, and its answerable *Actings* towards them.

And as it is the New Creature's *Eye*, being *fitted* for Converse with its glorious *Object* Christ; so it *looks unto him* alone for Salvation. *As* Moses *lifted up the Serpent in the Wilderness* (says our Lord) *even so must the Son of Man be lifted up; that whosoever believeth in him should not perish, but have eternal Life,* John iii.14, 15. Believing, in this Text, is put for a poor Sinner's looking unto Christ for Salvation, with the spiritual Eye of Faith; as the stung *Israelites* looked with their bodily Eyes to the Serpent, appointed of God to be the Means of their Cure. And it's the Father's Will, that every one that thus *seeth the Son, and believeth on him, may have everlasting Life,* John vi.40. Seeing and Believing, are here synonimous; which shews the *Fitness* of this Grace of Faith, as an *Eye*, to look unto Jesus. And thither was the poor Jailor directed by *Paul* and *Silas*, when in his Soul-Distress, he cry'd out, *Sir, What must I do to be saved? Believe* (say they) *on the Lord Jesus Christ, and thou shalt be saved,* Acts xvi.30, 31. And when they had preached the Gospel unto him, and to all that were in his House, and the Lord had wrought Faith in their Hearts, it is said, *he rejoiced, believing in God, with all his House*, Ver. 34. that is, in God the

Saviour, the Lord Jesus Christ, immediately; to whom he had been directed to look, *Ver. 31.* and in God the Father ultimately, as pardoning and justifying of him, in and through Christ. For *by him*, the New-Born *believe in God, who raised him from the Dead, and gave him Glory*, (in the Name and Room of his People) *that their Faith and Hope might be in God*, 1 Pet. i.21. Rom. iv.25. Heb. vi.20.

Again; As this Grace of Faith is the New Creature's *Hand*, so it's fitted to *receive* Christ, and all Life, and Blessings in him, as God's *unspeakable Gift*; and accordingly doth it, when the Soul is born again. Thus *John* i.11, 12. *He came unto his own*, (his own Countrymen, the unbelieving *Jews*) *but his own received him not.* As they had no Eye of Faith to see him, so they had no Hand of Faith to receive him); *but to as many as received him, to them gave he Power to become the Sons of God, even to them that believe on his Name.*

And as this Grace of Faith is the New Creature's *Foot*, so it's fitted for, and *follows the Lamb whithersoever he goeth*, Rev. xiv.4. And thus the *Walk* of the Heaven-Born Soul, while in this World, is said to be by *Faith*, 2 Cor. v.7. But I proceed;

In the next Place, The Grace of *Love*, in the New-Born Soul, as it's *fitted* for, so it *acts* towards its proper *Objects*, God, Christ, the Saints, &c. And thus it was graciously promised and foretold, *Zech.* xii.10. *I will pour upon the House of* David, *and the Inhabitants of* Jerusalem, *the Spirit of Grace and of Supplications, and they shall look on Me whom they have pierced, and shall mourn for him, as one mourneth for his only Son, and shall be in bitterness for him, as one is in bitterness for his First-born.* Here is, *first*, the Spirit of [*Grace*] promised to work all Grace; and as the Spirit of [*Supplications*] to teach them what to pray for, and how to pray, and to enable them to pray, so as no unregenerate Man in the World can do; whence it may be said of them, as of *Saul, Behold he prayeth*, Acts ix.11. *Saul* had made Conscience of Prayer while a Pharisee; but this was but natural Prayer to God, as the God of Nature, out of Form and Custom, and not out of any true Sense of his Soul-wants, nor Faith in Christ's Fulness to supply them: It did not spring from the *Spirit of Grace* dwelling in his Heart, *as the Spirit of Supplications,* (as he dwells in all the Regenerate) as so it was not *the Prayer of Faith*, of spiritual Faith, directed to God, as the God of all Grace in Christ. And the Lord made so little Account of this, that he speaks of him as beginning to pray, when he was New-Born, *Behold he prayeth.* 'Tis as if the Lord should have said, "See! *Ananias*, what a Wonder my Grace has wrought upon a poor Persecutor; I have poured out the Spirit of Grace and of Supplications upon him, have wrought the New Life in his Soul, and now he cried unto Me, in the supplication Breath of the New Creature." But further; As a Fruit of the Spirit's being poured out, it's said, *And they shall* [*look upon Me whom they have pierced*]; there's *Faith* in the New-Born Soul, looking unto Christ crucify'd, dying for it in its room and stead. And they shall [*mourn for Him*]; there's *Love*; Love to Christ in the Soul, flowing out in Gospel-Repentance, from believing Views of Christ's dying Love to *it*, in particular. And, oh, how *the Love of Christ constrains* such a Soul to love him again! Now it hates Sin, and mourns for it not merely as it is a Soul-destroying, Self-undoing Evil; but chiefly, in that it is a God-dishonouring, and a Christ-piercing Thing. It *mourns for him, and is in bitterness for him,* while it sees all its Sins, in the Light of redeeming Love, wounding and piercing its dear Redeemer. And the Greatness of its Love to Christ, in Sorrow for Sin, is expressed by its mourning for *him*, as for an [*only Son*] and being in bitterness for *him*, as for a [*First-born.*] And thus all the New-Born, under the sheddings abroad of God's Love in their Hearts, love him again. As, *1 John* iv.19. *we love him, because he first loved us.* And *he that loveth* (saith the Apostle) *is born of God*, Ver. 7. that is, that loveth God, his People, his Word and Ways, &c. And this Love to God in the Heart, shews itself in the Life; as, 2 Cor. v.14, 15. *For the Love of Christ constraineth us, because we thus judge, that if one died for all, then were all dead; and that he died for all, that henceforth they that live should not live unto themselves, but unto him that died for them, and rose again. And this is the Love of God, that we keep his Commandments,* 1 John v.3. But,

Further; The Grace of *Hope*, produced by the Spirit in the Soul, at the Time of Regeneration, and contained in that Principle of spiritual Life, then created in it, as it's *fitted* for, so it *acts* towards its proper *Objects*, Jesus Christ, and God in and through him displaying his Glory in his Word and Promises; and particularly those which relate to that great Salvation that shall be bestowed upon every New-Born Soul. And that Christ is the immediate Object of this Grace of Hope, is evident, in that he is stiled our *Hope*, 1 Tim. i.1. *and Lord Jesus Christ, which is our Hope*; that is, objectively so; in that the Sum and Substance of all we hope for, is *in* him; and therefore the Grace of Hope, acting towards him, is said to be in *him*, 1 Cor. xv.19. And this shews the *Fitness* of this Grace of *Hope*, to converse with Christ, its glorious *Object*, and the *Actings* of it towards him as such.

And as it acts towards Christ, in all his infinite Fulness and Fitness to save, so towards *God* in him. The *Hope* of the *New-Born*, is therefore said to be *in God*, 1 Pet. i.21. And it is in him, as displaying his Glory in his Word and Promise. *I hope in thy Word,* says the *Psalmist*, Psal. cxix.114. And *thro' the Comfort of the Scriptures, the New-Born have Hope*, Rom. xv.4. And particularly those which relate to the great Salvation promis'd. *Hope* looks for what's to come, even for that great Salvation, Faith sets before it in the Promise. As, *Rom.* viii.24. *For we are saved by Hope; but Hope that is seen, is not Hope: for what a Man seeth,* (i.e is in the present Enjoyment of) *Why does he yet Hope for?* And this *Hope* of the *regenerate* Man, is said to be *good Hope thro' Grace*, 2 Thes. ii.16. It is not only bestow'd of mere Grace on the Soul, but it is likewise founded on Grace; it has the Grace of God in Christ, display'd in the absolute Promises, for its *Object*. And thus, it *Specifically* differs from the Hope of all other Men. While others have a *false* Hope, founded on their own *Obedience*, which they think will recommend 'em to the Favour of God; the *Hope* of the *New-Born*, is founded on the mere *Grace* of God in Christ, without the Deeds of the Law, or respect had to their own Obedience, as a procuring Cause of Salvation. And therefore it's *Good;* or that that will Abide, that shall not be cut off. For it is *sure and stedfast, as it enters into that within the Veil;* the Grace, and Faithfulness of God in Christ, set before it in the absolute Promises, *Heb.* vi.18, 19. Thus this Grace of *Hope, acts* towards its proper *Objects*, at the Time of the Soul's *New-Birth*, and throughout its *New-Life:* For the whose Course of the New-Born Soul, thro' a World of Trials, is said to be, *in Hope of eternal Life, which God, that cannot Lie, hath promis'd,* Tit. i.2. It looks for all the Salvation promis'd, both in this World, and that to come; but especially regards that full and compleat Salvation, to be bestow'd at Christ's appearing. For, *if in this Life only, we have Hope in Christ,* (says the Apostle) *we are of all Men most Miserable,* 1 Cor. xv.19. Our Hope, says he, is in Christ, in whom all our Salvation is compriz'd, and from whom it shall be bestow'd. And if there was no more to be Enjoy'd in, and thro' Christ, than what we look for in this Life, we were of all Men most Miserable. How is that ? Why, as I conceive, it's not to be understood *Simply*, but *Relatively*.

Not Simply: As if the State of the New-Born in this World, under all their Afflictions, and Persecutions for Christ's Sake, in which they have his gracious Presence, is a worse State, in *itself*, than that of unregenerate Men, who are wholly at Ease in the Enjoyment of carnal, or sinful Pleasures. No:

take a Man that's Born again, in the worst of these outward Circumstances, when (thro' Divine Permission) Men and Devils rage most against him, and persecute him, even to Death, as they did *Stephen*, the first *Martyr* of the *Christian* Church; and even then his present State, consider'd in *itself*, is far preferable to that of an unregenerate Man, in the highest Station, Condition, and Enjoyments of Life. The *Views, Stephen* had of the Glory of God, and of Jesus Christ, while he was Suffering for him, fill'd him with unspeakably more Pleasure, and that of an higher Kind, than his Enemies could take, in venting their Rage by stoning him, *Acts* vii.55, &c. And thus the Apostles, and Saints of the primitive Church, *rejoic'd in Tribulations,* and took more Pleasure in their being *counted worthy to suffer* for Christ, than their Persecutors could, in inflicting Punishments upon them. *2 Cor.* i.4, 5. *Acts* v.41. And the *Martyrs* in the *Flames*, even here in *England*, in Queen *Mary's* Days, have been fill'd with inconceivably more Pleasure in their Torments for Christ's sake, than their Enemies could have in heaping Fire and Faggots upon them. Whence it is apparent, that the People of God, in their present suffering State, are not of all Men most Miserable, as that State is consider'd in itself, *Simply.*

And therefore, this Phrase, must be understood *Relatively*, or, as it relates to that future Glory, in, and thro' Christ, which the Grace of Hope looks for. *If in this Life only we have Hope in Christ, we are of all Men most Miserable.* 'Tis as if the Apostle should say, If there is no State of future Glory for us in Christ, we are *Miserable*; because we have *hoped* for such a *Thing*, and 'twould be a miserable Disappointment. Yea, if there be no such Thing, we are of all Men *most* Miserable; because all the natural Men in the World, have no more than a natural Appetite, which natural Things can fill; and accordingly, every Man in the World, hath some Satisfaction, more or less, in the Things of Nature: But as for us that are *Born again,* that are *Spiritual* Men, we have a *Spiritual Appetite*, the Grace of *Hope* created in our Souls, that earnestly looks for *spiritual* and *eternal* Glory; and if there is nothing to satisfy it, *we* are miserable indeed Yea, the Things we Hope for, are inexpressibly Greater, than what any natural Man in the World, has any Desire after, or Expectation of: (For tho' Natural Men desire Heaven, according to their own Notion of it, as a Place of Ease and Rest, &c. yet they neither see nor can desire it, as it is a State of perfect Conformity to, and Enjoyment of God) and therefore our Disappointment, if there be no such Things, must needs be unspeakably greater, and more miserable, than what can possibly befall any other Man. And thus it shews the *Fitness* of this Grace of *Hope*, to *act* towards *Christ*, and *God* in him, with Regard to the great Salvation promis'd in the Love to come, and its *Actings* towards these its glorious *Objects* in this Life, unto Hope is swallow'd up in Enjoyment, or turn'd into Fruition.

Again, The Grace of Patience, is likewise contain'd in that Principle of Spiritual Life, produc'd in the Soul, by the Spirit of God, at the Time of the New-Birth; which, as it's *Fitted* for, so it *Acts* towards its proper *Objects, Jesus Christ*, and *God* in him, as the Author of all *Salvation* for his People, both in this World, and that to come. When Faith, the principle Grace, like the main Spring in a Movement, sets all the other Wheels, the other Graces in Motion, this of *Patience* works among the rest. When Faith first gets a View of the Great Salvation of God in Jesus Christ, held forth in the Free Promise, as it's Infinitely Full, and every way suitable to that miserable, necessitous Case, the New-Born Soul sees itself to be in, by reason of Sin, it straightway brings Tidings of the Reality, and Certainty thereof; upon which, Love embraceth, Hope expecteth, and Patience waiteth for the Fulfilment of the Promise, and for the God of Salvation therein. And this *Waiting*, respects all the *Salvation* promis'd to the People of God, both in this Life, and that to come. The first, and great Concern of a Regenerate Soul, is about its Eternal Salvation; and the Acting of this Grace of Patience, with regard thereto, is proportionable to that Measure of Faith the Soul has, as to the Salvation itself, and its own Propriety in it. The more Faith sees of the Salvation of God in Christ, the more Love delights in it, the more Hope looks for it, and the more Patience waits for it. And if the Soul hath not at first, such an appropriating View, that it can say, this Salvation in Christ, is for *Me*; yet viewing it, as infinitely Full, and Free for the Chief of Sinners, and every way suitable to its own Case, it takes Pleasure in it, gathers Hope concerning it, and waits on, with a *who can tell* but this great Salvation may be *mine?* And when once a Soul is brought to this, that it has a deep Sight of its own Misery by Sin, and of its utter Inability to help, or relieve itself; and has all its Hope of Salvation fixt upon the free, rich Grace, and Mercy of God in Christ; resolving to cast itself at his Foot, to be dealt with according to his sovereign Pleasure, and to wait on the God of all Grace, for the Display of his abundant Mercy in its eternal Salvation; that Soul shall never be asham'd of its Hope in God, its Expectation from him, nor its waiting for him. For, *They shall not be ashamed* (saith the Lord) *that wait for me,* Isa. xlix.23. The Lord will certainly, in his own Time, manifest himself to that Soul, as the God of *his* Salvation. And till then, the Soul *waits* for him.

And as this Grace of *Patience, acts* towards Jesus Christ, and God in him, as the Author of eternal Salvation, at the Time of the Soul's Regeneration; so likewise, in its after Actings, it *waits* on God, s the Author of all those Time-Salvations, which he has promis'd to his People, and graciously gives them as an Answer to their Prayers. Nor doth it wait in vain; For, *The* LORD *is good to them that wait for him, to the Soul that seeketh him,* Lam. iii.25.

Again, This Grace of *Patience*, acts towards Jesus Christ, and God in him, as the Author of all that Bliss, that full Salvation, which is promis'd to, and shall be bestow'd upon the People of God, in the World to come. Hence the New-Born, are said to *wait thro' the Spirit, for the Hope of Righteousness by Faith*, Gal. v.5. That is, for eternal Life, or that compleat Salvation, which God will give unto all those who are found in Christ's Righteousness, at his Appearing. *And to wait for his Son from Heaven*, 1 Thes. i.10. *Who* (says the Apostle) *shall change our vile Body, that it may be fashioned, like unto his glorious Body, according to the Working, whereby he is able to subdue, even all Things unto himself,* Phil. iii.21. And when God the Saviour, *appears the second Time without Sin*, to the full *Salvation of his People*, They'll say, *Lo, this is our God, we have waited for him, and he will save us: this is the* LORD, *we have waited for him, we will be glad and rejoice in his Salvation*, Heb. ix.28. Isa. xxv.9.

And as this Grace of *Patience, waits* upon God, as the Author of all Salvation to his People, in the three Respects mention'd; So it's admirably fitted to endure *Afflictions*, and quietly *bears* whatever the Lord is pleas'd to exercise the Soul with, until the promis'd Salvation comes. Hence *Patience* and *Long-suffering*, are join'd together, when the Apostle prays for the New-Born, that they might *be strengthened with all Might* thereunto, *Col.* i.11. Because *Patience* is an enduring, a Long-suffering Grace. And thus the *Patience* of the *Thessalonians*, is commended, in all *the Persecutions, and Tribulations* which they endur'd, *2 Thes.* i.4. And the Apostle *James*, exhorts the Saints, he wrote to, to be *Patient*, under all their *Afflictions*, and stablish their Hearts unto the coming of the Lord. And to encourage them hereunto, he sets before them the Example of the Husbandman: *The Husbandman waiteth for the precious Fruit of the Earth, and hath long Patience for it, until he receive the early and the latter Rain. Be ye also Patient,* (says he) *stablish your Hearts, for the coming of the Lord draweth nigh,* Jam. v.7, 8. And thus he exhorts them to *take the Prophets, who had spoken in the Name of the Lord, for an Example of suffering Affliction, and of Patience.* And tells them, the enduring Christian, was the most Happy; giving an Instance in *Job: Ye have heard* (says he) *of the Patience of* Job, *and have seen the End of the Lord,* or the happy Issue, the Lord, of his tender Mercy, gave him out of all his Troubles, *Ver.* 10, 11. And thus, *Blessed is the Man that endureth Temptation; for when he is Tried, he shall receive the Crown of Life, which the Lord hath promis'd to them that love him,* Chap. i.12.

And as this Grace of *Patience,* is eminently *fitted* for *suffering,* the *passive* Part of Obedience; so likewise, for *doing,* the *active* Part of it also. Hence the Hearts of God's People, under the *Regenerating* Work of the Spirit, being set forth, as good Ground, having the Word of the Gospel, as a living Seed, cast into it, is said to *bring forth Fruit with Patience,* Luke viii.15. And *unto them, who by patient Continuance in Well-doing, seek for Glory, Honour, and Immortality,* God will give *eternal Life,* Rom. ii.7. But,

In the next Place, *Humility,* is another Grace, contained in that Principle of Spiritual Life, produc'd by the Spirit, in the Souls of the New-Born, at the Time of their Regeneration; which, as it is *fitted* for, so it *acts* towards its proper *Objects, Jesus Christ,* and *God* in Him. Man, by Nature, is a proud Creature: And as it is the great Design of God's Grace in the Gospel, to exalt him high, so, to lay the Creature low. And therefore it was prophecy'd, when the Gospel made its Approach, by the coming of *John the Baptist,* Christ's fore-runner, who was *sent before him to prepare the Way of the* LORD, what Work it should make in the Hearts of poor Sinners; *Isa.* xl.4. *Every Valley shall be exalted, and every Mountain and Hill shall be made low.* The Gospel of the Grace of God, *exalts* every humble Soul that is *low* as the *Valley* in its own Eyes, by reason of its own Ill-deservings, and Hell-deservings, and felt Inability to help or relieve itself; by shewing it that full, and free Salvation wrought out for it by the Lord Jesus, which every way suits the Case of such a miserable undone Sinner, as it sees itself to be. And it likewise *humbles* the *proud* Soul, which has such an exalted Sense of its own Goodness, that in its own Opinion, it stands fair for Heaven, and as far above others, for Acceptance with God, as the *Mountains* and *Hills* are above the *Plain,* or *Valley* for Height. And this it does, by shewing the Soul, the Glory of God, and of Jesus Christ, which breaking in upon it, with a Ray of its transcendent Brightness, makes all its own apprehended

Goodness, in its Nature Obedience, disappear, as the Moon and Stars, before the rising Sun. Thus it follows,

Ver. 5. *And the Glory of the LORD shall be revealed, and all Flesh shall see it together.* And the Glory of the [LORD] that is, of the LORD the Mediator, the Lord Jesus Christ, the great Messiah, and so, of the LORD the Father, and of the LORD the Spirit too, in, and through Him. Shall be [*revealed*], In the Ministration of the glorious Gospel, and by the Spirit of God therein. And all Flesh shall [*see*] it together, Either, 1. *Externally*, as all do where the Gospel Ministry comes, some of whom, being left in their Nature-Darkness, oppose the Light, finally reject the Lord Jesus, as the alone Saviour, and so perish from under the Sound of the Gospel; it being unto them, *a Savour of Death unto Death.* Or, 2. *Internally*, by a special saving Light set up by the Spirit of God in their Understandings; and so all Flesh, Sinners of all Stations, Conditions, Ranks and Sizes, which are *New-born*, see the Glory of God in Christ, thro' the blessed Gospel, to the *humbling* of their Souls, and making them to fall down before it, and gladly embrace the Lord Jesus, to their eternal Life and Salvation. For,

Ver. 6. *The Voice* of the Gospel *cries, all Flesh is Grass, and all the Goodliness thereof as the Flower of the Field.* It proclaims all the Goodliness of Nature, in Moral Performances, while the Soul is in an *unregenerate* State, which a natural Man is so *proud* of, to be, at best, but withering, fading Stuff; which can't stand before the blasting Wind of God's Wrath, breaking out upon it, thro' the Curses of a broken Law; nor yet, before the efficacious Breathings of the Spirit of God in the Gospel, and the burning Glory of the Lord Jesus, the Sun of Righteousness, arising upon it therein. And the Success of the Gospel, under the Breathings of the Spirit, to the *humbling* of God's People, was foretold.

Ver. 7. *The Grass withereth, the Flower fadeth*; (that is, all the Goodliness of unregenerate Nature, loseth its Beauty in the Eye of the New-born) *because the Spirit of the LORD bloweth upon it: Surely the People are Grass.* The People that are *New-born*, being cut down, by the Word of the Gospel, with respect to those high Imaginations, and tow'ring Conceits they once had, of their natural Abilities, and Self-Excellencies; these wither like the mown Grass, before a drying Wind, and the scorching Heat of the Sun. And then follows,

Ver. 8. *The Grass withereth, the Flower fadeth; but the Word of our God shall stand for ever.* The Prophet here has a View of the People of God, in their *natural* and *spiritual* Estate. And 'tis as if he should say, *See* what work the Gospel makes in the Hearts of God's chosen; it *humbles* them, cuts them down, they fall down before the irresistible Grace and Power thereof; but this is in order to *exalt* them. Their *natural* Excellencies, Wisdom, Strength, Righteousness, have lost their Beauty in their Eye: But it was to adorn them with the *superior* Glories of Christ, and his Righteousness, that beauteous, everlasting Robe, which can sustain no Change; but abides the same in its refulgent Glory, thro' all the Successes of Time, and to the endless Ages of Eternity. For, *The Word of our God* (the Christ of God, in all his infinite Fulness, as the great Saviour) *shall stand for ever:* And so the Glory of the saved Ones, in, and thro' Him, is *Permanent* and *Unchangeable*. Their State *in* Christ, with respect to their *Justification* before God, as they stand in the Obedience of his Son, is a *permanent* and *unchangeable* Glory. *For there is no Condemnation to them which are in Christ Jesus:* There is none at present, nor ever shall be; *They shall not come into Condemnation; but are passed from Death unto Life,* unchangeable Life, of an eternal Duration, *Rom.* viii.1. *Joh.* v.24. And their State *thro'* Christ, as *New-Born*, or, as having a Principle of spiritual Life, communicated to them out of Christ's Fulness, and wrought in their Souls by the holy Spirit, thro' the Word of the Gospel, is likewise a *permanent, abiding* Glory; For they're *born again, not of Corruptible Seed, but of Incorruptible, by the Word of God, which liveth, and abideth for ever.* As *1 Pet.* i.23. Where this Prophecy of *Isaiah*, is apply'd to the Gospel Dispensation, and particularly, to the Work of the Spirit thereby, in *regenerating* the Soul, and *humbling* proud Nature. And this Grace of *Humility*, in the Souls of the *New-born*, discovers itself, in its *actings* towards Jesus Christ, as a complete Saviour, in submitting to his *Righteousness*, in being beholding unto him for *Strength*, and dependent upon him for *Wisdom*, and in yielding unto his *Government*.

Proud Nature, will not *stoop* to the *Righteousness* of Jesus Christ, as it's appointed of God, to be the only justifying Righteousness of all that shall be saved. No: It thinks its own Works must have Place in its Acceptance with God. Thus *Paul* while a *Pharisee*, counted his Birth-Privileges, and his own Observance of the Law of *Moses*, to be his Gain, in Point of Justification and eternal Life. But when he was *born again*, and *humbled* by the Grace of the Gospel, he was quite of another Mind; And those things which he before esteem'd as his *Gain*, he then *counted Loss for Christ*, yea, esteem'd them no better than *Dung, for the Excellency of the Knowledge of Christ, as his Lord; that he might be found in him, not having his own* legal

Righteousness, but the *Righteousness of God* (of God the Father's appointing, of God the Son's working out, and of God the Spirit's revealing and applying) *which is by Faith*, as it stands oppos'd to the Works of the Law. Or that which is apprehended, and laid hold of by Faith, as the Soul's justifying Righteousness before God, exclusive of the Works of the Law, or any of its own Obedience, *Phil*. iii.7, 8, 9. And thus he tells his Country-men, the *Jews*, who had *a Zeal of God, but not according to Knowledge, being ignorant of God's Righteousness,* (*i.e.*, The strict Purity and Righteousness of God's Nature, and of his Holy Law, who, according thereto, requires perfect Obedience, and can accept no less) *went about to establish their own Righteousness, and have not* (says he) *submitting themselves to the Righteousness of God.* That is, unto the Righteousness of Christ, which is of God's appointing, working out, revealing and applying, *Rom*. x.2, 3. These poor *Israelites,* were too *proud* to *stoop* to Christ's Righteousness, they were unwilling that Christ should be *All* unto them, in Point of Righteousness; and therefore endeavoured to work out a Righteousness of their own, and so to exalt themselves as their own Saviours: On which Account they *attained not to the Law of Righteousness,* or to that they *sought after, viz.* a State of Justification before God; *Because they sought it not by Faith, but as it were by the Works of the Law. For they stumbled at that stumbling Stone,* Christ the only justifying Righteousness of all the saved ones, *Rom*. ix.31, 32. And so does every *unregenerate* Man to this Day: Whatever Profession, or Denomination he goes by among Men, he sees not the Excellency of Christ's Obedience to God's Holy Law, as it is the Matter of a Sinner's Justification before God; nor doth he see any Need of it for himself: But rises up against it, in the Ignorance and Pride of his Spirit, and will be working for Life, as being still upon Nature's Bottom, and under the Old Covenant; the Voice of which was, *Do, and live.* But it's far otherwise with the *New-Born,* who have the Grace of *Faith* and of *Humility* wrought in their Souls: These, *see* the transcendent Glory of Christ's Righteousness, and *bow* down unto it, with the highest Joy and Reverence; and say, in their very Souls, 'tis the Language of their Hearts, as well as Lips, as was long ago foretold, *In the* LORD *have I Righteousness*, Isa. xlv.24.

Again, This Grace of *Humility*, in the Souls of the *New-Born, acts* towards *Christ,* its *Object,* in being *beholding* unto him for *Strength.* Every Man while in an *Unregenerate* State, has a high Conceit of his own Ability to do that which is Well-pleasing unto God; and hence it is, that he sets about Obedience to the Law, to make himself acceptable in his Sight. And the most flagitious Sinner, thinks he has Power in himself to turn to God, whenever he pleases to exert it: Whence, under some Convictions of Sin, and Flashes of the fiery Law in his Conscience, he makes Resolutions to amend his Ways, and become a *New-Man*, And as he's ignorant of that Need he has of Omnipotent Power to be put forth, in delivering of him from Sin and Satan, and in giving of him a *New-Heart*, and then a *New-Life*, or, that true, Gospel-Reformation of Life, which is proper to a *New Creature*; so he likes not to be beholding to *another* for Strength; But in the Pride of his Spirit, *glories* in his apprehended Might. And therefore, the Lord says, *Let not the mighty Man glory in his Might*, Jer. ix.23. But when, by the Omnipotent Grace of the Gospel, any poor Soul is *Humbled*, this *high Imagination is cast down*. As says the Apostle, *2 Cor*. x.4, 5. *For the Weapons of our Warfare, are not Carnal, but Spiritual, and Mighty thro' God, to the pulling down of strong Holds: Casting down Imaginations, and every high Thing which exalteth itself against the Knowledge of God, and bringing into Captivity every Thought* (and so this, of Self-ability, among the rest) *to the Obedience of Christ*, who is the Lord our *Strength*. We are by Nature, *without Strength*, Rom. v.6. The Soul, by reason of Sin, is like a sick Man, void of Strength, and unfit for Labour. Yea, while *Unregenerate*, it is *Dead in Sin*, Eph. ii.1. And has no more Power to do any Thing that is *Spiritually Good*, than a *Dead* Man has to *act*, who wants a Principle of *Life* for *Motion*. And when once the Soul is *quickened* by the Grace of God, and so has Power of *Sensation*, it sees this was once its Case, and *feels* its natural Inability, or, the Weakness of its corrupt Nature, to do any *spiritual* good Thing: When it has a *Will* given it, yet it wants *Strength* for *Performance*. As, *Rom*. vii.18. *For to Will is present with me, but how to perform that which is Good, I find not*. And therefore it falls down in the Dust before the Lord, and implores Divine Assistance; and glad it is of the blessed Tidings, the Gospel brings it, that there is Strength for it in the Lord Jesus, and that *his Strength shall be made Perfect in his Weakness*, 2 Cor. xii.9. And therefore receiving the Testimony hereof, Rejoycing herein, and *Bowing* hereto, it says, *In the* LORD *have I Strength*, Isa. xlv.24. Strength for every Duty he calls me to, whether of Doing, or Suffering; as says the Apostle, *I can do all things thro' Christ which strengthneth me*, Phil. iv.13.

Further, This Grace of *Humility*, in the Souls of the *New-Born, acts* towards *Christ* its *Object*, in being *Dependant* upon him for *Wisdom*. Man by Nature, is a *Fool*, in respect of spiritual Things. And yet so proud is he, that, *vain Man,* (empty Man, destitute of all spiritual Wisdom) *would be Wise, altho' he's Born like the wild Asses Colt,* Job ix.12. Every *Unregenerate* Soul, has an high Conceit of his own Wisdom; of his Ability to know, and of the Knowledge he hath attain'd. Thus the *Pharisees* of old, prided themselves in their apprehended Wisdom, as if it was sufficient to know the *Messiah*; and thought those Fools, who believ'd on Jesus of *Nazareth,* as the Christ of God. And when the Officers they sent to take him, return'd without him, and gave this as the Reason of it, *Never Man Spake as this Man: Are ye also Deceiv'd?* (say they) *Have any of the Rulers, or of the Pharisees Believ'd on him? But this People who knoweth not the Law are Cursed,* John vii.46, 47, 48, 49. But whatever Wisdom any natural Man may have, whether he be *Jew* or *Gentile, Bond* or *Free,* which he prides himself in, as sufficient to guide him in the Way to Heaven, the Holy Ghost calls it no better than *the Wisdom of this World;* Which he says, *God hath made Foolish,* 1 Cor. i.20. *where is the Wise? Where is the Scribe? Where is the Disputer of this World? Hath not God made foolish the Wisdom of this World?* He hath made it appear to be so indeed, in the Revelation of Christ, as the alone Saviour. Which is a *Wisdom* too high, a *Glory* too bright, for all the *wise* and *prudent* Men in the World, while in a State of Nature, to behold. *We preach Christ crucify'd* (says the Apostle) *to the Jews a stumbling Block, and to the Greeks Foolishness, ver.* 23. There was not a Man of them then, nor is now, that by all their *natural,* or *acquir'd* Wisdom, (however proud they may be of it) is able to discern the *Wisdom* of God, in Saving his People by *a crucify'd Jesus.* No, says the Apostle, *the preaching of the Cross,* (the Gospel of Salvation by a crudify'd Saviour) *is to them which perish, Foolishness,* ver. 18. The Wisdom of God in the Gospel, *destroys the Wisdom of the Wise, and brings to nothing the Understanding of the Prudent,* ver. 19. And they, in their proud Wisdom, count the Wisdom of God *Foolishness,* ver. 21. But let Men, in their Ignorance and Pride, quarrel at the Cross of Christ, as long s they please, to their eternal undoing, God will save his own by it: These shall have a special, saving, internal Revelation of the *Wisdom* of God herein, to the *humbling* of their Souls, and making them shrink to nothing in their own Sight, and see all their *natural* Wisdom, with respect to the Way of Salvation, and the Things of Salvation, to be but mere *Folly:* And without such a *Revelation,* no Man can *see* Jesus, the Christ of God, to the Salvation of his Soul. And therefore, when *Peter* had made that brave Confession of his Faith, to our Lord, *Thou art Christ, the Son of the Living God: Jesus answered him and said, Blessed art thou Simon, Bar-jona; for Flesh and Blood hath not revealed it unto thee, but my Father which is in Heaven,* Mat. xvi.16, 17. And, *The natural Man*, says the Apostle, *receiveth not the Things of the Spirit of God; for they are Foolishness unto him; neither can he know them because they are spiritually discerned,* 1 Cor. ii.14. The *natural* Man (the Man of *Soul*, the Rationalist, with all his bright Parts, *natural* and *acquir'd*) receiveth not the Things of the Spirit of God; because they are *Foolishness* unto him: And they are so, because he cannot *know* them: And he cannot know them, because he has neither a spiritual *Revelation* to discover them, nor a spiritual *Eye* to take them in; for they are *spiritually discerned*, and only so. *But God has revealed them unto us by his Spirit,* says he, *ver.* 10. Unto Us, the *New-Born*, who have an Eye of Faith given, hath God reveal'd, or discover'd his *Things* by his *Spirit*. And Christ being made *Wisdom* to his People; is one of the *Things* which the *Spirit* of God reveals to the *New-born*, who being *humbled* by divine Grace, become as *little Children in their own Sight*, that have need of teaching; and are glad to *learn* of Christ, and be *dependant* upon him for all their *Wisdom*, becoming Fools, in their own Esteem, that so they *may be wise*, under his teaching, *1 Cor.* iii.18. And to these *Babes*, God the *Father reveals Christ, and his Things,* when he *hides them from the wise and prudent,* as the great *Sovereign of Heaven and Earth*, for which our Lord gave Thanks, *Mat.* xi.25.

In the next Place, this Grace of *Humility, acts* towards *Christ*, its *Object,* in *yielding* to his *Government.* And the Language of it is, in the Souls of the *New-Born, The* LORD *is our Judge, the* LORD *is our Law-giver, the* LORD *is our King, he will save us,* Isa. xxxiii.22. The Language of proud Nature, in *unregenerate* Men, is, *we will not have this Man*, the Man Christ, *to reign over us*, Luke xix.14. But when once the Soul is *humbled* by the Grace of God, it says with *Saul*, when humbled in Soul, and prostrate in Body on the Earth, by the majestick Glory of the Saviour's Voice, and Appearance to him from Heaven, *Lord, what wilt thou have me to do?* Acts ix.6. 'Tis as if he should say, I have been my own Lord long enough, and under the Dominion of Sin and Satan, to thy Dishonour, and my own unspeakable Misery; but now I see thee to be the alone Saviour, I bow down in my very Soul to thy Sceptre, and from henceforth, give up my self to be thy Servant. And thus the People of God, in submitting to the Government of Christ, are brought in speaking, *Isa.* xxvi.13. *O* LORD *our God, other Lords besides thee have had Dominion over us; but by thee only will we make mention of thy Name.* The Souls of the *New-Born*, see such a transcendent Glory in Christ, this great Lord, which makes them delightfully *bow* to his Sceptre, and count it their Honour to be his Servants. This was a Title the Apostle glory'd in, *a Servant of Jesus Christ*; as is manifest in their *Epistles*. And their entire Subjection to him is declar'd, *Rom.* xiv.8. *For whether we live,* (says the Apostle) *we live unto the Lord; or whether we die, we die unto the Lord: Living, and dying we are the Lord's* The *regenerate* Children of God, in the Exercise of this Grace of *Humility,* first *give themselves up unto the Lord, and then unto his People by the Will of God, 2 Cor.* viii.5. Submitting to all the Laws and Ordinances of Christ, the *King of Sion*, relating to their Behaviour, both towards *God* and *Men*, in the *Church* and in the *World.* Having learn'd of their *meek* and *lowly Master*, they, at his Command, *take his Yoke upon them*, and so they *find Rest unto their Souls, Mat.* xi.29. For his Service is perfect Freedom, his *Ways* to them *are Ways of Pleasantness, and all his Paths Peace, Prov.* iii.17. They love Christ's *Precepts*, and *yield* Obedience to his *Commands*; Whether such that are included in the *moral Law,* or those which peculiarly respect the *Worship* of the *Gospel.* They *serve the Law of God, Rom.* vii.25. But not now, as it is the Law of *Moses*, a Covenant of Works, for Life, that curseth for every Disobedience. No, so they are *dead to it*, ver. 4. But they *are under it to Christ, 1 Cor.* ix.21. who, as *King of Sion*, has given it to them as the *Rule* of their Obedience; that *Obedience,* which, as the saved of the Lord, they yield out of Duty and Thankfulness unto him that has loved them. Thus being *not their own, but bought with a Price,* (from endless Death, to endless Life) *they glorify God in their Body, and in their Spirit, which are the Lord's, 1 Cor.* vi.19, 20. As by Purchase and Possession, so by cheerful, *humble* Resignation. Thus the Grace of *Humility*, in the Souls of the *New-Born, acts* towards *Christ* its *Object,* in *submitting* to his *Righteousness*; in being *beholding* unto *him* for *Strength; dependant* upon *him* for *Wisdom*; and in *yielding* unto his *Government.* And in all, *proud Self* is *abased*, and the *Lord Christ exalted; who of God is made unto them Wisdom, Righteousness, Sanctification, and Redemption. That he that glorieth, might glory in the Lord, 1 Cor.* i.30, 31. And,

Further, as this Grace of *Humility*, in the Souls of the *Regenerate, acts* towards *Christ* its *Object*; so towards *God* in *him*, as the God of all *Grace* and *Salvation,* in and thro his *Son*; in being *beholding* to the Riches of his *Mercy, Love* and *Grace* herein; in *bowing* to his *Sovereignty*; in *adoring* his

Wisdom; in *depending* on his *Power,* and in *submitting* to his *Dominion,* in *Providence* as well as *Grace.*

Thus *Messiah,* when he humbled himself greatly before the God of his Fathers, on the account of his Transgressions, was glad to be *beholding* to the Riches of God's Mercy, Love and Grace in Christ, for his Salvation; and when *he besought the Lord his God, he was intreated of him, 2 Chron.* xxxiii.12, 13. And *David,* when he *humbled* himself before God, for the Sin of his Nature and Practice, *Psal.* li. Cried out, *Have Mercy upon me, O God, according to thy loving Kindness: according to the Multitude of thy tender Mercies blot out my Transgressions,* ver. 1. And,

The Apostle *Paul* expresseth the just Sense his *humbled* Soul had of God's *Sovereignty,* in saving some, of mere Grace, and in passing by others; where, in answer to the suppos'd Objection of an Adversary, he says, *Nay, but, O Man, who art that replieth against God? Shall the Thing formed, say unto him that formed it, Why hast thou made me thus? Hath not the Potter Power over the Clay, of the same Lump to make one Vessel unto Honour, and another unto Dishonour, &c. Rom.* ix.20, &c.

And thus all the *New-Born,* in the Exercise of this Grace of *Humility, bow* to the *Sovereignty* of God; which *Unregenerate* Men quarrel at, and oppose with all their Might.

And as they *bow* to divine *Sovereignty,* so they *adore* the infinite *Wisdom* of God, display'd in the Salvation of Sinners; saying, with the Apostle, *Rom.* xi.33. *O the Depth of the Riches both of the Wisdom and Knowledge of God! how unsearchable are his Judgments, and his Ways past finding out.*

Again, the Grace of *Humility* in the Souls of the *Regenerate, acts* towards God, in *depending* on his *Power.* They say, when surrounded with spiritual Enemies, as *Jehoshaphat,* when encompas'd with that Multitude of outward Foes, *2 Chron.* xx. *O our God, wilt thou not Judge them? For we have no Might against this great Company that cometh against us; neither know we what to do, but our Eyes are upon thee,* ver. 12. *And in thine Hand is Power and Might, so that none is able to withstand thee,* ver. 6. And as they *depend* on him for *Deliverance* from all *Evil,* so, for the *Enjoyment* of all that great *Goodness* he has spoken of concerning them; *being fully persuaded that what he has promised, he is able also to perform,* Rom. iv.21.

Once more, this Grace of *Humility, acts* towards God its *Object,* in *submitting* to his *Dominion* in *Providence,* as well as *Grace.* That it does so in *Grace*, has been hinted; and that it does so in *Providence*, appears, in that Acknowledgment made, *Psal.* cxv.3. *Our God is in the Heavens, he hath done whatsoever he pleased.* And, *It is the Lord,* (says old *Eli*) *let him do what seemeth him good, 1 Sam.* iii.18. And thus *Job, Shall we receive good at the Hand of God, and shall we not receive Evil?* Chap. ii.10. And *I have learned* (says the Apostle *Paul*) *in whatsoever State I am, therewith to be content. I know both how to be abased, and I know how to abound; every where, and in all things I am instructed, both to be full and to be hungry, both to abound and to suffer Need,* Phil. iv.11, 12. And as this Grace of *Humility*, in the Souls of the *New-Born, acts* towards *God*, its *Object*, in the respects mentioned, so it *acts* towards him, as the God of all *Grace* and *Salvation* in his Son.

It is thus, *Faith views* him, *Love cleaves* to him, *Hope expects* from him, *Patience waits* for him, and *Humility submits* to him. *God in Christ*, as the God of all *Grace* and *Salvation,* both for *Time* and *Eternity*, is the *Object* which all these *Graces act* towards; and so this Grace of *Humility*, in the Souls of the *New-Born*, differs from *all* that bears that *Name* in *unregenerate* Men. 'Tis the Grace of the *Gospel*, or of God in Christ, that *Humbles* the *New-Born;* and not the Terrors of the *Law*, as it denounceth Curse and Wrath against every Transgressor. And therefore when the Lord promiseth to give his sinful People *a New-Heart*, and says he *will be their God*, Ezek. xxxvi.26, *&c.* he foretells the Carriage of their *humbled* Souls, under the sweet Influences of his *Grace*, Ver. 31. *Then shall ye remember your own evil Ways, and your Doings which have not been Good, and shall lothe yourselves in your own Sight, for your Iniquities, and for your Abominations.* And thus, *Chap.* xvi.62, 63. *And I will establish my Covenant with thee, and thou shalt know that I am the* LORD; *that thou mayst remember, and be confounded, and never open thy Mouth any more, because of thy Shame, when I am pacify'd toward thee for all that thou hast done, saith the Lord* GOD. And as it is in *Christ* and in him *only*, that God can be pacify'd, or be the God of Peace to a poor Sinner; so it is the Display of this Grace in him, that is the Ground of all *Evangelical* Humiliation before God. 'Tis this draws out the Soul in the exercise of *Humility*, to *act* towards God all manner of Ways, as the Time of its *New-Birth*, and all along throughout its *New-Life*, during its stay in the Body. And with these *humble* Souls God will *dwell,* Isa. lvii.15. *For thus saith the high and lofty one, that inhabiteth Eternity, whose Name is Holy; I dwell in the high and holy Place; with him also that is of a contrite and humble Spirit, to revive the Spirit of the*

Humble, and the Heart of the Contrite ones. To *these* his Ear is open, for *these* his Hand is engag'd; *for he forgetteth not the cry of the Humble*, Psal. ix.12. To *these* he will *give Grace*, Jam. iv.6. And *these* he will *exalt in due Time*, 1 Pet. v.6. But to pass on:

The Grace of *Meekness*, is likewise contained in that Principle of spiritual Life produc'd by the Spirit of God, in the Souls of the *New-Born*; which likewise *acts* towards its proper *Objects, God, Christ,* the *Saints*, yea, all *Men. Patience, Humility,* and *Meekness* are Graces that are very near of kin, and therefore are join'd together in the sacred Writings. As, *Eph.* iv.2. *Col.* iii.12. But there is doubtless a Difference between them. The Grace of *Patience*, more peculiarly respects the Soul's *Endurance* under the Trials it meets with in God's Way, until promis'd Mercies, and hop'd for Salvation come. The Grace of *Humility*, respects the *Lowliness* of the Soul, in its Carriage towards God, while it waits upon him. And the Grace of *Meekness*, respects the *Stilness*, or Quietness of the Soul, under those Things which seem to make against it from *God*, and under real Injuries and Offences from *Men. Patience*, stands oppos'd to *Haste*, or a sinful Hastiness of Spirit in seeking Deliverance out of God's Way, and before God's Time. *Humility* stands oppos'd to *Pride*, or Haughtiness of Spirit. And *Meekness* stands oppos'd to *Anger*, or a tumultuous, wrathful Resentment of Spirit, under Things which make against our real, or apprehended Happiness. And this Grace of *Meekness, acts* towards its proper *Objects*, at the Time of the Soul's *New-Birth*. The Lord Jesus Christ, for wise and gracious Ends, doth oft carry it roughly to the Souls he designs Mercy for, when they *first* come to him for Salvation. As *Joseph* did to his *Brethren,* when they *first* came to him *to but Corn*; that so he might bring them to a greater Sense of their Sin, and commend his Love the more, in supplying their Wants, notwithstanding all that they had dome against him. And our Lord's Behaviour to the *Woman of Canaan*, when she besought him to have Mercy on her, and to heal her Daughter, is a sweet Resemblance of his Carriage to many whom he loves, when the come to him for the Salvation of their Souls. And her Behaviour towards hem, doth likewise shew the Carriage of a *meek* Soul, towards its frowning Lord.

In the Account we have of it, *Matt.* xv.22, &c. It's said, *And behold, a Woman of Canaan came out of the same Coasts, and cried unto him, saying, have Mercy on me, O Lord, thou Son of David; for my Daughter is grievously vexed with a Devil.* Here the Woman, having Faith given her, that our Lord was the true *Messiah*, the anointed one of God, and that he had Fulness of Power in himself to help and deliver her, she comes in the Anguish of her Soul, falls down at his Feet, and beseeches him to have Mercy upon her; or, to draw out the Compassions of his Heart, towards her in Misery, by extending the Power of his Arm, in her Deliverance. And thus a *New-Born* Soul comes unto Christ for Mercy. But how does the Woman succeed? Why, our kind Lord, who shew'd his Infinite Readiness to help all the Distressed that came to him for Relief, in this Instance, seem'd to take no Notice of her, *Ver.* 23. *But he answer'd her not a Word.* Oh Strange! What could the Woman think, but that there was no Mercy in him for her, and therefore she might go her Way, and seek no more for it? Well, Thus the Lord deals, sometimes, with a *New-Born* Soul, that seeks unto him for Mercy; he *answers it not a Word*. But this was not all the Discouragement the poor Woman met with. For, *his Disciples besought him,* saying, *Send her away, for she crieth after us,* ver. 23. And thus a poor Soul may meet with Discouragement from Christ's Followers, as well as from himself. And when *Jesus answer'd, he said, I am not sent but to the lost Sheep of the House of Israel*, ver. 24. Which the poor Woman might understand of *Literal Israel*; and so think herself excluded the Benefit of his Mission; she being one of another Nation. But lo, her Faith, strengthned by divine Power, surmounts this Discouragement also, *ver.* 25. *Then came she and worship'd him, saying, Lord, help me.* 'Tis as if she should say, I know not who thy Commission extends to, in particular; but I am a Creature of Misery, and I know thou art able to save and deliver me, as thou hast done others, and therefore, *Lord, help me.* And so, a Soul under the *first Work* of the Spirit, when it hears that Christ was sent to save God's *spiritual Israel*, or that *Remnant* which he chose out of all Nations, to be his peculiar People, of which *Literal Israel* was a Type, may have such Suggestions in its Mind, as if Christ did not come to save *him*. But as Christ strengthned this Woman's Faith by a *secret* Power, to *cleave* unto him, even when by his *open* Carriage, he laid Discouragements in her *Way*; so does he deal with a *New-Born* Soul; he *secretly* strengthens it to *follow* hard after him, when he *answers it not a Word*, seems to take no Notice of its Prayers, and nothing but Discouragements appear before it. And when Jesus answer'd to the Woman's Prayer, *Lord, help me,* What was it? Why, says he, ver. 26. *It is not meet to take the Children's Bread, and to cast it to the Dogs.* 'Tis as if he should say, Woman, thou art of the *Gentile* Race, which the *Jews* esteem no better than *Dogs*, and unmeet to share in the Privileges of God's *Children.* And now, one would think, the Woman had enough to dash all her Faith and Prayer, and stir up her *Resentment*, when Christ put her in Mind of this odious Name, *Dog*; which, tho' he did not apply to her, yet he lays it before her, to put her in Mind of her base Original, as a *Gentile*-Sinner, and to try how she could bear this Reproachful Term. And indeed, if almighty Power, had not given her mighty *Faith*, deep *Humility*, and great *Meekness*, she had never open'd her Mouth more. But lo! she replies, *ver.* 27. *Truth, Lord, yet the Dogs eat the Crumbs which fall from their Masters Table.* As if she should say, Lord, I acknowledge I am *Vile*, that I deserve no better Name than that of a *Dog*, that I am unworthy of *Children's Bread*, or to be dealt with as thou dealest with thy *own*; but let me have *Crumbs* of Mercy, the Off-fallings of that rich, and plenteous Board thou spreadest for thy *Children*. Oh the amazing *Meekness* of this Woman's Spirit! Here are no tumultuous Passions arising in her Soul, no angry Resentment chasing her Mind, when every Thing seem'd thus to make against her; but all in a sweet Calm, she still presses her Suit, and even makes *that* a Ground of her further Plea, which in all Appearance, was enough to have stopt her Mouth for ever; *the Dogs eat the Crumbs,* &c. And when the Lord had thus fully *try'd* her, then his Grace and Mercy breaks out, in an open Commendation of her Faith, and immediate Grant of her Request, *ver.* 28. *O Woman, great is thy Faith: Be it unto thee even as thou wilt. And,* divine Power going forth with his Word, *her Daughter was made whole from the same Hour.* Now the Woman had Mercy enough. She *fell* down at his *Feet*, apply'd to her self the opprobrious Name, *Dog*, and ask'd for *Crumbs;* but the Prince of Grace acts like *himself*, takes her up in his *Arms*, deals with her as a *Child*, sets her at his *Mercy-Board,* and bids her *take* her *Fill.*

And here, the *Wisdom, Grace, Mercy,* and *Power* of Christ, shone forth, in his Carriage towards her, when she sought to him for Mercy, and when he granted her Request. His *Wisdom*, in trying her Faith, Patience, Humility and Meekness; that so, in granting her Request, he might do it in such a Way, as to put a peculiar Honour upon her to all Generations. His *Grace*, in commending the Fruits of the Spirit in her Heart, which were his own Gift, and drawn forth into Exercise by his own Power: *O Woman, great is thy Faith!* And though her *Faith* is only mention'd, *that* being the leading *Grace*, yet the *other* are imply'd, they being all equally *Exercis'd.* His *Mercy*, in granting the Request of this miserable Object. And his *Power*, in working Deliverance of her. And thus the Lord Jesus, in infinite Wisdom, doth sometimes carry it *Roughly* to a *New-Born* Soul, when it seeks to him for Salvation. But yet, as he saves it be his Power in the End, so mean while, he strengthens it to the Exercise of every given Grace, and particularly, this of *Meekness:* So that it can be *Quiet,* and take all *Well,* when he seems to deny its Request, yea, when it *bears the Reproach of its Youth,* and is put in mind of the Name, *Dog*; and still go on, *Jacob like,* to *Wrestle* with him for the *Blessing,* and it comes off a *prevailing Israel*; under the Honour, Free-grace put upon it, of being *a Prince with God.* As, *Gen.* xxxii.26, *&c.* Thus the Grace of *Meekness,* in a *New-Born* Soul, *acts* towards *Christ* its *Object,* and takes all Well, when he carries it Roughly, and seems to take no Notice of it, yea, to load it with Reproach. Which no *unregenerate* Man in the World can do.

Again, This Grace of *Meekness,* hath *God* in *Christ* for its *Object.* And the Language of it, is, *Though he slay me, yet will I trust in him,* Job xiii.15. As, to *trust* in God, is peculiarly an Act of *Faith*; so to trust *when he slays,* or under slaying Dispensations, includes in it the Act of *Meekness.* And when the Soul first begins to believe in God, and to hope for his Salvation, it not only *waits* for it, in the Exercise of *Patience,* but waits *Quietly,* in the Exercise of *Meekness.* And it's *good for a Man* so to do, *Lam.* iii.26. *For he will beautify the Meek with Salvation,* Psal. cxlix.4. This Grace of *Meekness, giveth the Cheek to him that smiteth;* and the Soul in the Exercise hereof, can be *still,* when God *shutteth out its Prayer,* and appears against it as an Enemy: It makes no *Reply,* but is *still; knowing that he is God,* Psal. xlvi.10. As *David,* when fleeing from rebellious *Absalom, the Tabernacle and Ark of God,* saw his Hand against him in all this, and says, *If I shall find Favour in the Eyes of the* LORD, *he will bring me again, and shew me both it,* (i.e., the Ark) *and his Habitation. But if he thus say, I have no Delight in thee: Behold, here am I, let him do to me as seemeth good unto him,* 2 Sam. xv.25, 26. *And* thus *Aaron held his Peace,* when *there came Fire out from before the* LORD, *and devour'd his two Sons,* Lev. x.2, 3. His *calm* Soul made no *Reply,* but in the Exercise of this Grace of *Meekness,* kept a profound *Silence.* And as this Grace, doth first, and principally *act* towards *Jesus Christ,* and *God* in *him,* at the Time of a Soul's *New-Birth,* and throughout its *New-Life*; so for *his* Sake, it is extended unto the *Saints. In Meekness the New-Born, forbear one another, forgive one another, and restore one another when Fallen,* Col. iii.12, 13. Gal. vi.1. Yea, this Grace of *Meekness,* extends in all Exercise to *all Men,* to which the *New-Born* are exhorted, *Tit.* iii.2. *To speak Evil of no Man, to be no Brawlers, but Gentle, shewing all Meekness to all Men. Being Reviled,* (says the Apostle) *we*

Bless: Being Persecuted, we suffer it: Being Defamed, we intreat, 1 Cor. iv.12, 13.

Thus, that Principle of spiritual Life, produced by the Spirit of God in the Souls of his People, at the Time of Regeneration, contains in it all Kinds of Graces, fitted for, and acting towards their proper Objects. And so the *New-Born,* are inwardly adorned with the Grace of *Faith, Love, Hope, Patience, Humility,* and *with the Ornament of a meek and quiet Spirit, which, in the Sight of God is of great Price,* 1 Pet. iii.4.

I might likewise have mention'd the Grace of godly Zeal, of true Gospel Fervour of Spirit, as also, the Grace of Self-denial, which are Concomitant with the rest: For Christ *gave himself for us, that we might Purify to himself a peculiar People, zealous of good Works,* Tit. ii.14. And has said, *If any Man will come after me, let him deny himself, and take up his Cross, and follow me,* Matt. xvi.24. Yea, has declar'd this Grace so necessary, that without it, a Man *cannot be his Disciple,* Luke xiv.26, 27. But I pass on, having explain'd, and prov'd the Definition given of the New-Birth, to

The *Third* Thing propos'd: Which was, to shew what we may learn by this Phrase of being Born again. In which I shall be very Brief. And

First, We may learn hence, That as no Man can give himself an Existence in *Nature,* or the *First-Birth*; so neither can any Man give himself a Being in *Grace,* or the *New-Birth.* As God, as the God of *Nature,* is the sole *Author* of the one; so God, as the God of *Grace,* is the sole *Author* of the other. This appears, from *John* i.13. Where, speaking of the *Regenerate,* who had special *Faith* wrought in their Hearts, to *receive* the Lord Jesus, he says, *which were Born, not of Blood, nor of the Will of the Flesh, nor of the Will of Man, but of God.* Here's a *Denial* of all Creature Power, or Efficiency in the *New-Birth,* and an *Assertion* of God's being the only Author hereof. The Heaven-Born Soul, an Heir of Glory, is not Born of (*Blood*) of high, and noble Parentage; from whence proud Nature, may think itself, either more worthy, or capable of the *New-Birth,* than those of the meanest Rank. No; to stain the Pride of all Flesh. *God has chosen the base Things of this World, and Things which are not, to bring to nought Things which are.* Or, 'tis his usual Method, to work upon the *Base,* that *are not,* in Men's Esteem, when he passeth by the *Noble,* those Things which *are,* in their own Account; to make it appear, that all the great and honourable of the Earth, are nothing, and can do nothing towards making themselves *New-Creatures,* any more than the most despicable Man, upon the Face of the Earth, *1 Cor.* i.28. Thus it's not of Blood. Nor of the Will of the *(Flesh,)* or, of corrupt Nature, in its vain Resolutions to make itself *a New-Creature; for not of him that Willeth,* &c. *Rom.* ix.16. Nor of the Will of *(Man),* of the bright *Rationalist,* the Man of *Intellect,* that acts most agreeably to the Name, and Nature of a *Man*; and thinks thereby to exalt himself into the high Dignity of a *New-Creature. For God has made Foolish the Wisdom of this World, and confounded the Things which are Mighty in their own Esteem,* 1 Cor. i.27. But *(of God.)* Of his omnipotent Power, and of him as a *Sovereign,* working upon *base, sinful, foolish, weak* Men; that himself might have all the *Glory,* in the *New-Creation,* which was his due in the *Old,* 1 Cor. i.29, 30, 31.

Secondly, From this Phrase, of being Born again, we may learn, That it is as absolutely necessary for a Man to be *Born* into the World of *Grace,* in order to enjoy *this,* as it is that a Man should be *Born* into the World if *Nature,* before he can enjoy *that.* And therefore, none need marvel at what our Lord said, *Ye must be Born again:* And, *except a Man be Born again, he cannot see the Kingdom of God,* John iii.3, 7. For, as it is in the Works of *Nature,* so it is in the Works of *Grace.*

In the Works of *Nature,* the All-wise Creator, first made the *World,* with a Variety of Creatures and Things in it, for the Service and Delight of Man; and then made *Man,* every was *Fitted* for the Enjoyment thereof. In his *Mind,* he was every way *Fitted* to contemplate the wonderful Goodness of his Maker, in the large Provision he had made for him; and to give him the Glory due unto his Name. And his *Body,* in the several *Senses* thereof, was *Fitted* for *Converse* with their proper *Objects.* As, his *Sight,* to *behold* visible *Objects,* the Glory of Light, the Variety, and Beauty of *Colours*; his *Hearing,* to *take* in *Sounds;* his *Taste,* to *relish Meats;* his *Smell,* to *receive Scents*; and his *Feeling,* to *judge* of *solid Bodies.* Thus *Man* was *Fitted* for the Enjoyment of this *World.* And as it was with him in his first *Creation,* so, in some Measure, it is in his *Generation.* A Child must be first *Born* into the World, and in these respects *Fitted* to the various *Objects* thereof, before it can *Enjoy* them. And thus it is in the Works of *Grace.*

God, as the God of all Grace, has made vast Preparations for his People; even so Great, that *Eye hath not seen, nor Ear heard, nor have they entered into the Heart of Man to conceive of them.* 1 Cor. ii.9. *He prepared for them a Kingdom, even from the Foundation of the World,* Matt. xxv.34. And *it is his good Pleasure to give them the Kingdom,* Luke xii.32. And this Kingdom consists of two *Branches,* viz. The *Grace-part,* and the *Glory-part* of it. And both these Branches, *Comprehensively* taken, make up but one *Kingdom*, or that Kingdom, which it is the Father's good Pleasure to give unto his *little Flock*. And yet each of these Branches, *Distributively,* bear the Name of the *Kingdom*. The *Grace-part* of this *Kingdom*, contains in it, all those gracious Privileges which God has prepar'd for his People, in his Church Militant, under the *Government* of Christ, as *King of Sion*. And the *Glory-part* of it, contains, all those inconceivable Glories which he hath prepar'd for the Church Triumphant, under the open, glorious *Reign* of *Christ the Lamb, at his next appearing;* and *of God the Father, when the Son shall deliver up the Kingdom* to him, that *God may be all in all,* in all the saved ones, to the endless Ages of Eternity. And except a Man be *Born again,* he cannot *see* the *Kingdom* of God, in either of these its *Branches.*

For, even in the first *Branch* hereof, or the *Grace-part* of it, it is a distinct *Kingdom* from the *World*; tho' it is *in* the World, yet not *of* the World, *John* xviii.36. As for the *World*, it is said to *lie in Wickedness,* 1 John v.19. And, that *Satan, the Prince of the Power of the Air, is the God,* or Governor *of it; who,* as such, *Worketh in the Children of Disobedience,* the Subjects of his Kingdom. *Among whom,* (says the Apostle) *We all had our Conversation in Times past,* &c. 2 Cor. iv.4. Eph. ii.2, 3. That is, whilst we were in an *unregenerate* State. And as to Christ's *Kingdom* in the World, it is said to consist, of *Righteousness, Peace, and Joy in the Holy Ghost,* Rom. xiv.17. Here *Grace Reigns thro' Righteousness unto eternal Life, by Jesus Christ our Lord,* Rom. v.21. *Grace Reigns thro' Righteousness, by Jesus Christ, to the eternal Life* of all those happy Subjects, who have him for *their Lord.* Thus these *Kingdoms* are *Distinct.* And as no *Subject* of another Kingdom, can share the Privileges of *this,* unless he be first *Naturaliz'd*; so neither can any *Subject* of *Satan's Kingdom,* (and by Nature, we are all such) partake of the Privileges of Christ's *Kingdom,* before he be *Translated,* or carried over, into it. And as the Privileges of Christ's Kingdom, are *Heavenly,* and *Supernatural*; so no Man can enjoy them, before he is *Born* from *above,* or has a *supernatural Life* wrought in his Soul; no more than a Child in Nature, can enjoy the natural Privileges of this World, before it is *Born* into it, or *Fitted* for it. And the Reason on both Sides, is the same; because there must be an *Agreeableness* between the *Subject* and the *Object,* or between the Persons and Things *Enjoying,* and the Persons and Things to be *Enjoy'd,* or there can be no *Communion* between them. Christ's Kingdom is *Light,* and an *unregenerate* Man is *Darkness:* And *what Fellowship hath Light with Darkness? or Christ with*

Belial? 2 Cor. vi.14, 15. The Things of Christ's Kingdom are *spiritual*; and therefore the *natural Man,* with all his highest Attainments, cannot *know* them, *1 Cor.* ii.14. As for the *Righteousness* of the Kingdom, that is, the Obedience of Jesus Christ, imputed by God the Father, to every Subject thereof, as the Matter of his Righteousness before him, unto his compleat Justification in his Sight; this every natural Man is *ignorant* of, and *stumbles* at, *Rom.* ix.32. and x.3. As for the *Peace* of this Kingdom, that is, *Peace with God thro' our Lord Jesus Christ*; as it is alone by the Obedience and Sufferings of Christ, without regard to the Creature's Doings, or Sufferings, as the procuring Cause thereof, this a natural Man *understands* not. *The way of Peace, they have not known,* Rom. iii.17. And as for the *Joy* of this Kingdom, that is, *Joy in the Holy Ghost*; which flows from God's *Love* being *shed abroad in the Heart,* Christ's *Blood* being *sprinkled* on the *Conscience,* and an appropriating *View* of future Glory, this no natural Man is *capable* of. Because he hath not the *Holy Spirit* of God dwelling in him, nor yet, a *spiritual* Appetite, suited to the *spiritual* Things rejoiced in. *Sensual* Men, *have not the Spirit,* Jude 19. And *they that are after the Flesh, do mind the Things of the Flesh,* and those only, *Rom.* viii.5. 'Tis the *New-Born,* and only *they,* who have *spiritual* Senses, fitted for *Converse* with the *spiritual* Things of Christ's Kingdom, 'tis *these* only, that have an *Eye* to *behold the Glory of God,* as it *shines in the Face of Jesus Christ,* 2 Cor. iii.18. and iv.6. 'Tis *these* only, that have an *Ear* to *hear* Christ's *Voice,* John x.27. 'Tis *these* only, that *smell* Christ's Fragrancy, *the Savour of his good Ointments; his Name* being to them, *as Ointment poured forth*; in which they delight exceedingly, *Song* i.3. 'Tis the *New-Born* only, that have *Tasted that the Lord is Gracious,* 1 Pet. ii.3. And 'tis *these* only, that *have Handled of the Word of Life,*1 John i.1. And have *Felt* the sweet Impressions of omnipotent Power, touching their Hearts; while the *Gospel came unto them, not in Word only, but in Power, in the Holy Ghost, and in much Assurance,* 1 Thes. i.5. And those who have spiritual *Senses,* this *exercis'd* about spiritual Things, are such, that in order hereto, have been *deliver'd from the Power of Darkness,* the Dominion of Sin and Satan, *and Translated into the Kingdom of God's dear Son; brought out of Nature's Darkness, into God's marvellous Light,* or, into the World of *Grace,* Col. i.13. 1 Pet. ii.9. In which, all Things, in *Grace, appear New,* to the *Heaven-Born* Soul, as all Things in *Nature,* to a *New-Born* Infant. Whatever Notions a Man may have had of the Grace of God, or of the Things of the Kingdom of Grace, whilst in an *unregenerate* State, when God comes to work a saving *Change* on his Soul, in the *New-Birth*, he presently finds, that he never *saw* them before; nor had any *spiritual* Sensation of those excellent *Objects*, which now appear Marvellous, in their Reality and Glory, to all his spiritual *Senses*. For *if any Man be in Christ, he is a New-Creature: Old Things are past away, behold, all Things are become New*, 2 Cor. v.17. Thus it appears, that *except a Man be Born again, he cannot see the Kingdom of God,* in the first *Branch* thereof, or the *Grace-part of it*. And therefore,

Secondly, An *unregenerate* Man, cannot see the Kingdom of God, in the second *Branch* thereof, or the *Glory-part* of it. For, as the Work of Divine Grace on the Soul, in the *New-Birth*, is a *Preparation* for Glory; so, without *this*, there can be no *Enjoyment* of Glory. And therefore the Apostle, when he speaks of the glorious State of the Saints, in their heavenly House, or Kingdom of Glory, when *Mortality shall be swallowed up of Life*, says, *now he that hath wrought us for the self same Thing, is God: who hath also given unto us the earnest of the Spirit*, 2 Cor. v.5. 'Tis as if he should say, that Kingdom of Glory, which we shall ere-long inherit, is manifestly sure unto us, in that we have the *Earnest* of it now; *God's* Earnest, whose *Gifts are without Repentance:* He hath given us his *Spirit*, as the *First-fruits* of that full *Harvest* of Glory, he'll bestow upon us at Christ's appearing. And he hath likewise *wrought us,* prepar'd us for Glory, in giving us a Principle of Grace, in the *New-Birth*, and the Increase of Grace, by all the various Exercises thereof, throughout our *New-Life*, and therefore this Work of Grace in Us, must needs *Issue* in Glory; inasmuch as it is a *Preparation* for it; or God's preparing of us, for that *Glory*, which he hath prepar'd for us. And the All-wise God doth nothing in vain; nor can be frustrated in his End design'd: But when the prepared *Subjects* of Glory, shall have the *Glory* prepar'd, put upon them, the whole will appear to have a Design worthy of a GOD! And thus the Apostle gives *Thanks unto* God *the Father, who,* says he, *hath made us meet to be Partakers of the Inheritance of the Saints in Light*, Col. i.12. 'Tis the *New-Born*, and only *they*, who have a *New-Nature*, or the *Light* of *Grace* given them, that are prepar'd for the *Light of Glory*. 'Tis *these* only that are *pure in Heart*, and *their* peculiar Blessedness is to *see God*; or to have the transforming Displays of his Glory in the Church below, and the Beautifick Vision of his Face in the Church above, *Mat.* v.8. Grace and Glory, differ not *specifically*, but *gradually*; Grace is Glory *begun*, and Glory is Grace made *perfect*. And we may consider this, both *objectively*, and *subjectively*.

1. *Objectively. Objective* Grace *begun*, or the present Displays of the Grace of God thro' Christ, in the Church below, are of the same *Kind*, with the perfect Displays thereof in the Church above; tho' it's vastly different in *Degree:* The one, being but as the Brightness of the Morning-Star, and the other, like the Noon-tide Glory of the Sun.

2. *Subjectively. Subjective Grace begun*, in the Souls of the *New-Born*, is the same for *Kind*, that dwells in the perfect Saints in Heaven; but it differs as much in *Degree*, as the State of Infancy, or childhood, from the Perfection of Manhood. And as *Subjective* Grace *Inchoate*, or begun in the *New-Born, fits* that Soul for the present Enjoyment of *objective* Grace, display'd in the Church below; so, *subjective* Grace *consummate* in the Soul, at the Time of Death, *fits* the Soul for the full Enjoyment of *Objective* Grace, in its perfect Displays in the Church above, in the Kingdom of Christ, and of God the Father. Whence it's evident, that unless *a Man be Born again, he cannot see the Kingdom of God*, either in Grace, or in Glory: And that it is as absolutely necessary, that a Man be *Born* into the World of *Grace*, in order to enjoy *this*, as it is, that a Man be *Born* into the World of *Nature*, before he can enjoy *that*. But thus much may suffice for the *third* Thing propos'd: which was to shew, what we may learn from this Phrase of being Born again. I shall now,

Fourthly, With a Use or two, conclude the whole. And,

1st, Unto the *New-Born*. Oh happy Soul! From this Doctrine of the *New-Birth*, learn you these *three* Things especially. As,

1. To give all the *Glory* of your *heavenly Birth*, unto God, your *Heavenly Father*, who was the sole Author of it. You are *his Workmanship, created in Christ Jesus unto good Works,* Eph. ii.10. Your *New-Life*, was a Work of *Almightiness*. None of all the Creatures, either in Heaven or Earth, could form Christ's Image in your Souls, or work a Principle of Grace, and spiritual Life in your Hearts. No; 'twas nothing less than the omnipotent Arm of *JEHOVAH*, that made you *New Creatures in Christ Jesus. None Eye did*, nor could *pity you,* to do this, so great, so necessary a Work for you; until *he* pass'd by you when dead in Sin, and in boundless Mercy, by an All-creating Voice, said unto you, *Live.* therefore, give all the *Glory* of your *New-Life*, unto GOD the glorious Author of this wonderful Work. And say continually with the Apostle, *Blessed be the God, and Father of our Lord Jesus Christ, which according to his abundant Mercy, hath begotten us again unto a lively Hope, by the Resurrection of Jesus Christ from the Dead.* 1 Pet. i.3.

2. Learn hence, you *New-Born* Souls, the Necessity of your *Growth.* You are *born again* indeed; and that is your great Mercy, your peculiar Happiness, and unspeakable Privilege. But consider, you are yet but *New-Born Babes*, or if in some Measure grown up in Christ, you are still very far from that full *Stature*, that *Perfection* of Grace and Holiness which his design'd for you; for which your New Life was first given, and is still maintain'd, and to which it daily tends: And therefore be diligent in the Use of all the Means of divine Appointment, that so you may continually *grow in Grace, and in the Knowledge of Jesus Christ.* Do not think it enough that you are *New-Born*, that you have a Principle of Grace implanted in your Hearts, and have once believ'd in Jesus; and so sit down in carnal Security: But be as much concern'd about your daily *Growth* in Grace, as you were at first about the *Being* of it in your Souls. We can't expect to have thriving Souls, that we should grow in Grace, without a diligent Use of all those Means of it, which the God of Grace has appointed; no more than we can expect to have healthful Bodies, without the Use of those Means, which the God of Nature hath appointed for that End. The *Means* and the *End* are closely connected; and therefore we are exhorted, *to grow in Grace,* 2 Pet. iii.18. To grow in Grace, is a special *Blessing* from God; and we could in no wise be exhorted thereto, were it not that this Blessing was to be convey'd to us, thro' the *Means* which he hath appointed. And so it is an Exhortation to the Use of Means; inasmuch as our *increasing with all the Increase of God*, will be proportionable to our diligent Use of those *Means* of Grace which he hath appointed, such as Prayer, hearing, and reading God's Word, Meditation, &c. Therefore, *as New-Born Babes, desire the sincere Milk of the Word, that ye may grow thereby: If so be ye have tasted that the Lord is gracious,* 1 Pet. ii.2, 3. And whatever your present Attainments are, think not your selves to have *apprehended, or that you are already perfect*; but let this be the one Thing you do, *forgetting the Things which hare behind, and reaching forth unto those before, press towards the Mark; for the Prize of the high Calling of God in Christ Jesus,* Phil. iii.12, 13. 14. Which is no less than an absolute Perfection in Holiness, and Happiness; or a full Conformity to Christ, both in Grace and Glory.

3. From this Doctrine of the *New-Birth*, you who are *New-Born*, may learn, the Security of your *State,* for endless Life and Glory. 'Twas an abiding Principle of spiritual Life, which the Holy Ghost produc'd in your Souls at the Time of Regeneration. And *he which began the good Work in you, will perform it until the Day of Jesus Christ:* He'll *maintain*, and

increase the Life of Grace in your Souls, until it's *perfected* in the Life of Glory. Fear not then, you trembling Hearts, who once have had a blessed Experience if the begun *Life* of Grace in you, fear not *losing* this your spiritual Life; for it is a Life that shall *conquer* and *outlive* all those *Deaths*, and *Contrarieties*, with which it is surrounded; until it triumph over all, until *Mortality is swallow'd up of Life*, until all Sin, Sorrow and Death, re swallow'd up of perfect Holiness, Joy and Life for evermore! what tho' the Life of Grace in you, be but as a *Spark* in the Midst of the *Ocean*; yet it shall not be *extinguish'd* by that Ocean of Sin that dwells in your corrupt Nature, but shall *live*, and *triumph* over all Opposition. And this because it is in *Union* to the *Life* of *Jesus*, to that boundless, endless Fulness of *Life* in him; and also because, *the Spirit of Grace,* from Christ, who was the immediate Author of this Life in your Souls, doth, and shall *abide* in you, as a never-failing *Spring* of every *Grace*, to maintain, and raise the Life thereof, into the Life of *Glory.*

Here then, you *New-Born* Souls, *see* your *Security:* The Life of Grace in you, is more properly *Christ's* Life, than *yours! I am crucify'd with Christ,* says the Apostle, *nevertheless I live; yet not I, but Christ lives in me*, Gal. ii.20. I am *crudify'd* with Christ, here's his being *dead* with him; nevertheless, I *live*, here's his *New-Life* from him; yet not *I*, but *Christ* lives in me, here's *Christ* the *Life* of his *Life*, or his *Life*, Christ's *living* in him. And thus Christ is stiled, *our Life*, Col. iii.3. And because he *lives, we shall live also,* John xiv.19. *The Power of an endless Life* in him, will maintain the *Life* of *Grace* in us, and ripen it into the endless *Life* of *Glory!*

And as Christ is our Life, as the Ocean-fulness of it dwells in him, so it is and shall be communicated from him, by his holy Spirit; who, having taken Possession of our Souls, *abides* there, as the Spring of our Life, or as a Well of living Water, springing up unto everlasting Life, as saith our Lord, *John* iv.14. *Whosoever drinketh of the Water that I shall give him, shall never thirst; but the Water that I shall give him, shall be in him a Well of Water springing up into everlasting Life.* And it is *the Spirit of Grace*, as the *Life* thereof, that our Lord intends by this Water, as *Chap.* vii.38, 39. *He that believeth on me, as the Scripture hath said, out of his Belly shall flow Rivers of living Water. This spake he of the Spirit, which they that believe on him should receive.* Be joyful, and thankful then, you *New-born* Souls, and walk as the *Heirs* of *Glory*; for you are *begotten again, to an Inheritance incorruptible, undefiled, and that fadeth not away; which is reserved in Heaven for you:* And as the *Inheritance* is *reserved* for you, so *you* also *are*, and shall be *kept by the Power of God thro' Faith, unto that Salvation,* which is *ready to be revealed in the last Time,* 1 Pet. i.3, 4, 5. But,

2dly, A Word or two of use to such who are yet *unregenerate*. And what shall I say to you? Oh poor Souls! be convinc'd, that unless a special, gracious, universal *Change* pass upon you, you must perish for ever. If you go out of this World, as unholy, as destitute of a *Principle* of saving *Grace*, as you came into it, your *Life*, your Soul, will for ever *remain among the unclean*; And you must be Companions with Devils in everlasting Torment, and have your *Portion in the Lake that burneth with Fire and Brimstone.* Oh miserable Souls! you are *dead* in Sin, and *dead* in Law, you are under the Dominion of *Sin*, and the Condemnation of the *Law*; and such is the strict Justice, and flaming Holiness of Jehovah, that he will not, cannot suffer an *unrighteous*, an *unholy* Person to *inherit* his *Kingdom*, to enter into the *New Jerusalem. Marvel not* therefore, that our Lord has said, *ye must be born again*; But be convinc'd of the absolute *Necessity* thereof. And as the *Spirit* of God is the Author of the *New-Birth*; so be convinc'd likewise, that this so great, so necessary a *Work* is altogether out of the Reach of your own *Power*; that you have *destroy'd* your selves, and that all your *Help* is only in the Lord; and *seek* to him for it accordingly. For *Prayer* is a Part of natural Worship, which is every Man's Duty to perform. And even a *Simon Magus*, who was *in the Gall of Bitterness, and in the Bond of Iniquity*, was exhorted to it, *Acts* viii.22, 23. And tho' an *unregenerate* Man can't pray *with* the Spirit; yet he ought to pray *for* the Spirit, to *renew* his Nature, and *sanctify* him throughout. And since it is the Pleasure of God, to *quicken* dead Sinners by his *Word*, to beget them to a New *Life*, with the *Word of Truth*, the *Gospel of his Son*; it is the Duty of every unregenerate Soul, to attend upon the *Ministry* thereof. And this especially, he ought to do, in relation to the *New-Birth*; because it is God's usual Method to make use of the *preaching* of his *Word*, in this great *Work. Faith comes by hearing*, saith the Apostle, *Rom.* x.17. And if it is the Duty of Christ's Ministers, to *preach the Gospel to every Creature*, as by his Commission they are authoriz'd to do; then it is every Creature's Duty to lend an *Ear* to the Sound thereof. And great is their Encouragement so to do; in that the Ministration of the *Gospel*, is *the Ministration of Life. That* which is so *indeed*, the *pure* Gospel, preach'd by Christ's *sent* Servants; and not *that* which is so only in *Name*, a *mixed* Gospel, or rather the *Law*, instead of the *Gospel*, advanc'd by those, that are *sent* only by Men; who have never had the glorious Gospel of Christ, *shine* into their own *Souls*, and so can't *preach* it to *others*. 'Tis a *Gospel Ministry*, and not a *legal* one, that the Spirit of God works by, to the Salvation of Sinners. As, *Gal.* iii.2. *Received ye the Spirit by the Works of the Law, or by the hearing of Faith?* 'Tis under the Ministry of the Gospel, that dead Sinners, hear Christ's Voice, and live, *John* v.25. *Verily, verily I say unto you, the Hour is coming, and now is, when the Dead shall hear the Voice of the Son of God, and they that hear shall live.* 'Tis the *Hour* of the *Gospel*, that our Lord here speaks of, and of his Almighty *Voice*, which goes forth therein, to the *Quickening* of Souls dead in Sin. Here therefore, *dead* Sinners should *wait;* tho' they have no *Power* to *quicken* their own Souls, to *renew* their own Nature, or to give themselves the *New-Birth*; since the *creating Power of God*, goes forth in the *Gospel*, to the *Saving* of Multitudes. It's therefore the *Duty*, and *Privilege* of every poor Sinner, where the *Gospel* comes, to *lie* under the *Sound* of it; and there to *wait* for the saving Operations of the Spirit upon his *Soul*, by those living Waters, of free, Gospel-Grace, which proceed from the Lamb's Throne in his Church, as the poor *impotent Folk*, at the *Pool of Bethesda*, for the *moving of* those healing *Waters*, John v.2, *&c. Now therefore,* says our Lord, *hearken unto me, O ye Children; for blessed are they which keep my Ways. Hear Instructions, and be wise, and refuse it not. Blessed is the Man that heareth me, watching daily at my Gates, waiting at the Posts of my Doors; for whoso findeth me, findeth Life, and shall obtain Favour of the* LORD. *But he that sinneth against me, wrongeth his own Soul; all they that hate me, love Death,* Prov. viii.32, *&c.* And as it is the Duty of an *unregenerate* Man, to *hear* the Word of God; so likewise to *read* it, and therein to *wait* for the divine *Energy* of the *Spirit*, to give the *Word* an *Entrance* into his Heart, and make it effectual to the *illuminating,* and *quickening* of his *dark*, and *dead So*ul. *Search the Scriptures,* (saith our Lord) *for in them ye think ye have eternal Life, and they are they which testify of me,* John v.39. Thus it is the *Duty* of every one that is yet in an *unregenerate* State, to make use of all the *Means* of Grace, which God affords him; and therein to *wait* for the *Grace* of the Means, as a *Blessing* from Heaven: And if he neglect the same, 'twill be found to be a *neglecting* of *this great Salvation*; and his Condemnation, if he perish, will be so much the greater. *This is the Condemnation that Light is come into the World, and Men have loved Darkness rather than Light, because their Deeds were Evil,* John iii.19.

But let it be observ'd, that tho' it is the declar'd Will of God, to save Sinners by the Gospel of his Son, and so, that it is the *Duty* of every one to attend the same, and to make use of all the Means of Grace; yet when a *natural,* an *unregenerate* Man, performs what, in these respects, is *requir'd,* and meets with *Salvation* therein, he is not sav'd for *doing* his Duty; as if *that* was either a meritorious, or a moving *Cause* of his Salvation. No; *Works*, of all Kinds are excluded in the Point of *Salvation;* whether such as are merely *legal*, or such that are materially *Evangelical.* For tho' God requires *Obedience* under the Gospel; yet he doth not require it for this *End*, that a Sinner should *save* himself thereby, either in *Whole*, or in *Part*; but that Salvation may be *freely* bestow'd, in that *Way*, in which his infinite Wisdom has thought fit to *give* it; which is agreeable both to the Sovereign *Pleasure* of God, and to the Nature of his *rational* Creature. And every Soul that is *sav'd*, is sav'd of mere *Grace,* without the least Regard to his own *Works.* And yet, as was said, it is the *Duty* of every Creature to *obey* his Creator's *Command,* and as Law-condemn'd, and Self-ruin'd, to *wait* upon the God of all Grace under the *Gospel.* And great is his Encouragement so to do, for no one knows, but *he* may be the *Man* that shall find Mercy; since God upon his *Throne of Grace* in the *Gospel*, grants Pardon and Life, and that abundantly, to thousands of poor Souls, *dead* in Law, and *dead* in Sin, to their present *Life* in Grace, and future *Life* in Glory. That so his own Name may have the *Honour* of *Salvation*, from the Foundation, to the Top-stone, among all the *saved* ones. Who, when the *Head-stone thereof* is brought *forth with Shoutings,* in the highest *Joy* and *Duty*, as being rais'd to the highest *Glory*, will together *Cry, GRACE, GRACE unto it,* Zech. iv.7.

A P O E M on Salvation in Christ
   by Free Grace,
   for the Chief Sinners.

The D E D I C A T I O N.

To th' Soul that sees its Need of Christ,
   And longs in him t' have Interest,
And 'cause its vile, is full of Fear,
The following Lines presented are;
Being a *Poem*, made by One,
Sav'd by Free Grace, thro' God's dear Son.
The Author wishes 't may be blest,
To give some Soul a Glimpse of Christ.

Come, trembling Soul, Oh! come and see,
   What Grace there is in Christ for Thee.
What dost thou *want?* there's All in *Him*,
Prepar'd to fill thee to the Brim.
Art thou with th' *Guilt* of Sin opprest?
Christ bore its Weight, to give thee Rest:
And calls, ev'n Thee, as if by Name,
To Look to Him, the Bleeding Lamb.
And were thy Sins of Crimson Dye,
Christ's *Blood* can *cleanse* thee perfectly:
What's all thy mighty Guilt, before
His Godlike *Blood!* that paid thy Score?
He'll cast thy Sins in this vast Sea,
Whose Depths Unfathomable be:
And as th' *Egyptian* Host was drown'd,
They'll sink as Lead, and ne're be found.
Doth Sin's *Defilement* thy Heart grieve?
Christ's *Blood* alone can thee relieve.
There's Virtue in it, Infinite!
To wash thee clean, and make thee bright.

Doth Sin in 'ts *Being*, Sin in 'ts *Power*,
Afflict, and threaten to devour?
Christ's mighty *Arm* will Sin *subdue*,
And slay it in its *Being* too.
Look then to *Jesus* on the *Tree*,
Dying for Sinners, such as *Thee:*
Oh see! Christ made an *End of Sin*,
For every Soul that looks to Him.
Cast then *thy Burden on the Lord*;
And he'll sustain, as says his Word.
That Soul shall never *sink*, or *die*,
Who doth on Christ, for Life *Rely*.
Doth thou want *Strength*, and *Righteousness?*
Dost see thy Need of every *Grace?*
Christ's *Strength*, his *Grace*, his *Robe* is full;
To fill, to cloath the naked Soul.
And in a Word, there's All in *Christ*,
That thou canst want to make thee blest;
To raise thee now, and set thee high,
In Glory, to Eternity.
    What hinders then thy Joy in Him?
Is it because thou'st *Nought* to bring?
Is it because thou art so *vile*,
 Thou fear'st thou ne're shalt have a Smile?
Why, Christ needs none of all thy *Good*,
To join with his most precious *Blood:*
His full *Salvation* is so great,
That it is every Way *compleat*.
And this he freely *gives* away,
To them that ha'n't a *Mite* to pay.
And that Soul pleaseth Jesus well,
 That comes most *Poor*, for him to fill.
The Rich are *empty sent* from Him,
While th' poorest Souls are *fill'd* to th' Brim.
Christ saves, with th' greatest of Delight,
The Soul that comes in 'ts wretched Plight.
True *Faith*, by which a Sinner *lives*,
It nothing *brings*, but all *receives:*

Its *Nature* sweetly doth agree
With God's *Salvation*, that is *Free*.
It's *empty* Hand doth take up *Christ,*
As th' Father's *Gift*, with which it's blest;
And all that *Life* that's in him too,
Which God doth of *Free Grace* bestow.
Says *God*, I will give all away;
And thus my boundless Grace display,
In saving Sinners, thro' my Son,
That in themselves are quite undone.
Says, *Faith*, I like this well, *O Lord*,
I'm *glad* of this Soul-saving Word:
I *take* thy Great Salvation, Free;
And give the *Glory, Lord*, to Thee.
Thus God, and th' Soul are well *agreed*,
And meet in *Christ*, that once did *bleed*.
Sweetly each other they embrace,
Displaying, and *Receiving* Grace.

    Well then, Dear Soul, what shall I say?
Would'st thou be sav'd in God's own *Way?*
And if Salvation was not *Free*,
Dost think, it ne're would be for *Thee?*
And yet afraid that thou shalt die,
When th' Well of Life is brought so nigh!
Oh! Ope thy Mouth, and take thy *Fill*;
Since 'tis for *Whosoever will.*
And wouldst thou honour Jesus's *Blood!*
Then do not stay for any *Good,*
In thine own Heart, before thou *come*;
Lest thou should'st put it in Christ's *Room.*
But come to Christ, *just* as thou art;
With all thy Griefs, with all thy Smart,
With all thy *Vileness*, how e're great;
And cast thy self down at his *Feet;*
And say, with the poor leprous Man,
If thou wilt, thou canst make me clean.
I come, *Lord Jesus,* in my *Need,*
To Thee, who did for Sinners *bleed*.

I come to th' *Fountain, ope for Sin;*
Oh *wash* my filthy Soul therein!
I come to Thee for *Righteousness,*
And for Supply of every *Grace:*
Lord, I am *Empty*, thou art *Full,*
And with a *Word* canst *save* my Soul.
Thou know'st I fain on Thee would *rest;*
Let thy *Salvation* make me *blest.*
Let me not perish from thy Sight,
Since thou in Grace dost much *Delight:*
Oh! let thy Mercy bid me *Live*;
That I to thee may *Glory* give.
      Thus crowd thro' thy Unworthiness,
To try the Riches of his Grace;
And Christ will say, what ere's thy Guilt,
Soul, be it to thee as thou wilt.
Thou'st overcome me with Faith's Eye;
I can't thy great Request deny.
My *self*, and all that is in *Me,*
In boundless Love, I give to *Thee.*
Fear not, I'll *keep* thee from all *Harms,*
 Enclos'd in *Everlasting Arms.*
I *joy* to *save* thee, Oh my *Bride!*
This was the *End* for which I dy'd.
It glads my Heart to see thy *Face,*
Thou welcome art to all my *Grace.*
I, in my Love, will *rest* in thee;
Who art for ever *one* with me.
In *Me* therefore take up thy *Rest,*
Till thou, *with me*, art fully *blest.*
For thou hast *All*, in having *Me,*
For *Time*, and for *Eternity.*
Thy *Riches* thou canst never spend,
To *Ages* that shall have no End.
Such *Life*, and *Glory* I will give,
That Tongue can't tell, nor Heart *conceive!*

A H Y M N on the Mercy and Grace of God in Christ.

POOR *Sinners*, hark! what Voice is this
    That soundeth in your Ears?
        JEHOVAH speaks, in boundless Grace,
    To banish all your Fears.

The LORD doth speak from *Sion's* Mount,
    To Sinners in Distress,
Thro' his own Son, his *Mercy-seat*,
    Array'd in all his *Grace.*

The LORD, *the* LORD *God, merciful,*
    And gracious, is He,
Long-suffering, and abundant too
    In Goodness, rich, and free:

Forgiving Sin, Transgression,
    And all Iniquity;
For Thousands keeping Mercy still,
    By th' Truth that is in Me.

This was the bright Display he made,
    To *Moses*, of his *Name,*
When he i'th' *Rock* was *put*, while God
    His *Goodness* did *proclaim.*

Poor Sinners, hark to th' Voice of *Grace:*
    Here's none of *Sinai's* Roar,
Altho' you have deserv'd to die,
    That threatens to devour.

No, God in Christ, is *reconcil'd,*
    And sweetly doth *invite*
Lost *Sinners* to return to Him,
    Who doth in Grace delight.

In's Word, he thus to th' *Wicked* Speaks;
    Let him forsake his Way,

And the unrighteous Man his Thoughts;
    And turn without Delay,

Unto JEHOVAH, who will shew,
    On Him his *Mercy* Free,
And to that *God, who pardon will,*
    And that *Abundantly.*

Well then, poor Soul, art thou by *Sin,*
    Brought into sore *Distress?*
Obey God's *Call, come* to his *Throne;*
    For 'tis *a Throne of Grace.*

Are thy Sins *great?* and dost thou fear
    There is no Grace for *Thee?*
Why, what's thy *Sin*, if once compar'd
    To *Mercy's* boundless Sea!

They're Great indeed, but *Finite* still;
    God's Mercy's *Infinite:*
And far exceeds them all, as far
    As th' Heavens th' Earth for Height.

JEHOVAH*'s Mercy* never *fails,*
    And doth no *Limits* know:
To th' worst of *Sinners*, it streams down,
    In one Eternal *Flow!*

It drowns their *Sins*, those Mountains tall,
    Tho' numberless they be;
Yet without *Waste*, abides the *same,*
    Unto Eternity.

And since God's *Nature* cannot *change,*
    Nor yet his gracious *Will;*
Thousands of *Sinners*, thro' his Son,
    Shall find his *Mercy* still.

And tho' their *Sins* are multiply'd,
    Like Sands upon the Shore;
He'll *pardon* All, and they shall see,
    His *Grace abounds much more.*

God's Thoughts, and Ways in Mercy free,
  Our highest Thoughts transcend:
And *Grace doth reign thro' Righteousness,*
  To Life without an End!

Oh this abundant pardoning Grace!
  'Tis rich, 'tis full, 'tis free;
Soul, if of *Sinners* thou art *chief,*
  There is *enough* for *Thee!*

Yea, there is far *more* than enough;
  For when thou hast thy Fill,
There's more in *God*, than's left i'th' Sea,
  When 't fills a *Cockle-shell.*

Run then, thou sinful Soul, to God,
  Whose Arms stand open wide,
T' embrace returning Prodigals,
  Thro' Christ, who for them dy'd.

Whate're thy *Sins*, whate're thy *Wants*,
  In thine own Sight appear;
Since *Mercy's* deep, and boundless too,
  Thou hast no Cause to *fear.*

God's boundless *Grace*, most readily,
  Forgives the greatest *Score;*
And God herein doth much *delight,*
  T' *commend* his *Love* the more.

And never any *perish'd,* that
  Did *come to God by Christ:*
Then *cast* thy self into his *Arms;*
  Thou'lt be for ever *blest.*

Oh *venture* on his boundless *Grace!*
  However *vile,* and *poor;*
And he'll thee *save* from *Death* to *Life,*
  To *praise* him evermore.

A POEM on the Safety and Duty of a Believer.

HOW is it, Soul? hast thou to *Jesus* fled
   For *Refuge*, from that Wrath hung o'er thy Head?
       Hast ventur'd in to Him, the *Hiding place,*
Prepar'd for Sinners, by the Father's *Grace?*
Then know, Thou art exceeding *safe* in Him,
From fiery *Wrath*, the just Desert of *Sin:*
There's not a Drop of that amazing Storm,
Shall ever light on thee to do thee Harm.
No: JESUS, He has born it once for Thee,
And born it off; that Thou in *Him* art Free.
As th' *Ark* secur'd *Noah* from the *Flood,*
So *Christ* hid *Thee,* when in thy Place he stood.
And being entered into *Him* by Faith,
There, thou art *safe*, out of the Reach of Wrath:
Thou'rt pass'd from *Death to Life*, ev'n full Salvation:
And never shalt come into *Condemnation*.
Thou needst not fear the dreadful Wrath to come,
Which shall on Sinners fall at th' Day of Doom:
'twill only light on those who are *Without*;
But those *in* Christ, for *Safety* then shall shout.
Thy JESUS, He, hath saved Thee from Sin;
And in that Day, thou shalt be found in *Him;*
In Him as pardon'd, and as justify'd:
And therefore shalt with Him be glorify'd.
And being saved from the *Guilt* of Sin;
Sin's *Power* shall be destroy'd, it shall not reign.
Yea, Christ its very *Being* will destroy,
From out of Thee, unto thy endless Joy.
And as for *Satan*, tho' with furious Rage,
He often doth against thy Soul engage;
Thy Christ will save thee from his Wiles and Pow'r,
And never let this Lion Thee devour.
He'll teach thy Hands to *War*, and use the *Shield*;
And bring thee up *victorious* from the Field.

He in the Fight will safely thee defend,
And make his Rage to thy Advantage tend.
As for the *World*, that shall not thee destroy,
Thy Lord has *overcome* it, to thy Joy.
Tho' with its Snares, entangl'd thou may'st be;
Thy Lord, ere long, will fully set Thee free.
None of thine *Enemies*, with all their *Bands*,
Shall ever pluck thee out of JESUS' *Hands*.
His *Power's* Almighty, and his *Love* is great;
And nothing from it shall thee *separate*.
See then, dear Soul, Oh see how *safe* thou art!
Safe in thy Saviour's *Love*, his *Pow'r*, his *Heart!*
Christ *lives* for thee; and therefore thou shalt *live:*
And unto Thee, Eternal *Life* he'll give.

And now, dear *Soul*, what *Duty* dost thou owe,
Unto thy glorious Lord, that lov'd thee so?
Surely thy Life, thy whole Life here shou'd be
A Life of Faith, and Love continually.

Oh, think it not enough, thou'st once *believ'd;*
But still *walk* on in Christ, thou hast receiv'd.
Wash in his *Blood*, put on his *Robe*, draw *nigh*
By *Him*, to God the *Father*, constantly.
Remember, God *accepts* thee in his Son,
Thy *person,* and thy *Works* in Him alone.
To please the *Father* then, to honour *Christ,*
Walk on in *Him,* in whom his Soul doth *rest.*
Oh live upon the *Fulness* of thy Head,
In all that *He*, to *Thee*, of God is made;
His Fulness, to *present* thee, always eye;
His Fulness, to *supply* thee, constantly.
For lo, in Him, all *Fulness* ever dwells;
A *Fulness*, that his needy Children fills.
A *Fulness*, that can ne'er exhausted be;
That without Waste, doth flow eternally.
Come to him then, Oh come with all thy Wants,
Come to him daily, tell him thy Complaints.
Come, bring thy empty Pitchers to this *Well,*
This Well of *Life*, which richly thee will fill.

'Tis deep, 'tis full, 'tis overflowing too:
Draw Water hence, and thou no *Want* shalt know.
Pass over from thy *self*, thou empty Thing,
To live in *Christ*, thy never-failing *Spring.*
Who wou'd be careful in the Year of Drought,
That has a *Well*, where more is than enough?
Dwell then in *Christ*, abide in him by *Faith;*
And so abundant *Fruit* thou shalt bring forth.

But if thou say, My Heart's with Fear opprest,
That I in Christ, have yet no *Interest*;
I'm sore afraid, I never yet *believed,*
But that I only have myself *deceiv'd.*

I answer, Soul, whenever that's thy *Case,*
Then listen well unto thy Saviour's *Grace;*
For lo, he calls thee, when thou'rt most opprest,
To *come* to him, and says, I'll give thee *Rest.*
And when thou canst not come as a *Believer,*
Come as a Sinner, to be a Receiver:
Come as at *first*, with all thy Misery;
The Saviour now, is still as *full* and *free.*
Stand not, with *Satan*, to dispute it out,
Whether thou hast believ'd on Christ, or not:
Nor yet to argue this with *Unbelief;*
For lo, this Course, will give thee no Relief.
But say, Well, if I ha'n't *believed* yet,
It's Time to do it, and its not too late.
Now I am *call'd*, and now I will begin
To *look* to Christ, to save me from my Sin.

Christ says, to th' *End of th' Earth, look unto me,*
You *Sinners*, who at greatest *Distance* be;
And *be ye saved; for I am God* alone,
A Saviour, and beside me there is none.

Now then, dear Soul, consider well this *Word;*
Obey this great *Command* of Christ the Lord:
Look unto *Jesus* now, to Him alone,
Ev'n for the whole of thy *Salvation.*
And when thou'st *look'd*, see what he says to *Thee,*
Be saved, Soul, or thou shalt saved be.

This Word, a Royal *Grant* is from his *Throne,*
Even to Thee, of all Salvation.
Then *take* him at his *Word*, accept his *Grace,*
For, lo, his *Word* shall certainly take *Place.*
The Saviour, he is *God*, and cannot *lie;*
This Word, once *spoke*, he will not, can't deny.
Then count him *faithful* to his sacred Word:
Set to thy *Seal*, that *True* is Christ the Lord.
Believe thou shalt be *sav'd*, since *He* says so;
And *hold* it fast, 'gainst all that dare say, *No:*
For lo, His *Honour* is concern'd herein;
Thou canst not doubt it, without heinous *Sin.*
The faithful God, cannot himself deny;
Then dare not thus, to give his Truth the *Lie.*
Besides, thy *Comfort* and thy *Joy* of Faith,
Doth lie in *crediting* what Jesus saith.
He speaks on Purpose that it may be *strong,*
To *stand* against the huge Gainsaying *Throng.*
And if thou *listen* well, and take good *Heed*
To what Christ *says*, it will be *strong* indeed.
Thou'lt then in *Faith*, be fit to *fight* it out,
Against all *Fears*, which compass thee about.
For if thou thus obey, and honour *Christ,*
He'll honour *Thee*, with Sight of *Interest:*
And a *fresh* Act of Faith, will bring to *Light*
Thy *former* Acts, which *hid* were from thy *Sight.*

    Well then, dear Soul, my *Counsel* is to thee,
When-e'er assaulted by the *Enemy;*
Look unto Christ *afresh, trust* in his *Name,*
Go *forward* still, thou'lt not be put to *Shame.*
Go on *believing*, till thou'rt got to *Heaven:*
This is the *Work* which here to thee is *given.*
And while thy Life, a Life of *Faith* is found;
Thy *Love* will flow, and every Grace abound.

    Then think again, what *Duty* dost thou owe,
What Debt of *Love*, to Christ that lov'd thee so?
Sure thy whole Life, a Life of *Love* shou'd be,
To *Him*, that so immensely hath lov'd thee!

Oh think it not enough, thou once hast *lov'd,*
And in some *lower* Sphere of Action *mov'd.*
But still *reach* forth unto the high'st Degree;
And never *rest*, till Love shall *perfect* be.
Forget the Things *behind*, press *forward* still
To *love* the Lord, and to *obey* his Will:
And ne'er think thy Obedience is *compleat*,
While in this *Life*, this low, imperfect *State.*
But oh, pass on, *increasing* every Day,
In *Love* and *Labour*, while thou here dost stay.
Esteeming Christ's *Commands*, his *Yoke* to Thee,
To be most perfect, glorious *Liberty.*
Indeed his Yoke is *easy*, Burden *light*;
Found so by *All*, that take it on them right.
The more it *binds* 'em, they the more are *free*;
For Love-constraints the most delightful be.
Try then, dear Soul, *begin*, begin *again*,
To *love*, and *serve* the Lord, with *Might* and *Main:*
The more thou'rt in his *Work* and *Service* found,
The more thy *Happiness* will still abound:
Yea, let me say, the more thou'lt *honour* God,
And *Jesus*, who hath bought thee with his Blood.
And is not this, even *this*, thy chief *Desire*,
When with his Love, thy Soul is all on *Fire?*
Then think upon his boundless Love to *thee*,
Till into the same *Image* chang'd thou be:
And then his *Precepts* will be thy Delight,
As in *themselves*, they natively are *sweet.*
Oh follow then the *Lamb*, where'er he goes,
Thro' *Life*, thro' *Death*, whatever doth oppose.
In *Doing*, and in *Suffering* be thou free,
For Him who *did*, and *suffer'd* much for Thee.
Much! Aye, *How* much, soul, canst thou tell?
'Twill take *Eternity* to count it well!
The Greatness of his *Person*, think upon,
As he was God the Father's only *Son.*
Think likewise on the Greatness of his *Love*,
That brought him from his Royal *Throne* above;

T' *obey*, and *die* for such a Wretch as Thee!
Yea, so to die on the accursed *Tree!*
And *this*, that thou might'st not to *Hell* go down,
But that with endless *Life* he might thee crown!
Yea, this he did, to make thee *One* with Him;
One with Him *here*, and at the End of *Time!*
So one, that He and Thee might ne'er be *twain*;
But that thou, as his *Bride*, with him might'st reign!
Yea, Soul, thy *Jesus*, now in's Royal *State*,
In Love, still serves thee, as thy *Advocate!*
Behold then, all his *Love*, his wond'rous *Deeds*;
For's *Love*, and *Works*, all *Knowledge* far exceeds!
Such great Love-service, ne'er was *heard* before;
And 'twill be Heaven's *Wonder* evermore!

    Think then, what *Duty* this Love calls thee to!
Oh, canst thou pay the *Half* of what is *due!*
But Soul, *do* all thou *canst*, cast in thy *Mite*;
Thy *Lord*, he will *accept* it with *Delight*.
Sure nothing he commands thee can seem *hard*;
If thou his *Love*, or *Works* dost ought regard.
Remember thou thy *self*, to Him dost owe,
As thy *Creator*, and *Redeemer* too.
He bought thee from thy *Foes*, and set thee *free*;
That thou, henceforth, might'st *His* peculiar be.
Oh, don't deny him of his *Purchase*-right,
But give thy *self*, thy *All*, with great Delight.
In Ordinances, Providences too,
Follow thy Lord, where-ever he doth go.
Do what he *bids* thee, with the greatest Joy,
Bear what he *calls* thee to, without Annoy.

    Be diligent in all the *Means* of Grace;
For thou therein will often see his *Face*.
He thro' the *Lattess* of his Ordinances,
Doth give his People Soul-reviving *Glances*.
And when he *hides* himself, believe his Love;
Pray for, and wait fresh *Visits* from above.
For lo, as sure, as Christ doth go *away*,
He'll *come* again, and fill thy Heart with Joy.

Only with Care, Him seek in every *Street*,
In every *Duty*, till thou Him do meet.
And then thou shalt see thy Beloved's Face;
And be made joyful with his Words of Grace.
All Christ's *Commands*, Regard in every *Station*,
And yield th' *Obedience* due in each *Relation*.
Thou'rt saved by *Grace*; now love *Morality*,
That so Free Grace, may *glorified* be.
Shew forth the Praises of thy Saviour's *Name*;
Watch, keep thy Garments, lest Men see thy Shame.
Oh let thy *Walk* 'fore them, thy Conversation,
Be as becomes the *Gospel* of Salvation.
      Converse with Christ, in *Providences* too;
Trace all his Footsteps, where they are in *View.*
And when his Way's i'th' *Sea*, out of thy Sight,
Adore his wondrous Paths, *believe* them right.
Give him the *Glory* of each Providence,
That crowns thy Life with *Love*, to th' View of *Sense.*
Oh, when he *smiles*, and showers *Comforts* down,T
hen *bless*, and *praise* him, give him all *Renown.*
And when with awful *Frowns* he clothes his Face,
And brings thee into very great *Distress*,
Then be thou *still*, and know that he is God,
Adore, submit, and kiss thy Father's *Rod.*
Yea, Soul, in *darkest* Season's, *joyful* be,
Let *bitterest* Portions *pleasant* be to Thee:
For *greatest* Crosses, be thou *thankful* still;
In all give *Thanks*; for 'tis thy Father's *Will.*
      But if thou think this Lesson *hard* to learn,
And want'st a *Reason* for it, to discern;
I'll offer *four*, to help thee in this Strait,
Which, unto me, substantial are, and great.
      First then, know thou, that God doth all Things make
In Providence, for his own *Glory's* Sake:
His Glory is the *End* of all he doth,
Which He, by all, doth gloriously *bring* forth.
      Now then, If thou dost *love* him, Soul, rejoice,
In all thy Father *doth*, since 'tis his *Choice:*

'tis what he has *chose* for the bright Display
Of his own *Glory*, in that very *Way*.
Hast thou not *Cause* of highest Thanks and Praise,
Since God by all, doth his own *Glory* raise?
Wilt thou not *love* the Lord, and *bless* his Name,
For all, whereby he doth *exalt* his Fame?
The Greatness of his *Being* think upon;
His bright, essential Glory, search can none!
Then is 't not *meet*, that he should cast his *Rays*,
And make his Glories *known*, for his own Praise?
And while, in all his *Works*, his Glories *shine*,
To *bless* him, with all Saints, wilt thou not *join*:
Aye, tho' he *slay*, and seem to *cast* thee off,
'tis for his *Glory*, and that is *enough*.

    Another Reason, why thou shou'd'st be *glad*,
And *thankful*, for those Things which thou call'st *sad*,
Is *This*: The Works of God have *native* Excellence;
They're *glorious* all, of great *Magnificence!*
Then is the LORD not worthy of all *Praise*,
From thee, dear Soul, for all his *Works* and *Ways?*
His Work is *perfect*, in no *Part* amiss,
And nothing could be *better* than it is.
His Works are like *himself*, all wond'rous *great*,
And well become the God of Glory's *State!*
They're founded on his *Counsel*, wonderful;
And lo, they excellently *wrought*, are all!
If Works of Men, are *excellent* and *great*,
According to their Author's *Worth* and *State:*
Of what must those Works be, where th' *Art* of GOD,
For his own *Glory*, is display'd abroad!
The Works of God, in *Glory* are so bright,
That in them, He *himself* doth take Delight.
Wilt thou then *joy* with him, *thankful* be,
For all his *Works*, however *cross* to Thee?

    And yet *again*, I've something more to *add*,
As *Cause* of Joy and *Praise*, when thou art *sad:*
Know then, that God works all Things for thy *Good*,
I' th' Virtue of thy dear Redeemer's Blood.

Aye, thou wilt say, If this I cou'd but *see*,
I shou'd *rejoice*, and always *thankful* be;
But I, alas, think nothing's on my *Side:*
How can it be for *Good*, that I'm thus *try'd?*
Be joyful, thankful then, whate'er *befal*;
What canst thou wish for more than to have *All?*
Things present, Things to come, they all are *thine*;
And lo, for thy *Advantage* they combine.
Soul, God has *said* it; he'll *fulfil* his Word;
For th' *Way* and *Manner* leave it with the Lord.
If thou wou'dst *see* this Truth, open *Faith's* Eye;
For *Sense*, when Clouds are dark, can't *this* espy.
Let *Faith* but in the Light of promis'd Grace,
See All for *Good*, then straightway *Love* takes Place.
The bitter'st *Cup*, thou'lt take into thy Hand,
And freely *drink* it off at God's Command:
Yea, then thou'lt with a joyful, glorying Voice,
Give *Thanks* to God, and make his *Will* thy *Choice:*
Thou'lt like his *Way* of Working, best of all;
Before his *Wisdom* down thy *own* shall fall.
On Soul, thy *God,* doth work by Things *contrary*,
Fulfils his Word, by Things which seem to *vary*.
He brings the greatest *Good* from seeming *ill*;
This was, and is his Way of working still.
Perhaps, in some Respects, thou'lt see it *here*;
If not, *hereafter* 'twill be fully clear:
Then thou shalt see how *good* it was for thee,
To have thy Graces *tried* as they be.
How good it was, to make thy Graces *strong*,
How good it was, to *fit* thee for thy *Crown*.
The *Curse* is gone; an Things are *Blessings* made,
All work together, to make thee *like* thy Head:
All Things to thee the God of *Peace* doth send,
And all to thee, in glorious *Peace* will end.
Then enter into *Peace*, anticipate
The peaceful *Glories* of a future State.
Dear Soul, rise up, from Deeps of sore *Distress*,
Exult in *Joy*, abound in *Thankfulness*;

Love, and *bless* God, for th' darkest *Dispensation*;
For lo, ev'n *this*, shall turn to thy *Salvation*.
 Once more, I'll give to thee another *Reason*,
Why thou should'st bless thy God i' th' *darkest* Season:
'Tis *this*; hereby thou'lt glorify him more,
Than thou canst do, when this sad Time is *o'er*.
 Now then, dear Soul, if thou God's *Glory* love,
If *this*, ev'n this *alone*, thy Soul doth move;
Then rise in Haste, from all base *Selfishness*,
To *love* thy God, and him at all Times *bless*.
What is it? Surely 'tis a Thing but *small*,
To love, and bless thy God, when all goes *well:*
I do not say, that in it *self*, 'tis so;
But if *compar'd*, with what I'd bring thee to,
To bless the Lord, when *Smiles* are on his Face.
And he surrounds us with Displays of *Grace*,
This is a Thing that we can *easier* do,
Than when we think all Things *against* us go.
For when the Lord with *Frowns* arrays his Face,
We think we want a *Cause* of Thankfulness:
When thus it is, if we can but *submit*,
We're apt to think it's all that *then* is *meet*.
But oh, dear Soul, if thy God thou dost *bless*,
When he doth bring thee into great *Distress*,
This *glorify* him will abundantly,
And set his *native* Excellency high.
This will proclaim him to be what he *is*,
In *himself*, and *Works*, the *Sum* of all *Goodness:*
And that he's worthy of all *Love* and *Praise*,
At all Times, for *Himself*, and all his *Ways:*
Then if thou *lov'st* the Lord, rise up in Haste,
Thy heavy, selfish *Frames*, far from thee cast,
And *love*, and *bless* him with the great'st *Delight*,
Ev'n when against thee he seems most to *fight*.
Oh run into his *Arms*, when most extended
To *chasten* thee, because thou hast offended;
And *clasping* fast about him, do thou say,
Lord, here I *am*, I will not *run* away:

Do with me just according to thy *Will*,
Whate'er thou *dost*, I'll *love*, and *bless* thee still.
I know thou canst not do me any *Wrong*;
No, tho' to *Hell* thou wast to cast me down:
But, Lord, since *this* shall never be my Case,
I'll ever *bless*, and *magnify* thy Grace.
I'll *love* and *bless* thee, when thou *smit'st* me most;
My *Pain*, shall in the *Love* of *Thee*, be lost.
I'll *love* thy *Stroke*, because, dear Lord, they're *thine*;
They're for thy *Glory*; and I'll with it *join*:
In Thee I'll lose all my *Self-interest*;
Thine shall be *Mine*; in this I'll *joy* and *rest*.

   If thus thou dost, dear Soul, 'twill plainly prove,
That thou thy God, ev'n for *Himself*, doth *love:*
Yea, let me say, this *Glory* to him given,
Will be a *Kind* thou canst not give in *Heav'n*.

   'Tis true, the Glory thou shalt give him *there*,
In 'ts perfect *Bulk*, it will be greater far;
But to *love* and *bless* a *smiting* God, this is
A *Glory*, which thou canst not give in *Bliss*.

   Indeed, when thou in Heav'n shall clearly see,
That all his *Strokes* meer *Kindness* was to thee;
Thou then wilt *love*, and *bless* the Lord for *All*,
More than for *any* thou here art capable.
But lo, the *Pain* and *Smart* will then be gone,
And nothing but a *Sense* of *Love* comes on:
No *Frowns*, no *Strokes*, no *Crosses* there will be,
But bright Displays of *Love* t' Eternity.

   Now then arise, while *Pain* and *Smart* abide,
While *Darkness* lasts, and God his *Love* doth *hide*,
And *love* and *bless* him; for 'twill *praise* him more,
In some Sort, than thou *canst* when these are *o'er*.
Oh, count each *trying* Time, a precious *Season*,
To *praise* thy God; for which thou hast such *Reason*:
Improve it well; let this be all thy *Care*,
Since Trials well improv'd, thus *fruitful* are.

   To what I've said, I'll add another *Word:*
Hereby, thou wilt not only *praise* the Lord;

But this will be to thy *Advantage* great,
Both *here*, and also in a *future* State.
    Soul, if thou *bless* thy God in every Thing,
The *sharpest* Trials soon will lose their *Sting:*
Sweet *Peace* in *Trouble* shall to thee be given;
T' be one in *Will* with *God*'s little *Heaven.*
If thou the Lord dost *love*, and all Times *bless*,
Thou'lt likewise find a rich *Increase* of Grace.
And as thy try'd *Graces* will abound,
They all to *Praise* and *Honour* shall be found,
In that bright *Day*, when Jesus shall *appear*,
To *own* the *Service* thou hast done him here.
And as thou'st *serv'd* him in this present State,
He'll then give thee a *Crown* of Glory great.
    Now I'll return, and 'gain to thee will say,
Soul, *joyful*, *thankful* be i' th' *darkest* Day:
Go on to *walk* with God in Providence,
By *Faith* and *Love*, when all looks *dark* to *Sense.*
    But now, perhaps to me thou thus wilt speak,
You talk of *Duty*; but alas I'm *weak:*
I'm so *enfeebl'd*, and with *Weights* born down,
That I can't *stir*, nor gain an *Inch* of Ground.
    I know, dear Soul, that thus 't will be at *Times*;
But even *then*, strive *Duty's* Hill to climb:
God often gives us *Strength* ere we're aware,
When in his *Service* we engaged are.
And when all's *done*, if thou canst in no wise
Lift up thy *self*, and unto *Duty* rise:
Then know, thy Father's *Bowels* yern on thee;
And *he'll* thee *raise*, in boundless Mercy, *free.*
It is *His* Work, to *raise the Bowed down,*
To bind their Sorrows, and heal every Wound:
Then *wait* for *Him*, and he'll *renew* thy Strength,
To run again, in *Duty's* Way at Length.
    Upon the *Whole*, oh let thy *Life* be found,
A Life of *Faith* and *Love*, till thou art *crown'd!*
Thus *walk* with God, in every *Dispensation*;
Thy Course will *end*, in glorious, full SALVATION!

Now I commit thee to the *Grace* of Christ;
Oh may his *Spirit* always on thee rest!
That thou in all good *Works*, may'st fruitful be,
Till thou shalt *rest*, in blest ETERNITY!

F I N I S.

E R R A T A.

[Editor's note. Errata corrected in text.]

A

D I S C O U R S E

CONCERNING

God's Act of Adoption.

To which is added,

A

D I S C O U R S E

UPON THE

INHERITANCE

OF THE

Adopted Sons of God.

L O N D O N:

Printed for the Author: And Sold by *E. Gardner* in *Coleman-street* near the *Old Jewry*, 1737.

THE

PREFACE.

AS *to the Publication of my Thoughts upon the ensuing Subjects, what I have freely received of the Lord, I have freely imparted to the dear Saints. And tho'* I am less than the least of *them* all, *yet have I humbly offer'd my* Mite, *endeavouring to* speak the Truth in Love, *Eph.* 3.8. and 4.15. *as knowing that the same Spirit from Christ the Head, runs thro' every the least Member and Joynt of his Body, to the Edification of the whole, which is so* fitly joined together, and compacted by that which every Joynt supplieth, according to the effectual working in the measure of every part, *as to* make increase of the Body, to the edifying of itself in Love, *ver.* 16. *And if the Lord will please to use me, tho' one of the least Members, to do any Service to his Body, by what I have wrote, verily I have my Reward.*

In what I have offer'd in the ensuing Discourse, concerning God's Act of Adoption, I have not so much insisted upon it as a transient *Act, that passeth upon the Elect in Time, but rather as it is an* immanent *Act from Eternity: Because, I judge this to be the Foundation of the other, and, necessary, to be doctrinally laid, as the* Basis *of that which is more commonly treated of. We should not* conceal the Truth *of God, nor the Eternity of his* Loving Kindness *herein from his dear Children,* Psal. 40.10. *For the Grace of the everlasting Gospel, in every of its Branches, sweetly constrains the Saints to Holiness, in Heart, Lip, and Life.*

From blesses Experience, I can say, thro' Grace, That the Displays of God's everlasting Love, *in electing, adopting, and Settlement-Grace under the Holy Ghost's Witness of my particular Interest herein, have always been attended with strong influential Drawings of my Soul unto God in Christ, and to an holy, humble, thankful Walk before him. If the* Lord, *the Spirit,* direct the Heart into the Love of God, *2 Thess.* 3.5. *as it's great, free, distinguishing, unchangeable, and eternal, how doth it attract the Soul, in a moment, into the swiftest Motion after God, as the Center of all its Blessedness! The Holy Ghost's Light, in his saving Illuminations of his own, is always attended with the Holy Ghost's Fire. If in his Light I see what room I had in God's Heart before the World was, and what rich Provision he then made for me, in his* everlasting Covenant *with his Son; I straight- way feel the Heat of this Bright Shine, melting my Soul down, to run into any Form for God. If I know* the Truth, *in its Light and Heat, Purity and Power,* as it is in Jesus, *Eph.* 4.21. *my Heart is cast into the Truth I know, just as the melted Metal is cast into the Mold, and fashioned like it,* Rom. 6.17.

As to the other Discourse, I have added, upon the Inheritance of the Sons of God; I have endeavour'd to declare, *what I* have seen and heard *under the Light and Teachings of the Blessed Spirit,* 1 John 1.3. *The free, absolute, and irreversible Nature of the eternal Settlement of the Inheri- tance, upon the Sons of God, in Christ their Head, above the Consideration of the Fall, together with the way infinite Wisdom found out, for this* Grace *to* reign thro' Righteousness, by Jesus Christ, *Rom.* 5.21. *as a Saviour, in the Conveyance of it to the Children of God, notwithstanding their being Sinners, has been to me both delightful and amazing. The majestick Glory of Divine Grace, I have seen herein, has made my Soul, with* Moses, make haste, bow down, and worship, *Exod.* 34.8.

And now, dear Saints, what you shall see of the Truth of God in the following Pages, receive in the Love of it: What of Weakness appears, pass by, and cover, in brotherly Kindness, remembering that these Lines are but the Chatterings of a Child, *that* cannot speak, *Jer.* 1.6.

I conclude, committing the whole to God; who alone can give the Increase *to the Labours of his People,* 1 Cor. 3.6. *And if he will please to use the Hints I have given, to any of his Children, for their further Fellowship with the Truth; as it will be an Addition to my Joy, so I desire he may have all the Honour, who alone doth* build the Temple of the Lord, *and is worthy to* bear the Glory, *Zech.* 6.13.

A

DISCOURSE

CONCERNING

God's Act of Adoption.

MY Design in this Discourse, being to speak somewhat concerning the *Adoption of Children,* as it is a special gracious Privilege conferr'd upon the Elect of God: I shall

First, Give a Definition of it, (according to the Measure of Light received)

Secondly, Endeavour to explain it. And,

Thirdly, Improve it.

The Definition take thus: Adoption, is a gracious, immanent, eternal Act of God's Sovereign Will: Whereby he has taken a certain Number of Persons from among Mankind, as consider'd in the pure Mass, into a Supernatural, Covenant-Relation of Children to himself, by Christ Jesus, to the Praise of the Glory of his Grace.

In order to explain this Definition, I shall consider it in its Parts, and several Branches. As,

First, That Adoption is God's Act. 1 John iii.1. *Behold what manner of Love the Father hath bestow'd upon us, that we should be called the Sons of God.* Adoption is here set forth as God's Act: 'Tis the [Father] saith he, hath bestow'd this Privilege upon us. And the Lord himself declares this as his own Act, *2 Cor.* 6.18. *And I will be a Father unto you, and ye shall be my Sons and Daughters, saith the Lord Almighty.* We could no more bring ourselves into this Grace-Relation of Children, than we could bring ourselves into our natural Being. And therefore,

Secondly, Adoption is an Act of God's Sovereign Will, Eph. 1.5. *Having predestinated us unto the Adoption of Children by Jesus Christ to himself according to the good Pleasure of his Will.* The good Pleasure of God's Will, is the only Reason that's here assign'd, as the original Cause of this Relation.

Thirdly, Adoption is a gracious Act. 1 John 3.1. *Behold what manner of* [*Love*] or what manner of Grace, the Father hath bestowed upon us, in calling us Sons. The Grace of God, in its distinguishing Nature, differencing the Objects it fixt upon, from all the rest of Mankind, in its immense Riches, conferring such a high Dignity upon 'em, in its Sovereignty without Motives, in its Freeness without Conditions, and in the Eternity of its Duration, doth gloriously shine forth in this Act of Adoption.

Fourthly, Adoption is an Immanent Act, Or, an Act of God's Will, that always abideth the same in God. We say concerning it, as the Wise Man, Eccles. 3.14. *I know that whatsoever God doth it shall be for ever: Nothing can be put to it, nor any thing taken from it.* This is eminently true of what he doth in the Acts of his Grace, especially his Immanent Acts: Which are so perfect that nothing can be put to 'em, nor any thing taken from 'em. No, though the Grace of Adoption, as a transient Act, doth pass upon a Child of God in time, whereby he is brought into a visibility of Sonship, 1. In Grace, And, 2. In Glory, Yet this puts nothing to this Immanent Act of God's Will, so as to make it to be what it was not before. And as nothing can be put to it, so nor can any thing be taken from it. It is not our *Receiving the Adoption* by Faith, *Gal.* 4.5. and thereby entering into all the Immunities, and Grace-Privileges of the *Sons of God*, Joh. 1.12. nor yet our receiving the *Adoption* in the open Glory of *the first Resurrection*, When we shall enter into all the Glory-Privileges of this Relation, in the Sight of Men and Angels, *Rom.* 8.23. *1 Cor.* 15.43. *Rev.* 20.5. and 21.1. that will take any thing from this Act of God's Will, so as to make it cease to be what it is. For it is not our actual Enjoyment of all the glorious Fruits of adopting Love, that can take any thing from this Act of Adoption. It will abide the same to all the Ages of Eternity; which can't be said of a bare Decree: As for Instance, God decreed to make the World, which when effected, the Decree, as a Decree, ceased: But it can't be so said of an Immanent Act.

Fifthly, Adoption is not only an Act of God, an Act of his Sovereign Will, a Gracious, an Immanent, but it is also an Eternal Act: Or an Act that was from Everlasting in Commencement, and will be to Everlasting in Duration. Jer. 31.3. *I have loved thee* (saith the Lord) *with an everlasting Love.* 'Tis as true of Adopting as it is of electing Love. I shall insist a little upon the Eternity of this Act. And,

It must needs be, That Adoption is an eternal Act, since God's Chosen had an Inheritance settled upon 'em in Christ, before the Foundation of the World. From which Position, two things will follow by undeniable Consequences, as,

1. That in this very Act of Settlement, the Persons on whom it was made, were thereby constituted Heirs before the World began. And,

2. That if they were made Heirs, they must needs be made Children before the World began.

But because some Persons may scruple the Truth of the Position, I shall endeavour to prove it.

And that God's Chosen had an Inheritance settled upon 'em in Christ, before the Foundation of the World, is evident, by what stands upon Record in the Sacred Scriptures. We may begin with that Text, *2 Tim.* 1.9. *Who hath saved us, and called us with an holy Calling, not according to our Works, but according to his own Purpose and Grace which was given us in Christ Jesus before the World began.* Here's Grace said to be given us in Christ before the World began: By which we may understand, 1. The Grace of Relation; and 2. All that comprehensive Fullness of Grace that was settled upon us, as standing in that Relation. Our Grace-Relation was first given; and then our Grace-Portion bestow'd: And both before the World began.

Again, Another Scripture that bears Witness to this Truth, is, *Eph.* 1.3, 4. *Blessed be the God and Father of our Lord Jesus Christ, who hath blessed us with all spiritual Blessings in heavenly Places in Christ: According as he hath chosen us in him before the Foundation of the World.* Which we may understand in a two-fold Respect, as,

1. That the Elect were then blest with all spiritual Blessings Comprehensively; in that God himself did make over himself to them in Christ, as their eternal Portion. As saith the *Psalmist, My Flesh and my Heart faileth: But God is the Strength of my Heart, and my Portion for ever:* Or my eternal Lot, *Psal.* 73.26. This was the great Blessing of the Covenant made with *Abraham*, the Father of the Faithful, as a Type of Christ and his Seed. *Gen.* 17.7. *And I will establish my Covenant,* &c. *To be a God unto thee and to thy Seed after thee.* This makes the *Psalmist* pronounce God's People

happy, with a *Yea, happy is that People whose God is the* LORD, *Psal.* 144.15. Because this is the Origin of all our Blessedness, The Source and Fountain whence all the Streams flow, The Sum Total, in which all particular Blessings are comprized.

2. The Elect were blest with all spiritual Blessings Distributively. God did, as it were, distribute, or lay out his own Riches of Grace and Glory (which were first settled comprehensively) into so many several Parcels of Blessings; according to the Infinity of his *Wisdom. Eph.* 1.8. whereby he has made a full Provision in his *well-order'd Covenant*, to answer all the Designs of his Grace towards us, *2 Sam.* 23.5. and to *supply all our Wants*, *Phil.* 4.19. in every State and Condition, thro all those Ways and Means *the Counsel of his Will* has ordain'd, *Eph.* 1.11. And thus all spiritual Blessings in the Heavenlies, as a vast Inheritance, were settled upon the Elect in Christ, before the Foundation of the World. And God's eternal Act of Blessing [In] Christ Representatively, is the Foundation of his Blessing us [Through] Christ communicatively. For by this Act of Settlement, all God's Riches of Grace and Glory, were stored up in Christ, as in an immense Treasury; whence the Saints *receive* all Supplies, through Time and to Eternity, *Col.* 1.19. *Joh.* 1.16. And when we in Faith, do approach the Divine Throne, for *Grace to help in Time of Need,* Heb. 4.16. We come to God as our Father, in believing Views of that full Provision which he has made for us in Christ: And we don't ask for any new Blessings to be settled upon us, but only for the Communication of those Blessings [Thro'] Christ, which he hath already blest us with [In] Christ.

A *third* Scripture that bears Witness to this Truth, is *Titus* 1.2. *In hope of eternal Life which God that cannot lie, promised before the World began.* Eternal Life is here said to be promised, that is, given by Promise; for *God gave* the Inheritance to Christ *by Promise*, as he did to *Abraham* his Type, *Gal.* 3.18. Eternal Life then, which contains in it the whole of our Inheritance, both in Grace and Glory, was settled upon Christ, for the Elect, and upon the Elect in Christ, by an absolute Promise-Grant in the everlasting Covenant, by a God that cannot lie; even before the World began. Thus the Truth of this Position is abundantly evident: And as to the Consequences drawn from it, I think they are so clear they cannot be deny'd. For, if an Inheritance was settled upon the Elect before the World began, then they must be made Heirs before the World began: For Heirs and an Inheritance are Cor-relates. Again, if the Elect were made Heirs, they must needs be made Children before the World began: For Heirship depends upon Sonship: *If Children, then Heirs,* &c. *Rom.* 8.17.

Again, it may be farther prov'd, That Adoption is an eternal Act, by the Order in which it stands; as it comes in between our being chosen in Christ, and our being blest in him. For when the Apostle had set forth our Inheritance in the Matter of it, as it lies in all spiritual Blessings, *Eph.* 1.3. And also in the Time of its Bestowment, which was before the Foundation of the World, according as we were chosen in Christ, *Ver. 4.* he next proceeds to shew the Manner if its Settlement upon us, and that is as we were Children, *Ver.5.* [*Having*] *Predestinated us unto the Adoption of Children.* And were blest as being adopted.

This Predestination is an Immanent Act of God's Will; whereby he has absolutely determin'd us unto, or into the Adoption of Children, in this Resolution of his Divine Mind, *I will be unto you a Father, and ye shall be my Sons and Daughters,* 2 Cor. 6.18. Which predestinating Act of his Will, did give an immediate Being to this Relation, to, and in the Mind of God, and a remote Being unto it, or a Being of Futurity, in respect unto Men. No sooner did this Act pass in the Divine Mind, *I will be unto you a Father*; but the immediate Effect of it was, our being his *Sons and Daughters:* For this Act of God's Will, is the very Essence of Adoption. It was done to God secretly, as an Immanent Act from Eternity; as the Foundation of doing it to Men openly, as a transient Act of Time.

Once more, Adoption may be further evinced to be an eternal Act, in that the Elect not only sustain the Relation of Sons in the Mind of God; but also bear the Name of Sons in the Word of God, before the Spirit is sent into their Hearts crying, Abba, Father. *Gal.* 4.6. *And because ye are Sons, God hath sent forth the Spirit of his Son,* &c. Their Relation is not only antecedent to the sending of the Spirit; but it is also a Cause of his being sent: As is plain from this *Galatian* Text. The Elect are also called the Children of God, even before Christ died to *gather 'em together* in one. *John* 11.52. Because they never lost their eternal Relation, though *scattered abroad* in the Fall. Yea, on this Account they are likewise stiled Children, even before the Son of God assumed their Nature to set them free: *Heb.* 2.14. *Forasmuch then as the Children are Partakers of Flesh and Blood, he also himself likewise took part of the same.* And again, they are called the Sons of God, before their gathering to Christ by regenerating, and converting Grace: *Isa.* 43.6. *I will say to the North, Give up; and to the South, Keep not back: bring my Sons from far, and my Daughters from the*

Ends of the Earth. We may understand these Words, 1. Literally: And so they are a Prophecy of the *Jews* Return from Captivity, and Conversion to Christ. Whence we may observe, That the Royal Word of Command comes forth for their Deliverance, upon this bottom of their being the Sons of God secretly, in order to make them the Sons of God openly, by conferring on them the Privileges of this Relation in the View of all the World.2. We may take these Words spiritually: And so they respect the Elect of God among the *Gentiles*, as well as *Jews*, And their gathering to Christ by efficacious Grace. And thus the Royal Command comes forth for all Enemies to deliver 'em up, whether Sin, Satan, Law, or Conscience; when the Lord, the Spirit comes commission'd from the Father and Christ, to bring these Sons, upon the bottom of their antecedent Relation, out of the Bondage of a Nature-State, in which they are *afar off*, into a State of Freedom and influential Nearness, by Faith in *the Blood of Christ*, Eph.2.13. by which they are taken into the visible number of the *Sons of God*; and have a pleadable Right to all the Privileges of this Relation; as being *no more Strangers, but Fellow-citizens with the Saints, and of the Household of God*, Eph. 2.19. And God's Time-Act of Adoption, is but as it were a Copy taken from the Original of his eternal Act.

Thus I have shewn that Adoption is an eternal Act: 1. From the Nature of the Act itself. 2. From the Consequents of it, which are, 1. That the Elect hereupon sustain the Relation of Sons in the Word of God. And 2. That they bear the Name of Sons in the Mind of God, before the Spirit is sent into their Hearts, Yea, before Christ died for 'em; And lo, before their being gather'd to him by Faith: As is clear from this Text in *Isaiah*, which I last insisted on; and should now leave, but that some, perhaps, may object, and say,

Objection. That this Text affords no clear Proof for the Elect being called the Sons of God before their Conversion to Christ: Because in the very next Verse, as soon as the Lord had said, *Bring my Sons from far,* it follows, *Even every one that is called by my Name*, Isa. 43.7. From whence the Objector may conclude, that the Persons here styl'd Sons, are none but such that have pass'd under a saving Work of the Spirit in their Hearts.

Answer. In Answer to which I do readily grant, that the Persons here denominated Sons, are all such, and none but such that are called by God's Name: And yet I don't think, that this will in the least invalidate my Argument for eternal Adoption. I shall therefore endeavour to remove this Objection, by shewing

In what Sense calling by God's Name, creating for his Glory, &c. in the *seventh Verse* of this *forty-third* of *Isaiah*, may be understood, agreeably with God's eternal Act of Adoption. But before I come to open the several Phrases herein, I shall hint something concerning the Extensiveness of the Divine Command, consistent with other Scriptures, and also with the Sense I have given of the former Verse.

Bring my Sons from far, says God, *and my Daughters from the ends of the Earth: Even every one that is called by my Name.* This Divine Command extends itself to every Son of God, and secures his being brought home to his Father's House. Our Father will not leave one of his Children to perish in the distant State of Nature. For having *given 'em* to Christ, he expects to have 'em all brought safe home at last: As our Lord witnesseth, *John* 6.39. *And this is the Father's Will which hath sent me, that of all which he hath given me, I should lose nothing, but should raise it up against at he last Day.* Our Lord *receiv'd Commandment of* his *Father* to *lay down his Life for the Sheep*; that so he might lose none, *John* 10.18. And because it was both His and his Father's Will, he therefore makes Request for their being brought home, even all of 'em. *John* 17.20, 21. *Neither pray I for these alone, but for them also which shall believe on me through their Word: That they [All] may be one,* (or gather'd into one) *as thou Father art in me, and I in thee; that they also may be one in us.* And not only did our Lord pray to his Father who *always* heard him, *John* 11.42. for every Child of his, that it might be brought home according to his Will: But he also declares a Necessity was upon him concerning this thing, *John* 10.16. *And other Sheep I have which are not of this Fold: Them also I [Must] bring.* And doubtless one Reason why our Lord says, *I must bring* 'em, was, because it was his *Father's Will,* which he *came down from Heaven* on purpose to fulfil, *John* 6.38. And thus when he was to gather the *Samaritan* Woman, and bring her nigh by efficacious Grace, it's said, *John* 4.4. *He must needs go through* Samaria. This being the Will of his Father, which to do was his *Meat,* as himself says, ver. 34. And thus the *Apostle Peter, The Lord is Long-suffering to us-ward, not willing that any should perish, but that all should come to Repentance,* 2 Pet. 3.9. I apprehend that the whole Election of Grace is intended in these Words [*Us-ward*]. And so, his not willing that any should perish, is, that any of [Us] should perish, but that all of [Us] should come to Repentance: Which is the very Language of this Text in *Isaiah. Bring* 'em nigh, saith God, *even every one that's called by my Name.* From whence we may learn, That every one that is a Child of

God by adopting Grace secretly, shall certainly in God's own Way and Time, be brought nigh, and made a Child of God openly *by Faith in Christ Jesus* Here, and by Kingdom-Glory Hereafter, *Gal.* 3.26. *Rev.* 21.7.

I shall now take a little Notice of what is intended by the Sons of God being said, To be called by his Name, in the *seventh Verse* of this *forty-third* of *Isaiah.* And I humbly conceive, that hereby in the primary Sense of it, we are to understand, That Act of God's Will, whereby he has call'd 'em [His] People, in the Counsel-Language that pass'd, and Covenant-Transactions which were made, between his three glorious Persons, concerning the whole Body of the Elect before the World began.

And hence it is that they are called [His] People in his Word, even before Christ dy'd to redeem 'em: (and so before they could be made the Sons of God by Faith, as a Fruit of Christ's Redemption:) which we may see in that Message the Angel brought to *Joseph*, concerning the Virgin *Mary*, when he came to acquaint him what manner of Child she should bring forth, and what his Name should be, *Mat.* 1.21. *Thou shalt call his Name Jesus: For he shall save [His] People from their Sins.* And as they are called His People, before our great High-Priest offer'd up himself a Sacrifice in their room and stead: so also before the Holy Spirit is sent into their Hearts, to subdue their stubborn Wills, and bring 'em into a willing Subjection to Christ's kingly Sceptre, by his own creating Power. As we may see in that Promise of the Father made to Christ, *Ps.* 110.3. *[Thy] People shall be willing in the Day of thy Power.* Thus they are called by God's Name, in his Counsel and Covenant, Prophecy and Promise concerning 'em, upon the bottom of his eternal Choice and Foreknowledge of 'em as his [Own], *2 Tim.* 2.19. before effectual Grace reacheth their Hearts. So that here, *every one that is called by my Name,* is as much as if the Lord should say, every one that I have a special Right to and Propriety in. But,

I proceed to the *latter Part* of the *Verse*, which gives us the Reason why the Command for gathering, extends itself to every one that's called by God's Name: *For I have created him for my Glory, I have Form'd him, yea, I have Made him,* Isa. 43.7.

I have [Created] him for my Glory, is as much as if the Lord should say, I have given him his Being in the State of Creatureship, in Subserviency to all the ends of my Glory, in my vast Designs concerning him: And for this Reason he must be gathered from the East and West.

I have [Formed] him, as a *Vessel of Honour,* in his Grace-Relation and Glory-Designation. And having thus *prepar'd him unto Glory,* Rom. 9.21, 23. he must be brought from the North and from the South; *for my Counsel shall stand, and I will do all my Pleasure,* Isa. 46.10.

Yea (says God) *I have [Made] him,* or, I have given him already his Grace, and Glory-being in my own Son Representatively: *In whom it has pleased* me *that all fullness should dwell,* Col. 1.19. a fullness for Representation, as well as a fulness for Communication. I have [Made] him in the Upper-fall Acts of my Grace, in my own Son, his Head, Pattern, and Exemplar. Yea, I have [Made] him in the Under-fall Acts of my Grace to: For though he has *destroy'd himself* by Sin, *Hos.* 13.9. yet, I have [Made] him in his glorious Head, as a Saviour: Whom I have *made unto him Wisdom, Righteousness, Sanctification and Redemption,* 1 Cor. 1.30. So that, upon the bottom of what I have [Made] him, in all the Acts of my Grace concerning him, he must be brought from far; that this Representative-Life, which he now has in Christ his Head, may become a communicated Life, and enjoy'd in his own Person by a Derivation out of the communicable Fulness of my Son.

And thus I humbly conceive, That the Elect may be as truly said, to be [Made] in Christ, when he was constituted their *Common-Head,* and *Root;* as the Children of the *First Adam* may be said to be [Made] in him, when he came out of his Maker's Hand in the Capacity of a Common Person.

What *Adam* then was, that all Men were who were in him: And it is from this their being in him radically, and seminally, as the Life of the Branch is in its Root, or the Plant in its Seed, that they derive both his *Nature* and corrupt Image, by a Communication of Influence: Even as the Root communicates Life and Sap to the Branches. *And as we have born the Image of the Earthly, we shall also bear the Image of the Heavenly,* 1 Cor. 15.48, 49.

The Fountain-cause of our bearing *Adam's* Image, was our Union to him, when we were representatively made in him. So, our bearing the Image of the Heavenly, is secured by that Union we had to the Person of Christ, when representatively made in him; who was constituted our Head and Root *from everlasting, Prov.* 8.23. And a Representative-Being in each of these Heads, doth not only secure, but is also antecedent unto, that personal Being, which is from them derived to each of their respective Seeds, in Nature, or Grace.

Thus I have endeavoured to remove the Objection, by explaining the Phrases in the *seventh Verse* of the *forty-third* of *Isaiah*, according to what I apprehend, in the primary Sense of 'em, to be intended, in the Elect being said, to be called by God's Name, created for his Glory, formed and made even before their gathering to Christ by converting Grace: All which do very well agree with God's eternal Act of Adoption, from whence they are called Sons, in the precedent Verse: Which was my first Assertion. But, to return from this Digression. In the *next* Place

I proceed to a further opening of the Definition I gave of God's Act of Adoption. And having already gone through the *first Part* of it, which more peculiarly respects the Act itself; I now come to the *second Part*, the immediate Effect of that Act. Which is,

That God, by this Act of Adoption, did take a certain Number of Persons from among Mankind, as consider'd in the pure Mass, into a supernatural, and Covenant Relation of Children to himself, by Christ Jesus, to the Praise of the Glory of his Grace. In which may be consider'd,

First, That this Relation into which we are taken by Adoption, is, a Supernatural and Covenant-Relation: It is a Relation unto God by Grace, which is far superior unto that we had by Nature.

We had, indeed, a natural Relation to God as his Children by Creation, in our Head *Adam:* Who upon this Account is called *the Son of God*, Luke 3.38. but this was a Privilege common to all his Posterity, as saith the *Apostle*, Acts 17.26. *And hath made of one Blood all Nations of Men, &c. for we are his Offspring*, Ver. 28. And there was an Honour in this natural Relation to God as a Father: For it did bespeak the noble Extract of Man, as endow'd with a rational Soul, of which God was the immediate Parent, when *he breathed into Man the Breath of Lives, and Man became a living Soul*, Gen. 2.7. Which Soul of his, as it is a Discoursive, Immaterial, and Immortal Spirit, capable of enjoying, and glorifying his Creator, and accordingly filled with a Perfection of moral Rectitude, was made *in the Image of God,* Gen. 1.27. and did bear a Resemblance of its Maker, both in its Essence and Qualities. Thus Man was made in the Image of God; or in the Likeness of Christ; who is expressly styl'd *God's Image*, Col. 1.15. Christ, as Mediator, was *set up from everlasting*, Prov. 8.23. in God's Counsel and Covenant, as the Head of the Creation; in whom all the Perfections of God did meet; that so in him might shine forth a perfect Image, or Representation of God, in all his Perfections, to all sorts of Creatures, by all sorts of Ways, in all their various Conditions, and designed

Ends. And Christ was the original Draught, after which Man, as a little Picture, was drawn: so as that, there was more of the Image of God to be seen in Man, than in all the rest of the Creation. And as we had a natural Relation to God in *Adam*, and did bear a natural Image, so likewise we had a natural Inheritance; which was God, as the God of Nature, to be enjoy'd through the Creatures in this lower World. For *the Earth has he given to the Sons of Men*, Psal. 115.16. which was eminently true of 'em as they stood in their Head *Adam*, When he was *crown'd with Glory and Honour*, made Lord of the Universe, all Creatures being *put under his Feet*, Psal. 8.5, 6. Thus there was a Glory in the natural Relation: But when compar'd with the supernatural, we may say of it, as the *Apostle* doth of the Law, when compar'd with the Gospel, *That which was made glorious, had no Glory in this respect, by reason of the Glory that excelleth*, 2 Cor. 3.10.

What glory was there in the natural Relation to God, as the God of Nature, if compar'd with the excelling Glory of a supernatural Relation to him, as the God of all Grace! What Glory was there in the natural Image, if compar'd with the outshining Glory of that spiritual Image, which we bear as standing in a supernatural Relation! Again, what Glory was there in the natural Inheritance, which lay in earthly Blessings, if compar'd with our supernatural Inheritance, which lies in all spiritual Blessings in the Heavenlies! Surely the brightness of the First Relation, must needs lose its Lustre, when once the superexcellent Glory of the Second appears! And tho' our Eyes are not yet Strong enough, stedfastly to behold the brightness of God's Grace, which illustriously Shines forth in this supernatural Relation; yet a glimpse of its Glory is enough to fill us with Admiration, at those *Great Things* the Lord did for us, *1 Sam*. 12.24. when he took us into *the Family* of Heaven, in his adopting Act of Grace, *Eph*. 2.19. by which he has *called us Sons*, *1 Joh*. 3.1. or made us to sustain this Relation of Children. Which I call Supernatural, 1. With Respect to the Relation itself conferred. 2. With Respect unto those Springs of Favour from whence it was bestow'd upon us. And 3. With Respect to the inseperable Consequents of it.

It's Supernatural with Respect to the Relation itself, Because every Way above Nature; or what was meet for the Creator to bestow, even in the highest Dispensations of his Kindness in a natural Way, towards perfect natural Man. God Communicates of himself to all his Creatures, agreeably to the Relation they stand in to him. And having *chosen* a Remnant in his

Son, unto eternal Glory, in order to *Bless* them with this supernatural Inheritance, he took them into a supernatural Relation. *Eph.* 1.3, 4, 5.

It's supernatural, with Respect to the Springs of Favour whence it flows. 'Twas *great Love* that bestow'd this great Relation, *Eph.* 2.4. a Love far higher than Creation-Love. So great that it could not have *enter'd into the Heart* of a Creature to conceive such a Thing, *1 Cor.* 2.9. if God who is great in Grace, had not conceiv'd it in his own Heart, and *reveal'd* it in his Word and *by his Spirit, ver.* 10. 'Twas Free-Love, or princely Grace, that took no Motives from the Creature in the bestowment of it. God acted herein every Way like a Sovereign, *according to the good Pleasure of his Will, Eph.* 1.5. Yea, it was distinguishing Love: God did not so love all the World, as to Adopt 'em for his Children, No, it's a special Privilege that none but *the Elect* share in, *1 Pet.* 2.9.

It's supernatural also, as to the inseperable Consequents of it: Which are, an indefeasible Right unto, and a compleat Enjoyment of the heavenly Inheritance. *Adoption and Glory* go together, *Rom.* 9.4. And as it is a Supernatural, so also a Covenant-Relation that we are taken into by Adoption.

This Relation, was not only bestow'd upon us in the immanent Act of God's Will, but also in his everlasting Covenant with his Son. God not only took up this Resolution in his Mind, *I will be unto them a Father, and they shall be my Sons and Daughters, 2 Cor.* 6.18. but he likewise pass'd this Act of his Will into a Covenant-Promise, made to Christ as the Head and Representative of his People. And hence this Promise comes forth to us in the Gospel as a Transcript from that Original. In the next Place, we may observe.

Secondly, That it was a certain Number of Persons from among Mankind, which were taken into this Relation. *For whom he did Foreknow, them he did Predestinate,* &c. *Rom.* viii.29. Here is the determinate Number exprest, by their being said, to be [Foreknown]: Which was by God's eternal Choice of 'em *in Christ, Eph.* 1.4. *1 King* 8.53. *seperating* them from the World, setting them apart for himself, as *his own peculiar Treasure; Psal.* 135.4. both in the certainty of their Number, and individuation of their Persons. And it was none but those whom God thus Foreknew, which he did *Predestinate to be conform'd unto the Image of his Son, Rom.* 8.29. 1. In a sameness of Relation. 2. In a sameness of Disposition. And 3. In a sameness of Inheritance. And as it was a certain Number of Persons, that were taken into this Relation, so these were taken from among Mankind. And therefore says *the Apostle, Behold, what manner of Love the*

Father hath bestowed upon us, 1 John 3.1. Us the [Chosen] Men, and not others, who were of the same Nature with us: Us [Men] and not Angels, tho' they are of a superior Make: For tho' the Angels are *the Sons of God* by Creation, *Job* 38.7. yet they are not the Sons of God by Adoption; so that in this respect we stand in a nearer Relation to God, than the very Angels in Heaven. Again,

     Thirdly, These Persons were consider'd in the pure Mass, when this Act of Adoption fixt upon 'em. For as they were Chosen, so they were Adopted; and both antecedent to their being blest in the Grace-part of the Covenant; which was the Foundation of their being Blest in the Redemption part of it. When I say the Grace-part of the Covenant, I intend the upper-fall Settlement of *all spiritual Blessings* upon us *in Christ* our Head, *Eph.* 1.3, 4, 5, 6. which merely sprang from Sovereign Love, princely Grace, or Favour. Not but that the Redemption-part of it, which respected the conveyance of all these Blessings *through* Christ as a Saviour, was of Free-Grace to Us, *ver.* 7. too: But then, 'twas Grace, shewing forth its Glory, and extending its Riches, in a Way of *Mercy*, Pity and Compassion, *Eph.* 2.4, 5. *Isa.* 49.6. respecting the Creature as miserable. So that for Distinction Sake, I think we may say, the Grace-part, and the Redemption-part of the Covenant, as we respect the same *everlasting Covenant* in its several Branches. Adoption was an upper-fall Act of Grace, an earlier Act than the Act of Justification, altho' both were from Eternity. Indeed strictly speaking, there is no First nor Second with God, whose vast Mind comprehends all Things at once. But we Creatures, must speak of his Acts in a successive Order, as our Capacities can take them in. And so one Act was before another, in Order of Nature at least, if not of Time. All Acts respect their proper Objects; and there needed no more than the [Being] of the Creature, for an Act of Adoption to pass upon it. We were far enough off even in the State of Creature-ship, for adopting Grace to bring us nigh. Low enough even in the Heights of a natural Relation, for this Grace to raise us unto the transcendent Dignity of that which is Supernatural. Thus the Act of Adoption respects the Creature merely as such: But the Act of Justification, did not only pre-suppose the Being, but also the [Fall] of the Creature. And, that Adoption did fix upon the Creature as consider'd Pure, will further appear, if we consider.

     Fourthly, That Christ Jesus was the Pattern by which God did proceed in this Act of Adoption: *Having prededestinated us unto the Adoption of*

Children of Christ Jesus, Eph. 1.5. It was by Christ, 1. As the Relation-Pattern. 2. By him, as the Conveyor of Relation-Privileges.

1*st*, It was by Christ, s the Relation-Pattern. Our Lord Christ is the Son of God in a two-fold Respect. As,

1. In his Divine Nature, by his eternal Generation of the Father. And so he is God's [Own] Son; the Son of his Nature: His [Only] begotten Son: For in this Respect God hath no Son but him; who is co-equal, co-essential, and co-eternal with his Father. And as thus consider'd, his Relation is not the Pattern of ours. No, this is so high that it's incommunicable to any Creature; and peculiar to the Second Person in God; whose Name and Nature is as ineffable as the Father's, *Prov*.30.4. *What is his Name, and what is his Son's Name if thou canst tell?*

2. Our Lord Christ is not only the Son of God in his Divine Nature, as Second Person in the Glorious Trinity; but he is also the Son of God, as Mediator, in his Human Nature. In the first Sense he is God's Natural, in the second, (as I humbly conceive) his Adopted Son. Nor doth this make two Sons in the Person of the Mediator: for as his Person is but One, so he is but One Son of God; and yet he is the Son of God in these two Respects, answerable unto his two distinct Natures. Which to me is evident from the *first Chapter* to the *Hebrews*. The *Apostle's* Intent in this *Epistle*, is, to set forth the transcendent Glory of the Gospel above that of the Law: And he does it *first,* by setting forth the Dignity of its prime Minister. *God* (saith he) *who at sundry times, and in divers manners spake in times past unto the Fathers by the Prophets, hath in these last Days spoken unto us by his Son, whom he hath appointed Heir of all things, by whom also he made the Worlds. Who being the Brightness of his Glory, and the express Image of his Person, and upholding all things by the Word of his Power, when he had by himself purged our Sins, sat down on the right Hand of the Majesty on High.* Heb. 1.1, 2, 3. Christ is here set forth as the Son of God, in the two respects mentioned. As,

1. In his Divine Sonship, by his being said to be, *The Brightness of his Father's Glory, the express Image of his Person,* and to *uphold all things by the Word of his Power.* And,

2. His Adoptive Sonship, is as evidently intended, in that this Son of God is said to be, *The Appointed Heir of all things:* Which can't be predicated of him as the Second Person in God: For so considered, he had an equal and essential Right to all things with his Father. And therefore his Covenant Sonship must be intended; which was in order to a Covenant-

Appointment of him as Heir of all things. Again, Christ's Adoptive Sonship is further set forth, *Ver*. 5. *I will be unto him a Father, and he shall be unto me a Son.* Christ's Divine Filiation can't be here meant: for that is by Necessity of Nature, but this by an Act of the Divine Will. It's the Language of Covenant-Grace, constituting this Covenant-Relation. And so it runs, first to him the Head, *I will be his Father, and he shall be my Son, 1 Chron.* 17.13. And then to us the Members in him, *I will be unto You a Father, and Ye shall be my Sons and Daughters, saith the Lord Almighty, 2 Cor.* 6.18. Thus it appears, That Christ's Relation, in this respect, and Ours is the same for [Kind]; in that they both flow from the same Covenant-Grant, and also in that both Christ and we partake of the same Spirit of Adoption: And therefore God is said, To *send the Spirit of his Son into our Hearts, crying, Abba Father,* Gal. 4.6. We are *anointed* with the same *Oyl of Gladness,* Psal. 45.7. Which Words doubtless intend, in one Sense of 'em, the pouring out of the Spirit as a Comforter, to Witness Relation, and enable us to cry, *Abba Father.* And thus it was graciously promised in the Covenant, and foretold of Christ, *Psal.* 89.26. *He shall cry unto me, my Fahter, my God, and the Rock of my Salvation.* And the Grace of this Promise, not only respects the Head, but it reacheth to the Members also: For concerning them the Lord says, *Thou shalt call me my Father, and shalt not turn away from me,* Jer.3.19. For so run all the New Covenant-Promises, to *David, and to his Seed for evermore,* Psal. 18.50.

And as our Lord Christ, doth stand in this Adoptive-Relation upon the bottom of absolute Grace, so this Act of Grace was primarily fixt upon his Person, as God-Man, peculiarly respecting his Man-Nature, when he was *set up from everlasting,* Prov. 8.23. in Counsel and Covenant, as the great Mediator and *Head of the Church, Eph.* 5.23. which was antecedent to his being *the Saviour of the Body.* For though his being *Declared to be the Son of God by his Resurrection, Rom.* 1.4. and glorious Exaltation at the Right-Hand of the Father, was given him as his Due, upon his being *Obedient unto Death,* as the Saviour of the Body, *Phil* 2.8, 9. yet this glorious Relation, in this Branch of it whereof I now speak, with all the Privileges thereof, was originally settled by mere Grace upon his Person, as Head of the Church. And thus he was the Relation-Pattern; for as God's Act of Adoption did fix upon the Person of Christ, as Head, so upon our Persons, in the pure Mass, as Members of that Head.

Again, it will further appear, that Christ was the Pattern by which God did proceed in this Act of Adoption, if we consider some *Scriptures* where

Christ is set forth as standing in a sameness of Relation with, and yet in a Transcendency of Glory above us. We may begin with *Rom.* 8.29. *For whom he did foreknow, he also did predestinate to be conformed to the Image of his Son, that he might be the First-born among many Brethren.* Here is, first, A sameness of Relation, in that the Elect are said to be Christ's [Brethren]: As they are also stiled, Heb. 2.12. *I will declare thy Name unto my Brethren.* And Christ is *not ashamed* to own us in this Relation, *ver.* 11. *For both he that sanctifieth, and they who are sanctified, are all One: For which cause he is not ashamed to call them Brethren.* Christ, and we have one and the same Father, sprang from one and the same Fountain of pure Grace; and were design'd for one and the same Glory: And for this Cause he is not ashamed to own us.

Again, this sameness of Relation doth further appear, in that Christ, in that *Roman* Text, is said to be the [First-born] among many Brethren. And thus he is called *God's First-born, Psal.* 89.27. and his *First-begotten, Heb.* 1.6. which Phrase doth necessarily imply, that there are other Sons that stand in the same Relation with him. For there can be no First, where there is not a Second, &c. And therefore when Christ's Divine Sonship is intended, in which he stands[Alone] in a Relation infinitely above all the Creatures, he is never set forth by this Character of the [First] but always by that of the [Only] begotten Son of God, *John* 1.14. 18. *chap.* 3.16. 18. And as this Style of First-born, doth necessarily imply, that there are others that stand in the same Relation with him; so it doth as plainly denote, that Transcendency of Glory which he hath above them. For, as the First-born, he's the Head of the Family, The Pattern to which all the younger Brethren are conform'd, both in Relation, Disposition and Inheritance.

Again, this will further appear, if we look into the *Twentieth* of *John*, where our Lord, when risen from the Dead, and full of Thoughts about his own Glory, did yet own his Disciples as his Brethren. *Ver.* 17. *Go to my Brethren, and say unto them, I ascend unto my Father and your Father, to my God and your God.* 'Tis as if he should say, "Go tell my Brethren, that I am indeed Risen from the Dead, and just entering into my Glory; but I don't forget my Relation to them as I am their Brother. I own them for my Brethren still, though all of them have forsaken, and one deny'd me: Yet, say unto them, I ascend unto my father and your Father, to my God and your God: You and I have one and the same Father; are lov'd with the same Love, and Blest in the same Covenant, and therefore I ascend to [Your] Father, as well as my Father, to [Your] God, as well as my God: And yet he is first [My] Father, and [My] God, as I am his First-born Son, and your Head, and then he is [Your] Father, and [Your] God, as you are his younger Children, and my Members. The Father *hath loved* You *as he hath loved Me, John* 17.23. with the same Love of [Kind] tho' not in the same [Degree]. He loved me first, so as to make me the First-born and Head of the Family: And then he loved you next, so as to make you my younger Brethren. His Love to you, is but an overflow of his Love to me: And (as if he should further say), herein lies your Security, in that he is first my Father and my God in Covenant, and then your Father and your God in me by the same Covenant; so that you can never Lose your Relation and Interest, because *the Covenant stands fast with* me *for ever. Psal.* 89.28. And so long as it stands fast with me, so long it will stand fast with you; because it stands fast with me [For] you, and so with you [In] me."

And hence it is that we can draw nigh to God *with Boldness*, since he is the God and Father of our Lord Jesus Christ, and so our God and Father in him, *Eph.* 3.14. The Saints of old, dealt with God as a Covenant-God, and put up their Supplications to him as *the God and Father of Abraham, Isaac, and Jacob, 1 Chron.* 29.18. whose Seed they were: For God did make Covenant with them, and their Seed in them, *Gen.* 17.7. as Types of that everlasting Covenant that was made with Christ and his Seed. And the Believers that were among them then, did look thro' the Type to Christ the great Antitype: But yet they did not see him with that Clearness, and in that unvail'd Glory, which the Saints now do, *2 Cor.* 3.13, 18. and therefore they went to God, in the Relation and Interest of their Father *Abraham.* Whereas we, in the Advance of New-Testament Faith, draw nigh to God, as *the God and Father of Christ, Eph.* 1.3. and so our God and Father in him; who was the Pattern by which God did proceed in all the wondrous Grace bestow'd on us. But

Secondly, It was by Christ, also, as the Conveyer of Relation-Privileges, Which are oft put for the Relation itself. If we view the Sons of God as *scatter'd Abroad* in the Fall, they look very unlike his Children, *John* 11.52. Yea, by Nature, as consider'd in *Adam*, and under a broken Law, they were *Children of Wrath even as others, Eph.* 2.3. deservedly, tho' not designedly. They were under the same declarative Wrath in the Sentence of the Law with others, as it curs'd every Transgressor. But Christ taking their Law-place, putting himself in their Room and Stead, he endured its Penalty, as the just desert of their Sin; satisfied Justice, and Redeemed them from the Curse of the Law, *that they might receive the Adoption of Sons, Gal.* 4.5. or the open Admittance into all the Privileges of this Relation. But notwithstanding the Sons of God were, all at once, *Redeemed* by Christ *from the Curse of the Law,* by his being *made a Curse for* them, *ch.* 3.13. yet still while they lye here and there in the distant State of Nature, there is no apparent Difference between them and others. They are *without Christ, Aliens from the Covenants of Promise, having no Hope, and without God in the World, Eph.* 2.12. Estranged from him and Haters of him. And as such, there is an absolute necessity for the Application of Christ's Redemption by his Holy Spirit; that so these Strangers might become *Fellow-Citizens with the Saints, and of the Household of God, Ver.* 19. *i.e.,* his visible Household. For while the Elect of God remain in Unregeneracy, their open State by Nature, as related to *Adam*, is a State of Alienation and Wrath; tho' at the same Time their secret State by Grace, in Christ, is a State of Nearness to God, and perfect Freedom from all Guilt and Curse. For God's chosen, even while in a State of Nature, are not one Moment under his real Wrath, or the Affection of Wrath in his Heart; tho' they are under the Declaration of Wrath in *the Curse of the Law, Gal.* 3.10. as it sets forth the just Desert of every Transgression. And as such it is impossible for them either to know, or enjoy the Privileges of their high Relation, until they are brought *nigh by the Blood of Christ, Eph.* 2.13. under the saving Operations of the Holy Ghost, working Faith in their Hearts, enabling them to *lay Hold* on Christ, *Heb.* 6.18. and *eternal Life in* him. *1 John* 5.11. And to plead their Freedom by *the Son, John* 8.36. as such that are *passed from Death to Life, Ch.* 5.24. or from an open State of Wrath under the Law, into a visible State of Favour, and full Salvation, under the Declarations of Grace in Christ, whither they have fled for Refuge, and are Safe: When it is that they first Appear to be the Sons of God, but not first Begin to be so; unless it be in respect of Visibility. We are to distinguish between secret and open Adoption: The one is the Foundation of the other. Secret Adoption respects the Relation itself, bestow'd of mere Grace, in the immanent Act of God's Will, and in his everlasting Covenant with his Son. Open Adoption respects the Visibility, or Manifestation thereof by a transient Act of Time: Which I look upon to be no new Act in God, but only his eternal Will herein, in the Declaration of his Word, passing upon an elect Vessel at the appointed Season; whereby the Person is admitted into the enjoyment of all the Privileges of this Relation, as a Fruit of Christ's Redemption, and free Justification by his Blood. Thus *John* 1.12. it's said, *To as many as received him, to them gave he Power to become the Sons of God.* And *Gal.* 3.26. *Ye are all the Children of God by Faith in Christ Jesus.* We are not from hence to infer, that the Elect of God are in no Sense his Children before Faith, because they are here said to be so by Faith: For it is an apparent visible Sonship that is here spoken of. The Manifestation of the Thing is put for the Being of it: Which is frequent in the sacred Writings. Thus *Rev.* 22.7. the Lord says, *He that overcometh shall Inherit all Things, and I will be his God, and he shall be my Son.* We are not to understand this as a Promise of the Being of Sonship to an overcoming Believer, as if he had no such Relation to God before: But of the Manifestation thereof, as the *Apostle's* Phrase is, *Rom.* 8.19. *He shall be my Son,* says God; that is, he shall openly and gloriously Appear to be my Son, when thus advanc'd to inherit all Things: And visible Adoption, both in the Grace, and Glory-parts of it, we receive as a fruit of Christ's Redemption. *To him,* saith our Lord, *that overcometh, will I give a white Stone, and in the Stone a new Name written, Rev.* 2.17. The new Name of Adoption, is written in the white Stone of Absolution. And thus our Adoption, in the Conveyance of Relation-Privileges, is by Christ, as Jesus, a Saviour: but the Relation it self chiefly depends upon his Person, as our Head.

Fifthly. As our God, did predestinate us to the Adoption of Children by Christ Jesus, so it was unto [Himself.]

1. Unto himself in respect of special Right and Propriety. We were in this Predestinating Act of his Grace, set apart for himself, as his [Own] Children, in distinction from all the World beside: As he saith concerning his Typical People of old, *Israel is [My] Son, Exod.* 4.22. My Son by peculiar Grace in Distinction from all the other Works of my Hands.

2. Unto himself in respect of Communion: That so his infinite Heart-Love might flow forth in the Grace and Bowels of a Father, to the full *Supply* of *all our Need, according to his Riches in Glory by Christ Jesus,* through Time and to Eternity, *Phil.* 4.19.

3. Unto himself in respect of Delight and Pleasure. For as a *Father delighteth in his Son,* Prov. 3.12. so, and much more doth the Lord delight in his Children, and *take Pleasure in them that fear him,* Psal. 147.11. He delights in us now, as we stand mystically *compleat* in Christ, *Col.* 2.12. and when we are personally *wrought* up into a full Conformity to his *First-born* Son, our elder Brother, *2 Cor.* 5.5. *Rom.* 8.29. and by him *presented before the Presence of his Glory,* 'twill be *with exceeding Joy,* Jude 24. Oh the inconceivable Delight our Father will take in us when his *many Sons* are

brought *to Glory, Heb.* 2.10. *He will rest in his Love, and rejoice over us with singing* to an endless Eternity, *Zeph.* 3.17. And,

4. Unto himself in respect of Honour. The Lord, in setting apart his Children for himself, design'd such great things for them, that might get himself Honour as the great God, *Jer.* 33.9. And he expects peculiar Honour from them, answerable to that nearness of Relation they stand in to him, and the amazing Favours they receive from him. *If I be a Father, where is mine Honour?* Mal. 1.6. But this brings me to consider

The last Thing in the Definition: Which is, That God's ultimate End in this Act of Adoption, was, The Praise of the Glory of his Grace. And that 1. as display'd. And 2. as ascribed.

1. As display'd. It was the love-reign good Pleasure of *Jehovah's* Will, to manifest that Infinity of Grace that was in his Nature; that so the Glory of it might shine forth before all intelligent Beings: Which set his infinite Wisdom on work to find out Ways and Means to effect it. And here first, The Man Christ Jesus was *brought forth* in the Counsels of Jehovah, into Union with the Second Person in God, as the glorious Project of infinite Wisdom; to answer all the Ends of infinite Grace: And as the great Mediator, he was *set up from everlasting*, Prov. 8.23, 25. Isa. 49.3. in whom Grace resolv'd to glorify itself to the utmost, in all its out-goings towards Him first as an Head, and then in him towards Others as his Members. And there was a glorious Display of Grace in the Bestowment of this adoptive Relation: So glorious that it transcends the Capacity of our present Sight, either to look stedfastly upon it, or fully to take it in. In the Contemplation of which we may well be lost as in a sweet Surprize; and cry out with astonishing Wonder, *Behold, what manner of Love the Father hath bestowed upon us,* in that he hath given us the Relation, Disposition, and Inheritance of his Children; so that *we [Now] are the Sons of God!* 1 Joh. 3.1, 2. We now bear, in our Soul-part, the glorious Impress of this Relation, as we are the *Workmanship* of the Holy Ghost, *Eph.* 2.10. God having *sent the Spirit of his Son into our Hearts, crying, Abba, Father,* Gal. 4.6. who as a *Spirit of Glory resteth upon us,* 1 Pet. 4.14. But *the World knoweth us not,* 1 Joh. 3.1. because we han't yet *received the Adoption* of our Body, in the Glory-Image of the *first Resurrection,* Rom. 8.23. 1 Cor. 15.43. 49. Rev. 20.5. which will be such a writing our Father's *Name* in our *Foreheads,* that he that runs may read, whose Children we are, Rev. 22.4. And then the World shall [*Know*] that the Father *hath loved* us so, as to make us Christ's Brethren, even *as he loved* him, *Joh.* 17. 23. to make him the *First-born,*

and Head of the Family; when once we are the *Sons of God* as being *the Children of the Resurrection*, Luke 20.36. But till then our glorious Relation will not appear to the World: No, nor doth it *yet appear* fully to the Saints themselves, either what they now *are*, as raised up by Grace to the unspeakable Dignity of Sonship; or *what they shall be,* when they *appear with* Christ in all that Glory, which this Relation doth bespeak, *1 John* 3.2.

'Tis true we have now and then some Glimpses of it here: But how distant and imperfect are our Views? how short our sweet Glances? our clearest Apprehensions how soon clouded? so that it don't yet appear; because *we see but through a Glass darkly, 1 Cor.* 13.12. But the time's a coming when we shall see, with the vail cast off; our imperfect Faith-Views being swallowed up of perfect Glory-Vision. And Oh the Soul-ravishing Prospects we shall then have of the Glory of God's Grace, that shines forth in this Relation!

2. God's End in this Act of Adoption, was, the Glory of his Grace, as ascribed. It's because we see no more of its Glory, that we abound no more in its Praise: For surely here's Matter enough, to fill Heaven and Earth, with astonishing Wonder. We have now and then *a Song* of Praise *put into* our Mouths here, *Psal.* 40.3. though our Hearts are too often out of Tune: But when in the Resurrection-Morning, we *appear with* Christ in the Glory of this Relation, our Souls shall be as a well-strung Instrument, while we cry, *Grace, Grace unto it,* Zech. 4.7. *Eye ha'n't seen, nor Ear heard, neither hath it enter'd into the Heart of Man* (fully) to *conceive* those *unspeakable Joys* that will fill the Hearts of the Sons of God, *1 Cor.* 2.9. when in his glorious *Lamb*, the *New Jerusalem Temple*, Rev. 21.22. we shall with one united Voice, for ever shout forth our loudest *Hallelujahs*, to him who hath *predestinated us unto the Adoption of Children, by Jesus Christ unto himself, according to the good Pleasure of his Will,* (which to the endless Ages of Eternity, will be) *to the Praise of the Glory of his Grace,* Eph. 1.5, 6.

The Improvement.

First. Is it so, That Adoption is a gracious, immanent, and eternal Act of God's sovereign Will: Then let the Saints admire the Earliness, Sovereignty, Eternity of *Jehovah's* Grace herein. Dear Souls, you had room in God's Heart, and he *put* you *among the Children*, Jer. 31.3. in order to bring you to Glory, before he made the Worlds. Give God your Heart, prefer his Glory, Honour, and Interest, before the World, and your dearest Enjoyments in it. Let your Love, manifested to him in all the Paths of

Obedience, be cast as a Drop into the infinite Ocean of his Grace, *1 John* 5.3. and 4.19. Our God is infinitely worthy of all our Love, were our Souls capable of ten thousand times more than they are, because of *the great things he hath done for* us in Christ, *1 Sam.* 12.24. and especially because of his own infinite Excellencies, the immense Glories of his Being, *Psal.* 148.13, 14.

Secondly. Is this Relation we are taken into by Adoption, a Supernatural, and Covenant-Relation: Let's think upon the Greatness, and Freeness of that Love which bestow'd this high Relation, till we are swallow'd up in it, with the Apostle, *1 John* 3.1. *Behold what manner of Love,* &c. If the Man *Adam* in his Paradisical State, might say for Himself and all His, *Lord, what is Man, that thou art mindful of him? Psal.* 8.4. much more might the Lord Christ say so for Himself and all His, when he was exalted as the *Heavenly Man,* Prov. 8.23. 1 Cor. 15.47. and had an heavenly Seed given him, *Heb.* 2.13. who together in and with him were advanced unto an heavenly Relation to God, *John* 20.17. and so invested with a supernatural Right to all the Privileges of their *Father's House* in Heaven, *Ch.* 14.2. which secured the full Enjoyment of that glorious Inheritance, *1 Pet.* 1.4. settled upon the *Heirs of Promise,* Heb. 6. 17. *Lord, what is Man,* that Mean Low Thing, that thou should'st be thus *mindful of him, Job.* 25.6. Who could have thought, That the Creature Man, who was but of an *earthly* Make, *1 Cor.* 15.47. and as such could sustain but an earthly Relation to God, and have but a natural Right to, and Enjoyment of earthly Blessings, (which was the highest Dignity he was capable of in his earthly State) should ever have been thus advanced to an heavenly Relation, Title, and Inheritance! *What is Man,* whose Original was of the Dust, *Gen.* 2.7. that he should be taken up to dwell in Heaven, *Job* 14.3. the Place of God's immediate Glory-presence, *Isa.* 57.15. And not only to dwell in the Place of Glory, but also to possess the State of Glory, *1 Pet.* 5.10. which consists in the most close and intimate Communion with God in Christ, that finite Beings are capable of, without the least Interruption to an endless Eternity. *John* 17.21. So that, if we take a View of those Springs of supernatural Grace, whence the adoptive Relation flows, of the Relation itself bestow'd, or of the inseparable Consequents of it, which reach as far as our eternal Glorification; and see all secur'd in an everlasting Covenant; we may well say, *Behold, what manner of Love the Father hath bestowed upon us, that we should be called the Sons of God!* 1 Joh. 3.1.

Think, dear Saints, how securely you *stand in this Grace!* Rom. 5.2. The Glory of the natural Relation might be lost: But the supernatural cannot. The Fall could not mar it: Though thereby we were brought into a State of Slavery to *Satan, 2 Tim.* 2.26. Servitude to *Sin, John* 8.34. and Bondage to *the Law, Gal.* 4.3. But *because we were Sons* by supernatural Grace, *Ver.* 6. God, *in the fullness of Time sent forth his Son, to Redeem* us *out of the House of Servants*, Mic. 6.4. *That we might receive the Adoption of Sons* by Faith, which was previously ours by absolute Grace. And has also *sent forth the Spirit of his Son into our Hearts.* To witness our Relation to God, and work in our Souls filial Dispositions towards him: That so being *Deliver'd out of the Hands of our Enemies we might serve him without Fear, in Holiness and Righteousness all the Days of our Lives. Luke* 1.74, 75. from a Principle of Love, and Gratitude, surpassing the highest Principles of Obedience found in pure Nature, and every way agreeable to the transcendent Dignity of the supernatural Relation in which we stand. Our Relation don't depend upon our Obedience, But upon the *immutable* Will, *Promise*, and *Oath* of *Jehovah, Heb.* 6.17, 18. And as this affords *strong Consolation to the Heirs of Promise*; so let it Teach us daily to hate Sin intensely, and to flee from every *appearance of Evil, 1 Tim.* 6.11. *1 Thes.* 5.22. How shall [We] Sin against that Love, that will never Disinherit us! Oh, what Childlike Ingenuity, should this work in our Hearts towards our dear Father, since we are *no more Servants*, to return to Servitude, *Gal.* 4.7. but Sons, *Free* Children that shall *Abide in the House for ever. Joh.* 8.34, 35.

Thirdly, Was it a certain Number of Persons from among Mankind, which were taken into this Relation: Then let's Adore distinguishing Grace each one for our-selves, while Thousands are pass'd by, And we our individual Persons absolutely *predestinated unto the Adoption of Children, Eph.* 1.5. And being raised up to this unspeakable Dignity of Sonship, let's *Forget* our *own People, and* our *Father Adam's House. Psal.* 45.10. We are called to walk in daily Fellowship with the Family of Heaven, as such that are *no more Strangers and Foreigners, but Fellow Citizens with the Saints, and of the Household of God, Eph.* 2.19.

Fourthly, Were the Persons adopting Grace fixed on, as then, consider'd in the pure Mass: Let's learn hence, the Height of adopting Love. The Heights of natural Bliss were low Things, compar'd with the superexcellent Glories adopting Love design'd, *1 Cor.* 15.47, 48. *Rom.* 8.29, 30.

Fifthly, Was Christ Jesus the Pattern, by which God did proceed in this Act of Adoption: This informs us, as, of the transcendent Dignity of the

Adoptive-Relation, so, that it is an higher Glory we are to be *wrought* up to, than the first *Adam* in his pure State was capable of. Not *Adam's* Nature-likeness, but Christ's Grace, and Glory-Image is the Pattern to which we shall be comform'd. For the Relation, Disposition, and Inheritance of God's adopted Children, are inseperably join'd together. They are all of them Glory-Sons, *Heb.* 2.10. i.e., absolutely ordain'd to Glory, in, and with himself for ever: Christ the eldest Son, as the Supreme Heir; and We the younger Brethren, as *Joint-Heirs with* him of this vast Inheritance. *Rom.* 8.17. Oh amazing Project of infinite Wisdom! Did God advance our Nature into personal Union with his own Son, that so the Man Christ, constituted *Mediator*, and *Head*, might become the great Receptacle of all Grace, both of Relation, and Communication; that so he, as the *First-born* of the Family, might be the comprehensive Pattern of all the beautiful Lineaments to be drawn upon the younger Brethren! *1 Tim.* 2.5. *Col.* 1.18, 19. *Rom.* 8.29.

And further, Was it by Christ, as the Conveyor of Relation-Privileges, as he is Jesus, a Saviour: Let's adore infinite Wisdom herein; that subservient to the Glory of all the Divine Perfections, and particularly of adopting Love, did see it meet, that Christ's younger Brethren, belonging to the Family of Heaven, should yet sustain an earthly Relation to God, in their first *Adam*-Head, and in him be permitted to Fall with all Mankind; and thereby Marr the Glory of their natural Relation, setting themselves further off from God than ever, by becoming Strangers and Enemies, *Eph.* 2.3, 12. *Col.* 1.21. that so adopting Love might be the more commended, in raising up the Sons of God by supernatural Grace, from the Depths of Misery, to the ultimate Heights of their designed Glory! And oh! the marvellous Difference, this same Grace put between the Sons of God, and *the Rest, Rom.* 11.7. which in the Fall were irrecoverably Lost, *2 Cor.* 4.3. while these never lost their eternal Relation to God in Christ, tho' by Nature in *Adam*, they *were Children of Wrath even as others, Eph.* 2.3. Nor that amazing Security they had under all, to be Redeem'd both by Price and Power, *Hos.* 13.14. *1 Cor.* 6.20. *Eph.* 1.19. thro' the Son's, and Spirit's Work; 'till at last wrought up into a compleat Conformity to God's *First-born*, their elder Brother, the amazing Glory-Pattern, to which they were first Predestinated! *Rom.* 8.29. Oh the *Heights, Lengths, Depths*, and *Breadths* of this Grace! *Eph.* 3.18.

Sixthly, Did our God Predestinate us unto the Adoption of Children by Christ Jesus, unto himself: How Marvellous is this Wonder! Let's think upon his infinite Greatness, as *God Blessed for evermore*, 2 Cor. 11.31.

together with our own Littleness, *Job* 25.6. and 'twill fill us with Astonishment, that we should be set apart for himself! Our *Jehovah*, might for ever have took up his Satisfaction in his own great [SELF]; Resting in that high Communion which was held between his *Three* glorious Persons, *1 John* 5.7. *John* 14.10. and never have gone forth into Creature-Converse: For this *high and lofty One that inhabiteth Eternity, whose Name is Holy*, Isa. 57.15. needed none of his Creatures. *And he that comes to God, must believe that he [IS]* Heb. 11.6. That Self-existent, Independent, and Self-sufficient Being, whose essential Blessedness none of his Creatures can add any Thing to, or take any Thing from. Look we to this terrestrial Globe: What's the spacious Earth? *Before him, all Nations, are but as a Drop of the Bucket, a dust of the Balance*, Isa. 40.17. Yea, less than nothing and Vanity. Let's ascend to the Celestial Bodies, and *behold even to the Moon, and it shineth not; and the Stars are not pure in his Sight,* Job 25.5. Yea, if we rise as high as the Place of his immediate Presence, behold, *the Heavens are not clean in his Sight; and he charged his Angels with Folly*, Job. 15.15. *and* 4.18. 'Tis infinite Condescension in the great God, to *Behold the Things* done *in Heaven,* by those noble Creatures, the Holy Angels, *Psal.* 113.6. How adorable then is that Grace, which cast a look of Favour upon sorry Man, whose *Foundation is in the Dust!* Job 4.19. Yea, that set us apart for his great [Self] notwithstanding our [Littleness]! Yea, notwithstanding all our foreseen [Vileness]. *Isa.* 48.8. And our Father's Love abides still unchangeably the Same towards us. *Mal.* 3.6. And having predestinated us unto himself, he'll *cleanse* us *from all* our *Filthiness*, Ezek. 36.25. and set us *Holy, and without Blame before him* in *Love*, as the Objects of his eternal Complacency, *Eph.* 1.4. *Who*, or what are We, oh Lord, God? or *what* is our Father's *House, that thou* shouldst *bring us hitherto?* 2 Sam. 7.18.

Lastly, Was God's ultimate End in this Act of Adoption, the Praise of the Glory of his Grace, both as display'd and ascrib'd:

Then let's Admire that Grace which illustriously Shines forth herein. Well may we each one for our selves, cry out, *Lord, what is Man!* Psal. 8.4. with Heb. 2.6, 7, 8, 9. Yea, we may go higher, for the Words are spoken of the Man Christ in his Type *Adam.* Our Lord Christ was astonish'd at the Glory of Free-Grace in taking such Notice of him: And if this is the Language of the Head, well may it be of the Members.

And let our Wonder at this Grace, engage us, to ascribe unto God, the Glory due unto his Name. Christ's Heart is more taken with Free-Grace than any of ours. 'Tis he only has a perfect Knowledge of its Glory, *Mat.*

11.27. and is therefore able to give it its adequate Praise. And when the *Apostle* brings him in, saying, *I will declare thy Name unto my Brethren,* his next Words are, *in the midst of the Church, I will Sing Praise unto thee,* Heb. 2.12. Our Praises are very imperfect, and it's well for us that they ascend to God in the Perfection of Christ's Praises. 'Tis hence they become an *acceptable Sacrifice*, to his and our Father, *1 Pet.* 2.5. *By him therefore,* as our great high Priest, *let's offer unto God the Sacrifice of Praise continually,* Heb. 13.15. Let's Praise adopting Love, in Heart, Lip and Life.

My Son, give me thine Heart, says God, *Prov.* 23.26. Let's in Faith then *consider* daily, *what great Things the Lord hath done for us,* in *putting* us *among the Children,* 1 Sam. 12.24. Jer. 3.19. to enkindle our Love, and inflame our Praises.

Let no corrupt Communication proceed out of our Mouth, Eph. 4.29. but let our *Speech be always with Grace, season'd* as *with Salt, that it may minister Grace to the Hearers,* Col. 4.6.

Yea, in the whole of our Lives, let's *be Holy in all manner of Conversation,* 1 Pet. 1.15. that so we may Praise adopting Grace, all sorts of Ways.

Our Father, is a God, *Glorious in Holiness,* Ex. 15.11. and hath bidden us, *be Holy as he is Holy,* 1 Pet. 1.16. *Holiness becometh* his *House for ever,* Psal. 93.15. his House below, as well as his House above. Yea, our Father hath but one *whole Family,* Eph. 3.15. tho one part of it be on Earth, and the other in Heaven. We *are come to the general Assembly, and Church of the First-born, to the Spirits of just Men made perfect, and to an innumerable Company of* Angels, *Heb.* 1.2, 22, 23. Then let us not, by Sin, dishonour our *Holy Father,* John 17.11. the *Holy Jesus,* Act. 4.30. our elder Brother, nor the *Holy Spirit* our Comforter, *Eph.* 4.30. Debase our *Heavenly* Birth, *Heb.* 3.1. nor act unbecoming the *Holy Angels,* Luke 9.26. our Attendants, *Heb.* 1.14. 'Tis the most unbecoming Sight, to see an High-born Son of God, defiling himself with that low, base *abominable Thing* [Sin], Jer. 44.4. *We are* made *a Spectacle unto the World, to Angels, and to Men,* 1 Cor. 4.9. The Holy God, Angels, and Men, expect to see us Holy: Wicked Men and Devils watch for our Halting: What need then have we to *Watch, and keep our Garments?* Rev. 16.15. We are *Called unto Holiness,* 1 Thes. 4.7. let's make it our Business to *Perfect* the same daily, *2 Cor.* 7.1. that so our *Father* may be *Glorify'd,* John 15.8. and we appear like his Children, by the nobleness of our Spirits, and whiteness of our Robes, *Mat.* 5. 45. *Rom.* 6.2. *Rev.* 3.4. In a Word, let the Grace of Adoption, engage us in Faith to abound in its Praises here, 'till in superior Strains we Adore its Wonders, as the Glory of it opens in perfect Vision above. For *now we see through a Glass darkly; but then Face to Face: Now we know in Part; but then shall we Know even as also we are Known* 1 Cor. 13.12.

F I N I S .

A

DISCOURSE

UPON THE

Inheritance of the Adopted Sons of God.

H AVING in the foregoing Discourse, chiefly insisted upon God's Act of Adoption, predestinating us into a supernatural Relation: And also therein given some Hints, of what the Inheritance is that was settled upon the Sons of God, as standing in that Relation: I shall now farther take it into Consideration, and make it a distinct Head of Discourse. The Method I propose, is,

First, To prove that the adopted Sons of God have an Inheritance.
Secondly, To enquire what their Inheritance is, or wherein it consists.
Thirdly, When it was made theirs.
Fourthly, How it was settled upon them.
Fifthly, Which Way they come to enjoy it.
Sixthly, When they enter upon the Possession of it. And,
Seventhly, Something by Way of Reflection. I begin with the
First, To prove that the adopted Sons of God have an Inheritance. The Truth of this might be evidenced from many Scriptures: But two or three express Tests, may be sufficient to establish the same. *The Lord knoweth the Days of the Upright: And their [Inheritance] shall be for ever,* Psal. 37.18. *In whom we have obtain'd an [Inheritance] being predestinated according to the Purpose of him who worketh all things after the Counsel of his own Will,* Eph. 1.11. And Ver. 14. *Which is the Earnest of our [Inheritance]. To*

an [Inheritance] incorruptible, undefiled, and that fadeth not away, 1 Pet. 1.4. From these *Texts* it is fully proved, That the Sons of God have an Inheritance. I proceed,

Secondly, To enquire what their Inheritance is, or wherein it consists. But Oh, who can set it forth! Neither Men nor Angels can fully tell what it is. The Words of *Elihu* are very applicable here; *If a Man speak, surely he shall be swallow'd up,* Job. 37.20. The Inheritance of the Sons of God, is so great, that Words can't set it forth; yea, so vast, that our Thoughts cannot take it in. We are so far from delineating its Glory in our clearest Expressions, and highest Conceptions, that we rather *Darken Counsel, by Words without knowledge,* Job 38.2. But though we can't fully comprehend it, no, not when grown up *to the Stature of a perfect Man in Christ Jesus,* Eph. 4.13. yet it is our Duty to lisp out its Glory, even while we are like *Children* in this imperfect State, *1 Cor.* 13.11.

Quer. What then is the Inheritance? This Query may be answered by shewing, 1. *Negatively,* What it is not. And 2. *Positively,* What it is.

Answ. 1. *Negatively,* The Inheritance of the adopted Sons of God, doth not lie in worldly Pleasures, Riches, Honours, *&c.* For these outward and temporal Blessings, are Favours which God out of his common Bounty vouchsafes to *all,* Psal. 145.9. yea, even to his greatest *Enemies,* Mat. 5.45. which things indeed are their All: And therefore the *Psalmist* speaking of the *Men of* this *World, Their Portion,* says he, *is in this Life,* Psal. 17.14. And it was said to the rich Man, who *in Hell lift up his Eyes, Remember, that thou in thy Life-time receivedst thy good things,* or thy Portion of good; *Luke* 15.25. And where their *Treasure is,* their *Hearts* are also, *Mat.* 6.21. This being the Language of 'em continually, *Who will shew us any good,* Psal. 4.6, 7. that is, any temporal worldly Good, whereby we may encrease our Store of Corn, Wine, Oyl, *&c?* But the Portion of God's Children doth not lie in these things.

And as their Inheritance doth not consist in the perfect Enjoyment of outward and temporal Blessings since the Fall: So neither did it consist in that Fulness of Nature-good, which in a perfection of natural Blessings, was settled upon us in our Head *Adam, Psal.* 8.5. This was indeed our natural Inheritance: And it was every Way suited to make us perfectly happy, as natural Men in the State of Innocence. But this was a Privilege common to all *Adam's* Posterity; and the Portion of the Sons of God, is peculiar to them. What then is their Inheritance? Which may be answer'd,

Answ. 2. Positively. It is no less than GOD HIMSELF, as the God of all Grace and Glory, making over himself to them, as their Eternal ALL. And here, as in an heavenly Rapture, we may cry out concerning it, as the Children of *Israel,* about their *Manna, What is it? What is it?* Exod. 16.15. Yea, lost in a sweet Surprize, we may even sit down in Silence. *For who by searching can find out God? Who can find out the Almighty to Perfection?* Job. 11.7. There are such *Heights, Depths, Lengths,* and *Breadths* of boundless Love display'd herein, which infinitely surpass the highest *Knowledge* of the most intelligent Creatures, *Eph.* 3.18, 19.

The Saints swim in this Ocean; and find it to be an immense Sea of Life, Love, Joy, and Glory: The Depths of which are unfathomable; its Breadths immeasurable; its Lengths eternal; and its Heights infinite.

Yea, the very Angels in Heaven, with intense Desire, *stoop down to look into* these *things,* 1 Pet. 1.12. That Jehovah should be the Portion of his People, is indeed Matter of Astonishment: And yet it is a most glorious Truth that shines forth in the Sacred Records.

Thus when the Lord by the *Prophet,* doth speak of himself as the God of his People *Israel,* and their transcendent Glory, in this Respect, above those Nations that served dumb Idols; *The Portion of* Jacob (says he) *is not like unto them: for he is the Former of all things,* Jer. 10.16. It is as if the Lord should have said, There can be no Comparison between the *Portion* of my People, as I, *the Former of all things,* am their Inheritance, and *the Portion* of those Nations that serve Idol-gods; which are the Work of Mens Hands; that can neither See, nor Hear, nor in the lease wise save them that call upon them. Nay, so far are they from saving others, that *these gods that have not made the Earth and the Heavens, shall themselves perish from under these Heavens,* ver. 11. And *the Nations* that serve 'em shall *Tremble* at the fierce Wrath of Jehovah, and shall *not be able to abide the Indignation* of him, who is *the living and true God, and an everlasting King,* ver. 10. *But the Portion of* Jacob *is not like them: For he is the Former of all things,* ver. 16. As if the Lord should say, It's I, I my self, whose Name alone is [JEHOVAH] that am the Portion of my People. It's I the Former of all things, the Creator and Possessor of Heaven and Earth, *Isa.* 42.5. *Gen.* 14.19. whose Name is [I AM] *Exod.* 3.14. that have Fulness of Being in myself; and give Life and Being to all Creatures and things at my Pleasure, *Heb.* 11.8. *Act.* 17.28. *Rev.* 4.11. and am therefore well able to give the most substantial Being to all that vast Happiness, I have ordained for my People, in Nature, Grace, and Glory: So that in [Me] they have a transcendent and an everlasting Portion.

That *Jehovah*, is the God and Portion of his People, is a Truth oft inculcated in the Sacred Scriptures. *I will be unto them a God*, is the great Promise of the New Covenant, *Heb.* 8.10. And how often doth the Lord comfort his Children with this spiritual Cordial? When in their Fainting-fits, he says unto them, *Fear not, for I am with thee: Be not dismay'd, for I am thy God, Isa.* 41.10. Thus he spake to his Servant *Abram: Fear not*, Abram; for *I am thy Shield, and thy exceeding great Reward:* or thy exceeding great Portion, *Gen.* 15.1. And to *Aaron, I am thy Part, and thine Inheritance*, Numb. 18.20.

And when once this joyful Sound is proclaim'd by the blessed Spirit in the Hearts of God's Children, Oh how doth it revive their drooping Souls! It raiseth them up from under all sorts of Discouragements, into an holy Boldness, and joyful Triumph of Faith, with the *Psalmist, My Heart and my Flesh faileth: but God is the Strength of my Heart, and my Portion for ever,* Psal. 73.26. And with the Church in the midst of Distresses, *The LORD is my Portion, saith my Soul, therefore will I hope in him,* Lam. 3.24.

And as God, himself is the Portion of his Children, so it is himself as the God of all Grace and Glory. And he is so, 1. Essentially. 2. Provision-ally. And 3. Communicatively.

1. *Essentially.* Grace and Glory are the essential Perfections of God's Nature. And thus he proclaim'd his Name (or the Perfections of his Nature by which he would be known) to *Moses*, Exod. 24.6. *The LORD the LORD God, Merciful, Gracious,* &c. Mercy and Grace, here, are his Nature. And *Acts* 7.2. he is said to be, The *God of Glory*. That is, the God of Glory essentially. Grace and Glory in God, are HIMSELF: He IS all his Perfec-tions, *1 John* 4.16.

2. He is the God of all Grace and Glory *Provisionally.* In that he has made a full Provision of all sorts of communicable Grace and Glory, and stor'd up all these Riches as an immense Stock, or Portion for all his Children in his own Son, as the great Mediator and Head of the Church: *For it hath pleased the Father, that in him all Fulness should dwell,* Col. 1.19. And,

3. God is the God of all Grace and Glory, *Communicatively.* In that he communicates all Grace and Glory out of the infinite Riches of his own Nature, and out of his Covenant-Provision in his Son: As saith the *Apostle, My God shall supply all your Need according to his Riches in Glory, by*

Christ Jesus, Phil. 4.19. The Original of all our Supply is according to, or out of, the Riches of *Jehovah's* Nature: And it's by Christ, as the Way of Communication. Thus *the Lord God will give Grace and Glory,* Psal. 84.11. or communicate Grace and Glory, to all his Children, through Time, and to Eternity. And in these *three* Respects, *Jehovah*, as the God of all Grace and Glory, is the Inheritance of his Children. All the infinite Perfections of his Nature are made over to us for our Good and Advantage. And what he is in his incommunicable Attributes, he is For us: And what he is in his communicable Attributes he is both For us and To us.

And, as I humbly conceive, we may safely retain the Distinction of communicable, and incommunicable Attributes in the Divine Being: Because some of the Divine Perfections casting the Rays of their Glory thro' Christ upon the Creature, transform it *into the same Image,* 2 Cor. 3.18. And others there are which the Creature can bear no Resemblance of. 'Tis true, indeed, that even God's communicable Attributes are, in some Sense, incommunicable; that is, as to the Infiniteness of 'em as they are in God: So that God is gracious, and glorious infinitely as God: And when he communicates out of his own Nature, to make a Creature gracious or glorious, he doth not communicate infinitely; because the Creature is not capable of it, and so he doth not deify that Creature; but the greatest Perfection of its Grace and Glory, is still limited and finite, answerable to its Creature-Being. And yet there is a real, tho' not an infinite Communication, in these as well as other his communicable Attributes. So as that, it is still *the Fulness of God*, in Nature, Grace, and Glory, that is the infinite Ocean that filleth all in all, *Eph.* 3.19. *and* 1.23. in all sorts of Creatures, according to their distinct Natures, and different Ends, Thus God, as the God of Nature, did at first make, and still doth uphold, and fill all Things in the old Creation: And as the God of Grace and Glory, he makes, upholds, and fills all Things in the new Creation. *Acts* 17.24, 25, 28. *Eph.* 4.6. *Rom.* 11.36.

Further, I Judge this Distinction not only Safe, but Necessary. For, if our Portion did only consist in Grace and Glory, as created Communicables in the Person of Christ; 'twould fall far short of JEHOVAH, Himself, who is *our Portion,* Lam. 3.24. We are *Heirs of GOD*, Rom. 8.17. of all [His] Riches, and *Joint-Heirs [With] Christ.* The Riches of Christ, as Mediator, and Ours in him are Unsearchable, as the Man Christ, stands personally United to the Godhead; and we United to the Person of Christ. Christ stands in [God], the infinite Ocean of Grace and Glory; and We in [Him] as the *Medium* of Communication.

And to this purpose Dr. *Owen* speaks in his Book *of Communion with God:* where setting forth the Excellencies of Christ, as the Husband of the Church, he hath these Words, *pag.* 78, 79.

"It is not the Grace of a Creature, nor all the Grace that can possibly at once dwell in a created Nature, that weill serve our turn. We are too indigent to be suited with such a Supply. There was a fulness of Grace in the humane Nature of Christ; *He receiv'd not the Spirit of Measure*, John 3.34. A fulness like that of Light in the Sun, or of Water in the Sea, I speak not in respect of Communication, but Sufficiency. A fulness incomparably above the Measure of Angels, yet it was not properly an infinite Fulness; it was a created, and therefore a limited Fulness. If it could be conceived as separated from the Deity, surely so many thirsty, guilty Souls as every Day drink deep and large Draughts of Grace and Mercy from him, would (if I may so speak) sink him to the very Bottom: Nay, it could afford no supply at all, but only in a moral Way. But when the Conduit of his Humanity is inseperably united to the infinite, inexhaustible Fountain of the Deity, who can look into the Depths thereof? If now there be Grace enough for Sinners in an al-sufficient God, it is in Christ. And indeed in any other there cannot be enough."

But oh, the unspeakable Blessedness of te Heirs of God, in that they have [Himself] as the God of all Grace and Glory for their Inheritance! With what inexpressible *Joy*, may *we draw Water out of these Wells of Salvation!* Isa. 12.3. When *the Vessels of Mercy*, Rom. 9.23. are cast into the endless, boundless, bottomless Ocean of *Jehovah's* Glory in Christ, for which they were *prepar'd*; with what inconceivable Pleasure will they take in a full variety of Glory to the utmost of their vast Capacities, without the least fear of Waste, or Diminution to Eternity; while their GOD, is their GLORY1 *Isa.* 60.19. It must needs (as one well hints) be enough for us, for it's enough for God himself to Eternity. Dr *Goodwin* 4 Vol. 2 Book Page 123. &c. But to proceed,

Since *Jehovah*, the God of all Grace and Glory, is the Inheritance of his Children; as such, we should live upon him continually, both with respect to Acts of Grace without us, and to the Work of Grace within us. We should live upon *Jehovah* as our Portion, in the Infiniteness of his Love towards us.

1. In the Acts of Grace without us. For there are infinite Riches of Grace and Glory, display'd in the Acts of Election, Adoption, Pardon, and

Justification. The Love of God is infinitely Rich, Free, and Unchangeable as it is his Nature: And therefore it is so in all the Acts of his Will. *Jehovah changeth not, and therefore* it is that we *are not Consumed*, Mal. 3.6. *The Lord our God in the midst of us is Mighty; he will Save, he will Rejoice over us with Singing, he will Rest in his Love,* Zeph. 3.17. And therefore well may we Rest in it. *The Gifts and Calling of God are without Repentance.* Rom. 11.29. His calling us his *People,* Psal. 78.52. his *Sons and Daughters,* 2. Cor. 6.18. his *Jewels,* Mal. 3.17. together with all the Gifts of Grace and Glory that were bestowed upon us as such, are absolutely without Repentance; either as to the Settlement, or Communication of 'em. *The Counsel of the LORD will stand for ever, and the Thoughts of his Heart,* in his everlasting Kindness to us in Christ Jesus, will endure *to all Generations.* Psal. 33.11. And as Faith may Feast on all the Riches of Mercy, Love, and Grace that are in *Jehovah's* Nature, as they are made Ours in the Acts of Grace without us, to Delight us infinitely; to bestow all Blessings upon us freely; to Pity and Pardon us continually; so we should Live upon Jehovah, as our Portion, with Respect

2. To the Work of Grace within us. we need abundance of Grace, not only to begin, but also to carry on our Conformity to Christ, in his Grace and Glory-Image: But there is an Infinite Fulness in the God of all Grace and Glory, that is every way sufficient for us, in Time and to Eternity. What ever *Jehovah* IS in his own Nature, that he is to Us in Christ, as he is Ours in an everlasting Covenant.

Is he *Good,* Luke 13.17. That he is for us. The infinite goodness of his Nature, as made ours in Covenant, is the Source of all our Happiness, *Psal.* 119.68. And as God is good for us, as the immense Ocean whence all our Supplies come: So he is good to us, in that he communicates of his Goodness through Christ, to *make us Good.* Mat. 12.33. in his new-Creation *Work* upon us, *Eph.* 2.10. whereby he implants, and maintains a Principle of *Goodness* in our Hearts, *Gal.* 5.22.

Is God *Love,* 1 John 4.16. This he is for us, in all the out-goings of his Heart towards us. And he is also Love to us, in that he Communicates, or *sheds abroad his Love in our Hearts,* Rom. 5.5. whereby he Forms his Love-Image there; and causeth our Souls to *Love him* again, as being enkindled with his own Love, *1 John* 4.19.

Is Jehovah *Merciful,* Exod. 34.6. This he is for us. And it is from the greatness, freeness, fulness, and eternity of his *Mercy,* as made ours in *Covenant,* Psal. 89.28. that he pardoneth all our Sins, *Psal.* 103.3. healeth all our Backslidings, *Hosea* 14.4. pitieth us in all our Weakness, *Psal.* 103.13. and delivereth us out of all our Distresses, *Psal.* 107.13. And as in the infiniteness of his Bowels he is Mercy for us: So also he is Mercy to us, in that he makes us as his Children, to bear some Resemblance of our merciful Father, *Luke* 6.36.

Is he *Gracious*, Exod. 34.6. He is so for us, in all the Acts of his Grace without us: And as such he is the Fountain of all Grace to us, in all the Works of his Grace upon us.

And is our God, Glorious in himself, or *the God of Glory*, Acts 7.2. Isa. 60.19. As such, he is an Ocean of Glory for us to Swim in: And an Ocean of Glory to us, so as to fill us with Glory.

Again, is he *Light*, 1 John 1.5. The uncreated Fountain of it: This he is for us in Christ: As such he'll be the Object of our eternal Complacency, *Eccles.* 11.7. And he is also Light to us, when as *the Father of Lights*, Jam. 1.17. he communicates Light, by creating a Divine Principle of Light in our Hearts, and by carrying on, and encreasing this *Light of Life* here in Grace, *John* 8.12. 'till we enter upon the full Possession of our *Inheritance in* the *Light* of Glory, *Col.* 1.12. God, as Light, darting forth the Rays of his Glory thro' Christ, is Light for us, to be beheld, *2 Cor.* 4.6. And he, by the transforming Glory of his Light display'd, is Light to us, by way of Communication, so as to make us *Light in the Lord*, Eph. 5.8.

Again, is he *Life* or the *living God,* John 5.26. Acts 14.15. This he is for us, as he is ours in Christ: *Our Life is hid with Christ in God,* Col. 3.3. And as he is the original Fountain of Life for us, Natural, Spiritual, and Eternal: So also he is to us, in the Communications of it thro' Christ.

Is he, the *Lord God Almighty*, Gen. 17.1. This he is for us, in all his Works of Nature, Grace and Glory. And as the Lord God Omnipotent, is Strength for us: So also he is Strength to us, 1. Defensively, in that as the strong God, he is *our Rock* to Secure and Defend us, *Psal. 94.22. And 2. Influentially, he is our Strength* to make us Strong, *Psal.* 73.26. He *puts Strength* into us, *Job* 23.6. we derive all our Nature-Strength from him, and all the Degrees of our Grace-Strength, either to live upon him, or to him: To Walk with him in sweet Communion and Fellowship, or to Fight his Battles against all Enemies. And we shall derive all our Glory-Strength from him, when in the Resurrection-Morning, the Bodies of the Saints shall be raised in Power, *1 Cor.* 15.43. and so their intire Persons, be made capable to bear that *Weight of Glory* which shall then be conferr'd upon them; *2 Cor.* 4.17.

Again, Is he *the only wise God*, 1 Tim. 1.17. This he is for us; in that, in the Infinity of his Wisdom, he hath *abounded towards us* in all his Riches of Grace and Glory, *Eph.* 1.7, 8. Hence, it is, that in his wise Counsels he hath dispos'd of all things in such an excellent Order, as shall most effectually subserve all the Ends of his Glory, *Prov.* 16.4. and our Good, *Rom.* 8.28. And he is Wisdom to us, in that he makes us wise, *Dan.* 12.3. All our Wisdom is but a Communication out of his Fulness: And therefore we are bid, to *ask Wisdom* of him *who gives* it *liberally*, Jam. 1.5.

Farther, Is he *a just God*, Isa. 45.21. This also he is for us. Hence he's true and faithful in all his Covenant Promises, and Engagements to his Children, as well as in all his Threatnings to his Enemies. *He abideth faithful* in both, whether we are in the Exercise of Faith about it, or not; *for he cannot deny* himself, *2 Tim.* 2.13. He is Just for us, in that he declares us *Just* in the imputed Righteousness of his Son, *Rom.* 3.26. His Justice is our Friend, and constantly dischargeth us in the highest Court; notwithstanding all the Accusations that may be brought against us by Satan, Men, Law, or Conscience, *Rom.* 8.33. And he is also Just, or the Fountain of Justice for us: In that he makes us *Just, Isa.* 26.7. by creating a Principle of Justice in our Souls, and maintaining it in our Hearts and Lives.

Is he a God, *glorious in Holiness, Exod.* 15.11. This also he is for us, *in all his Ways and Works*, Ps. 145.17. 'Tis from the infinite *Purity* of his Nature, that he *Hates* Sin infinitely, *Hab.* 1.13. and will therefore destroy it perfectly in all those whom he loves, *Jer.* 44.4. *Isa.* 1.25. And as he is Holiness for us, so also to us, in the Communications of it through Christ. Hence the new Creature in us, which is his Image, is said to be *created in true Holiness*, Eph. 4.24. And as the first Principle of it is from him, so are all the Increases of it in this Life; and the Perfection of it in the Life to come. All the shining Holiness of Saints and Angels, is but as it were the Reflection of his Glory cast upon 'em. JEHOVAH, Glorious in Holiness, is the infinite Sun, who by darting forth his piercing Rays thro' Christ, in the Place of his immediate Glory-Presence, transforms all the Royal Courtiers that are round his Throne, into this same Image of him, the King of Glory.

Again, Is he the *Omniscient* God, *Psal.* 147.5. He sees all things for us. And because he sees what is best for us, he gives what is best to us, and that in the best Season. And as he sees what is good for us to bestow it, *Psal.* 8.12. So he sees what is Evil, or would hurt us to prevent it, *Psal.* 19.10. He sees the Rage and Malice of Hell, Isa. 37.28. the Enmity of wicked Men, the

Seed of the Serpent, the Lustings of the Flesh against the Spirit: And how often doth he discover their Plots, and disappoint their Designs? And when he suffers their Projects in any Measure to take place, he always bounds their Rage, and rules their Madness, as he doth the foaming Ocean, *Psal.* 76.10. and 89.9. *Hitherto shalt thou come, and no farther: And here shall thy proud Waves be staid,* Job 38.11. And it is because he knows how to make all those *things work together for good,* Rom. 8.28. which in their own Nature tend to harm us, that he at any time suffers our Enemies to prevail. And because he sees 'em perfectly, as his and our Enemies, he'll destroy 'em throughly. *The eyes of the Lord are in every place, beholding the Evil and the Good,* Prov. 15.3. He beholds the Evil that is in Hell among the Devils, and that is in the Earth among the reprobate Part of Mankind; and he'll *reward* these *Evil Doers* that have been fighting against him and his, *according to their Wickedness,* 2 Sam. 3.39. And *make them as a fiery Oven in the time of* his *Anger*; when he *swallows them up in* his *Wrath,* Psal. 21.9. Yea, his omniscient Eyes, behold all the Evil that is in the Hearts and Lives of his Children, *Hos.* 5.3. and therefore he'll *chastise* 'em for it *in Measure,* Psal. 89.32. Isa. 27.8. *Purge* 'em from it more and more here; and root the very Being of it out of their Nature hereafter, *Ver.* 9. *Rev.* 21.27. And as it's the Saints Privilege that he beholds the Evil to destroy it; so that he beholds the *Good* to maintain and reward it, *Phil.* 1.6. *2 Cor.* 5.10. Wicked Men are so blinded by Sin and Satan, that they can't see the Saints Goodness; but are ready to charge them as Hypocrites. And how oft doth Satan represent the matter thus to themselves? While their own unbelieving Hearts are apt to join with him. So that at times they know not what to think of it, when in the Views of their own Vileness; but are ready to fear, that there never was any thing truly good, either wrought in 'em, or done by 'em. But the omniscient God, sees all that Good which was the Work of his own Spirit in 'em, and which by his Assistance they have been enabled to act either in Heart of Life: And will therefore own and crown it *in the Day of Christ,* 1 Pet. 1.7. He'll not suffer the Saints Goodness to be lost, in those Mists of Darkness that have been raised to obscure it; either by evil Angels, evil Men, or that evil Principle of Unbelief, in the Hearts of his Children; but he will *bring forth* their *Righteousness as the Light,* (or as the Sun from under all its Eclipses,) *and their Judgment as the Noon-day,* Psal. 37.6.

Again, Is our God the omnipresent Being, *Psal.* 139.7, 8, 9. and *Jer.* 23.24. He fills all things for us: The World with his general, the Church with his gracious, and Heaven with his glorious Presence; yea, and Hell with his wrathful Presence, in a Way of just Revenge, of all that Malice and Hatred, they have shewn towards his Children.

And is JEHOVAH, immense, incomprehensible, unchangeable, and eternal, in his Goodness, Love, Mercy, Grace, and Glory; in his Light, Life, Power, and Wisdom; in his Justice, and Holiness; in his Omniscience, and Omnipresence; and as such the Portion of his Children: Oh how vast is their Inheritance! They have All in GOD, for their All, in having Him as the God of all Grace and Glory for their Inheritance. For all the Perfections of God's Nature, are jointly concern'd in projecting, carrying on, and finishing this vast Design of his free Grace; which in the Perfection of it will open in the Heighths of eternal Glory. And therefore when the Saints, as *Vessels prepar'd for Glory*, Rom. 9.23. are made to *comprehend*, that is, to hold, in their Measure, that Love which is incomprehensible in itself; and so to know its *Heights* and *Depths*, which are infinitely past Knowledge; they are said to be *filled with all the Fullness of God:* Inasmuch as all the Divine Perfections, appear for us in Christ, in this one Form of Love, *Eph.* 3.18, 19.

Thus the Children of God should live upon him as their Portion, with respect to the Work of Grace in 'em. We may well be *confident of this very thing, that he which hath begun* it, will also carry it on *until the Day of Christ*, Phil. 1.6. since all the Divine Attributes are angaged in this Design.

The Inheritance of the Sons of God, lies in Grace and Glory: And thus it specifically differs from the Portion of all other Men. 'Tis true, indeed, that the Saints, in having God for their Portion, have him comprehensively; as the God of Nature, as well as the God of Grace and Glory; and as such he is the Fountain of their natural Supplies, Psal. 111.5. and in that they are *Heirs with Christ*, Rom. 8.17. who is *Heir of all things*, Heb. 1.2. they have a Right to all things in this *World*, 1 Cor. 3.22. yet so, as that their Portion, especially, lies in Grace and Glory. This being that Inheritance, or Kingdom that was *prepared for them*, Mat. 25.34. and all natural Blessings are but as things that are *added*, as subservient Means to that great End, *Ch.* 6.33. Our God, indeed, *gives us all things* in this World *richly to enjoy*, 1 Tim. 6.17. Even all that his infinite Wisdom sees best for us, and the Means of our comfortable Subsistence in a natural Life; but this is in order to our being filled with spiritual, and fitted for eternal Life. 'Tis the enriching us with all Grace and Glory, is the great Design our Father's Heart is engaged in: And all natural Blessings are afforded, or restrained, as either doth most conduce to this great End. The Lord never empties his Children of earthly Blessings, but in order to fill 'em with heavenly, *Hos.* 2.6, 7. And when he cuts short their Enjoyment of outward Favours, he doth not in the least infringe their Right to all things: But so disposeth of them in the Infinity of his Widsom, as to make them subserve all the Ends of his Glory, in the greatest Advantage of his Children. So that the poorest Saints, *as having nothing* in an Eye of Sense, may yet by Faith *possess all things*, 2 Cor. 6.10. for *All* that our Father hath is ours, *Luke* 15.31. And it's our unspeakable Privilege that our God hath the chusing of our Portion, *Psal*. 47.4. we may hance be sure, that as he will always give us what is *good* in itself, *Psal*. 85.11. so in the best Way and Time, when it shall do us the greatest Kindness, *Isa*. 30.18. So that it's impossible we should *want any good thing*, to make us truly blessed in this World; or perfectly glorious in the World to come, *Psal*. 34.10. Thus having given some broken Hints, What the Inheritance of the Sons of God is; I come to enquire,

Thirdly, When it was made theirs. In answer to which, we may observe, That

It was very early settled upon them. For all *Grace* was *given* them *in Christ before the World began*, 2 Tim. 1.9. The Children of God, were *blesses with all spiritual Blessings in the Heavenlies, according as* they are *chosen in Christ before the Foundation of the World*, Eph. 1.3, 4. *Eternal Life*, which is the whole of their Inheritance was given 'em by *Promise, even before the World began*, Tit. 1.2. That *Kingdom* of which the Sons of God are Heirs, was *prepared for them from the Foundation of the World*, Mat. 25.34. The Inheritance of the Sons of God in general, and every Child's *Lot*, Dan. 12.13. and Portion in particular, was got ready for 'em, and settled upon them, in the Preparations of infinite Wisdom and Grace, from the Foundation of the World, in its first Creation: That was done before this begun. God's *Works* of Grace *were finished* in his Counsels, and Covenant Settlements, before he gave Being to the Works of Nature, *Heb*. 4.3. And the Creation, Preservation, and Government of all things in this World, were in Subordination to the Glory of God's Grace, in the Advancement of his Children to that Inheritance he ultimately design'd for them, *Heb*. 2.10. So that if we enquire of the Date of God's Loving Kindness, in making the Inheritance theirs, we must say with the *Psalmist*, That *it has been ever of old*, Psal. 25.6. In the next Place,

Fourthly, I would enquire, how it was settled upon them. In answer to which, we may observe, That

This Inheritance was settled upon the Persons of God's Children, in Christ their Head, by a free, absolute, irreversible Grant of the Father. I shall take a little Notice, distinctly, of the Nature of this Settlement.

1. This Inheritance was settled upon the [Persons] of God's Children. We were first chosen to all Blessings, then taken into the Relation of Children, in order to their Bestowment, and then blessed in the Settlement of 'em upon us. And as in Election, God did not choose Qualities, but Persons, *Rom.* 9.11, 12, 13. so nor in this great Act of Settlement, did *Jehovah* make over himself as the Portion of his Children, and leave it at Uncertainty (to be determined by the Will and Goodness of the Creature) who these should be. No, *The Foundation of God standeth sure, having this Seal, The Lord knoweth them that are his,* 2 Tim. 2.19. He knew 'em distinctly from all the World beside, *Jer.* 1.5. when he wrote down *their Names* in his eternal Choice of 'em, *Luke* 10.20. And they were as distinctly blessed as chosen, *Eph.* 1.3. *Blessed be the God and Father of our Lord Jesus Christ, who hath blessed us,* &c. *according as he hath chosen us,* Ver. 4. *Having predestinated us*, &c. *Ver. 5.* He hath Blessed [Us] saith the Apostle, even the same [Us] which he did choose, and predestinate. Thus, *Rom.* 8.30. *Moreover, Whom he did predestinate, Them he also called: And Whom he called, Them he also justified: And Whom he justified, Them he also glorified.* And if we take this Word, *Glorified,* to intend either, 1. The Settlement, or, 2. The Conveyance of a glorious Inheritance, or both, it will afford a full Proof to the Point in Hand: That God hath glorify'd none but those whom he eternally Predestinated unto Life. They were all *Known by* [*Name*] in God's Electing, and adopting Love, who, in the Settlement of this Inheritance, *have found Grace in his Sight.* Exod. 33.17.

2. This Inheritance was settled upon the Sons of God, as standing [In] Christ their Head. It pleased the Father to *give* Christ *to be the Head of the Church*, and in him, as such, they were both *Chosen* and Bless'd, *Eph.* 1. 22. *ver.* 3.4. This great new Covenant-Grant, of God, as the Portion of his Children, was first made to Christ as the Covenant-Head; who was constituted *the everlasting Father,* Isa. 9.6. of that Remnant that were Chosen in him, and *given* to him, as his Seed and Children, *Heb.* 2.13. and then to us in him as our great Representative. And thus the Covenant ran, *to thee and to thy Seed,* with *Abraham,* Gen. 17.7. and with *David:* Psal. 18.50. who were Typical of Christ and his Seed. God, is first the God of Christ; and then our God in him. Christ is the eldest Son, the *First-born* of the Family, *Rom.* 8.29. and as such the Prime-Heir; though we as younger

Brethren are made *Joint-Heirs with* him, of the same Glorious Inheritance, *Ver.* 17. This seems to be intimated in that Message our Lord sent his Disciples just after his Resurrection, *I ascend,* says he, *to my Father and your Father, to my God and your God,* John 20.17. First [My] God, in that I have a more immediate, and transcendent Interest in Jehovah, as my Portion; as I am his First-born Son: And then [Your] God, as you are made Heirs with me, as his younger Children. My God and your God, in one and the same Covenant: Yet so, as that the Grant of this Inheritance, was originally and transcendently made to me; and then to you in me: So that yours is a derived Interest, from mine. And as this Inheritance was settled upon the Persons of God's Children, as standing in Christ their Head: so

3. It was by a Grant of the Father. *In hope of eternal Life, which God that cannot Lie, promis'd before the World began,* Tit. 1.2. Promis'd, or granted by Promise, to Christ and all his Seed. And this Grant was, 1. Free. 2. Absolute. And 3. Irreversible.

1. *Free.* God took no Motives from without himself herein. 'Twas the Sovereign *good Pleasure of his own Will,* going forth in a Way of Free-Love, that was the original Cause of this Grant, both to Christ and us. *Eph.* 1.3, 5. The Father's Love to Christ, in this Respect, was the Pattern of his Love to us, *John* 17.23. *And hast loved them, [As] thou hast loved me.*

2. It was *Absolute*, without Conditions. When the Father first said to Christ, I will be thy God, and the God of thy Seed, there were no Works included as the Condition of this Grant. For then it had been of the Law, and not of Grace. *For to him that Worketh, the Reward is not reckon'd of Grace, but of Debt,* Rom. 4.4. Whereas this Inheritance was given by Promise. And as the Grant of it was Free and Absolute, so

3. It was *Irreversible.* And the *Apostle* argues its irreversibleness, from the free and absolute Nature thereof, *Gal.* 3.17, 18. *And this I say, that the Covenant which was confirmed before of God in Christ, the Law which was four Hundred and thirty Years after, cannot disannul, that it should make the Promise of none effect. For if the Inheritance be of the Law, it is no more of Promise; but God gave it to Abraham by Promise.*

Now, as I conceive, we are to look upon *Abraham, the Father of the Faithful,* Rom. 4.16. with whom God made Covenant, as a Type of Christ; who was constituted the *everlasting Father* of all God's Chosen, who were given to him as his Seed and Offspring; with whom God's everlasting Covenant was originally, and substantially made. And as *all Nations,* or some of all Nations were typically Bless'd in *Abraham,* Gal. 3.8. so the

Elect among all Nations were substantially Bless'd in Christ. And as the Promise of the Inheritance was given to *Abraham*, before the Promulgation of the Law at Mount *Sinai*; so likewise, this Promise-Grant, as it was originally made to Christ, was above, and before the consideration of all Laws. So that it must needs be irreversible, being thus made by *a God that cannot Lie*. Tit. 1.2. Who is *not a Man that he should Lie, nor the Son of Man that he should Repent,* Numb. 23.19. Whose *Gifts and Calling are without Repentance*, Rom. 11.29.

And if this Inheritance was thus settled upon the Persons of God's Children, in Christ their Head, by a free, absolute, irreversible Grant of the Father; it will necessarily follow from hence, that it was impossible these *Heirs of Promise*, Heb. 6.17. should lose their Title, or forfeit their Right to this Inheritance, when they Sinn'd in, and Fell with the first *Adam*, because it was not put into his Hands; and so could not be Lost, or forfeited by his Sin.

We were, indeed, Bless'd in *Adam* with a natural Inheritance, Which did consist in a Perfection of natural and earthly Blessings: and with this Stock he was entrusted. This Portion was put into his Hands for all his Posterity, whom he then Represented. And this Inheritance was not given absolutely; but conditionally. So that if he had continued in his Obedience to his Maker's Law, both himself and his, were to have lived for ever, in that Paradisical Estate he then possest, *Gal.* 3.12. but if he fail'd herein, nothing but Death and Wrath were to be expected, as *the Wages of Sin*, Rom. 6.23.

And oh, how soon did *Adam* lose this natural Inheritance, put into his Hands, *Psal.* 49.12. For though he was a Perfect Man, and had Power to have Stood if he would, *Eccles.* 7.29. yet being a mutable Creature, and left to the freedom of his own Will, in his own Strength to grapple with the Temptations of the Devil; he quickly fell in with his Suggestions; and turn'd Rebel, and Traitor against his Prince: by which his Estate became forfeited to the Crown: And instead thereof, all kinds of Death became due to him and his, according to the just Penalties of the broken Law of his Sovereign Lord. So that, if the Inheritance of the Sons of God by supernatural Grace, had been put into *Adam's* Hands, it had been lost: for he lost all he was entrusted with.

But this was the unspeakable Privilege of the Children of God, the elect remnant, that they were, not only chosen in *Christ*, but, *Blessed in Christ* too, *Eph.* 1.3, 4. Our Portion was exceeding safe in his Hands: *Our Life* being *hid with Christ in God*, Col. 3.3. So that, tho' we were robbed and spoiled of that Portion of goods, our Father gave us in *Adam*, for our accommodation in the lower Room of this World; yet our Jewels, our Treasure in *Christ* were locked up in a safe Cabinet; *Reserved for us in Heaven*, 1 Pet. 1.4. where *Thieves* could *not break thro' nor steal*, Mat. 6.20. Those terrestial Blessings, we had in the *first Man*, who *was of the Earth earthy,* 1 Cor. 15.47, 48. we forfeited and lost in his fall; tho' our right thereto is again restored: but our supercelestial Blessings in *Christ, the heavenly Man,* lay far above all spoil.

'Tis true, the adopted Sons of God, did equally with others, by the fall, lose that Estate of Favour, and natural Communion with God, which they had in their Head *Adam:* and by Sin did really deserve, and bring themselves under *the Curse of the Law*, Gal. 3.10. And in themselves considered, they became obnoxious to the fierce *Wrath* of a Sin-revenging God, *Eph.* 2.3. which by reason of the infinite *Purity* of his Nature, and hatred of Sin, must necessarily feed upon all Sinners; who are like dry *Stubble* to *devouring Fire,* and fit Fuel for everlasting Burnings. *Mal.* 4.1. *Isa.* 33.14. So that, if we consider the Inheritance as antecedently settled upon the Sons of God, and ultimately designed for them; and then view them as lapsed Creatures, together with the Impossibility of Sinners, as such, being taken into the Enjoyment of God, either in Grace, or Glory, it will make room to enquire.

Fifthly, Which way they come to enjoy their Inheritance. Ay, which way indeed? Had God summoned the whole Host of Creatures, and told them, that, from everlasting, he had settled himself as a Portion upon a Remnant of Mankind, whom he had loved in his Son; and here withal have laid before them the Difficulties that did occur in carrying on this Design, by reason of the Fall: Who of them all could have found out a way, to glorify all the divine Perfections in the Salvation of Sinners, from the Depths of Misery, to the ultimate Heights of their designed Glory!

Had God stated the matter thus, "How shall my Children, that are now turned Transgressors, and deserve my Wrath, ever come to enjoy that glorious Inheritance I have settled upon them, and reserved for them in the greatness of my Love? 'Tis true, my Love is the same towards them as ever; and *the Thoughts of* my *heart*, in my everlasting Kindness, will abide the same *to all Generations* Ps. 33.11. Yea, *my Covenant* with *Christ* their Head, *doth stand fast for evermore*, Ps. 89.28, 34, 35. *Once have I sworn by my Holiness, and I will not lie unto* David; *nor alter the thing that's gone out of my Mouth.* But *how shall I put them among the Children, and give* them *a pleasant Heritage,* Jer. 3.19. that have thus rebelled against me? *I am JEHOVAH, and change not,* Mal. 3.6. as not in my Love, so nor in any of my infinite Perfections. I am a *great,* as well as a gracious God, *Isa.* 57.15. *The high and lofty one,* whose infinite Majesty they have affronted, whose Honour they have injured, whose Sovereignty they have despised, and have done what in them lies to pull me from my Throne. And as I am a great, so a *just God,* Isa. 45.21. My Justice to my own Greatness, obligeth me to do my Being right, for the wrong they have done me. And I must have an infinite Satisfaction, for the Injury done to my infinite Majesty: and how must I come at this, when lo, they have *nothing to pay?* Luke 7.42. Yea, I am just and righteous to the threatnings of my holy Law: the Word is gone out of my Mouth, *in the Day thou eatest thereof, thou shalt surely die,* Gen. 2.17. And I am *a God of Truth,* Deut. 32.4. Faithful, and *can't deny* my *self,* 2 Tim. 2.13. as not in the Promises of my Grace, so nor in the threatnings of my Law. How then shall I give Life, to such that are thus sentenced to Death, as the just *Wages of Sin?* Rom. 6.23. And as I am a great, just, and true God, so I am a God of infinite Holiness, *Of purer Eyes than to behold Iniquity,* Hab. 1.13. and cannot look on Sin: And *without Holiness* it is impossible for any *to see God,* Heb. 12.14. How then shall I take such filthy, abominable Creatures, and set them before my Face for ever as the Objects of my eternal Complacency?"

Had God, I say, thus stated the Question, and referred it for answer, to al the Men that ever have been since *Adam,* or shall be to the end of the World; how would it have nonplus'd the most bright, illustrious Souls that have moved in the highest Orb of human Understanding? None of them all could have given the least Intimation of a Way, in which all the divine Perfections might be glorified, in the Salvation of Sinners.

Nay, so far is the Wisdom of the Flesh, from contributing any thing to this Design, that it always stands diametrically opposite. *The Redemption of the Souls* of Sinners, was a Work so *precious,* that it must have *ceased for ever,* had either the Contrivance, or Performance of it, in the least depended upon our Wisdom or Strength, *Ps.* 49.8.

And as this Question would have nonplus'd the whole Posterity of *Adam;* so also it would have been far above the Sphere of angelick Understanding. Neither Angels, nor Archangels, among all their bright Orders, could ever have given God a positive Answer hereto. No: For tho' these pure, piercing, and intelligent Spirits, do move in the highest Orb of created Understanding; yet none of those bright Seraphs, in all the flaming Glories of their Wisdom, but must here have confest their profound Ignorance. So that none of the whole Host of rational Creatures, either in the upper or lower Worlds, could have returned any more than a negative Answer to this Question: and must have remained in eternal Silence as to the positive part of it.

And here, the Project of Eternity, for the Glory of God's Grace, in the Bestowment of this Inheritance upon his Children, must for ever have been stopped in the Conveyance, had not infinite Wisdom stept in, and found out a Way in which to carry it on, unto its ultimate Glory Heights in the Perfection of an endless Life, thro' all those vast Mazes of Sin, Curse, Wrath, and Death, thro' which it was to pass.

Now then, let's resume the Question, *viz.* which way these Sons of God come to enjoy their Inheritance? And hear it answered by the Lips of Truth, the eternal WORD, who came down out of the Bosom of the Father, to acquaint us with the Court Record about this Matter.

And, behold, how the Mystery opens, in him, who is *the Wisdom of God in a Mystery*, 1 Cor. 2.7. *I am the* [Way] says *Christ, no Man cometh unto the Father but by me,* John 14.6. Here then let's stand Agast! That our Lord *Jesus Christ* should be the Way, fills the Saints on Earth, with astonishing Wonder and Joy, Heaven above, with eternal Amazement and highest Acclamations, and Hell below, with the blackest Horror and everlasting Confusion.

But, I would a little enquire, how *Christ* is the Way? And he is so, 1. In respect of Title: 2. In respect of Meetness: And 3. In respect of Communication.

1. *Christ* is the Way of our Enjoyment of the Inheritance in respect of Title. He was the Way in which this Inheritance was first settled upon us: and so our original Title stands in him. And he is the Way by which it is conveyed to us by a secondary Title: Of which I now speak. And had it not been so, we could never have come at the Enjoyment of it, so great were the Obstacles which came in by the Fall. But here, irresistible reigning Grace, which at first shone gloriously in the Settlement of this Inheritance upon the Sons of God, (even in him who was *set up from everlasting*, Prov. 8.12, 23. as the Wisdom of the Father, and the great Head of the Church) did again break forth in its triumphant Strength, from under all that Darkness that covered it by the Fall, like the Sun from under an Eclipse, in a new amazing Glory; with an, *I have* [Found] *David my Servant; I have laid* [Help] *upon*

one that is mighty, Ps. 89.19, 20. This mighty Head of the Church, in whom the Inheritance was first settled, shall now become the mighty *Saviour of the Body,* through whom it shall be enjoyed, *Eph.* 5.23.

And in order hereto, the Father resolved, to *prepare* Christ *a Body*, Heb. 10.5. demanded, and took Satisfaction at his Hands *for our Offence*, Rom. 4.25. by making him *Sin for us,* 2 Cor. 5.21. and consequently *an offering* for our Guilt, *Isa.* 53.10. Yea, and he did do it in Covenant, from everlasting: from whence, even in Old Testament-times, it's put in the past Tense: *He* [Was] *wounded for our Transgressions; he* [Was] *bruised for our Iniquities; and the Lord* [Hath] *laid on him the Iniquity of us all*, Isa. 53.5, 6.

Nor was this done without Christ's Consent: For God the Son, in the Covenant Capacity of Mediator, did from everlasting engage with God the Father, as our Surety, that *in the Fulness of Time*, he would take our Nature, sustain our Persons, stand in our Law-room, obey and die in our stead; to *make Reconciliation for Iniquity, finish Transgression, bring in an everlasting Righteousness*, and answer all the Ends of the Father's Glory, *Gal.* 4.4, 5. *Col.* 1.18. *1 Pet.* 3.18. *Dan.* 9.24.

Whereupon, the Father promised, that he would take him *from Prison and from Judgment*, Isa. 53.8. *Raise* him *from the Dead,* Acts 13.34. Acquit him from all Law-Charges, and publickly *justify* him as righteous, *Isa.* 50.8. in the Name, and Room of all those for whom he engaged, and whom, as their publick Head, he then represented, *Rom.* 4.25. And that upon the Account of his meritorious Blood and Righteousness, he would freely pardon all their Sins, *Eph.* 1.7. justify their Persons, *Tit.* 3.7. admit 'em into the highest Favour and Fellowship, *Rom.* 5.2. and at last compleatly save them out of the Hands of all their Enemies, *Isa.* 45.17. So that hereupon he should *See*, *i.e.*, Enjoy *his Seed,* in their being raised up from the Depths of Misery, to the Heights of Glory, to be for ever with him in the full Enjoyment of their Inheritance, as the Fruit of the *Travail of his Soul*, in which he should be satisfied, *Isa.* 53.10, 11. For so great was the Love of Christ, our everlasting Father, to his Seed and Children, our Elder Brother, to his younger Brethren, our Head and Husband, to the Members of his Body, his Bride and Spouse, that he could not have been satisfied, if he had not been to have had us all about him. Whereupon the Father told him, that he would satisfy *his Heart's Desire*, by giving him to see his Seed, *Psal.* 21.2.

And further, That upon his Ascension into Heaven, having finished the Work he gave him to do on Earth) he would advance him to *his own right*

Hand, far above Principalities, and Power, and Might, and Dominion, and every Name that is named, not only in this World, but in that which is to come. Eph. 1.20, 21. That *in the Name of Jesus every Knee shou'd bow, and every Tongue confess* his universal Lordship, and sovereign Domination, as having all *Power* committed to him, as King of Saints, and King of Nations, *Phil.* 2.10, 11.

And further, the Father told him, That as the Reward of his Obedience, he would give him *the Heathen for his Inheritance, the uttermost Parts of the Earth for his Possession,* Psal. 2.8. And that he should not only for a Time, govern all things in his vast Empire of this World, by a Secret, though an Almighty Hand; setting up, and pulling down at Pleasure; Managing all the Affairs of Providence in a real, though invisible Glory, by his Ministers of State, the Angels. But that also, at the appointed time, he would, in an open and visible Manner, give him *the Throne of his Father David, Luke* 1.32. *Dominion, Glory, and a Kingdom, that all People, Nations, and Languages* might *Serve him,* Dan. 7.14. And that he would set his *many Crowns* upon his Head, *Rev.* 19.12. and in all his Royalty make a *Shew* of him openly, to Saints and Angels, Men and Devils, as *King of Kings, and Lord of Lords, the only Potentate,* and Ruler of Princes, *1 Tim.* 6.15. And that when he himself should thus *take* the *Power, and Reign, Rev.* 11.17. all Nations should *bow before him, and his Enemies lick the Dust,* Ps. 72.9, 11. all the People seeing his Glory, to the Terror of Hell, and the *confounding all* those that *serve Graven Images,* Ps. 97.6, 7. While Heaven and Earth, harmoniously sing his Praise, as the *Judge of quick and dead, at* this *his Appearing and Kingdom,* 2 Tim. 4.1. *Appearing and Kingdom,* 2 Tim. 4.1. proclaiming *the Lamb, worthy to receive Blessing and Honour, Glory, Wisdom, Riches, and Strength,* Rev. 5.12.

Nor was *Christ* to have all this Glory as the just Reward of his meritorious Sufferings for himself only, but for us also; according to the decreed Proportion of Head and Members: so that, having obtained Life, Glory, and a Kingdom, by the infinite Worth of his Obedience unto Death; he was to be the Donor of this *Life,* Glory, and Kingdom, as being his own Right by Price, *to as many as the Father gave him,* John 17.2, 22. And thus *Christ Jesus,* as the Saviour, was verily *foreordained* to be the Way, in which the adopted Sons of God, as considered Sinners, should enjoy their Inheritance, *1 Pet.* 1.20.

And not only from everlasting, was he fore-appointed, in *Jehovah's* Counsel and Covenant; but in the fulness of Time, he did actually come down, and perform all his Covenant-engagements; by answering the Demands of Law and Justice: and so removed all the Objections, that could be made against our Enjoyment of the Inheritance, upon the Account of our being Sinners.

And having paid our Debts, he ascended to Heaven, demanding entrance, and was admitted into Glory both for himself, and all his; as that which in strict Justice was due to his Obedience. Thus the Sons of God come to enjoy their Inheritance, by Purchase-right.

The Inheritance, as was before observed, is, God himself, as the God of all Grace and Glory, essentially, provisionally, and communicatively considered. Grace and Glory essentially considered, are God's Nature: and in this first Sense, I think they cannot be said, to be purchased: nor yet in the second: for the Provision of Grace and Glory, in Counsel and Covenant, was an Act of God's Will; and so can't be said to be purchased; but it was, *the Father's* mere *good Pleasure to give the Kingdom*, Luke 12.32. It remains then, that in the *third* and last Sense, only, we are to apprehend the Inheritance as purchased: that is, the Communication of all Grace and Glory unto us.

And that the Inheritance, in this Sense, is purchased, is clear to me, from the Nature of *Christ's* Obedience and Reward. Our Lord's Obedience, in emptying himself of Glory, by reason of the Dignity of his Person, had an infinite Value in it; which did deserve all the Grace and Glory, that were to be given out to him and his to Eternity. And as there was an intrinsick, so also an extrinsick Worth in it; by virtue of the Father's Covenant, to give him all Grace and Glory, as the just Reward of his Obedience.

And thus our Lord, prayed the Father to *glorify* him, upon his having *finished the Work* he gave him to do. *I have glorified thee on Earth: I have finished the Work thou gavest me to do.* Whereupon he proceeds, *And now, Father, glorify thou me with thine own self, with the Glory which I had with thee before the World was,* John 17.4, 5. Having finished the Work of his Humiliation, for the Salvation of Sinners, (in the active part of it, and just entering upon the passive part, with full Resolution to become *obedient unto Death, even the Death of the Cross,* Phil. 2.8. Both which are put into the word finished) and therein fulfilled his own Covenant-engagements; he prays the Father to fulfil this, in glorifying of him, in his humbled Man-nature; by exalting him to his own right Hand, and installing him openly, into all that vast Dignity, he had with him secretly, in the Covenant before the World was.

Our Lord Christ, as I conceive, had all his Mediatorial Glory, originally settled upon his Person, as God-Man, the Head of the Church, by an absolute Grant of the Father's free Love, in the Grace-part of the Covenant, answerable to Upper-fall Designs.

And, Again he had all this Glory given him by Promise as his Due, upon the Account of his worthy Undertaking to become the Saviour of the Body, in the Redemption-part of the Covenant, agreeable to the under-fall Counsels. And in both these Respects our Lord Jesus, had all this Glory with the Father before the World was.

In the *first* Sense, he pray'd for the Communication of it, having finish'd the Work which the Father gave him to do: Inasmuch as infinite Wisdom upon the Account of the Fall, did appoint him to pass through *Sufferings* before he thus *entered into his Glory*, Luke 24.26.

In the *second* Sense, he pray'd for it as the just Reward of his Work.

Christ's vast Inheritance in God, with all those Revenues of Glory, which arise from his being admitted into the highest Glory Communion with JEHOVAH , answerable to his transcendent Union; And also from his universal Dominion over all Creatures, as Head of Nature, Grace, and Glory; were all originally settled upon his Person of mere Grace: And of these Riches the Apostle speaks, *2 Cor.* 8.9. *For ye know the Grace of our Lord Jesus Christ, that though he was rich, yet for your sakes he became poor,* &c. 'Tis evident to me, he here speaks of Christ's Riches, as originally settled upon his Person, as God-Man, Mediator, by the Father's Free Grace; in that he makes 'em antecedent to his Poverty: For as these same Riches were given him as the just Reward of his Obedience, they became not his Due, as such, until he had so obey'd. And as in this *Text* the *Apostle* asserts his Riches before his Poverty: So on the other Hand he declares, that all his glorious Dignity, was given him as the just Reward of his deep Humility. *Wherefore God hath highly exalted him,* &c. Phil. 2.9. *And to him that worketh,* he says, *the Reward is not reckoned of Grace, but of Debt,* Rom. 4.4. Now Christ did really work for Life: And his Reward, as such, take it in the largest Sense, was not of Grace, but of Debt.

And thus I humbly conceive, that *Christ*, the first born Son, the prime Heir, and we the younger Brethren, as joint Heirs with him, shall for ever enjoy God as our everlasting Portion, in the same Way of Interest and Propriety. Our original Right lies in the Father's Gift: Our secondary Right in the Son's Purchase. Our original Title by the Father's Gift, stands in absolute Grace both to *Christ* and us too. Our secondary Title by the Son's

Purchase, stands in Justice to *Christ*, by reason of that valuable Price he paid into the hands of his Father: Ay, and in Justice to us too, inasmuch as the Price was paid upon our Account. Though it was pure Grace that both provided, and accepted of it for us. And so indeed there is a Difference: For *Christ* enjoys the Inheritance in this secondary Title, as his own proper Desert: We only as interested in his Merit: So that in both Respects it is of Grace to us, in the first only to *Christ*.

Our original Title by the Father's Gift, we never lost, nor mar'd by Sin; tho' thereby we laid ourselves under the greatest Impossibilities of enjoying our Portion. But this was our unspeakable Privilege, that we were not left as single Creatures, to stand *alone*, Eccles. 4.10. but being in Relation to *Christ*, when we fell, there was *one to help* us *up:* even our strong Lord *Jesus*, who had before engaged to open a Way for all Grace and Glory, to flow unto us through his own bleeding Wounds: And so fully redeem us to the Enjoyment of our Inheritance, to which we had an indefeasible Right. And to do this also in such a Way, as thereby to make us another Title, for our farther Confirmation and Consolation: That so we might inherit Glory upon a double Right.

And thus he sounds his Intercession-pleas, as our righteous Advocate with the Father. He pleads for our full Deliverance from all Evil, Preservation from all Dangers, and compleat Glorification with himself for ever: First, upon the bottom of Grace, and then of Justice.

Father, says he, *I pray for those thou hast given me*, first as they are [Thine] in Electing, Adopting, and Settlement-Grace: And so I ask but according to thine own Heart, and what in the Riches of thy Grace, thou hast already Provided for 'em; and in the unchangeableness of thy Love, canst not but bestow upon them: *For thou hast loved them as thou hast loved me*, John 17.9, 23. And as I Pray for these as Thine, upon the bottom of thy Free-Love, so again, I pray for 'em as [Mine] both by Gift and Purchase, *ver.* 10. and not only have I a Right to their Persons, but also unto all that Glory which they shall enjoy. And so in strict Justice thou canst not deny my Request for them: For upon this very bottom *I* [*Will*] *Father, that they be with me where I am, to behold my Glory*, ver. 24. And thus he gives *Eternal Life, to as many as the Father gave him*, ver. 2. Having made them *Rich*, (or made a Title, to all the Riches of their vast Inheritance,) by his own *Poverty*, 2 Cor. 8.9. 'Tis in this Sense, That being *justified by Grace, we are made Heirs according to the Hope of eternal Life*, Tit. 3.7.

And by the way, I think that these things, being thus consider'd, may serve in some measure to reconcile the different Opinions of those Persons, who on the one hand assert, That the Saints have their Inheritance by virtue of the Father's Gift of it to 'em in Christ; which they never lost by the Fall; although it was impossible that as Sinners, they should enjoy it, until Christ by his Death had remov'd all Obstacles out of the Way: But they don't think that they have it by Right of Purchase, because their Title by Gift was never lost. And again those other Persons, who on the contrary assert, That the Saints Title to their Inheritance, stands in the Purchase of Christ. For though those that are for Title by Purchase, do generally miss it, in that they apprehend, That Heaven and eternal Glory were contain'd in the Promise of Life by the Law, as it was given out to *Adam:* And so, that all his Posterity did lose it by his Fall: And Christ purchasing it for the Elect, their original Title stands in his Purchase; and in the Father's Gift only as consequent thereupon. In this, indeed, they miss it: And here the first are right, who say, that they did not lose their Title to the Inheritance, by the Father's Gift, when *Adam* fell: Because it was absolutely settled upon 'em in Christ, above the Consideration of the Fall, and never put into *Adam's* Hands. But yet, this hinders not there being a Truth in what the other say, when they assert Title by Purchase, If taken in a right Sense. For I don't see but both are very consistent; if the first Title be plac'd in the Father's Gift, and the second in the Sons of Purchase.

But here, perhaps, some may be ready to start a Question, and ask me, What need there was for this Title by Purchase, if our Title by Gift was never lost?

Which I shall answer, by putting another Question to these Querists: *viz.* What need was there of *Two immutable Things*, God's Oath, and his Word? *Hebrews* 6.18. Was not his Word sufficient of the *Confirmation* and *Consolation of the Heirs of Promise,* Seeing he is a *God that cannot lie?* Tit. 1.2. Yea, surely they can't say but it was. And yet it was the Pleasure of God, not only to pass his great Word, but also to *Swear* by his great *Self,* for this End, as the *Apostle* declares, *that the Heirs of Promise might have strong Consolation,* Heb. 6.13, 18. So say I in this respect: Our first Title by Gift was so firm, as that our Inheritance was eternally secur'd by it: and had it been the Pleasure of God, this [Alone] had been sufficient for our Enjoyment of the same. God might have created us, and at once have taken us up into the Enjoyment of himself, upon this bottom only; and never have suffer'd Sin to enter. But it was the Pleasure of JEHOVAH, to permit the

Fall, 1. To glorify his Grace the more, in giving his Son to die for us: And not only redeem us to the Enjoyment of the Inheritance; but also to make us another Title; that so we might inherit Glory upon a double Right. And as it was for the Glory of the Father, so 2. For the Glory of the Mediator. The Dignity of his Person, as the great High-priest and Sacrifice, the Greatness of his Love and Grace, Power and Faithfulness, resplendently shining forth herein. And 3. It was also for our Advantage: For the corroborating of our first Title, and for the strengthning of our Faith, who are Expectants of this Inheritance, which we shall enjoy through our Lord Jesus Christ, as he is our [Way] in respect of Title.

But having been so large in this first Part of my Answer to that Query, *viz.* Which Way the Sons of God come to the Enjoyment of their Inheritance, I must endeavour Brevity in what remains. To proceed then,

2. Our Lord Christ is the Way in respect of Meetness. That the Sons of God, as consider'd Sinners, might come to the Enjoyment of their Inheritance; there was a Necessity, not only that the Guilt of Sin should be taken off their Persons, but also that the Filth of it should be removed out of their Nature: For they that *Ascend the Hill of God,* and *stand in* his *holy Place*, must have *clean Hands* and *a pure Heart*, Psal. 24. 3, 4. We had indeed, all at once, a mystical cleansing from all Sin, both in the Guilt and Filth of it, upon the great Day of Attonement, when our Lord *put away Sin by the Sacrifice of himself,* Heb. 9.26. and rose from the dead, discharged from all our Debts, and compleatly justify'd in our Name and Room, *Rom.* 4.25. And this mystical cleansing is the Foundation of that personal Cleansing, of which I here intend to speak.

Our Lord declares, that the Blessing of *Seeing*, i.e., enjoying God, belongs to such that are *Pure in Heart*, Mat. 5.8. And no *Unclean* Thing can be admitted into his Glory-Presence, *Rev.* 21.27. For *how can two walk together unless they be agreed?* Amos 3.3. God is *Light*, 1 John 1.5. And an unregenerate Man is *Darkness*, And *what Fellowship hath Light with Darkness?* or what Communion can a holy God have with an unholy Soul? *2 Cor.* 6.14. For though the Guilt of Sin was taken away by the Death of Christ; and so Justice is satisfy'd that we should have our Inheritance; and also oblig'd to give us the Enjoyment of it: Yet still there was a Necessity that the Filth of Sin also, should be taken away by Power, in the Virtue of its being taken away by Price; that so God's Holiness might not oppose our nearest Approaches to him, and Enjoyment of him. And as there was a Necessity, on God's Part, that Sin should be taken out of our Nature, in order to his full Communion with us; so also on our Part, in order to our full Enjoyment of him. For if it was possible, that an unholy Soul could be taken up to the Place of Glory, yet Heaven would be no Heaven to him; not having an holy Principle, he could not enjoy the State of Glory: the Beauties of its flaming Holiness, would rather consume, than delight him.

There being then a Necessity, that all the Heirs of Glory, should first be made *meet* for, before they are made *Partakers of,* their *Inheritance in Light,* Col. 1.12. Our Lord Christ becomes the Way in respect of Meetness: And this as he is our Grace-Head. *For it pleased the Father that in him all Fulness should dwell,* Col. 1.19. that *of his Fulness we might receive, and Grace for Grace,* John 1.16. Christ is *made of God unto us Sanctification,* as well as *Righteousness,* 1 Cor. 1.30. And the Sons of God, in and by Christ, have a two-fold Meetness for their Inheritance.

1. We have a Representative-Meetness in the Person of Christ. Which consists in the inherent Holiness of his Nature being imputed to us, and we look'd upon by an holy God, as perfectly Holy in the shining Glories of our holy Head, *Col.* 1.22. 1 John 4.17. And,

2. We have an Influential-Meetness in our own Persons, by and from Christ. Which consists, 1. In the Communication of an holy Principle from Christ, our holy Root, by his Holy Spirit, in the Work of Regeneration. And, 2. In all those after-Supplies of Grace, which we receive continually from Christ, as our Root of Influence, by the Spirit of Holiness; as he carries on his begun Work, both in Mortification and Vivification; from our Infant State in Grace, until we *grow up unto a perfect Man, to the Measure of the Statrue of the Fulness of Christ*, Eph. 4.13. And then in our Soul-part, we are made perfectly meet for the Inheritance, Christ's Grace-Image, having been compleatly form'd in us, and we, in this respect, wrought into a full Conformity to the Son of God, under the new Creation-Work of the Holy Ghost; Who all along wrought by Rule, while he kept his Eye upon Christ, the glorious Pattern; and drew every Part of the new Creature, in all its Grace-features, exactly according to the beautiful Lineaments which were first drawn in Christ.

Thus Christ is our Way in respect of Meetness, as it concerns our Souls: I should also hint something of his being the Way in this respect, as it regards our Bodies. For Glory being settled upon our whole Man, and the Body to be taken up into a joint Participation of it with the Soul, There is a Necessity, that it should first be fitted for, before it is taken up into Glory.

The Apostle tells us, *that Flesh and Blood cannot inherit the Kingdom of God,* 1 Cor. 15.50. The Meaning of which, I humbly conceive is this, that Flesh and Blood, in its ntural, mortal, and corruptible Estate, cannot inherit Glory: Because, as such, it is no way capable of it. And we being *in* our *Flesh* to *see God*, Job. 19.26. and to dwell in his Presence for ever, in the Glory of the heavenly State: Hence there was a Necessity, that all those impediments should be removed out of the Way, which came in by our being put into a first *Adam*, and permitted to fall in his first Sin: And so to derive our Nature from him, who was the common Stock, or Fountain of it, in all its Weakness, Mortality, and Corruptibility: Which render it incapable to enjoy Glory. *Forasmuch then as the Children were Partakers of Flesh and Blood*, Christ *also himself took part of the same,* being *made like unto his Brethren in all Things*, Sin only excepted: That so he might make them like him, in which their Meetness for Glory consists, *Heb.* 2.14, 17.

The divine Person of the Son of God, took our Nature, in all its sinless Frailties, into personal Union with himself; that so he might exalt it above the Sphere of its own natural Weakness; and free it from all those sinless Infirmities, such as Hunger, Thirst, and Weariness, arising from a Decay of vital Spirits; together with that liableness to Sorrow and Death, which attended it even in its pure State. Nor did our Lord *Christ,* by this Assumption, as he is our *heavenly* Head, 1 Cor. 15.48. free our Nature only, from all those sinless Frailties which attended the Man *Adam*, in his paradisical State, as he was of an earthy Make: But

Further, also, *Christ*, as our great Saviour, in his assumed Nature, has *born our Sins,* 1 Pet. 2.24. was *made a Curse for us,* Gal. 3.13. endured divine Wrath, *Mark* 15.34. and died in our Room, *1 Pet.* 3.18. and by the Merit of his Death, has given us *the Victory* over Death, even as it respects our Bodies, *1 Cor.* 15.57. For though the Bodies of the Saints are still subject to all Kind of Diseases in this Life, Death itself, with Putrefaction and Rottenness in the Grave, and all this in common with others: yet this hinders not but that the Saints [Now] have the Victory over Death, as they stand in *Christ* their conquering Head: Who has already destroyed Death in its Root and Principle, *2 Tim.* 1.10. so that there remains no *curse* in their sharpest Afflictions, *Gal.* 3.13. nor any *sting* in their Death, *1 Cor.* 15.55. Yea, he has already destroyed Death in its very Being, in his own Person, as our great Representative, when he rose from the dead, as a triumphant Conqueror over Death, and *became the first Fruits, of them that sleep,* ver. 20. So that *Christ* being *raised from the Dead, dieth no more, Death hath no more Dominion over him,* Rom. 6.9. No, nor over us as represented in him. For we were all mystically *raised up together with him,* Eph. 2.6. and had a Representative Meetness for Glory, in the Resurrection-Body of *Christ.* And we shall also, e're long, have an influential Meetness in our own Bodies, when by virtue of Union to him, who is *the Resurrection and the Life,* Joh. 11.25. they shall be raised from the Dead, *spiritual, immortal, and incorruptible,* 1 Cor. 15.44, 45. every way *fashioned like unto* Christ's *glorious Body,* Phil. 3.21. And then in our whole Man we shall compleatly *bear the Image of the heavenly,* 1 Cor. 15.49. (which will be a far higher Glory, than the first Man was capable of in his earthly State:) And so shall be made perfectly Meet, for the full Enjoyment of our glorious Inheritance.

And when thus our entire Persons, shall be made perfect in Holiness, without the least Adhesion of a Stain, not so much as the Shadow of a Spot of Sin being left in us: yet even then, this influential Meetness in us, shall be as it were swallowed up in our Representative Meetness in *Christ:* I mean, in respect of its Acceptance with God; while he complacently looks upon our perfect personal Holiness, thro' the spotless Purity, and splendid Holiness of his own Son. Thus the holy Members, in and with their holy Head, shall for ever stand *holy, and without blame before* God *in Love,* Eph. 1.4. or in the Love-Delights of an eternal Glory-Communion with *JEHO-VAH.* Thus *Christ* is our Way, in respect of Meetness. Again,

3. *Christ* is the Way, in which the Sons of God come to enjoy their Inheritance in respect of Communication: *Christ was set up from everlasting,* as the great Mediator between God and all his Creatures, even in *the beginning of his Way, before his Works of Old,* Prov. 8.22, 23, *&c.* When God went forth by his wise Counsels and firm Decrees, into Creature-Converse, *Christ* was then by him, as the great *Medium,* in and thro' whom it was to be held. All divine Communications were first made unto *Christ,* as Head of Nature, Grace, and Glory, and so through him are made unto all Creatures, in their Nature, Grace, and Glory-Relations. The being and well-being of Creatures, are but a Derivation out of his Fulness. *For by him were all things created that are in Heaven, and that are in Earth, visible and invisible, whether they be Thrones, or Dominions, or Principalities, or Powers,* Col. 1.16. And as all things were made by him, so *by him* also *all things do consist,* ver. 17. and are fixedly held together, in all those Enjoyments which their distinct Natures, and different Conditions do admit of. *Christ* is an interposing Mediator between God and all his Creatures: And would have been so if Sin had never entered. The holy Angels in

Heaven, receive all their Glory from God, thro' *Christ*, as the *Medium* of Communication: And stand everlastingly fixed in their high Stations, by virtue of his being their confirming Head. And *Christ* is also an atoning Mediator between God and Elect-Sinners: And in both respects he is the *Medium* of all Glory-Commucations to us. 'Tis *in the Face*, or Person, *of Christ*, 2 Cor. 4.6. that the Saints now see the Glory of the Father: And that Knowledge of God in which *eternal Life*, and the highest Enjoyment of our Inheritance consists, *John* 17.3. will for ever flow unto us in the same Way: For *eternal Life*, both as to the Right and Enjoyment of it, is only *in his Son*, 1 John 5.11.

And it is our unspeakable Privilege, that when advanced to the highest Glory in Heaven, yet, that even then, we shall not be left to stand there alone, to enjoy God in our own single selves; but shall for ever converse with him in *Christ*, our glorious Head. Our *Inheritance in Light*, consists in the highest Enjoyment of God as he is *Light:* And God in his abstracted Essence *dwelleth in that Light* that is inaccessible, and can only be approach'd to in his Son, *1 Tim.* 6.16. God's essential Glory, is a Light too strong for the Creatures weak Sight, to have any immediate converse with: And can only be seen in the human Nature of *Christ*, as the Glass of Representation. 'Twill be a *pleasant Thing* for our Eyes thus *to behold the Sun*, Eccles. 11.7. The Eyes of our glorious Souls, yea, and the strong immortal Eyes of our Bodies too, will be every way fitted to converse with the Light of the Father's Glory, as it will for ever shine, in and thro' the Mediator. The Glory of *JEHOVAH*, will first cast its Rays upon *Christ* our glorious Head, and then thro' him, upon us, as the Members of his Body: All our Light will be but as it were the Reflection of his Glory cast upon us. 1. *In them*, says our Lord, *and thou in me, that they may be made perfect in one*, John 17.23.

Thus *Christ* is the Way in which the Sons of God, come to enjoy their Inheritance, 1. In respect of Title. 2. In respect of Meetness. And 3. In respect of Communication. And in all these respects he is the Way of God's Contrivance and Appointment, to answer all the Ends of his Glory in the Salvation of his Children.

Here all the Divine Attributes are perfectly reconciled: *Mercy and Truth* are *met together, Righteousness and Peace have kissed each other*, Psal. 85.10. Well may Christ's Name be called *Wonderful*, Isa. 9.6. His Person is wonderful in its Constitution, his Offices wonderful in their Design, the Execution of them wonderful in their Effects; which fills Heaven and Earth with joyful Surprize. The holy Angels with intense Desire, *stoop down to look into*, and learn of the Church the manifold Wisdom of God, as it shines forth in the Person and Work of our Great *Immanuel*, 1 Pet. 1.12. and Eph. 3.10. The Saints, both in the upper and the lower Worlds, caught up into an Extasy of joyful Wonder, while they look into this *Mystery* of God *manifest in the flesh*, 1 Tim. 3.16. break forth as in an heavenly Rapture, with a *What hath God wrought!* Numb. 23.23. And when our Lord appears the second time without Sin unto Salvation, he'll come, as to be *glorify'd in his Saints*, so to be *admir'd in all them that believe*, 2 Thes. 1.10. We shall then admire Christ in himself, as having the most compleat Revelation of his Glory: Yea, we shall admire him in our ownselves as being compleatly changed into his Glory-Image: And we shall also admire him in one another, while we look upon the Saints in all their different Glories, as shining forth in the Fulness of his Light; who is the Glory-Sun from whence they receive all their starry Lustre, *1 Cor.* 15.41, 42. and *Rev.* 21.23. And as in the Kingdom-State, so unto the endless Ages of Eternity, we shall admire Christ, both as our Way to the Father, and the Father's Way unto us. Thus having shewn, which Way the Sons of God come to enjoy their Inheritance: I proceed,

Sixthly, To enquire, When they enter upon the Possession of it. In answer to which we may observe,

1. That the Sons of God did enter upon the Possession of their Inheritance in Christ, when he ascended to Heaven as their great Representative. For as the High Priest of old did enter into the holy Place, as the Representative of the People, having *the Names of the twelve Tribes upon* his *Breastplate*, Exod. 28.29. So likewise our great High Priest, the glorious Anti-type of that Figure (when he had *put away Sin by the Sacrifice of himself*, Heb. 6.29. went *with his own Blood into the holy Place*, even *into Heaven itself, having obtain'd eternal Redemption for us*, ver. 12. *that* so *he might receive the Promise of eternal Inheritance* in the Right of his Obedience, *ver.* 15. and he enter'd into Glory, not as a single Person for himself alone, but for us also. For we were all mystically in him, when as our *Forerunner, he for* [*us*] *enter'd*, Heb. 6.20. And as he first took Possession of Glory in our Name and Room, so he still keeps it: for *he* [*now*] *appears in the Presence of God for us*, Ch. 9.24. Hence it is that we are now said, *to sit together in heavenly Places in Christ Jesus*, Eph. 2.6. Again,

2. The Sons of God, in their own Persons, do enter upon the initial Possession of their Inheritance, when the Spirit works Faith in their Hearts, and enables them to lay hold on Christ, and eternal Life in him. Faith views Christ as the Father's *Salvation* for lost Sinners, *Isa.* 49.6. and eternal Life in him: And *fleeing for Refuge to lay hold on this Hope set before it,* Heb. 6.18. takes God at his Word, in *the Record he hath given of his Son. And this is the Record that God hath given to us eternal Life; and this Life is in his Son,* 1 John 5.9, 11. Thus the Soul, by Faith, possesseth the Inheritance, as our Lord witnesseth, *John* 6.47. *Verily, verily, I say unto you, he that believeth on me [hath] everlasting Life.* And to give us this Possession by Faith, is one great End of the Gospel Ministry, As appears by that Commission our Lord gave unto the *Apostle Paul,* when sent unto the Gentiles, *Acts* 26.18. *To open their Eyes, and to turn them from Darkness to Light, and from the Power of Satan unto God, that they may receive Forgiveness of Sins, and Inheritance among them which are sanctify'd by [Faith] that is in me.*

And as the Holy Spirit, at first, gives us a real Possession of our Inheritance by Faith, so also *after that* we *have believed,* he further *Seals us up unto the Day of Redemption,* Eph. 1.13. by which he gives us a more sensible Possession of it. And this he doth as he is the Comforter, by giving us the fullest Assurance of the Inheritance, and sweetest Communion with all the Fulness of God as our own; to the filling us with those unspeakable Joys, which are the First-fruits of Glory. Yea, further,

The Person of the Spirit himself, as the Spirit of Grace and Sanctification, the Spirit of Liberty and Consolation, Light, Life, and Glory, is given unto us as *the earnest of our Inheritance,* Eph. 1.14. Thus the Sons of God do initially enter upon the Possession of their Inheritance, in the Right and Title, first-Fruits and earnest of it. Again,

3. The Sons of God, do enter upon the compleat Possession of their Inheritance, in their Soul-part, as the Time of their Death. This makes 'em have a *desire to depart,* Phil. 1.23. and *willing rather to be absent from the Body,* 2 Cor. 5.8. because that then they are taken up to be *with Christ,* in his immediate Glory-Presence: Which, indeed, is *far better* than all the Enjoyment of him which they had here by Faith.

But tho' *the Spirits of just Men made perfect,* Heb. 12.23. are now put into the compleat Possession of their glorious Inheritance: yet so, as that it is but partial, respecting their Souls only. For their Bodies remain still in the Grave, under the Dominion of Death. So that if we will see 'em in the full

Possession of their Inheritance, we must look further. In the next place then let us observe,

4. That the Time when the Sons of God, in their whole Man, shall enter upon the compleat Possession of their Inheritance, will be at *the Resurrection of the Just*, Luke 14.14. Then their Bodies shall be raised from the Dead, re-united to their Souls, and so their whole intire Persons, taken up into the Enjoyment of that Glory which is prepared for them. And that, 1. In the Glory-Kingdom of *Christ:* And, 2. In the ultimate State of Glory after the last Judgment.

The Sons of God, as the blessed of the Father, shall then *inherit* that *Kingdom* that was *prepared for* them *from the Foundation of the World,* Mat. 25.34. *For when* Christ *who is our Life shall appear, we also shall appear with him in Glory,* Col. 3.4. And *sit with* Christ *in* his *Throne,* Rev. 3.21. And *then the Righteous shall shine forth as the Sun, in the Kingdom of their Father*, Mat. 13.43. *The wise shall* then *inherit Glory,* Prov. 3.35. and they that *overcome inherit all Things,* Rev. 21.7. And so great will be the Glory of this happy Day, that the Saints now, at best, can have but some imperfect Glances of it, while in this distant State: Which yet are sufficient to enable them to *reckon*, with the great *Apostle, That the Sufferings of this present Time, are not worthy to be compared with that Glory which shall then be revealed in us,* Rom. 8.18. It will be a massy *Crown of Righteousness, Life* and *Glory,* that will then be set upon the Saints Heads, *2 Tim.* 4.3. *Jam.* 1.12. *1 Pet.* 5.4.

And though the [Manner] of our possessing Glory in the Kingdom of *Christ*, will be but Temporary: It being to end when the Son *delivers up the Kingdom to the Father,* 1 Cor. 15.24. Yet even this will be but in order that both *Christ* and we, may further enter upon the fullest, and most immediate Possession of GOD himself as our eternal Lot.

The Son will lose no Glory by becoming *subject unto the Father,* 1 Cor. 15.28. as the sole Administrator of all that vast Blessedness, which both he and his shall possess to Eternity: But Glory will rise to much the higher, by how much the more immediate it will be both to *Christ,* and us too; when God in HIMSELF will be [ALL] in all, our Glory to an endless Eternity. But how great this Glory will be, together with the Manner of our possessing it, is yet to be revealed.

When we attempted to view the Sons of God possessing their Inheritance in the Kingdom-State, their Glory is, even there, so bright, that our weak Eyes can't look stedfastly upon it, so as to take in an Idea of it in all its resplendent Rays: But if we further attempt to cast an Eye upon 'em in the ultimate State, their Glory there, is heightened out of our Sight! What I shall further add, is,

In the *Seventh*, and last place, something by way of Reflection. From the Whole, then, Is it so, that the Sons of God have an Inheritance, that this is no less than GOD HIMSELF; that this Portion was early made theirs, freely, absolutely, irreversibly settled upon them, and that they initially now do, and compleatly shall, e're long, enter upon the Possession of it: What manner of Lives then should the Saints live in this World!

How should we admire the Care and Kindness of God our Father, in that he hath not left us *Orphans*, or like fatherless Children, that have none to provide for 'em! *John* 14.18. But *having predestinated us unto the Adoption of Children*, Eph. 1.5. in the same infinite Grace, he hath also made a rich Provision for us; every way answerable to his own Greatness as God, and that Nearness of Relation we stand in to himself! *He is not ashamed to be called our God: for he hath prepared for us a City,* Heb. 11.16.

Again, How should we adore the Greatness of God's Love, that would give us no less for our Portion, than his great SELF! Oh, the immense Depths of JEHOVAH's Grace, that because he could give us no greater, he gave us HIMSELF! Oh, what are we, vile, despicable Worms, that the great God should thus set his Heart upon us, and make over himself to us!

Further, Is GOD HIMSELF, *Our Portion,* Lam. 3.24. While the far greater Part of Mankind have the Creatures for theirs; *their Portion in this Life,* Psal. 17.14. What Reason have we to admire distinguishing Grace! The Lord might have given us a Portion of outward good things, and have sent us away from himself for ever. And how miserable then had our Case been! Let's think upon the unspeakable Misery of those that are *without God in* this *World,* Eph. 2.12. and shall be sent away from him in the next, with a *Depart from [Me] ye cursed, into everlasting Fire, prepared for the Devil and his Angels,* Mat. 25.41. To raise our Admirations of distinguishing Grace: For this might have been our Lot. We were the same *by Nature as others,* Eph. 2.3. nothing but sovereign Grace made the Difference. And while, of *the same Lump, some are made Vessels unto Honour, and others unto Dishonour,* Rom. 9.21. How adorable is Divine Sovereignty! Did God set his Heart upon us, when he passed by others; put us among the Children, when they were left in a State of Alienation: And reserve the Inheritance for us, as *the Children of Promise,* Gal. 4.28. while on the rest he only bestows common Gifts, and sends them away! even as *Abraham gave all that he had to* Isaac: *But unto the Sons of the Concubines he only gave Gifts, and sent 'em away*, Gen 25.5, 6. What Thanks shall we render for this Grace!

Again, Is JEHOVAH, our Portion: Who then can count up our Riches, or tell what vast Stores we have in GOD! Riches, beyond the Comprehension of Men and Angels! *Durable Riches*, Prov. 8.18. *that neither Moth nor Rust can corrupt, nor Thieves break through to steal*, Mat. 6.20. Enough for Time, and enough for Eternity! Yea, though JEHOVAH's Riches have been ever flowing forth to the Supply of thousands of poor, indigent, starving Creatures; yet are they not subject to the least Waste, or Diminution!

Again, Is the LORD our Portion: How is it, dear Saints, that being *the King's Sons*, Heirs of God, and Joint-Heirs with Christ, we are so *lean from Day to Day*, 2 Sam. 13.4. Let's be convinc'd of our Folly in setting our Hearts upon Trifles, *Things which are not*, Prov. 23.5. How oft through Unbelief, do we *forsake the Fountain of Living Waters, and hew out* to ourselves *broken Cisterns that can hold* none, *Jer.* 2.13? Is the LORD HIMSELF, our Portion: Then let us not, in depth of Ingratitude, set our Hearts upon any thing else as such.

Are we in the Enjoyment of Creatures, let us labour to enjoy God in 'em, and glorify him for them: But let us not set our Hearts upon 'em, for *wherein* are they *to be accounted of? Isa.* 2.22. We may have them one Day, and want 'em the next: *Vanity* and Uncertainty, are wrote upon all Creatures, *Eccles.* 12.8.

God's best Children are sometimes stript *naked* of Creature-Enjoyments, *Job* 1.21. And should this be our Case, let us not murmur, and repine at the Hand of our Father. He's but pursuing his own Glory, and our Good, in the most emptying Dispensation. With the deepest Submission and highest Chearfulness, let's bow to divine Sovereignty; and bless our God when he taketh, as well as when he giveth. And surely we have the highest reason to do so, since whatever he takes, he'll never take away [HIMSELF] from us. And in having him, we have ALL. Ay, tho' we were stript naked of every thing else; yet even then, *as having nothing*, in an Eye of Sense, we may, by Faith, *possess all Things* in GOD, *2 Cor.* 6.10.

Again, Is GOD our Portion: We may hence be assured, that we *shall not want any good Thing*, Psal. 34.10. *The LORD liveth, and blessed be our Rock*, Psal. 18.46. And because he liveth ever, we can never want. If Prosperity be good for us, we shall not want this: And if Adversity be good for us, we shall not want that: For having given himself in Covenant to be *our God*, 2 Cor. 6.16. all the divine Perfections stand engaged to do us good. Everlasting Mercy, boundless Grace, abundant Goodness, Almighty Power, are joyntly engaged to supply all our Wants, thro' Time and to Eternity; in that Way and Manner, Degree and Measure, which infinite Wisdom sees blest, for the Glory of JEHOVAH's Name, and our highest Blessedness.

Once more, since JEHOVAH HIMSELF, is the Inheritance of his Children: How should this Engage us to *walk worthy of God unto all pleasing?* Col. 1.10. To an holy, humble, becoming Conversation, Trusting in the Lord for ever, *Isa.* 26.4. rejoycing in him always, *Phil.* 4.4. earnestly expecting that happy Day, when we shall enter upon the compleat Possession of his own great SELF, *Rom.* 8.23. *Rev.* 21.7. glorify him perfectly, and enjoy him fully; which will fill us with inconceivable Blessedness, while our GOD, will be our Glory, Life, Light, and all in all unto Eternity, *Isa.* 60.19. *1 Cor.* 25.28.

Thus according to the Measure of Light received, I have endeavoured to prove, that the Sons of God have an Inheritance, to shew what it is, when it was made theirs, how settled upon them, which way they come to enjoy it, And when they enter upon the Possession of it: And have given some hints by way of Reflection. But nothing less than the full Enjoyment of our Inheritance, can fully acquaint us with these Things: Our Conceptions now are but weak, and our Expressions childish, *1 Cor.* 13.11.

For my own part, I often compare myself unto a Child that begins to learn Letters. It first with difficulty learns one, and then another: And when it has learned the Alphabet, yet still it remains greatly ignorant of its use; and knows not how to put Letters together and make Words. And when a little further advanced in Knowledge, so that it begins to spell here and there a Word; yet still it is at a loss how to put Words together to make Sentences. And when it can do that, yet still it is a great while e're it becomes a Master of Language; and knows how to speak in all the Elegancies of the Tongue it has been Learning. Just thus it is with me. I am taught here one Piece of Truth, and there another: But yet I find but little Skill in putting Letters of Truth together, so as to form intelligible Words out of 'em. And if I now and then make out a few Words, yet still I find much difficulty, in putting Words together into apt Sentences: I mean, in joyning the several Parts of divine Truth together, so as to make out the great Doctrines of the Gospel, in their Order, Beauty, and Consistency, like apt Sentences, in a just Dependence upon each other.

And even those Saints that have made the greatest Proficiency in the School of *Christ*, and are best skilled in the heavenly Tongue, do yet *know but in part*, 1 Cor. 13.9. and are far from expressing heavenly Things in their own *Idiom*, or proper Form of Speech: So that the Perfection of the Language is yet unknown; while it is as it were translated into an earthly Form: Heavenly Glories being described by Earthly. The *Apostle Paul*, indeed, was *caught up into Heaven*, and heard the Language in its pure naked Glory, unclothed of all its earthly Forms: But when he descends into this low Land, he declares, that the Words he had heard, were both *unspeakable* in themselves, and *unlawful to be uttered* in this present State, *2 Cor.* 12.2, 4.

But, it's our unspeakable Mercy, that things will not be always thus with us. For *that which is perfect* shall *come:* And then our imperfect *Knowledge shall be done away. And we shall know, even as also we are known,* 1 Cor. 13.10, 12. Mean while the Sons of God have the highest Cause of unspeakable Joy, in that now, being *Children*, they are *Heirs of God, and Joynt-Heirs with* Christ, *Rom.* 8.17. tho' *it doth not yet appear what* they *shall be*, 1 John 3.2. when they enter upon the full Possession of their *undefiled, incorruptible,* and *unfadeable Inheritance;* which is *reserved in Heaven for* them: Who *are kept by the Power of God, through Faith unto Salvation, that's ready to be revealed in the last Time,* 1 Pet. 1.4, 5.

F I N I S.

THREE

LETTERS

ON

I. The MARKS of a Child of GOD.

II. The SOUL-DISEASES of GOD's Children;
and their SOUL-REMEDIES. And

III.   God's PROHIBITION of his Peoples unbelieving
FEAR; and his great PROMISE given for
the Support of their FAITH, unto their
Time-Joy, and Eternal Glory.

By ONE *who has tasted that the* LORD *is* GRACIOUS.

L O N D O N:

Printed by J. HART, in *Popping's-Court, Fleet-Street:* And
sold by G. KEITH, at the *Bible and Crown,* in *Grace-
church-street;* and J. FULLER, in *Blow-bladder-street,*
near *Cheapside.*

M.DCC.LXI.

[Price Three-Pence.]

THREE
L E T T E R S, *&c.*

L E T T E R I.

The MARKS *of a* CHILD *of* GOD.

Dear Sir,

Y OU ask me to give you some genuine *Marks* of a Child of God. According to my weak Lisping, please to take the following.

 First. A Child of God is one, That hath been conceived by the Divine Law in the Hand of the Spirit, of his *lost* and *undone State*, by Nature and Practice, as a Transgressor of God's Law both in Heart and Ways; and thence, of his extreme Misery as a Law-breaker, as being under its awful Curse now, and in apparent Danger of the Wrath to come; and of his utter Inability to keep its righteous Precepts. Whence he is made to cry out, under a deep Sense of present, and an awful Fear of future Misery, "Wo is me, for I have sinned! Wo is me, for I am undone! What shall I do to be saved?"——Thus a persecuting *Saul*, when a Self-righteous *Pharisee*, was convinced of Sin by the Law, and says of himself, "I had not known Sin, but by the Law. But when the Commandment came, (i.e., in its strict Purity and Spirituality, as extending both to Heart and Life, unto Tho'ts, Words and Actions, in its righteous Precepts; and thus condemning all Sin and Sinners, by its righteous Curse:) Sin revived; (in its Guilt, Filth and Power:) and I died." That is, was fully convinced of my exceeding great Misery as a Law breaker, and of my utter Inability to be a Law-keeper.—This is the first Work of the Spirit of God, as a Spirit of Bondage by the Law, binding Sin upon the Conscience, unto a thorough Conviction of Self-Guiltiness, and Self-Weakness, which passeth upon every Child of God, in order to the Soul's Preparation to receive a free and full Salvation by the Gospel. At least, the regenerating Work of the Holy Ghost, which is instantaneous, and unknown to us, as to the exact Moment, is thus discovered at first, in his he was chosen of God in Christ from Eternity; as it is Conformity to , the First-born Son, of the noble Family, unto which he was of old tinated, and a special End, for which by the Blood of the Lamb, he deemed; as it is the great Design of the Holy Spirit, in his Work on art; and as it is the Soul's Felicity, and hath with his hew Nature, the leasing Congruity. He loves the Law of God, for its innate Excel- its native Purity; and serves it in the Hand of Christ, from a Spirit of ity, for God's Glory, and his own Joy. The Law of God, is written in art; and thence he copies after it in his Life. To please God; is g to a Child of God. To be enabled to do, or to suffer, any Thing for Honour; he accounts his Honour. To walk with God, in every Path ; to a Child of God, is ineffable Felicity! He desires, and follows oliness; not to make him a justifying Righteousness, *that* he hath in ; but that thereby, he might enjoy, and glorify GOD upon the Earth undantly; and as it is his inherent Meetness, for the full Enjoyment, fect Service of him in Heaven, eternally: And can never rest, till he perfect Purity, unto God's highest Glory, and his own full and ing Felicity.——Thus a Child of God, "Delights in the Law of God, inner Man." "Having in him this good Hope thro' Grace, of seeing reafter, as HE is; he purifyeth himself here, even as HE is pure."— ts it his "Reasonable Service, To glorify God, in his Body, and in , which are His." The Business it is, of a Child of God, an Heir of as assisted by Grace, "In the Fear of God, to perfect Holiness." tever be his present Attainments, "He counts not himself to have But follows after, if that he may apprehend *That*, for which he is ded of Christ Jesus:" viz. Perfect Holiness, and Eternal Glory.— hese Ends,

athly. A Child of God is one, That "*Desires* to depart, and to be st:" In his Spirit, at his Body's Dissolution: And that *Loves*, and Christ's Appearance: "Unto his full Salvation. When in his entire the Glory of the First Resurrection, he shall "See CHRIST as HE like him:" In perfect Holiness, unto GOD's eternal Praise, and to Bliss.

Vord, then, A Child of God is one, That hath been convinced by n the Hand of the Spirit, of Sin and Misery, of his lost State by a Heart, Lip, and Life Sinner, and of his Inability to keep the Law ure: That hath had an internal Revelation of Christ by the Spirit, to the Gospel; that from an alluring Sight of Christ, as the All-

enlightening the Mind to discern Sin and Misery, and the Soul's Inability.——For as "We are all the Children of God by Faith in Christ Jesus:" As we thus are bro't into a declarative visible, & pleadable Relation: So, in order unto Faith in Christ, for Life and Righteousness, the Soul must be convinced of Sin & Death, of its Nakedness and Unrighteousness. For, "The Whole need not a Physician, but they that are sick." This therefore is the Soul's Remove, from Nature's sandy Bottom; in order to its being built upon that sure Foundation which God hath laid in *Sion*.

Secondly. A Child of God is one, That hath had an internal Revelation of CHRIST by the Spirit of God, unto Faith in Him, according to the Gospel. Or, He is one that hath seen JESUS, as the only and allsufficient SAVIOUR in his Person & Office, in his Fulness of Grace, and in the Glory of his great Performances, as able and willing to save the chief of Sinners, and in his exceeding Suitableness to the Soul's miserable Case. Whence Christ appears *altogether lovely* in the Soul's View, & is made above all Things desirable, and exceeding *precious* to the Heart.——And thus the Apostle *Paul*, gives us an Account of this Part of the Lord's Work upon his Heart, in making him a Child of God, "It pleased God to reveal his Son in me." And says of all the Lord's Children, "We see JESUS." And this *Seeing of the Son*, by the Eye of Faith, thro' the Spirit's Gospel-Revelation of the SAVIOUR, is absolutely necessary, in order to other concomitant Acts of Faith, which in order of Nature, if not of Time, are consequent upon it, such as Coming to him by Faith's Foot, and Receiving of him by Faith's Hand: Upon all which, the Grant of Sonship, in the written Word, proceeds. And this Order, is making a Child of God, our Lord intimates, "He that seeth the Son, and believeth on him; shall have everlasting Life." A Child of God, then, is one, That from an alluring Sight of Christ, as the All-sufficient, able & willing SAVIOUR of Sinners, comes to him, upon the free Invitations of the Gospel, & ventures his Soul upon him, for a whole Salvation by him: He receives the SAVIOUR, as held forth in the Word of Promise, to be received by the Faith of a miserable, unworthy, vile & guilty, & every way perishing Sinner. He receives CHRIST, in all his glorious Offices, in all his immense Fulness, in all his great Performances, in his Sin-cleansing Blood, & Soul-justifying Righteousness, unto all the Ends of Grace; and all Salvation in and with him, from all Sin and Misery, unto all Holiness, Joy and Glory, present and eternal; & gives up himself to be the Lord's entirely, & to be saved by him in his own Way, unto God's Glory, in his Felicity.— And, "To as many as see Christ, come to him, & receive him, & thus believe on his Name: He gives them Power, Right or Privilege, to become the Sons of God."

Thirdly. A Child of God is one, "That after he hath thus believed in Christ, is, more or less, sensibly *Sealed with the Holy Spirit of Promise:*" Unto a pleasing, Soul-staying Hope, in all Believers, & to a prevailing Persuasion in others, That they are the Children of God.—"Because they are Sons, both by God's immanent, & transient Act of Adoption; He sends forth the Spirit of his Son into their Hearts, crying, Abba, Father!" "They receive not the Spirit of Bondage, again unto Fear; but the Spirit of Adoption; whereby they cry, Abba, Father!" "The Spirit Himself, beareth Witness with their Spirits, That they are the Children of God." And consequently, "That being Children, they are Heirs; Heirs of GOD, and Joint-Heirs with CHRIST. And, having thus received the Spirit of Adoption, to witness their Relation, & to work in them a filial Disposition, their Souls are struck with an Holy Wonder and Admiration, and while in the Faith of their Adoption, they cry, with exulting Joy, unto God's Glory, "Behold what manner of Love, the Father hath bestowed on us; that we should be called, The Sons of GOD!"

Fourthly. A Child of God is one, That from Faith in JESUS, and the Love of GOD, shed abroad in his Heart by the Holy Ghost, in this his great Adopting Act, and in all his Acts & Works of Grace, is drawn out thereby, to *Love the* LORD fervently. To love GOD, in all his Persons, Father, Son & Spirit, for his own infinite Excellency, & All-surpassing Glory; & for all his Love, Grace & Mercy, as display'd by each of the Divine Persons respectively. To love GOD, in all his infinite Persecutions, in his wise Counsels, & firm Decrees, in his precious Word, & wondrous Works, in his righteous Law, & gracious Gospel, in his Cause & Interest, in his Ordinances & Appointments, & in his Saints & Servants; to love all that are begotten of HIM, of all Denominations, chiefly because of their Relation to GOD, & of their bearing his Image upon them; & they shew this their Love to GOD, by keeping his Commandments. All which they approve of as Right; unto every of which they have Respect; & none of which they account Grievous: But judge it their glorious Liberty, to be thus bound unto Duty; and find it their exceeding Joy, when their Hearts are enlarged, to run the Way of God's Commandments; and they esteem it their greatest Misery & Slavery, when they are straitned & fettered by Sin, & thus prevented from pursuing their chosen, desired, & delightful Course, of universal Obedience.—Thus the Faith of the Children of God, is said to "Work by Love." And their Character as such is, "That they love HIM; because he first loved them."

That they "Love GOD, & keep his Commandments." Lord Jesus Christ in Sincerity." That "Loving HIM w him that is begotten of him." And "By this we know, s that we are passed from Death unto Life; because w And, "This is the Love of GOD, that we keep his Con

Fifthly. A Child of God is one, That from Love o hates all Sin, as Sin. Not only for its Soul-destroyin upon a Child of God present Misery, & as every Sin eternal Misery; but chiefly, for its own Deformi Contrariety, to a GOD of infinite Purity, of All–a unbounded Glory! And especially, as it is against a Grace & Mercy! A Child of God, from Love to Go God-dishonouring, a Christ-piercing, & a Spirit-grie this his Hatred of Sin, he prays, watcheth, & strivet Efforts. He proclaims continual War, against this E Peace. He grones, under Sin's Inbeing, under Sin's Prevalence; and thro' forgiving Grace, and renewing Cross, he stands again to his Arms, and lifts up the S against Sin, in all its combined Forces. And so great of God, against Sin, that he desires nothing more, th & can never rest, till its full Extirpation; he rejoyce accounteth that, as a great & essential Part, of his S the Children of God, who have been convinced o have seen Christ, as the only Remedy, unto Faith upon him entirely, who have received the Spirit of their Relation, and to work in them a filial Disposit God, are said to "Hate Evil." While they love & se hate Sin, which is the Breach of the Law, accordin & holy Nature, and yet do those Things which they old, carnal, corrupt Nature: They cry out of this t wretched Man that I am, who shall deliver me Death!" They "Grone, being burdened under Si Prevalency, and after the glorious Liberty of the Purity, full Joy, and eternal Glory: That all that works in their Spirits, unto partial Death, may b swallowed up, of full and endless Glory-Life."

Sixthly. A Child of God is one, That Loves, an for Holiness Sake. As it is the Image of God's Pur enlightening the Mind to discern Sin and Misery, and the Soul's Inability.——For as "We are all the Children of God by Faith in Christ Jesus:" As we thus are bro't into a declarative visible, & pleadable Relation: So, in order unto Faith in Christ, for Life and Righteousness, the Soul must be convinced of Sin & Death, of its Nakedness and Unrighteousness. For, "The Whole need not a Physician, but they that are sick." This therefore is the Soul's Remove, from Nature's sandy Bottom; in order to its being built upon that sure Foundation which God hath laid in *Sion*.

Secondly. A Child of God is one, That hath had an internal Revelation of CHRIST by the Spirit of God, unto Faith in Him, according to the Gospel. Or, He is one that hath seen JESUS, as the only and allsufficient SAVIOUR in his Person & Office, in his Fulness of Grace, and in the Glory of his great Performances, as able and willing to save the chief of Sinners, and in his exceeding Suitableness to the Soul's miserable Case. Whence Christ appears *altogether lovely* in the Soul's View, & is made above all Things desirable, and exceeding *precious* to the Heart.——And thus the Apostle *Paul*, gives us an Account of this Part of the Lord's Work upon his Heart, in making him a Child of God, "It pleased God to reveal his Son in me." And says of all the Lord's Children, "We see JESUS." And this *Seeing of the Son*, by the Eye of Faith, thro' the Spirit's Gospel-Revelation of the SAVIOUR, is absolutely necessary, in order to other concomitant Acts of Faith, which in order of Nature, if not of Time, are consequent upon it, such as Coming to him by Faith's Foot, and Receiving of him by Faith's Hand: Upon all which, the Grant of Sonship, in the written Word, proceeds. And this Order, is making a Child of God, our Lord intimates, "He that seeth the Son, and believeth on him; shall have everlasting Life." A Child of God, then, is one, That from an alluring Sight of Christ, as the All-sufficient, able & willing SAVIOUR of Sinners, comes to him, upon the free Invitations of the Gospel, & ventures his Soul upon him, for a whole Salvation by him: He receives the SAVIOUR, as held forth in the Word of Promise, to be received by the Faith of a miserable, unworthy, vile & guilty, & every way perishing Sinner. He receives CHRIST, in all his glorious Offices, in all his immense Fulness, in all his great Performances, in his Sin-cleansing Blood, & Soul-justifying Righteousness, unto all the Ends of Grace; and all Salvation in and with him, from all Sin and Misery, unto all Holiness, Joy and Glory, present and eternal; & gives up himself to be the Lord's entirely, & to be saved by him in his own Way, unto God's Glory, in his Felicity.—— And, "To as many as see Christ, come to him, & receive him, & thus believe on his Name: He gives them Power, Right or Privilege, to become the Sons of God."

Thirdly. A Child of God is one, "That after he hath thus believed in Christ, is, more or less, sensibly *Sealed with the Holy Spirit of Promise:*" Unto a pleasing, Soul-staying Hope, in all Believers, & to a prevailing Persuasion in others, That they are the Children of God.—"Because they are Sons, both by God's immanent, & transient Act of Adoption; He sends forth the Spirit of his Son into their Hearts, crying, Abba, Father!" "They receive not the Spirit of Bondage, again unto Fear; but the Spirit of Adoption; whereby they cry, Abba, Father!" "The Spirit Himself, beareth Witness with their Spirits, That they are the Children of God." And consequently, "That being Children, they are Heirs; Heirs of GOD, and Joint-Heirs with CHRIST. And, having thus received the Spirit of Adoption, to witness their Relation, & to work in them a filial Disposition, their Souls are struck with an Holy Wonder and Admiration, and while in the Faith of their Adoption, they cry, with exulting Joy, unto God's Glory, "Behold what manner of Love, the Father hath bestowed on us; that we should be called, The Sons of GOD!"

Fourthly. A Child of God is one, That from Faith in JESUS, and the Love of GOD, shed abroad in his Heart by the Holy Ghost, in this his great Adopting Act, and in all his Acts & Works of Grace, is drawn out thereby, to *Love the* LORD fervently. To love GOD, in all his Persons, Father, Son & Spirit, for his own infinite Excellency, & All-surpassing Glory; & for all his Love, Grace & Mercy, as display'd by each of the Divine Persons respectively. To love GOD, in all his infinite Persecutions, in his wise Counsels, & firm Decrees, in his precious Word, & wondrous Works, in his righteous Law, & gracious Gospel, in his Cause & Interest, in his Ordinances & Appointments, & in his Saints & Servants; to love all that are begotten of HIM, of all Denominations, chiefly because of their Relation to GOD, & of their bearing his Image upon them; & they shew this their Love to GOD, by keeping his Commandments. All which they approve of as Right; unto every of which they have Respect; & none of which they account Grievous: But judge it their glorious Liberty, to be thus bound unto Duty; and find it their exceeding Joy, when their Hearts are enlarged, to run the Way of God's Commandments; and they esteem it their greatest Misery & Slavery, when they are straitned & fettered by Sin, & thus prevented from pursuing their chosen, desired, & delightful Course, of universal Obedience.—Thus the Faith of the Children of God, is said to "Work by Love." And their Character as such is, "That they love HIM; because he first loved them."

That they "Love GOD, & keep his Commandments." That they "Love the Lord Jesus Christ in Sincerity." That "Loving HIM which begat; they love him that is begotten of him." And "By this we know, saith the Apostle *John*, that we are passed from Death unto Life; because we love the Brethren." And, "This is the Love of GOD, that we keep his Commandments."

Fifthly. A Child of God is one, That from Love of God, *Hates Sin*; that hates all Sin, as Sin. Not only for its Soul-destroying Nature, as it brings upon a Child of God present Misery, & as every Sin has in it the Desert of eternal Misery; but chiefly, for its own Deformity, as it is an entire Contrariety, to a GOD of infinite Purity, of All–amiable Beauty, & of unbounded Glory! And especially, as it is against a GOD of infinite Love, Grace & Mercy! A Child of God, from Love to God, haves Sin, as it is a God-dishonouring, a Christ-piercing, & a Spirit-grieving Thing. And from this his Hatred of Sin, he prays, watcheth, & striveth against Sin, in all its Efforts. He proclaims continual War, against this Enemy to the Prince of Peace. He grones, under Sin's Inbeing, under Sin's Working, under Sin's Prevalence; and thro' forgiving Grace, and renewing Strength from Christ's Cross, he stands again to his Arms, and lifts up the Standard of Free-Grace, against Sin, in all its combined Forces. And so great is the Hatred of a Child of God, against Sin, that he desires nothing more, than its utter Destruction, & can never rest, till its full Extirpation; he rejoyceth in Hope thereof, and accounteth that, as a great & essential Part, of his Soul's Salvation.—Thus the Children of God, who have been convinced of Sin and Misery, who have seen Christ, as the only Remedy, unto Faith in him, and Soul-Rest upon him entirely, who have received the Spirit of Adoption, to witness their Relation, and to work in them a filial Disposition, by which they love God, are said to "Hate Evil." While they love & serve the Law of God, and hate Sin, which is the Breach of the Law, according to their new, spiritual, & holy Nature, and yet do those Things which they hate, according to their old, carnal, corrupt Nature: They cry out of this their Misery, with an "O wretched Man that I am, who shall deliver me from the Body of this Death!" They "Grone, being burdened under Sin's Being, Working, & Prevalency, and after the glorious Liberty of the Sons of God, in perfect Purity, full Joy, and eternal Glory: That all that Mortality , which now works in their Spirits, unto partial Death, may be perfectly and for ever swallowed up, of full and endless Glory-Life."

Sixthly. A Child of God is one, That Loves, and follows after *Holiness*, for Holiness Sake. As it is the Image of God's Purity, and a great End, unto which he was chosen of God in Christ from Eternity; as it is Conformity to Christ, the First-born Son, of the noble Family, unto which he was of old predestinated, and a special End, for which by the Blood of the Lamb, he was redeemed; as it is the great Design of the Holy Spirit, in his Work on the Heart; and as it is the Soul's Felicity, and hath with his hew Nature, the most pleasing Congruity. He loves the Law of God, for its innate Excellency, its native Purity; and serves it in the Hand of Christ, from a Spirit of Ingenuity, for God's Glory, and his own Joy. The Law of God, is written in his Heart; and thence he copies after it in his Life. To please God; is pleasing to a Child of God. To be enabled to do, or to suffer, any Thing for God's Honour; he accounts his Honour. To walk with God, in every Path of Duty; to a Child of God, is ineffable Felicity! He desires, and follows after Holiness; not to make him a justifying Righteousness, *that* he hath in CHRIST; but that thereby, he might enjoy, and glorify GOD upon the Earth more abundantly; and as it is his inherent Meetness, for the full Enjoyment, and perfect Service of him in Heaven, eternally: And can never rest, till he attains perfect Purity, unto God's highest Glory, and his own full and everlasting Felicity.——Thus a Child of God, "Delights in the Law of God, after the inner Man." "Having in him this good Hope thro' Grace, of seeing Christ hereafter, as HE is; he purifyeth himself here, even as HE is pure."—— He counts it his "Reasonable Service, To glorify God, in his Body, and in his Spirit, which are His." The Business it is, of a Child of God, an Heir of Promise, as assisted by Grace, "In the Fear of God, to perfect Holiness." And whatever be his present Attainments, "He counts not himself to have attained: But follows after, if that he may apprehend *That*, for which he is apprehended of Christ Jesus:" viz. Perfect Holiness, and Eternal Glory.—— And for these Ends,

Seventhly. A Child of God is one, That "*Desires* to depart, and to be with Christ:" In his Spirit, at his Body's Dissolution: And that *Loves*, and *looks* for, Christ's Appearance: "Unto his full Salvation. When in his entire Person, in the Glory of the First Resurrection, he shall "See CHRIST as HE is; and be like him:" In perfect Holiness, unto GOD's eternal Praise, and to his eternal Bliss.

In a Word, then, A Child of God is one, That hath been convinced by the Law in the Hand of the Spirit, of Sin and Misery, of his lost State by Nature, as a Heart, Lip, and Life Sinner, and of his Inability to keep the Law for the Future: That hath had an internal Revelation of Christ by the Spirit, according to the Gospel; that from an alluring Sight of Christ, as the All-sufficient SAVIOUR, comes to him, ventures his Soul upon him, and receives him, for a Whole Salvation by him: That hath received the Spirit of Adoption, to witness his Relation: That from Faith in JESUS, and the Love of GOD, shed abroad in his Heart, is drawn out to love the LORD: That from Love to God, hate Sin: That loves and follows after Holiness, for Holiness' Sake: And that desires to depart, and to be with Christ; and that loves, and looks for his Appearance.

These, Dear Sir, I judge to be the genuine Marks of a Child of God. That they are upon *all* the Children of God, and upon them *only*. And whoever they be, that experience these Things in themselves; they may with the greatest Certainty conclude, "That now they are the Sons of GOD:" Tho' it doth not yet appear what they shall be, who now are advanced to the unspeakable Dignity of this High Relation, when they shall receive the Adoption of the Body; at the Morning of the Resurrection, to their full Salvation, and See, and Appear with CHRIST, in immortal Glory!

But, Sir, If a Child of God, wou'd *try himself*, by these Scripture-Marks, to know if he is indeed of the blessed Family: He must seek to find them in himself, as a *new Creature*, in his new, and holy Nature, according to the Mind of the inner Man, or of his Soul, so far as it is renewed by Grace, and he is enabled to act accordingly. For, From his better Part, and his general Course, altho' he fail in some particular Steps of his Walk, a Child of God, in the Word of God, is thus described. And as in his new Nature, & when he acts accordingly, he must seek to find these Marks upon him, to his Heart's Joy: So likewise, he must seek to find them, just when, and so far as he is under, the Holy Spirit's Influence; and when the Graces of Faith & Love, were, or are in Exercise: And then, so far as the Spirit shines upon his own Work, and witnesseth the Truth thereof to his Spirit; they will be perspicuous.—But if a Child of God, shou'd seek to find these Marks upon him, while he judgeth of himself according to his *old, corrupt Nature*, and when he is drawn aside to act according to the Motions & Prevalence of Sin, either in Heart or Life; when he is not under the Holy Spirit's Influence, nor in the Exercise of Grace; if at such Times of Darkness, he seeks to find these Marks: He will be tempted, from the Want of these, from the Contrary to these, which at those Times he doth sadly experience, to question, if not to conclude, That he is *not* a Child of God, by regenerating & adopting Grace.

And this, Sir, is a Point of great Moment: The Glory of God, & the Faith & Joy of his Children, are much concerned in their seeking to find these Marks in themselves, from their new, & gracious Nature, & at those Times, when they are under the Holy Spirit's Influence, & their Graces are in Exercise. A great Piece of spiritual Wisdom it is, in a Minister of Christ, thus to direct Christians, to seek for these Marks of their being the Children of God, from their proper *Springs*, & at their proper *Times:* And so of Christian Prudence, to seek for Marks of Grace, when they *were*, or *are*, in the Exercise of Grace. Else, a Minister of Christ, will rather wound, than help, the Faith of Christians: And a true Believer, by Unbelief, will enter thro' the Gate of seen & felt Carnality, into an endless Maze, of Doubt & Perplexity, concerning his Spirituality, & so of his being a Child of God truly.—It is sufficient to Prove any one to be such, if he ever *hath* found, or *doth* find in him, these Marks of Grace, when he *was*, or *is*, under Divine Influence, & in the Exercise of Grace: For none but *God's Children*, are ever *thus* wrought upon.——And if a Child of God at Times, is sunk by Corruptions & Temptations into a sad Degree of the Contrary; by which his New Nature is opprest, & the Actings of his Graces at best, are now chiefly, by Grones under Carnality, & faint Desires after greater Spirituality: He may learn thereby, his awful Degeneracy; & ought to be concerned in a Way of Duty, by a diligent Use of all appointed Means, to "Strengthen the Things which remain, (in the Actings of Graces, & Performance of Duties:) that are ready to die:" By which his spiritual Frame will be renewed, his Evidences cleared, & his Soul abundantly comforted.——"The Grace of our Lord Jesus Christ be with your Spirit!" In Him, with all due Respect, I am, Dear Sir,

Your Humble Servant, &c.

L E T T E R II.

The SOUL-DISEASES *of* GOD's *Children; and their* SOUL-REMEDIES.

Reverend and Dear Sir,

WE have cause to lament that this old Guest, or rather this old inhabitant, this troublesome Inmate, this grieving Opposite, *Pride*, abides & works, in humble Souls. And that like the Leprosy, in the Walls of the leprous House, it will abide & fret, until the House be taken down. We have reason to cry out on account of this Sin, & others, even of a whole indwelling Body of Death, *Unclean! Unclean!* And to admire & praise that Grace, which has devised & provided a Way, for the cleansing of our Persons & Services, unto perfect Purity before God, & Acceptance with him, tho' the attoning Sacrifice & perfect Holiness of his crucify'd Son, presented for us before him, by JESUS our Great High Priest upon the Throne. Yea, and to long for that happy Day, when the whole of old *Adam's* Image, as corrupt, shall be destroyed in us, and the holy, glorious Image of the new *Adam*, introduced: Unto personal Purity & ineffable Glory, of absolute Perfection, of endless Duration; to God's eternal Glory by us, & unto our everlasting Joy in HIM.——And mean Time, asking Help of GOD, let us in the Strength of Christ, watch and oppose the Motions of this abominable Sin of Pride, this *spiritual Wickedness*, which attacks us in *High Places*, as being mustered up by the King of it, the *Prince of Darkness*. And whenever it makes its Appearance, Hissing-hot for GOD, let us instantly say, "*Away!* vile Pride: "I am the Lord's, not my Own; a Dependent, not a Sovereign. An Instrument, not an Agent. And shall the *Ax*, exalt itself against *him* that heweth therewith? Or the *Saw*, against *him* that shaketh it? Or the *Staff*, lift up itself, as if was *no Wood? Away!* thou vile Affection: My Feet too long already, have been swift to shed Blood; to wound and pierce my Lord, by Thee! To slay the Life of GOD, the Life of his Glory in Himself and Works! And thus to slay the Life of CHRIST, the Life of his Grace in me! I will henceforth be *Nothing:* And the LORD shall be ALL! *Away!* Thou Hellish Monster, thou shalt not have Dominion over me: I refuse Subjection to thy Sovereignty. I am under the *Prince of Grace and Peace*; and his Subject will I be, in Spite of Thee: *Away, Away!*"——Oh my Brother, let us set ourselves with the greatest Fervour against this Hellish Usurper! This *Christ*, this *God-Excluder!* For we cannot yield in the least Degree, to this vile Iniquity; but we affront and dethrone thereby, Infinite Majesty! Yea, we despise infinite Mercy! We say, "No GOD! No Divine Glory!" We say to CHRIST, *Away! Away!* I have "no Need of THEE! I receive Nothing from THEE! I am under no Obligation to THEE! To SELF I bow down, as an All-Sufficiency! And MYSELF I admire as the most amiable Beauty! In SELF I joy; & to SELF be the Glory!" Oh Horrid Language, of a saved Sinner, to GOD the Saviour! And yet this is the Voice of Pride's Iniquity! And lo, it is against Christ, & God in him, an irreconcileable Enmity! And shall *We*, that are the Favourites of *God's Heart*, of Father, Son & Spirit, yield to it! No:—if there is in Us, the least Spark of Ingenuity, let us resist this Enmity, with the greatest Vehemency!

For so much as we set up Self, in any of its vile Shapes, depend on Self-Fulness, or take Pleasure in Self Performance: Just so much, we pull down CHRIST, to take his Place! And what an egregious Folly is it, That any little Creature, shou'd please itself with its being, of doing *That*, which was wrought in it, & by it, wholly & solely, by the Almighty Energy of its Great Creator! Pride's Iniquity, is Madness of Folly, & the vilest Robbery!—May the God of all Grace, fill us, & clothe us with all Humility: To his Praise, & our Happiness! And when any elating Thought, presents itself to our Minds: Let us ask it, What it aims at, *Christ*, or *Self?* What it proposes, Whether *Self-Pleasure*, in Self-Reflexion; or *Christ's Honour*, to give *Him* the Glory of Salvation? And insisting on an Answer; if we cannot find our Lord there: Let us not give Place to it for a Moment; but instantly & strongly, resist & reject it. And if we are surprised e'er we are aware: As soon as we discern the Enemy, let us rise up in Arms against it presently. For the Lord our GOD goeth before us, in the Triumphs of his Grace towards us, & in his mighty Vengeance against our Enemies, for the Subduction, & Destruction, of this Giant-like Iniquity: To our Joy in Victory, & unto his eternal Glory.

But how, Sir, shall I answer your Letter? Is it fit a little Child, shou'd be a Dictator? I am glad you look to the God of all Grace, for an Answer. And depending upon his All-Sufficience, & promis'd Assistance, in his Fear, & under his Favour, I most humbly attempt, what you request.

And as I rejoyce with you, Dear Sir, for that wondrous Display of Divine Favour, in daily Fellowship with God, Father, Son & Holy Ghost, with which for so long a Time you have been blest: So I mourn with you, for your present Distress, for your Bridegroom's Absence, in which you see your Soul-Diseases, your Weakness, Deadness, Coldness, towards the God of Grace in Christ.—You ask me the Causes, Sir, "Why the Lord speaks not to you by his blessed Spirit & Word, as formerly? Why Reading & Meditation, are not so comforting as they were? And, Why Prayer is begun & ended coldly, & in a very Languid manner?"—And this I suppose you will take for a general Answer: Because the LORD is *gone*, the LORD is not *there*. That is, Not with you, not there, in such a sensible manner, as heretofore, in the Manifestations of his Favour; nor in the Communications of his Light, Life & Heat, as the Sun of Righteousness: To make Divine Ordinances a Mirrour of his Glory, nor a Burning-Glass, to enkindle your Heart instantly.—But you will say, *Why, wherefore* doth the Lord thus hide his Face, & suspend the Influence of his Grace, from me, & others, who are the Children of his Favour?—To which yourself may answer:

I. Because of *Original Sin*. As, If there was no Sin, there wou'd b no Sorrow: No Distance between GOD & his People. And with Respect to the Sin of our Nature, GOD may, & doth hide his Face, & withdraw the Influence of his Grace, from his Dearest Favourites, in a Way of Divine Chastisement. Not that HE is particularly provoked thereby, thus to grieve, the Souls HE loves. But HE may, on Account thereof, withdraw in a Way of Sovereignty: To shew them more fully, their own universal Depravity; that they may confess & bewail it, to his Glory: Their own Nothingness and Vileness; their Need of continual Dependance, upon His All-Sufficience; to endear the more, Christ and His Fulness; and to make them Partakers of His Holiness. Thus the Lord withdrew from, and tried his Servant *Job*.

And when this is the Case, which is attended with the least Guilt we can imagine, as the Cause, of a Suspension of Divine Influence: We ought to humble ourselves before GOD, for our Original Guilt; to flee by Faith afresh to Christ, as the Great Sacrifice; to deprecate Divine Anger; and to intreat the Lord's renewed Favour.—When I say, This Case is attended with the least Guilt: I mean not, That the Sin of our *Nature*, is less than the Sin of our *Practice*. No:—*That* is the Horrid Fountain, from which all the filthy Streams flow. And from that Fountain, that Ocean of Sin in the Heart, it is, that all the Streams of Sin in the Life, receive an additional *Guilt*. But this is my Sense of it: That the Sin of our Nature, is not a Provocation of GOD's Anger, in *particular*. As of *Job*, the Lord said to Satan, "Thou movest me against him, to destroy him without Cause." Not without Cause, from his *Original Sin*; but without Cause, from any particular *Sin of Life*, that shou'd incurr Divine Displeasure.—GOD's Anger, towards his sinful People, is Fatherly: It flows from, and ends in Love. He loves their Persons, tho' He is displeased with their Sins. And from his Love to their Persons, He will display his Anger against their Sins, as a Chastisement for their Guilt, for the Manifestation, & Mortification of Corruption. And thus He may, & doth at Times, display his Anger, against the Sin of their Nature.—And indeed, *Job's* Chastisement, tho' it appeared to him, to be in wrathful Anger; was rather a Cast for him, of infinite Favour. To humble him more deeply for all Iniquity; to give him an Opportunity of Trust in GOD, When HE appeared to slay him; of being a bright Example of Patience, unto all tried Believers; & thus to prepare him for the Double, of GOD's manifestative Favours. Which gracious Designs of his Trial, were happily & visibly answered at the End of it. And yet, with respect to Original Sin, *Job's* Affliction, might be styled a *Chastisement*.——But,

II. GOD may, & doth hide his Face, & withdraw the Influence of his Grace, from the Favourites of his Heart, as a Chastisement for *actual Sin*, in Heart & Life, and especially for the Sin of Unbelief. According to that Proviso in the Covenant. "If his Children forsake my Law, & walk not in my Judgments; If they break my Statutes, & keep not my Commandments: Then will I visit their Transgression with the Rod, & their Iniquity with Stripes." And, "I will go, & return unto my Place, until they acknowledge their Offence,& seek my Face."

And when this is the Case, the Lord usually by the *Chastisement*, points as with a Finger, to the *Sin* which was the Cause of it. And tho' at first, the Soul may be in a great Measure insensible; the Lord will contend, until by his Blessing upon the Rod, HE has bro't it to a due Sense of its Evil; a true Humiliation for it, & a Disposition to forsake it.——And when thus the Lord's Dear Children, thro' the Subtilty of Sin, the Malice of Satan, & the Snare of this World, have lost their GOD; as to the Soul-rejoycing, and Heart-quickning Influence of his manifested Love: They are called to humble themselves before him most deeply; to confess & bewail their Iniquity; to wash by Faith in the Blood of Christ, that Fountain set open for Sin & for Uncleanness; to intreat their Father's Forgiving Grace, & the renewed Smiles of his glorious Face.

It were endless to enumerate particular Sins, which provoke the Lord to hide his Face, and to withdraw the Influence of his Grace, from his special Favourites. But these are some of the Sins which displease him: 1. The Sin of Unbelief; that Root of all Evil. 2. Insensibility of Divine Mercy. 3. A Walk unworthy, of a GOD of infinite Bounty; in not Rendring to the LORD, his due Glory, according to the Greatness of his bestowed Mercy. 4. Heart-backsliding from GOD, to the Creatures: Or, *Forsaking the Fountain of living Waters; & hewing out broken Cisterns, that can hold no Water.* 5. The Want of maintaining a strict Watch against Sin, in all its various Motions, & a vigorous Resistance of the Enemy's Incursions. 6. The Neglect of a becoming Observance, of the lesser Withdraws, of GOD's quickning Presence. 7. Sloth and Indolence, when call'd by Absence, to seek the LORD with Diligence. And on the other Hand, 8. The Neglect of a Life of pure Faith on Christ, according to his Word, when highly favoured with the Enjoyment of GOD, unto the vigorous Exercise of other Graces: Or the Sinking insensibly, into spiritual Idolatry, into Idolizing of our own Graces, into Self-Dependance, Self-Evidence, or Self-Praise.

And when this last is our Guilt: As a proper Chastisement, for our Amendment; The LORD hides his Face, and withdraws the Influence of his Grace: To shew us more fully, the Sin of Self-Idolatry; to wean us from an inordinate Addiction, to a Life of spiritual Sense, and to insure us to a Life of Faith on Christ.——At first Conversion, and while GOD eminently shines upon his Dear Children, they are apt to live too much by *spiritual Sense*. As to taking up their Faith of Interest in Christ, principally, from the Secondary Evidence, of *their Graces*; rather, than from the prime Evidence thereof, *The Faithfulness of* GOD, in his *Promise-Word*; which secures and declares, to every Soul that believes in JESUS, upon its first Act of Faith, an entire and eternal Interest in HIM, unto a full & everlasting Salvation by him. And while they thus live by Sense; they can *believe*, no longer than they *see*.——Again, a culpable Life of *Sense*, is, Trusting in our *inherent Beauty*, and going forth in Duty, as it were, in *Self-Sufficiency*; and in *Idolizing* GOD's *fair Jewels, our given Graces*.——When this therefore is the Case with GOD's Favourites: He *stretcheth out his Hand over them,* and *diminisheth their ordinary Food*; and gives them up, as it were, for a Time, into the *Hand of them that have them:* Who *strip them of their Clothes, take away their fair Jewels, & leave them naked & bare.*—And thus HE prevents their playing th Harlot, as before. HE *remembers for them his Covenant,* and speaks kindly to them; and thereby causeth them to *remember their evil Ways, & to open their Mouth no more,* in Self-Praise, or a Conceit of Self-Worthiness, *because of their Shame, when* HE *is pacify'd towards them, for all that they have done.*—And when *Self,* spiritual Self, is *abased:* The LORD alone is *exalted:* As their "Wisdom & Righteousness, & Sanctification, & Redemption." The Lord taketh them by the *Arms,* & teacheth them to *go:* In the Way of *Faith,* without the Props of spiritual Sense, on which they had used to lean. And his Dealing with them herein, appears so strange to them, that they know not what HE is doing with them: They *know not,* That HE *heals them:* They think it strange, That they must not be always dandled upon the Knee, & laid to the Breasts. But, "Whom shall HE teach Knowledge? (The Knowledge of Themselves, in their own Nothingness & Vileness?) And whom shall HE make to understand Doctrine? (The Doctrine of Christ's perfect Righteousness, unto their mystical Completeness; & of His All-Fulness, for the rich Supply of their Emptiness; & of GOD's Faithfulness to his Promise, notwithstanding their Unworthiness?)

Them that are *weaned from the Milk, & drawn from the Breast.*" Of sensible Enjoyments; with Respect to taking up their *Faith of Interest in Christ,* principally from *thence.* Not but that the Children of GOD, in their purest Life of Faith, shou'd earnestly long for, & seek after, the ineffable Sweets, & great Advantages of spiritual *Sense*; as their *Secondary Evidence,* of Interest in Christ, & an *additional Fitness,* for Divine Service: And when These are *superadded* to Faith; such Believers possess the *Double* of Divine Favour. But, weaned, Believers ought to be, from the Sweets of spiritual Sense, as their *prime Evidence,* & as that, without which, they cannot *believe* their Interest in Christ, & Acceptance with GOD.—And when the Dear Children of GOD, are thus *weaned:* HE will make them a *Feast.* When they have wearied themselves in vain, to find Rest in Themselves: HE will point the Eye of their Faith to CHRIST, by his Word & Spirit, & to the faithful Promise of his Free Grace in HIM; yea, will take them by the Hand, & lead them to HIM, & say, "This is the Rest, & This is the Refreshing, wherewith the Weary may be caused to rest!" And thus the Life which they live in the Flesh, shall be more eminently, a *Life of Faith* on the SON of GOD. Who loved them, and gave Himself for them; who loveth them, and gives Himself to them, in all his Fulness, of Righteousness & Strength. For whatever the Lord doth with his Children; HE is always bringing them on, *From Faith to Faith.* From believing *upon* Sight, unto Believing *without* Sight: Which, with Respect to his Glory, & their solid Joy, hath a peculiar *Blessedness* attending it.—And when stript of spiritual Sense, to convince them thoroughly of Self-Nothingness, & Self-Insufficience, for Divine Service: The Lord thereby, prevents their *Self-Idolatry,* in Self-Dependance, & Self-Praise; & allures their Hearts to HIM, & into a greater Adoration of, & a stricter Adherence to, *His Infinite All-Sufficiency.* And thus secures to HIMSELF the *entire Glory:* Which, to Them, is an Advance of *their Felicity.*

Thus, The Cause of GOD's Hiding his Face, & suspending the Influence of his Grace, from His Favourites: Are their *Sins,* Original, & Actual, of Nature & Practice. And this his Fatherly Anger, in the Chastisement of their Guilt, as it flows from his Infinite Favour, doth & shall work for their Good. Tho' HE sees it meet, during the Season of Chastisement, That they should be *in Heaviness, tho' manifold Temptations,* from within & without, and especially from the Sight and Feeling of, their Weakness, Deadness, Darkness, & Coldness.

But, You ask me, Sir, "To point out the *Cause* of these *Diseases.*"— And in General, I wou'd answer:

I. That the proper *Cause*, of every *Soul-Disease:* Is the *Universal Disorder,* of our *whole Nature.* "The whole Head is sick, and the whole Heart faint. From the Sole of the Foot, even unto the Crown of the Head, there is no Soundness in us: And therefore Wounds & Bruises, and putrifying Sores are upon us:" All manner of Soul-Diseases attend us.—And

II. As from our general Disorder: So from the Neglect of every Disease in particular, as to a proper Application of Remedies for its Cure: That Disease is increased upon us, that Malady, is strengthned by us.

And these Soul-Diseases, which we have bro't, and bring upon Ourselves: must be discovered, in order to their being cured. And as Soul-Malady, affects us with great Stupidity, and frequently prevails insensibly: The Lord our Father, the Lord our Physician, who is displeased with our Sins, as they are great Offences to his Infinite Majesty; from his tender Mercy, and kind Sympathy with us under them, as they are our Miseries: Is pleas'd to hide his Face, and to suspend the Influence of his Grace: In order to bring us to a due Sense, of our native Weakness, Deadness, Darkness and Coldness: For these are not so sensibly known, when He affords his strengthening, quickning, illuminating and comforting Presence.—As in Nature, When the Sun goes down, Night comes on; when Light and Heat depart, Darkness and Coldness, is seen and felt: So, When the illuminating, warming Beams, of the Sun of Righteousness are gone; a Night of Darkness and Coldness, upon the Soul, comes on.——And tho', as in Nature, The Sun's Withdraw from the Earth; is not the *positive*, but only the *privative* Cause, of that Darkness and Coldness, which is after seen and felt: Nor in Grace, is The Lord's Withdraw of his sensible Presence from his Saints, the *positive*, tho' it may be styled the privative Cause, of that Darkness and Coldness, which succeeding, as their Soul-Griefs and Diseases, fill them with sad Complaints: Yet, As, if the Earth, was not to be deprived of the Sun: Darkness and Coldness, wou'd not be so sensibly known: So, Nor wou'd the Souls of the Saints, be so sensible of these their Diseases, if they were not at Times deprived of GOD's enlightening, comforting Presence. And the more sensible we are of *Soul-Diseases*; the more welcome will be that *Physician*, whose Name is, "The LORD which healeth us." Darkness and Coldness, are *natural* to the Earth and Air, without the Sun's Presence: And Darkness and Coldness, are *natural* to the Soul and Spirit of a sinful Man, without the Presence of the GOD of all Grace. But as Darkness and Coldness, are not so sensibly *known* by us, till GOD withdraws from us: He is pleased to hide his Face, and suspend the illuminating, and comforting

Influence of his Grace: That by his gracious Teaching with, and his Blessing upon the Chastisement; He might bring us to that due Sense of our Guilt and Misery, of our Iniquities and Soul Maladies, which must be previous, unto Soul-Healing. For the *Whole*, need not a *Physician*; but they that are sick.

Thus, Sir, Having pointed out the *Causes*, of GOD's Hiding his Face, and suspending the Influence of his Grace, from His Favourites: Which are, *Our Sins*; Original, and Actual Sin. The Causes of our Soul-Diseases: Which are, Our *universal Disorder of Nature*; with our *Neglect* of those Remedies which are *proper*, for the Cure of our Diseases in *Particular*. And the Causes of our being bro't to that due Sense of our Maladies, which is requisite, in order to our Healing: Which, as specify'd, are, GOD's *Hiding his Face*, and *withdrawing the Influence of Grace*; as a Chastisement, with His Blessing upon it.——I should next attempt a short Answer, to what You ask me, about *Soul-Remedies:* "To direct to proper Remedies."—— And these are, as I humbly think, of Two Sorts. As, 1. *Effectual*. And 2. *Instrumental*.

I. Effectual Remedies for Soul-Diseases, are Those which respect *Divine Bounty*.—The *Grace of God the Father:* Which doth & will reign thro' Righteousness, unto our Salvation from all Sin and Death, & unto our spiritual & eternal Life, by Jesus Christ our Lord.—The *Grace of God the Son:* Who, having satisfied Divine Justice for our Offences, and bro't in for us an everlasting Righteousness, hath a Fulness of Grace treasured up on HIM, to be communicated to us; which from the Grace of his Heart, thro' the Grace of his Hand, shall descend upon us. Grace to forgive, & subdue every Iniquity, to heal our every Malady, & to raise us up from all Sin & Death, unto Purity, Life & Glory, initial, partial, & increasing Here; & complete, total, & undeclining Hereafter.—And the *Grace of God the Holy Ghost:* Who; as he is one in Essence, Will & Grace, with the Father & Son, & as he is the great Applier of Salvation, "Having begun this good Work in us, will perform it until the Day of Jesus Christ." Sick Believers, for a full & glorious Cure, are under the gracious Care, of the *Three-One* GOD. And they may & ought by Faith & Prayer, "To cast their Care, even all their Care, for a Soul-Cure, upon HIM that careth for them:" Who is & will be, "The LORD that healeth them."—And these effectual Remedies for Soul-Diseases, which respect Divine Bounty; are to be convey'd according to Divine Appointment, by & thro',

II. Instrumental Remedies, which regard *our Duty*. And tho' as to these, I have in part prevented myself: Yet under this Head, I may place some of them in Order. And they are such as, 1. Self-Examination: Wherefore the Lord contendeth with us? "Let us search & try our Ways; & turn again unto the LORD." 2. Confession of Sin, with a sincere Desire & Endeavour to forsake every evil Way. And this Confession is to be made in a fresh Exercise of Faith, in the infinite Merit of Christ's Blood, & in the infinite Mercy of God's Heart. By laying the Hand of Faith, upon the Head of the great attoning Sacrifice; as accepting of the sacrificed Lamb, as God's provided Remedy, for our great Misery; & as presenting a crucify'd Christ unto God, as the only & all-sufficient Attonement for our Guilt. And here confessing Sin freely, & bewailing it bitterly, to intreat Divine Mercy, in the Forgiveness & Subdual of all Iniquity, in the Removal of God's Anger, & in the Return of his Favour. For, "He that confesseth & forsaketh his Sin; shall find Mercy." And, "If we confess our Sins unto God: He is faithful & just to forgive us our Sins, & to cleanse us from all Unrighteousness." 3. Deep Humiliation, under such a trying Dispensation. "Humble yourselves in the Sight of the Lord; and HE shall lift you up." 4. Earnest Supplication, as having the Promise of Salvation. "Ask, and ye shall receive: Seek, and ye shall find: Knock, and it shall be opened." 5. Believing, patient Expectation. "I will wait for the God of my Salvation; my God will hear me." And, "Call upon ME in the Day of Trouble; I will deliver thee, and thou shalt glorify ME." 6. Reading and Meditation. For, "Blessed is the Man whose Delight is in the Law of the LORD, and that meditates therein Day & Night. He shall be like a Tree that is planted by the Rivers of Water, that bringeth forth his Fruit in his Season; his Leaf also shall not wither, & whatsoever he doth shall prosper." And above all, 7. Soul-Trust in the God of our Salvation; even in, & under the darkest Dispensations. For, "Who is among you that feareth the LORD, and obeyeth the Voice of his Servant, that walketh in Darkness, and hath no Light? Let him trust in the Name of the LORD, (In the LORD, the LORD *God, merciful & gracious,* &c who as such will deliver him out of his Distress, & bless his benighted Soul, with the fresh Shinings of the Sun of Righteousness:) and stay (when by inward & outward Temptations, he is just ready to be driven away from his Confidence in God; then let him stay,) upon his God." Let him rely upon that Almighty, All-sufficient GOD, who is *His God* still, tho' he hides his Face; and who will as such, in his infinite Grace & Faithfulness, again "bring him forth to the Light, and cause him to behold his Righteousness."

These, Sir, are some of the *Duties*, which God hath appointed, as proper instrumental Remedies, for our Soul-Diseases. And in a conscientious Performance thereof; those effectual Remedies, of God's free, rich, sovereign *Grace in Christ*, thro' the Almighty Energy of the Holy Ghost, shall most certainly, in the Lord's Time and Way, be ministred to us, and take place upon us, for the seasonable and sufficient *Relief* of our Soul-Maladies, and the *Restoration* of double spiritual Joys: To our unspeakable Bliss; and JEHOVAH's present & eternal Praise.

And tho' when God hid his Face, and suspends the Influence of his Grace; we cannot perform these Duties with a wish'd-for Fervency: Yet let us make Conscience of their Performance, as Means of Grace, with a Hoped-for Success, frequently and continually. For Nothing, Oh, Nothing like *This*, is so dishonourable and provoking to the Lord, and so dangerous and destructive unto us, as *carnal Ease & Carelessness*, when GOD *is at a Distance!* If we can't perform Duty as we would; let us do it as we can. And GOD, who knoweth our Frame, will pity our Weakness, pardon our Sinfulness, and accept thro' Christ our imperfect Service, and bless us with more Grace, for better Performance: Until, in the Infinity of his Mercy, HE returns again to deliver us gloriously; and to turn our Winter-Graces, and Seeds-Time Services, into a renewed Spring of Joy and Praise, and Summer-Fruits, of weighty Sheaves. If we *cannot* be content without GOD: We *shall not* be without him. If we seek HIM; HE will be found of us; and richly crown our Diligence, with a double Blessing, by his returning, gracious, quickening and comforting Presence. Yea, He will crown our Duty, with immortal Glory!

And to quicken our Diligence in Duty: Let us cast an Eye on our exceeding great Privilege, in *Christ's Advocacy*. With what cheerful Hope, & holy, humble Boldness, may *we* seek GOD *below*; while JESUS our great High Priest, pleads with Him for us, *above!* We Sin continually, & provoke the God of Glory: But JESUS with his *own Blood*, his All–attoning, Peace-making, & Grace-deserving Blood, for our Delivery, is entered into Heaven itself; *Now to appear in the Presence of God for us. Now, now, now,* we sin, as fast as Moments spring & fly: But JESUS for us, *now, now, now,* an inceasant perpetual Now, appears and presents before his Father's Face, his All-attoning, & Grace-procuring Sacrifice! " If any Man sin; we have an Advocate with the Father: Jesus Christ the Righteous." An *Advocate:* That for the Forgiveness of our Guilt, and the Multiplication of all Grace & Peace, unto our spiritual and eternal Life; pleads the infinite Merit of his own Death! A *righteous* Advocate, *The Righteous:* That is perfectly, infinitely Righteous, in his Person, & in his active & passive Obedience: which he pleads with God for us, who in ourselves are *unrighteous:* To our full Acquitance from all Law-charges, and from Satan's Accusations, and unto all Grace-Prevalence! We have an Advocate, whose Name is JESUS, a SAVIOUR, who is *mighty to save!* Able & willing, to save us to the *uttermost!* And whose Name is CHRIST, the *Anointed Saviour!* As for the whole Work of Salvation in general; so for the whole of Application of God's great Salvation, by and thro' this his Office-work, as *Advocate*, in particular. In which, as He *ever lives*, to plead and intercede, He is *able* to save. HE hath an infinite Ability of *Power*, Essential, and Authoritative, as God, and as the Mediator between God and us; an infinite Ability of *Merit*; and an infinite Ability of *Interest:* To save them to the *uttermost*, that *come unto* GOD *by* HIM! For He is an Intercessor, an Advocate, with *The Father!* With *his* Father; who can deny his *Son*, nothing that he asks: Who hath set him down at his own Right Hand, and bid him Ask, and hath promised to Give him, to the uttermost. We have an Advocate with *our* Father; who *Himself* loveth us. Who hath appointed and anointed his own Son, the Son of his Nature and Love, the Darling of his Heart: To be our Advocate. On purpose that he might communicate unto us, all the Fruits of his Love & Grace, in such a Way, thro' Christ's Advocacy, as is consistent with the Honour of *Jehovah's* Persecutions, with Infinite Majesty! With the whole of Divine Glory!

If then, in case of Sin, we have an Advocate; a righteous Advocate; an Advocate with the Father, with his and our Father; who, as our Jesus, is Christ, the Anointed of God, to save us by this his Office of Advocacy; if we have an Advocate, who hath such an infinite Greatness of Might, of Merit, and of Interest: Let us put our *Cause*, into our Great *Advocate's Hands:* And it shall succeed *well:* To GOD's Glory, and our Joy! HE will bring us off clear from Guilt, with Honour in open Court; and carry the Point for us, as to the Continuance, & renewed Displays of Divine Favour: Because by pleading & interceding, HE liveth for us, for Ever! And lo, we need not draw back from HIM, in our worst of Cases: For his Heart is made of Tenderness! And to the Grace of his Office, and Promise, HE is of Infinite Faithfulness! HE is faithful to GOD, and faithful to *us*; as an appointed, and employed Advocate.—Let us go on therefore, in the Way of Duty, with all humble & earnest Expectance of Divine Mercy; while Jesus Christ the Righteous, our Advocate with the Father, pleads prevalently, for the fullest Acquitance, and highest Acceptance, of our Persons and Services, before a GOD of infinite Purity, who delights in the native Displays of infinite Bounty: thro' his beloved Son, the Great Advocate of the Church; who for *our Sins*, is the *Propitiation!*—And by the Way, How much Work, hath our Lord to do, & doth HE do in Heaven continually, in Grace Unknown, for the whole Church, & for every of its Members, by his Advocacy!

What means my Reverend Brother, by saying, upon his performing Duty in a languid Manner, " Insomuch, that I can scarcely know myself?" Is he at a Loss to know, from the Weakness of his Faith and Love, if he is indeed a true Believer? Or hath in him, that Faith in Christ, which works by Love to God?—If so: This is to be known by former Acts of Faith, when in Love to Christ, he first ventured his Soul upon HIM, for all Salvation by him. Or if former Acts are vailed, by present Darkness, or present Acts, in their Liveliness suspended: This is to b known, if any Person is a true Believer, by the present Disposition of his Heart, towards Faith's Object. For, whoever he be, that sees himself to be utterly undone by Sin, devoid of all justifying Righteousness of his own, and without inherent Power for sanctifying Grace, to his present & future Bliss: That sees the Christ of God, as all-sufficient & willing to save; that sees a Suitableness in Christ, in all his Offices, in his Person, Blood and Righteousness, and in all his Grace-Fulness, to his own miserable Case: And that approves of, desires to be saved by, and looks to, the great & only SAVIOUR, *That Man*, is a *true Believer in the Son of God*, and hath *that Faith in Him*, which *works by Love*. "He hath the Son; and eternal *Life* in HIM:" In the *Right* of it now, and in Begun-Possession; and shall have most assuredly, its full Completion, that glorious Reversion, to a blest Eternity! However he may at present, want the *Joy* of it, in the Comforts of the Holy Spirit. And he should not, for want of Summer-Fruits, in a Winter-Season, think, or fear himself to be, a Lifeless, barren Tree. But abide in Christ by Faith, & wait for the Joy of Sense, till the next Spring of Divine Favour; which will certainly appear at its appointed Season, and new-robe his Heart and Life, with a fresh Greenness & Fruitfulness: To his desired Bliss, under the glorious Return of the Sun of Righteousness.

It was well, Dear Sir, That you put an IF, "IF the Lord cou'd change his Purpose, Grace & Love: I might justly fear, That he wou'd give me up totally & finally, to pursue the Ways of Sin & Ruin." For this IF, barrs a Hesitation, not to say a Conclusion, that is most inconsistent with, &

dishonourable to, the GOD of your Salvation.—No:—Sir, The LORD your God, is, "The Lord that changeth not:" And therefore you are not, shall not be consumed. The Love of God's Heart, is *Eternal*. Infinitely free and great, sovereign and immutable. His *Covenant*, in which he hath engaged to be your God, is *Everlasting. Well-ordered* in all Things, to pity, & bear with you under, and to relieve and save you from, all your Sins & Weaknesses, and to supply you with all Grace, unto all Joy & Glory: And lo, It is inviolably *sure*. The Word and Oath, of a GOD that *cannot lie*, wherein it is *impossible for* GOD *to lie*, are given therein, for your *strong Consolation.*— Your Lord's Redemption, obtained for you, by his meritorious Death, is *Eternal.*—And the Gift of the Holy Ghost, as the Spirit of Sanctification & Consolation, as the Earnest of your Inheritance; is a Gift of God thro' Christ, that is absolutely *without Repentance.* GOD the Father, will *rest* in *his Love* towards you, notwithstanding all your Unloveliness. GOD the Son, will *rest* in *his Love* toward you, notwithstanding you evilly requit him, for all his Grace. And GOD the Spirit, and never quit his Residence within you, nor forsake his Work of Grace upon you, tho' you grieve HIM daily, grieve him by Unbelief greatly, and grieve him by the Motions of Sin, in your corrupt Nature, which are too often yielded to, and which are directly contrary, to his Holy Person & Work, continually. Your Three-One GOD, in Mercy, Love & Grace, boundless, has said concerning you, "Here will I dwell *for Ever*; for I have desired it." Yea, The Lord your God, will *rejoyce over you with Joy:* With exulting Joy: With *Singing:* As if you was the most lovely One; the most amiable, excellent, a chief Treasure. And indeed, all *This*, hath God's Free Grace, made you in Christ. You are made *accepted*, you are graced, in GOD's *Beloved:* In the Father's *First-born Son.* "Of HIM are you in Christ Jesus; who of GOD is made unto you, *Wisdom*, to answer and cure, all your Folly: *Righteousness*, to cover all your Nakedness: *Sanctification*, to present you Holy, before infinite Purity, & to make you personally Holy, initially, increasingly and perfectly, and to keep you Holy, to an endless Eternity: And *Redemption*, to Rescue, in the virtue of Ransom, your enslaved Soul and Body, from every Kind and Degree of Thraldom and Misery." And made a Child, a Son, and Heir of GOD thro' Christ, yea, a *Joint-Heir with* CHRIST, of the GOD of all Grace, of the GOD of Glory: Is it possible now, think you, That you should be an *Outcast* from Divine Favour? No:—Loved with the same Love, for Kind, wherewith the Father loved his Son, as a Member of that glorious Head; GOD's Love towards you in Christ, must run on, and flow down, upon you thro' HIM, in its Time-Displays, and Eternal Glories, unto Endless Ages!

And even in the worst Case, that an Object of GOD's Love, can be in, when he provokes his heavenly Father most, to give him up to Ruin for Sin: When it comes to *That*; what is the Language of God's Heart and Mouth concerning him? "How shall I give *Thee* up, *Ephraim?* How shall I deliver *Thee, Israel?* How shall I make *Thee* as *Admah?* How shall I set *Thee* as *Zeboim?* Mine Heart is turned within me; my Repentings are kindled together. I will not execute the Fierceness of mine Anger; I will not return to destroy *Ephraim*; for I am GOD, and not Man, the Holy ONE in the midst of Thee, and I will not enter into the City."—Oh, Dear Sir, This great Grace, this superabounding Grace, should make our backsliding Souls, return speedily to our Father's Arms, to our Bridegroom's Embraces, to confess and bewail all our Iniquities: Who say, "Only acknowledge thine Iniquity, that thou hast scattered thy Ways unto the Strangers, and ye have not obeyed my Voice: Return ye backsliding Children: And I will not cause mine Anger to fall upon you: For I am merciful, for I am married unto you, saith the LORD."—*Great Grace be with you!* With all affectionate Esteem, I am, Reverend Sir,

Your most Humble Servant, &c.

L E T T E R   III.

GOD's PROHIBITION *of his People's Unbelieving* FEAR; *and his great Promise given for the Support of their* FAITH, *unto their Time Joy, and Eternal Glory.*

Dear Sir,

YOURS I received with Joy, and give Thanks to GOD with you, That my Letter on *The Application of the Holy Scriptures*, is so sweet and precious to your Soul. How blessed are *you*, in that you are an *Heir of Promise!* In that "All the Promises of God, are Yea, and Amen, unto you, in Christ!"—And as to that great Word of GOD, which has been a Support and Comfort to you many a Time; which you wou'd not have out of the Bible, for all the Gold in the World: And which you long to have my Thoughts on: Please to receive from the LORD, what HE will please to give, from that his precious Word: As it stands in his Sacred Book,

Isaiah XLI.10. *Fear thou not, for I am with thee: be not dismayed, for I am thy God: I am thy God: I will strengthen thee, yea, I will help thee, yea, I will uphold thee with the Right-Hand of my Righteousness.*

Briefly, then, Sir, I humbly think, That these Words, are the LORD's *Prohibition* of his Peoples unbelieving *Fear*; and His great *Declaration,* and All-comprehending *Promise of Grace*, unto their Time-Joy, and eternal Glory.——These precious Words are given to *God's People:* To his Church collectively, and unto all its living Members, even to every true Believer, particularly: Under the Words, *Thou*, and *Thee*.——They are the LORD's Prohibition of his Peoples unbelieving Fear: *Fear thou not: Be not dismayed.*——They are his great Declaration: *I am thy God.* ——And they are his All-comprehending Promise of Grace, unto his Peoples Time-Joy & Eternal Glory: *I* (as thy God) *will strengthen thee, yea, I will help thee, yea, I will uphold thee, with the Right-Hand of my Righteousness.*—And in them may be considered, 1. *Who* the People of God are, which are here spoken to 2. That these People are subject to unbelieving *Fear*, and sinful *Dismayment*. 3. That nevertheless, it is their unspeakable Privilege, To have God *with them*, and an Interest in HIM, as *their God.* 4. That as their God, HE hath given his great Word, That He will *strengthen* them, yea, *help*, and *uphold* them. And 5. That in dispensing all this Grace, HE engages to do it, With the *Right Hand* of *his Righteousness.* To each of these, a few Words, if the Lord will.—And we may consider,

First. Who the People of God are, which are here spoken to.—And literally considered, they are, The Seed of *Abraham*, God's Friend, his *Jacob & Israel*, that were of the Lineage of *Abraham*, the *Jews.*——And GOD's great Declaration and Promise, in these great Words, were literally fulfilled to the Body of that Nation as such, in *Temporals:* In respect of those Church-Privileges, and National Advantages, with which they were so singularly favoured, above all Nations of the Earth.——Spiritually considered, they are, The Lord's *Jacob*, the *Israel* of God, the Whole of God's People, consisting of *Jews & Gentiles:* And all those of both, who as the Effect of God's Eternal Choice, are called in Time by his special Grace, unto Faith in Christ. For God hath now manifested clearly, this great Love-Mystery, this Mystery of infinite Grace, according to the sovereign Pleasure of Jehovah's Will, "That the *Gentiles* should be Fellow-Heirs, & Partakers of his Promise in Christ by the Gospel." And told us HE hath, "That those who are of Faith, are *Abraham's* Seed, and blessed with faithful *Abraham*."

And thus of all Believers, both *Jews* and *Gentiles*, of the whole Church, with all its Members, called by Grace, unto Faith in Christ, the Lord saith in the Verses preceding that under Consideration, *But thou* Israel *art my Servant,* Jacob *whom I have chosen, the Seed of* Abraham *my Friend. Thou whom I have taken from the Ends of the Earth, & called thee from the chief Men thereof, & said unto thee, Thou art my Servant, I have chosen thee, & not cast thee away,* ver. 8, 9. And unto these his People, HE saith, ver. 10. *Fear thou not,* &c. And those great Things, in these great Words, have their Fulfilment to God's spiritual *Israel*, chiefly in *Spirituals* and *Eternals*.

But wou'd you know more particularly, Dear Sir, *Who* the Lord's People are? They are, then, All that are convinced by the Word and Spirit of God, That they have destroyed themselves, and are utterly undone by Sin. That see their own Righteousness, is as filthy Rags. That the righteous Law of God, which they have broke, curseth them to Death, to Eternal Death. That they have deserved this fearful Doom, and are in imminent Danger of the Wrath that is to come. And that in this miserable State, They have no Strength in Themselves, to help or save themselves: From the Guilt and Filth, Power and Being of Sin; from the Dominion of Satan; from the Curse of the Law, nor the Wrath of God. They are such, That see themselves to be deep in Debt, to the Law and Justice of God; and that they are so poor, that they han't a Mite to pay. That they are without Strength, of themselves, either to fulfill the Law, or obey the Gospel. They are such, That have their Mouth stopped, & are become guilty before God: So that they han't a Word to say, from any of their own Worthiness, why they should find Grace; nor yet, by reason of their great Iniquity, Why they should not be sent away instantly, into Everlasting Misery. In a Word, They are such, That under the special Work of the Holy Ghost, are convinced of *Sin*, of *Righteousness*, and of *Judgment:* That lothe themselves in their own Sight, for all their Iniquities, that fall down, as utterly undone, at the Feet of infinite Mercy, and that earnestly desire Grace, to turn from all Sin, unto God by Christ.

Again, They are such, that have had an internal Revelation of *Christ*, by the Word & Spirit of God, as the only and All-sufficient Saviour of lost Sinners. That approve of, and earnestly desire the Saviour, in his glorious Person, in all his great Offices, in his sweet Relations, and in his All-comprehending, and inexhaustible Fulness of Grace and Glory, for their own Salvation; and that actually flee, at the Gospel-Call, unto Christ by Faith, for Refuge from the Wrath to come, as the only Hope that is set before them. Upon which, by the Promise of God, They have a declared *Right to Christ*, and to *Eternal Life in* HIM.

And hence, they are such, that more or less, are blest with a sweet Persuasion, of their own Salvation by Jesus Christ, thro' God's free and faithful Promise, applied by his Spirit to their Hearts. And that from God's manifested Love to them, are strongly drawn to love HIM again; and to dedicate Themselves unto the Lord, to be *His* Forever, in all holy Obedience, unto his Praise.—These, Dear Sir, and every one of These, are the Lord's People; and unto Them, generally and particularly, do these great Words of Grace, belong.——But,

Secondly. These, tho' the People of God, by Faith and Holiness, are subject to unbelieving Fear, and sinful Dismayment.——This is imply'd, in the Lord's saying, *Fear thou not; be not dismayed.* Which wou'd be needless, if they were not subject to Fear, and Dismayment.——And this Fear, arising from remaining Unbelief, hath for its Ground, The Power and Prevalence of indwelling Sin; together with various, and numerous inward Temptations, and outward trying Providential Dispensations. And the Matter of their Fear, is, 1. That the Lord is not *their God:* And 2. That He is not *with them.* Or, From an Apprehension, That the Lord is not with them, by his Sin-subduing, and Soul-saving Grace, nor by his special Providence, as He is with his own People; they are apt to fear, That the Lord is not their God: Or, at least, That He hath forsaken them. And so, That they shall be left as a Prey, to the Power of the Enemy: Which dismays their Hearts exceedingly. Unbelieving Fear, whenever, and which way soever it works, exceedingly sinks their Spirits. And Dismayment, is the Height of unbelieving Fear: Or the Soul's sitting down, as it were inactive, under great Discouragement.——At such a Time as this, then, These glorious Words of Grace, as they stand in God's Book, and as apply'd by his Spirit to the Heart, are most suitable, precious, and joyous.—For, Tho' their Sins, Trials, Griefs and Fears are many: Yet,

Thirdly. It is, nevertheless, their unspeakable Privilege, To have God *with them*, and an Interest in HIM, as *their God.*——As saith the Lord, "Fear thou not, for I am with thee: be not dismayed, for I am thy God." Which is as if the Lord should say, "Thou poor, sinful, fearful, distressed, Worm, tho' many and great are thine Adversaries, thy Necessities, thy Griefs and Burdens; tho' various and numerous, are thine inward and outward Trials; and tho' in and of Thyself, thou art helpless; and from any other Creature or Thing, hopeless; Yet, fear thou not, for I am with thee. *I,* that am well able to destroy all thine Enemies, to supply all thy Necessities, to deliver thee from all thy Griefs and Fears, and to grant all thy Desires; I am *with thee*; engaged for thee; and therefore fear thou not, an Host that is against thee. I am thy God: I *am* thy God, whoever, or whatever, says to the contrary. I am *thine entirely*, and *eternally*; thine in an everlasting Covenant. All my Perfections, as GOD, are engaged for thy Good: And therefore be not dismayed; take up thy Rest, thy Solace in ME, who am thy Time-Portion, and thy Eternal LOT."——And thus,

Fourthly. The Lord as their God, has given them his great Word, That "He will strengthen them, yea, help, and uphold them." *Strengthen them*, under all their felt Weakness; and against all their potent Enemies. *Help them,* in the rich Supply of all their Necessities; and in the Grant of all their Desires, so far as is for his Honour and Glory, and for their Happiness and Joy. "Yea, saith the Lord I will *uphold thee*." Uphold thy Faith and Love, thy Hope and Patience, and every other Grace. Uphold thee by my Spirit and Word, and Providence. Yea, I will uphold thee in thy Christian Course, until thou hast run thy Race; and then comes on, thy eternal Glory-Crown; in and with ME, as *Thy God:* In which Glory, I will uphold thee, to Eternity.——And,

Fifthly. The Lord in dispensing all this Grace, engageth to do it, With the Right-Hand of his Righteousness.——*With the Right-Hand of my Righteousness*. Which is as if the Lord should say, "Not by the Virtue and Power of *thy Righteousness*; but of *my Righteousness*. By my Righteousness, for thy complete Justification; and by my Righteousness, my Covenant-Faithfulness, to my great Promise, which is given for thy Salvation. By the *Hand*, the Virtue and Power, of my Righteousness, will I strengthen thee, help thee, and uphold thee. Yea, with the *Right-Hand*, of my Righteousness, will I dispense unto thee, all my purposed and promised Grace. With the strong Hand, the working Hand, the embracing Hand, of my Righteousness, will I secure to thee, and confer upon thee, all my provided, and thy desired Bliss; unto thy Time-Joy, and Eternal Glory." For this Word, *Uphold thee*, reacheth all the Trials of Life, thro' the last Trial, Death, and will be a Truth of Eternal Duration: As it respects that *Sustentation*, which shall be afforded to the People of God, in immortal Bliss, to increasing Joys, and rising Praises, thro' Endless Ages. For thus, To an immeasurable, undeterminable Space, will the God of all Grace, with the Right Hand of his Righteousness, uphold his Saints, in, and to, Eternal Glory!——And when the Lord thus opens and applys to his People, this great Word of Grace, in any of its Parts, by his Spirit to their Hearts: Oh what Ease and Peace, what Joy and Victory, what Liberty and Glory, doth HE give them thereby!

How blessed, then, how ineffably blessed, is that People, is that Soul, who has the Lord with them; as their God; who will thus strengthen, help, and uphold them! Well might the *Psalmist* say "Yea, Blessed are the People, whose God is the LORD!"

And is it *you*, my Dear Sir, That convinced by the Holy Ghost, of Sin, of Righteousness, and of Judgment; have fell down helpless, as in and from yourself, and as hopeless, in and from any other Creature of Thing; for the whole of God's Salvation, by way of entire Dependance, upon His free, rich, sovereign Grace in Christ, according to his faithful Promise, given thro' the mighty Saviour, to believing Sinners? It is *you*, then, that are one of the Lord's People; and unto you as such, doth this great Declaration, and All-comprehending Promise of Grace, unto Time-Joy, and Eternal Glory, belong. It belongs unto *you*, as really and particularly, as if there was never another in the World, interested therein, besides yourself.

And tho' from remaining Unbelief, you are often subject to many Fears, thro' the Power of indwelling Sin, the Temptations of Satan, the Snares of the World, and the Trials of Life, which you meet with in the Dispensations of Divine Providence: Yet, unto *you*, the Lord saith, *Fear thou not, for I am with thee.* And if GOD is with you; most surely, with a slavish, Soul-tormenting Fear, you need fear nothing. If GOD is with you: Who, or what can be against you? Can be so against you, as to destroy you? Iniquity shall not be your Ruin: For the Lord is with you, as a Sin-pardoning, Sin-subduing, Soul-justifying, and Soul-saving GOD. The roaring Lion of Hell, shall not devour you: For, "The God of Peace, will shortly bruise Satan under your Feet." Nor shall the Trials of Life, no, nor the Sorrows of Death, be too hard for you: For, The Lord that is with you, is by far an *Over-Match*, for all Things that be, in their own Nature, or appear to be, in your View, against you. Omnipotence is on your Side: And the most potent of your Enemies, and Adversities, with respect thereto, are mere Impotence. GOD, with you! All Opposites, must fall before you. Yea, Those very Things, which seem to be most against you; must and shall work for you: Effectually over-ruled, by Almighty and All-wise Grace; they do, they shall, make for your Advantage, and turn to your present, and eternal Salvation.

And tho' at Times, You are greatly dismayed, and your Heart is ready to sink within you, thro' unbelieving Fear, thro' Heart and Hope-slaying Fear, *That the Lord is not your God:* Yet lay the Ear of Faith, to this precious Word of his Mouth: *Be not dismayed, for I am thy God!*——Does GOD *prohibit* your dismaying Fear: And will You *yield* to it? Does *Jehovah* say, *I am thy God:* And will You *doubt it?* The Word is gone out of his Mouth in Faithfulness; & it shall not return void. "Once hath HE sworn by His Holiness: And HE will not, cannot, lie unto *David:*" Unto *Christ* your Head, with whom God's Covenant was made, for all the chosen Seed. *If I lie*, unto *David!* The great and eternal *Jehovah*, doth as it were hereby, pledge his whole *Godhead*, for the Performance of his great Word. It is as if HE should say, "I swear by my Great SELF, That I will be a GOD, unto *David* and his *Seed:* And let me not be GOD, if I break my Word! All immense Perfections, and infinite Glories of my Great BEING, I engage, to perform my Word! *Once have I sworn by my Holiness: If I lie unto* David!" And little can we tell, How much there is, in this great IF! Oh the astonishing Condescension, of this great Abomination!—And to doubt it by Unbelief; How great is the Abomination!—And this great Declaration of Grace, Sir, which the Lord here makes unto You, *I am Thy* GOD! is made in CHRIST. In HIM it is confirmed: Confirmed by the *Oath of God!* Confirmed by the *Blood of God!* In HIM it is, *Yea, & Amen!* An Eternal YEA! And a Fixed AMEN! And thus, It's not an uncovenanted, but a solemnly confirmed Promise, An Oath, a Blood-confirmed Promise! Confirmed thus, stands *Jehovah's* Promise-Word, by the Oath of an *Infinite* GOD! Who, "Because HE could swear by no Greater, He sware, By HIMSELF!" And for what End? "That by Two immutable Things, the great Word, and the solemn Oath, of *Jehovah*, wherein it was impossible for GOD to lie: The Heirs of Promise, might have a strong Consolation; who have fled for Refuge, to lay Hold on the Hope set before them."——And have *You* fled, my Dear Friend, have You fled to Christ for Refuge, to lay Hold on HIM, for Eternal Life, as your only Hope? Then *You*, are an *Heir of Promise*, and of this great, and All-comprehending Promise, this Oath-confirmed Promise, *I am Thy God!* And confirmed thus it is, not only for your spiritual and eternal Salvation; but also, for your strong Consolation! That You might have a Cordial strong enough, to keep your Heart from Sinking, under the most depressing Fears. Yea, to raise your Heart, into an holy Triumph, and Joy of Faith, over your most potent Enemies, and all possible Adversities—And will You not receive this Cordial? This strong

Consolation? Does the Lord say, and say to You, *I am Thy God:* And will you, dare you, *disbelieve it?* And thus, and thereby, make GOD, the GOD of Infinite Truth, in this his Oath-confirmed Word, a *Liar!* Forbid it—Mighty GOD! No—Rather, Dear Sir, *Set to your Seal,* That GOD herein is *True!* And doubt your Interest in HIM, no more.——If Satan tempts You, if Sin terrifies You, if Trials perplex You, and your Heart is ready to sink within You: And all agree to say, *The Lord is not your God:* Put *their Lie,* in one Scale, and GOD's *Truth,* in the other, their Suggestion on one Side, and God's Confirmation on the other Side: And then see, by the Eye of Faith, What an infinite *Disparity,* there is between them! What a light Atome of Dust, a mere *Nothing,* your Enemies Suggestion is! And what a ponderous *Weight,* a solid Substance, a Soul-satisfying, and Heart-rejoycing ALL, *Jehovah's* Promise, is! And take it out of the Balance of the Sanctuary, by the Hand of Faith, and hold it fast, in the Face of all Opposition, from inward and outward Temptation: With a *"Thus saith the* LORD; *I am Thy* GOD: And *let* GOD *be True*; and all that oppose his Truth, *Liars!"*——Thus, Sir, stand fast, on GOD's Side, and in his Truth: And you shall find his Promise-Word, to be to your Enemies, a destroying Sword; unto You, a Sword of Victory, a Shield of Safety, and a cordial most spirituous, to sustain, revive, and delight your Heart, in the greatest Distress. For GOD's Honour, for your own Joy, while HE says in his Word, and has often said by his Spirit to your Heart, *I am Thy* GOD: Say after him, say to him, in Faith, and without Doubt, "Thou, LORD, art *my* GOD. Thou hast told me so; I believe it is so. Thou hast given *Thyself,* in all thy Persons, and in all thy Perfections, to be mine, entirely and eternally: Unto my Deliverance from all Misery, and Salvation unto all Joy and Glory. And, Drawn by Thee, in Love to Thee, I give *Myself,* my whole Self, and all that Thou hast given me, unto THEE, the Lord my GOD: To be unto thy Praise, both here and hereafter, for Time's, and for Eternity's Ever!"

And well you may, Sir, Speak thus in Faith: Since the God of Truth, as your God, hath said, "I will strengthen thee, yea, I will help thee, yea, I will uphold thee."——If GOD strengthen you, Sir: You shall not sink, under the most pressing Weights. If GOD will help you: You shall not want Supplies, in Thousands of Necessities. And if HE will uphold you: You shall not fail, in your Christian Course. You shall run and not be weary, and walk and shall not faint: Yea, You shall mount up by Faith, with Wings like an Eagle, thro' Life, and Death. Because, Tho' in yourself, you are all Unworthiness, mere Impotence, and utmost Weakness, yea, Vileness: You travel in

JEHOVAH's Strength; and shall be borne and carried in the sweet, strong Arms, of free, rich, reigning Grace, thro' every Difficulty, until Sorrow and Sighing shall flee away; & You, with exceeding Joy, shall be presented Perfect before the Throne of GOD and of the LAMB, to inherit in and with HIM, Eternal Glory! And in that ineffable Bliss, The Lord your own God, by his Free Grace, unto your Joy, & His Praise, will Uphold you, unto Endless Days!—For, HE that saith, *Fear thou not, for I am with thee:* Will thereby speak down Fear, powerfully, & will Speak up Faith, efficaciously. HE that saith, *Be not dismayed, for I am thy God:* Will thereby raise the most dejected Heart, deliver from Dismayment; & give Faith, to receive & believe, this glorious Promise-Grant, & Covenant-Settlement. And HE that saith, *I will strengthen thee, yea, I will help thee, yea, I will uphold thee:* Will as surely make These *good*, to the *Heirs of Promise*; as JEHOVAH, is the GOD *of Promise.*

Rich Enough, then, Sir, in the LORD, your own GOD: More than a Conqueror, thro' HIM that hath loved you: Able to do all Things, thro' CHRIST, which strengthneth you: Rejoyce in Him, & live to Him, until you shall live with Him, in full Joy, perfect Holiness, & immortal Bliss! Of which, by this great Promise, You have & shall have, a most form Assurance, a most certain Earnest, & a most sweet Foretaste. And may The Lord fill You thereby, with *Joy unspeakable, & full of Glory!*—I am, Dear Sir,

Yours in Christ Forever, &c.

F I N I S .

E R R A T U M.
[Editor's note. Erratum corrected in text.]

INDEX